Luther's Sermo
Lenker Editic
Volume 2

Edited by Pastor Gregory L. Jackson, PhD

Illustrated by Norma A. Boeckler

Dr. Gregory L. Jackson's blog:

http://ichabodthegloryhasdeparted.blogspot.com
Email: greg.jackson.edlp@gmail.com

Norma A. Boeckler's website:

www.normanoecklerart.com
Email: normaboeckler@charter.net

Interior, front, and back covers designed by Norma A. Boeckler.

ISBN-13: 978-1975689872

ISBN-10: 1975689872

Acknowledgements and Dedication

My wife Christina underwent cancer surgery when this series was being planned, and she has been a constant source of encouragement for promoting Luther's works. Virginia Roberts has worked tirelessly on removing the errors picked up by scanning and copying into Word. Numerous people are helping with this project, and they all report learning so much from Luther, even though they must focus on the glitches rather than the volumes. Their labor of love means more people can read Luther conveniently and at a very low cost.

When I became a Lutheran at the age of 16 and joined Salem Lutheran Church in Moline, Illinois, no one could foresee the changes ahead in the Lutheran Church. But I soon learned about Roland Bainton and read *Here I Stand: A Life of Martin Luther*. I took a course in Reformation history at Augustana College and soon had a unique opportunity to meet Bainton, hear him lecture, and photograph him with our newborn son, Martin. He responded by drawing a picture of Luther holding Martin and Bethany, our second child. Bainton impressed me with his kindness and generosity, once offering to Xerox pages for me when I was working on my dissertation. He was a historian who pursued the sources and learned the languages needed. I used his language methods to teach Latin, Greek, and Hebrew to Martin. Therefore, these volumes are directly connected to Bainton's influence on me and all Lutherans. Volume II is dedicated especially to Roland Bainton, honorary Lutheran, scholar and friend.

Table of Contents

Pastor Gregory L. Jackson, Trinity Season, 2017

Gems from Luther's Sermons, Volume II

Luther is discussed far more often than studied, so it is best to let his Biblical theology speak for itself. All the gems will be gathered for Volume IX.

He will not permit himself to be found…outside of his Word.

27. Behold, he punishes his parents because they had erred and had sought him among earthly and human affairs, among friends and acquaintances, not thinking that he must be in that which is his Father's. He wishes to indicate by this, that his kingdom and the whole essence of Christianity consists alone in the Word and in faith, not in external things (as the external and hypocritical sanctity of Judaism), nor in temporal and worldly ordinance or government. In a word; he will not permit himself to be found, either among friends and acquaintances, nor in anything outside of his Word. For he does not wish to be worldly, nor in that which is worldly, but in that which is his Father's, even as he always manifested himself from his birth through his entire life. He was, indeed, in the world, but he did not conform to the world, as he also said to Pilate, "My kingdom is not of this world." He was among friends and acquaintances and came to them, but did not identify himself with any of their affairs in the world, except that he sojourned in the world as a guest and used it to satisfy the wants of his body; but he waits alone on that which is his Father's i.e., the Word. There he can be found; there he who wishes truly to find him, must seek him.

First Sunday after Epiphany

God Directs Us to the Word, Not to Any Saint or Man

48. The same truth has been previously presented in many figures and examples, as in the Gospel for Christmas, Luke 2:12, where the angels give no other sign to the shepherds by which they might find Christ than the manger and the swaddling clothes. There they should find him lying and wrapped up, not in the bosom of the mother, nor on her lap, which would have seemed credible. That is, God does not wish to direct us to any saint or person of man, but only to the Word or Scripture, in which Christ is wrapped as in swaddling clothes, and in the poor manger (that is the preaching of the Gospel), which is so highly esteemed, and serves merely for the feeding of the cattle. Again, we have also heard from the aged and holy Simeon who, as had been promised him by God, should not die until he had seen Christ, but who does not recognize him until by the instigation of the Holy Spirit he enters the temple.

So also the wise men from the east who, when they came to Jerusalem and no longer saw the star, hear of no other sign concerning Christ, as to where he was born and where he could be found, than the Scripture of the prophet Micah. So much may be said concerning the most important teaching and the principal parts of this Gospel. Finally, it is also to be noted that the Evangelist says: "His mother kept all these sayings in her heart."

First Sunday after Epiphany, Second Sermon, p. 36

To Turn Water into Wine

31. To turn water into wine is to render the interpretation of the Law delightful. This is done as follows: Before the Gospel arrives everyone understands the Law as demanding our works, that we must fulfill it with works of our own. This interpretation begets either hardened, presumptuous dissemblers and hypocrites, harder than any pot of stone, or timid, restless consciences. There remains nothing but water in the pot, fear and dread of God's Judgment. This is the water interpretation, not intended for drinking, neither filling any with delight; on the contrary, there is nothing to it but washing and purification, and yet no true inner cleansing. But the Gospel explains the Law, showing that it requires more than we can render, and that it demands a person different from ourselves to fulfill it; that is, it demands Christ and brings us unto him, so that first of all by his grace we are made in true faith a different people like unto Christ, and that then we do truly good works. Thus the right interpretation and significance of the Law is to lead us to the knowledge of our helplessness, to drive us from ourselves to another, namely to Christ, to seek grace and help of him.

Second Sunday after Epiphany

Faith Inclines His Favor

12. This is what we have often said: we ought to believe without doubting and without limiting the divine goodness; but we ought to pray with the limitation, that it may be his honor, his kingdom and will, in order that we may not limit his will to time, place, measure or name, but leave all that freely to him. For this reason the prayer of the leper pleased the Lord so well and was soon heard. For where we submit to his will, and seek what is acceptable to him, he cannot refrain from doing in return what is acceptable to us. Faith inclines his favor to us, and submissive prayer inclines him to grant us what we pray for. As to the sending of the leper to the priests, why it was done and what it signified, enough has been said in the Postil of the ten lepers.

Third Sunday after Epiphany, p. 55

All Are To Be Equal in the Grace of God

15. By these and similar wonders he shows that he will not have his Spirit in his saints limited by us, and that we are not to judge according to the person. He wills to bestow his gifts freely, according to his pleasure and not according to our opinion, as St. Paul says in 1 Corinthians 12:11. Indeed even of himself he says in John 14:12: "He that believeth on me, the works that I do shall he do also; and greater works than these shall he do." The purpose of all this is to prevent men from being presumptuous toward others and from elevating one saint above another and creating divisions. All are to be equal in the grace of God, however unequal they are in his gifts. It is his will to do through St. Stephen what he does not do through St. Peter, and through St. Peter what he does not do through his mother; so that it may be he alone who does all in all without distinction of person according to his will.

Third Sunday after Epiphany, p.56

He Care More and Soon for Us Than We Do For Ourselves

1. In today's Gospel Christ gives us another lesson in faith, that we should not be overanxious about our daily bread and our temporal existence, and stirs us up by means of a miracle; as though to say by his act what he says by his words in Matthew 6:33: "Seek ye first the Kingdom of God, and his righteousness, and all these things shall be added unto you." For here we see, since the people followed Christ for the sake of God's Word and the signs, and thus sought the Kingdom of God, he did not forsake them but richly fed them. He hereby also shows that, rather than those who seek the Kingdom of God should suffer need, the grass in the desert would become wheat, or a crumb of bread would be turned into a thousand loaves; or a morsel of bread would feed as many people and just as satisfactorily as a thousand loaves; in order that the words in Matthew 4:4 might stand firm, that "Man shall not live by bread alone, but by every word that proceedeth out of the mouth of God." And to confirm these words Christ is the first to be concerned about the people, as to what they should eat, and asks Philip, before they complain or ask him; so that we may indeed let him care for us, remembering that he cares more and sooner for us than we do for ourselves.

Fourth Sunday in Lent

So Mighty is the Word

8. All this is done, I say, by faith. For if you believe that by this seed the serpent has been slain, then it is slain for you; and if you believe that in this seed all nations are to be blessed, then you are also blessed. For each one individually should have crushed the serpent under foot and redeemed himself from the curse, which would have been too difficult, nay impossible for us. But now it has been done easily, namely, by Christ, who has crushed the serpent once, who alone is given as a blessing and benediction, and who has caused this Gospel to be published throughout the world, so that he who believes, accepts it and clings to it, is also in possession of it, and is assured that it is as he believes. For in the heart of such a man the Word becomes so powerful that he will conquer death, the devil, sin and all adversity, like Christ himself did. So mighty is the Word that God himself would sooner be vanquished than that his Word should be conquered.

Easter Sunday, Second Sermon, p. 186

The Nature of Faith

12. The question now arises: If Christ has taken away death and our sins by his resurrection and has justified us, why do we then still feel death and sin within us? For our sins torment us still, we are stung by our conscience, and this evil conscience creates the fear of hell.

13. To this I reply: I have often said before that feeling and faith are two different things. It is the nature of faith not to feel, to lay aside reason and close the eyes, to submit absolutely to the Word, and follow it in life and death. Feeling however does not extend beyond that which may be apprehended by reason and the senses, which may be heard, seen, felt and known by the outward senses. For this cause feeling is opposed to faith and faith is opposed to feeling. Therefore the author of the Epistle to the Hebrews writes of faith: "Now faith is assurance of things hoped for, a conviction of things not seen." For if we would see Christ visibly in heaven, like the visible sun, we would not need to believe it. But since Christ died for our sins and was raised for our justification, we cannot see it nor feel it, neither can we comprehend it with our reason. Therefore we must disregard our feeling and accept only the Word, write it into our heart and cling to it, even though it seems as if my sins were not taken from me, and even though I still feel them within me. Our feelings must not be considered, but we must constantly insist that death, sin and hell have been conquered, although I feel that I am still under the power of death, sin and hell. For although we feel that sin is still in us, it is only permitted that our faith may be developed and strengthened, that in spite of all our feelings we accept the Word, and that we unite our hearts and consciences more and more to Christ.

Thus faith leads us quietly, contrary to all feeling and comprehension of reason, through sin, through death and through hell. Then we shall see salvation before our eyes, and then we shall know perfectly what we have believed, namely, that death and all sorrow have been conquered.

Easter Sunday, Second Sermon, p. 188

We Ought Not Cast Away the Weak

23. This is nothing but a sermon that teaches us not to be offended in the weak Christ. He does not rebuke the disciples harshly, does not say: Away with you; I do not want you. You should be strong and courageous, but here you sit and are dismayed and terrified! He does not do these things; but lovingly comforts them, that he might make them strong and fearless.

Hence they were also made strong and fearless, and not only this, but also cheerful and of good courage. Therefore we ought not to cast away the weak, but so deal with them that, from day to day, we may bring them to a condition that they may become strong and of good cheer. This does not signify that it is well, if they are weak, and that they should continue weak; for Christ does not stand among them for that purpose, but that they might grow in faith and be made fearless.

Third Easter Day, p. 240

The First and Highest Work of Love

13. The first and highest work of love a Christian ought to do when he has become a believer, is to bring others also to believe in the way he himself came to believe. And here you notice Christ begins and institutes the office of the ministry of the external Word in every Christian; for he himself came with this office and the external Word. Let us lay hold of this, for we must admit it was spoken to us. In this way the Lord desires to say: You have now received enough from me, peace and joy, and all you should have; for your person you need nothing more. Therefore labor now and follow my example, as I have done, so do ye. My Father sent me into the world only for your sake, that I might serve you, not for my own benefit. I have finished the work, have died for you, and given you all that I am and have; remember and do ye also likewise, that henceforth ye may only serve and help everybody, otherwise ye would have nothing to do on earth. For by faith ye have enough of everything. Hence I send you into the world as my Father hath sent me; namely, that every Christian should instruct and teach his neighbor, that he may also come to Christ. By this, no power is delegated exclusively to popes and bishops, but all Christians are commanded to profess their faith publicly and also to lead others to believe.

The Sunday after Easter, p. 276

True Peace of Christ, In the Midst of Misfortune

4. For the devil will not allow a Christian to have peace; therefore Christ must bestow it in a manner different from that in which the world has and gives, in that he quiets the heart and removes from within fear and terror, although without there remain contention and misfortune. And this we see in the example of these disciples of Christ, who are in great fear on account of the Jews; they are behind barred doors, not daring to go forth, and are in constant dread of death. Although they have peace without and are annoyed by no one, nevertheless their hearts are all aflutter, and they have neither rest nor peace. While they are thus in fear and terror, the Lord enters; he quiets their hearts and brings them peace, not by removing the danger, but by quieting their hearts. For the wickedness of the Jews is neither removed nor changed thereby, for they are as full of hatred and rage as before, and without there is no change whatever, but within the disciples are changed, they have become courageous and bold, and the hatred of the Jews is for them now of but little concern.

5. This is the true peace, which is able to calm the heart, not in time of good fortune, but in the midst of misfortune, when without there is nothing but contention. For here is the difference between worldly and spiritual peace. Worldly peace consists in removing the external evils which cause the contention, as for example, when enemies besiege a city, there is war, but when they are gone, peace returns. Thus also, when poverty and sickness are pressing thee, thou art not contented, but when they are removed, and thou art rid of the misfortune externally, thou art again at peace and rest. But he who endures this is not changed; he remains just as discouraged when these things exist as when they do not, the only difference being that he is feeling it and that it oppresses him when it is present.

Sunday after Easter, Third Sermon p. 292

First Sunday after Epiphany. Luke 2:41-52

Jesus Among the Doctors, or An Example of Cross-Bearing

Jesus in the Temple

TEXT: Luke 2:41 Now his parents went to Jerusalem every year at the feast of the passover. 42 And when he was twelve years old, they went up to Jerusalem after the custom of the feast. 43 And when they had fulfilled the days, as they returned, the child Jesus tarried behind in Jerusalem; and Joseph and his mother knew not of it. 44 But they, supposing him to have been in the company, went a day's journey; and they sought him among their kinsfolk and acquaintance. 45 And when they found him not, they turned back again to Jerusalem, seeking him. 46 And it came to pass, that after three days they found him in the temple, sitting in the midst of the doctors, both hearing them, and asking them questions. 47 And all that heard him were astonished at his understanding and answers. 48 And when they saw him, they were amazed: and his mother said unto him, Son, why hast thou thus dealt with us? behold, thy father and I have sought thee sorrowing. 49 And he said unto them, How is it that ye sought me? wist ye not that I must be about my Father's business? 50 And they understood not the saying which he spake unto them. 51 And he went down with them, and came to Nazareth, and was subject unto them: but his mother kept all these sayings in her heart. 52 And Jesus increased in wisdom and stature, and in favour with God and man.

1. This is a Gospel that presents to us an example of the holy cross, showing us through what experiences those have to pass who are Christians, and how they ought to bear their sorrow. For he who desires to be a Christian must expect to help bear the cross. For God will place him between the spurs and thoroughly test him that he may be humble and no one will come to Christ without suffering. Of this we have here an example, which we ought to imitate and shall now consider.

2. Although the holy mother Mary, who was highly blessed and upon whom many favors were bestowed, had undoubtedly the greatest delight in her child, yet the Lord so ruled that her joy was not without sorrow, and like all others, she did not attain complete blessedness until she entered heaven. For this reason she had to suffer so much sorrow, pain and anguish on earth. It was her first great sorrow that she had to give birth to her child in Bethlehem, in a strange town, where she found no room with her babe except in a stable. Then her second sad experience was that, soon after the six weeks of her purification, she was compelled to flee with her child into Egypt, a strange country, which was indeed a poor consolation. She undoubtedly experienced many more like trials, which have not been recorded.

3. One of them is related here, when her son caused her so much anxiety, by tarrying behind in the temple and letting her seek him so long, and she could not find him. This alarmed and grieved her so that she almost despaired, as her words indicate: "Behold, thy father and I sought thee sorrowing." For we may well imagine that thoughts like these may have passed through her mind: "Behold this child is only mine, this I know very well, and I know that God has entrusted him to me and commanded me to take care of him; why is it then that he is taken from me? It is my fault, for I have not sufficiently taken care of him and guarded him. Perhaps God does not deem me worthy to watch over this child and will take him from me again." She was undoubtedly greatly frightened and her heart trembled and was filled with grief.

4. Here you see what she experienced. Although she is the mother of a child in whom she might have gloried before all mothers, and although her joy was immeasurably greater than any she had ever felt, yet you perceive how God deprives her of all happiness, in that she can no longer call herself the mother of Jesus. In her great dismay she probably wished, she had never known her child and was tempted to greater sins than any mother had ever committed.

5. In the same manner the Lord our God can take from us our joy and comfort, if he so desires, and cause us the greatest sorrow with the very things that are our greatest joy, and, on the other hand, give us the greatest delight in the things that terrify us most. For it was the greatest joy of Mary that she was the mother of this child, but now he has become the cause of her greatest sorrow. Thus we are afraid of nothing more than of sin and death, yet God can comfort us so that we may boast, as St. Paul says in Romans 7, that sin served to the end that we became justified and that we longed for death and desire to die.

6. The great sorrow of the mother of Christ, who was deprived of her child, came upon her in order that even her trust in God might be taken from her. For she had reason to fear that God was angry with her and would no longer have her to be the mother of his Son. Nobody will understand what she suffered who has not passed through similar experiences. Therefore we should apply this example to ourselves, for it was not recorded for her sake, but for our benefit. She is now at the end of her sorrows; therefore we should profit by her example and be prepared to bear our sorrow if a similar affliction befall us.

7. When God vouchsafes to us a strong faith and a firm trust in him, so that we are assured he is our gracious God and we can depend upon him, then we are in paradise. But when God permits our hearts to be discouraged and we believe that he takes from us Christ our Lord; when our conscience feels that we have lost him and amidst trembling and despair our confidence is gone, then we are truly in misery and distress. For even if we are not conscious of any special sin, yet in such a condition we tremble and doubt whether God still cares for us; just as Mary here doubts and knows not whether God still deems her worthy to be the mother of his Son. Our heart thinks in the time of trial thus: God has indeed given me a strong faith, but perhaps he will take it from me and will no longer want me as his child. Only strong minds can endure such temptations and there are not many people whom God tests to this degree. Yet we must be prepared, so that we may not despair if such trials should come upon us.

8. We find many examples of this in the Scriptures, as for instance in Joshua 7:6-7. God had given to Joshua great and strong promises, telling him that he would exterminate the heathen and charging him to attack his enemies courageously and vigorously, which he also did. But what happened? When his faith was strong he,sent three thousand men against a city to take it. They were proud, seeing that it was a small city with only a few people to defend it. When the men of Israel approached, the enemy sallied forth from the city and defeated the people. Then Joshua fell to the earth upon his face before the ark of Jehovah until the evening, lifting up his voice and lamenting before God, saying: "Alas, O Lord Jehovah, wherefore hast thou at all brought this people over the Jordan, to deliver us into the hand of the Amorites, to cause us to perish?" His faith had become weak and he was utterly discouraged, so that God himself had to raise him up again. Thus God deals with his great saints, whom he sometimes deprives of Christ, that is, of their faith and confidence.

9. But God does all this out of his superabundant grace and goodness in order that we might perceive on every hand how kindly and lovingly the Father deals with us and tries us, so that our faith may be developed and become continually stronger and stronger. And he does this especially so as to guard his children against a twofold danger which might otherwise threaten them. In the first place, being strong in their own mind and arrogant, they might ultimately depend upon themselves and believe they are able to accomplish everything in their own strength. For this reason God sometimes permits their faith to grow weak and to be prostrated, so that they might see who they are and be forced to confess: Even if I would believe, I cannot. Thus the omnipotent God humbles his saints and keeps them in their true knowledge. For nature and reason will always boast of the gifts of God and depend upon them. Therefore God must lead us to a recognition of the fact that it is he who puts faith in our heart and that we cannot produce it ourselves. Thus the fear of God and trust in him must not be separated from one another, for we need them both, in order that we may not become presumptuous and overconfident, depending upon ourselves. This is one of the reasons why God leads his saints through such great trials.

10. Another reason is, that he wants to give us an example. For if in the Scriptures we had no examples of saints who passed through the same experiences, we should be unable to bear our trials and would imagine that we alone are thus afflicted, that God never dealt with anyone in this manner; therefore my suffering must be a sign of God's displeasure with me. But when we see that the Virgin Mary and other saints have also suffered, we are thereby comforted and need not despair, for their example shows that we should calmly and patiently wait until God comes and strengthens us.

11. We find many examples of similar trials in the Scriptures, and here we might refer to the words of David in Psalm 31:22: "As for me, I said in my haste, I am cut off from before thine eyes," just as we sometimes think that God does not want us. Such trials are unendurable and severe beyond measure, wherefore the saints passing through them lament greatly, for if God would not deliver them they would be in hell. Compared with these trials other temptations and sorrows are trivial, as for instance when our possessions and honors are taken from us, or when the innocent babes were murdered and Jesus was forced to flee into Egypt. The prophet speaks of this in Psalm 94:17: "Unless Jehovah had been my help, my soul had soon dwelt in silence." So great is the terror and anguish of such visitations. But God permitted them that we might lay hold of these examples, be comforted and saved from despair. At the end of our lives we must also pass through like trials. Therefore we must be armed and prepared for them.

II. An Example of Comfort Under the Cross

12. Such is the narrative and example of the great sorrow as it is portrayed in this Gospel, but we are also shown where comfort may be found. The parents of Jesus lost him, going a day's journey and seeking for him among their kinsfolk and acquaintance, but found him not. They return to Jerusalem and after a search of three days, he is found by them in the temple. Here God has pointed out how we can find consolation and strength in all our sorrows, and especially in these great trials, and how we can find Christ the Lord, namely by seeking him in the temple. Jesus said to his parents: "Knew ye not that I must be in my Father's house?

13. The words of Luke "and they understood not the saying which he spake unto them" are especially to be noted here. With these words he silenced the idle talk of those who exalted and praised the Virgin Mary too highly, asserting that she knew everything and could not err. For you see here how the Lord permits her to seek her child for a long time in vain, till she finds him in the temple after three days. In addition to this, Jesus seems to reprimand her when he says: "How is it that ye sought me? knew ye not that I must be in my Father's house?" She understood not the saying which he spake to her. Consequently all the idle talk to which we have referred is nothing but falsehood, and the Virgin Mary does not need this fabricated and mendacious praise. God concealed much from her and led her through many trials, so that she might remain humble and not think herself better than others.

14. But the consolation of which I have spoken is that Christ is only found in the temple, that is to say in the house of God. But what is the house of God? Is it not the whole creation? It is indeed true that God is everywhere, but he is especially present in the Holy Scriptures, in his Word, more than anywhere else. We learn therefore here that nobody can presume to derive any comfort from anything but the Word of God; you will find the Son only in the temple. Now look at the mother of Jesus who does not yet understand this and does not know that she must seek for him in the temple. When she sought for him among their kinsfolk and acquaintance, and not at the right place, she did not find him.

15. Therefore I have often said and say again, that in the Christian Church nothing should be preached but the pure Word of God. With this the Gospel agrees when it says that they did not find the Lord among their kinsfolk and acquaintance. It is therefore wrong to say that we must believe what the councils have decreed, or what Jerome, Augustine and other holy fathers have written. We must point out the place where Christ may be found, which he himself points out when he says that he must be in his Father's house, which means that he can only be found in the Word of God.

We should therefore not believe that our conscience may trust in the teachings of the holy fathers or derive comfort from them. Now if they say to you: Should we not believe the holy fathers? you may reply: Christ is not found among the kinsfolk and acquaintance. It would indeed be well if Christians generally were to heed this example from the Gospel and use it as a maxim against every doctrine that does not agree with the Word of God.

16. But in order to emphasize this more and to make it clearer, let us see what other doctrines have been proclaimed that do not agree with the Word of God. Up to this time we have had three different systems of doctrine. The first and coarsest is that of St. Thomas (if indeed he be a saint). This was taken from the system of pagan science and art which was written by that great light of nature, Aristotle. Now they say that his philosophy is like a bright, shining plate, and the Word of Christ is like the sun. And as the sun shines upon the plate, causing it to gleam and glitter all the brighter, so the divine light shines upon the light of nature and illumines it. With this beautiful simile they have introduced pagan doctrines into the Christian church, which have been taught and cultivated by the great universities and in which teachers and preachers have been instructed. The devil has taught them to speak in this way. Thus the Word of God is trodden under foot, for when it is given full play, it subverts all these satanic doctrines.

17. In the second place, they have taught and prescribed human laws, called the institutions and precepts of the holy Christian church. Thereby these fools have thought to lead men to heaven and to be able to comfort and pacify our conscience. These human laws prevail to such a degree that like a great deluge they cover the whole world and have submerged everything else, so that it is almost impossible that anyone may be saved from going down to hell. For they clamor unceasingly as though they were insane: This has been decreed by the holy councils and that has been commanded by the church; we have observed this a long time, shall we not believe it now?

18. Therefore we should reply to this from the Gospel, as I said: Even if Mary, the Holy Virgin, had done this, it would not be surprising if she had erred. She was the mother of God, and yet she did not know where to find Christ; she sought him among her kinsfolk and acquaintance and failed to find him. Now if she did not succeed in finding Christ among her kinsfolk, but had finally to come to the temple, how shall we expect to find him outside of the Word of God in human doctrines, in the decrees of the councils or the teachings of the scholastics? Bishops and councils have undoubtedly not possessed the gift of the Holy Spirit in as large a measure as Mary. If she erred, why should not they also be mistaken who fancy to find Christ elsewhere but in his Father's house, that is in the Word of God?

19. If therefore you find one who adheres to these two different systems of doctrine, believing them to be right and trusting in them, ask him whether he is quite confident that they will comfort his soul in the hour of death or under the judgment and the wrath of God, whether he will be able to say then with a conscience undaunted: This has been declared and decreed by the pope and the bishops in their councils, I depend upon that and am quite certain I shall not fail? He will soon be obliged to say: How can I be so certain of this? Thus, when it comes to the point and you are in the presence of death, your conscience will say: It is indeed true, the councils have decreed this, but what if they were mistaken, and who knows whether they were right? Then when you are in such doubts, you cannot hold out, and Satan will assail you and hurl you to the ground, so that you lie there helpless.

20. In the third place, besides these two theories they have also pointed us to the Holy Scriptures and said, that above every other doctrine the laws and decrees of the pope in matters of faith must be observed. But here they except the teachings of some of the holy fathers, who have interpreted the Scriptures, and whom they have exalted so highly that they place them on the same level with the pope of Rome, or a little above him, asserting even that they could not err, and clamoring: How could it be possible for the holy fathers not to understand the Scriptures? But let these fools say what they wish, always remind them of the words of Christ: "Knew ye not that I must be in my Father's house?" We must above all things have the Word of God and cling to it, for Christ will be there and in no where else. Therefore it is in vain that you seek him elsewhere. For how can you convince me that Christ must be found in the writings of the holy fathers?

21. This Gospel is therefore a severe thrust at every doctrine and every comfort of any kind that is not derived from the Word of God. You may therefore say: It matters not how highly you exalt reason and the light of nature, I reserve the right of not putting my trust in it. The councils have issued decrees and the pope or the holy fathers have taught what they wish, but that does not concern me; I will not depend upon them. We will soon agree if they decide and propose what they please, but grant me the liberty to say: If it pleases me, I shall observe it, but not as something that is especially meritorious. They will however not grant us this right; for they are not satisfied to let us use our own discretion in these things, but demand in addition that we base our trust and comfort on them, teaching that if we trust in them, it is as much as if we place our confidence in Christ and the Holy Spirit. We cannot tolerate their delusions according to which they think that they are doing a good work who keep their laws, and again, that it is a sin not to keep them. For they declare that the precepts and doctrines of the pope and the church come from the Holy Spirit and are the Word of God, for which reason we ought to believe and observe them. But this is an obvious and shameless lie; for how can they prove it?

22. But, they say, the Christian church is always led by the Holy Spirit, who will not permit the church to err or go wrong. To this we answer with what we said before: However good the church may be, it has never possessed the Spirit in as large a measure as Mary, who although she was led by the Spirit, erred nevertheless, so that we might learn from her experience. If she herself is uncertain, how can you make me certain?

Whither should we then go? We must also come into the temple, that is to say we must cling to the Word of God, which is secure and will not fail us and where we will certainly find Christ. I must therefore always be with the Word, if I cleave to it. If the Word of God goes conquering through death and remains alive, I must also pass through death to life, and nothing can hinder or destroy me, neither sin nor death, nor the devil. The comfort and boldness I derive from the Word of God cannot be engendered by any other doctrine, for none can be compared with it.

23. Therefore it is necessary that we understand this clearly and not place our confidence in human doctrines and the teachings of the holy fathers.

God has demonstrated this by many other examples in order to teach us not in the least to depend upon men, as the saints also may sometimes make mistakes. We read for instance in Acts 15:5-11 that not more than eighteen years after the Ascension of Christ, the apostles and the majority of the Christians held a conference. The question was raised whether the Gentiles should be compelled to submit to circumcision. There stood up the leaders of the sect of the Pharisees who believed and said: It is necessary to circumcise them, and to charge them to keep the law of Moses. There was a great commotion and all seemed to hold the same opinion. Only Peter, Paul, Barnabas and James were opposed to this view, and Peter especially rose up and said unto them: God has given the Holy Spirit unto the Gentiles who have heard the Gospel from me, even as he did unto us; and he made no distinction between us and them, cleansing their hearts by faith. Now if they received the Holy Spirit and were not circumcised, why would you force them and put a yoke upon the neck of the disciples which neither our fathers nor we were able to bear? But we believe that we shall be saved through the grace of the Lord Jesus, in like manner as they.

24. You notice that many Christians were at this council who were true believers, at a time when the church was in its youthful vigor and almost perfect, and yet God permits them all to err with the exception of three or four men. If these few men had not protested, erroneous doctrines would have been taught and a law not in accordance with the Gospel of Christ been established. Yet we are such blind fools as to say continually: The councils and the church have commanded this or that, and as they cannot be in error, their decrees must be observed.

25. Later on we read that even the most prominent leaders, both Peter and Barnabas, fell into error and all the other Jews with them. Then Paul alone rose up and rebuked Peter publicly, as he himself writes in Galatians 2:11. Now if these holy councils and holy men erred, why should we put our trust in our own councils? For they cannot for an instant be compared with the councils held by the apostles.

26. Why does God permit these things to occur? He does it that we may not depend upon or derive comfort from the words and doctrines of men, however holy they may be, but place our confidence only in the Word of God. If then even an apostle came or an angel from heaven, as St. Paul says in Galatians 1:8-9, who would preach another Gospel, we should openly declare it is not the Word of God and refuse to listen to it. Do not forget that the child can be found in no other place but the temple, or the house of God. Mary indeed sought him among the kinsfolk, who are the great, learned and pious people, but she did not find him among them.

27. There are many similar examples and types elsewhere in the Gospel which point out the same truth, namely, that nothing should be taught but the Word of God and no other doctrine should be accepted, because Christ can be found only in the Scriptures. Thus we read in the Gospel for Christmas, Luke 2:12, where the angel, who announced the birth of Christ, said to the shepherds: "And this is the sign unto you: Ye shall find a babe wrapped in swaddling clothes, and lying in a manger." Why does he not direct them to Mary and Joseph, but only points them to the swaddling clothes and the manger? The reason is that God will not point us to any saint, not even to the holy mother herself, for they may all err. Therefore a special place must be pointed out where Christ is, namely the manger, where he surely may be found, even if Joseph and Mary were not present.

This signifies that Christ is completely wrapped in the Scriptures, just as the body is wrapped in the clothes. The manger is the preaching of the Gospel, where he is lying and where he is apprehended, and from which we take our food. Now it would indeed appear that the child should lie where Joseph and Mary are, these great and holy people. Yet the angel points only to the manger, which he will not have overlooked or dishonored. It is an insignificant and simple expression, but Christ is found in it.

28. The same truth is also pointed out in other narratives, as for instance in that of holy Simeon, who had received a promise from God that he should not see death, before he had seen the Lord Christ. He came in the Spirit into the temple, found the child and received him into his arms. But here it is only emphasized that he finds Christ in the temple. From all this we learn that God would warn us against human doctrines, however excellent they may be, advising us not to depend upon them, but cleave to the only true guide, the Word of God. Lay aside everything else. Their declarations and decrees may indeed be good and right, but our heart cannot trust in them.

29. This then is the comfort we derive from this Gospel in our great trials, of which we have spoken above. We know that consolation may be found only in the Scriptures, the Word of God. For this reason God caused this to be recorded, so that we might learn these lessons, as St. Paul writes to the Romans: "For whatsoever things were written aforetime were written for our learning, that through patience and through comfort of the Scriptures we might have hope." Romans 15:4. Here he says that the Scriptures are comforting, that they impart patience and comfort. Consequently there can be nothing else that comforts the soul, not even in the most trifling temptations. For everything else with which man comforts himself, however great it may be, is altogether uncertain, and the heart inquires constantly: Who knows whether it is right? if I only were sure about it! etc. But when the heart clings to the Word of God, it may say without any wavering: This is the Word of God, which cannot lie nor err, of this I am certain. And this is our greatest struggle, that we keep and hold firmly to the Word; for if that is taken from the heart, man is lost.

30. Let us then be prepared for their representations and expostulations to the effect that the Christian church cannot err, so that we may know how to meet them, and say: Here is not the word of man, but the Word of God.

We read in this Gospel that his mother, Mary, was filled with the Holy Spirit, and yet she erred. Likewise we read in the Acts that there was a Christian council of such who believed and who had the Spirit, and yet they stumbled and would have established an unchristian law, if others had not protested. We should therefore not believe any council or, saint, if they come without the Word of God. This is then the sum total of this Gospel, and if anything else is to be said on it, we will let those explain it who have leisure; but he who studies it faithfully will easily understand it.

31. Some have broken their heads over the meaning of the words of Luke where he says that Christ advanced in wisdom and grace, for they assume that as true God he possessed all wisdom and grace from the time of his conception. But here they have shamefully altered the text with their commentaries. Therefore refrain from such idle talk and let the words stand just as they are without any commentary. We must understand them simply as saying that he grew continually and waxed strong in the Spirit, just as any other man, as we have explained it more fully in the Gospel for the Sunday after Christmas.

First Sunday after Epiphany Second Sermon. Luke 2:41-52

An Example of Severe Suffering

I am the way, the truth, and the life: no man cometh unto the Father, but by me. John 14:6

TEXT: Luke 2:41 Now his parents went to Jerusalem every year at the feast of the passover. 42 And when he was twelve years old, they went up to Jerusalem after the custom of the feast. 43 And when they had fulfilled the days, as they returned, the child Jesus tarried behind in Jerusalem; and Joseph and his mother knew not of it. 44 But they, supposing him to have been in the company, went a day's journey; and they sought him among their kinsfolk and acquaintance. 45 And when they found him not, they turned back again to Jerusalem, seeking him. 46 And it came to pass, that after three days they found him in the temple, sitting in the midst of the doctors, both hearing them, and asking them questions. 47 And all that heard him were astonished at his understanding and answers. 48 And when they saw him, they were amazed: and his mother said unto him, Son, why hast thou thus dealt with us? behold, thy father and I have sought thee sorrowing. 49 And he said unto them, How is it that ye sought me? wist ye not that I must be about my Father's business? 50 And they understood not the saying which he spake unto them. 51 And he went down with them, and came to Nazareth, and was subject unto them: but his mother kept all these sayings in her heart. 52 And Jesus increased in wisdom and stature, and in favour with God and man.

I. An Example of the Cross and of Severe Suffering

1. Hitherto, under the blindness of the papacy, nothing was taught concerning the blessed saints of God except to cover them with extravagant praise and laudation, and to praise them for exalted devotion and celestial joy, as if on earth they had not also been human beings and as if they had never suffered and felt the adversities, misfortunes and frailties of men; and as if they could not be honored sufficiently, unless they were represented in wood and stone. They have sought to strengthen this idea by means of false and shameful lies and idle tales, as if in this way the saints were highly honored and men spoke of them only in wonder and saw only such examples in them as no one could realize in this life, nor find comfort in them. In consequence, they have been turned into idols and men have been taught to call upon them, instead of the Lord Jesus Christ, as intercessors, mediators and helpers in need, to the shameless blasphemy and denial of our blessed Savior and high priest, Jesus Christ.

2. Thus they also falsely imagined to exalt the mother of Christ and know of no greater honor for her than to fill and overload her with graces and gifts, as if she had never suffered temptations, had never faltered nor failed in reason, nor in anything else. The holy Scriptures and this Gospel, on the other hand, show how God deals with his saints in a wonderful manner, according to Psalm 4:4 and in a way altogether contrary to human reason; and that the more highly he endows them with grace and exalts and honors them, the deeper he thrusts them into sorrow and suffering, yea, even into dishonor, shame and desertion.

3. Human reason would undoubtedly teach and advise God not to permit his own Son to be shamefully and ignominiously dealt with as a murderer and malefactor, and allow his blood to be shed, but rather see to it that the angels should bear him on their hands, all kings and nobles fall at his feet and render him all honor. For human wisdom consists in this, that it neither sees, nor seeks, nor desires anything except that which is high and precious, and that which brings honor; and, again, neither shuns nor flees from anything more readily than dishonor, contempt, suffering, misery, and the like. Thus God reverses the order and acts in a contrary way, deals so harshly and offensively, according to human reason and opinion, with his dearly beloved Son as he would not deal with any man on earth, as if he were not the Son of God, or of man, but the child of Satan! In the same way he also dealt with his well-beloved servant, John the Baptist, of whom Christ says, Matthew 11:11, that among those that are born of women there hath not arisen a greater than he, and yet upon him he conferred the honor of being beheaded by a knave. This was, indeed, a most dishonorable and shameful death.

4. In like manner he dealt with his dear mother, so that she was compelled to learn and experience how wonderfully God deals with his saints, and the Gospels point out with sufficient clearness, that he very seldom permitted them to see and experience what was noble, precious and joyous, but for the most part caused them to experience suffering and anxiety, as the aged and holy Simeon had foretold her, as a type for all Christians. Besides, he spoke harshly to her and repulsed her in an unfriendly manner.

5. Accordingly, this Gospel presents, first of all, the mother of Christ as an example of cross-bearing and of great suffering, such as God permits his saints to endure. For although the holy Virgin was greatly blessed with all grace and was a beautiful temple of the holy God and in preference to all was accorded the high honor of being the mother of the Son of God, and doubtless had the greatest possible pleasure and joy in her child, more so than any other mother, as was natural; yet God so ordered that she did not merely have exalted pleasure, but also great distress, pain and sorrow because of him. For her first distress was that she was in a strange place when he was born at Bethlehem, where she found no place for her child but a common stable. Her other distress was that within six weeks after his birth she was compelled to flee with the child and remain an exile for seven years. Besides she must have endured many things that are not recorded.
6. One of these afflictions, and not the least, is the misery he caused her to suffer when he permitted himself to be lost to her in the temple, and allowed her to search for him so long. By this he so terrified and saddened her that she might have despaired of finding him, as she confessed when she exclaimed, "Thy father and I have sought thee sorrowing." For let us think for a moment, how she must have felt and grieved. Every father and mother can easily understand the misery and sorrow caused by the unavoidable separation from a dear child, when they know only that the child is lost. And even if the separation should last only an hour, how great are not the sorrow and lamentation, and how many tears are not shed, without consolation, without strength to eat, drink, sleep or rest, and with such misery that they would prefer to die. How much greater the suffering, if this condition were to continue for a day and a night, or even longer, when each hour must seem like a hundred years!

7. Now, on the other hand, behold this mother who, first loses her only son, a son like whom neither she nor anyone else can have; who is alone her son and she alone his mother, without a natural father; yea, who is truly the only-begotten Son of God and in a special manner given and entrusted to her by God, that she, as his mother, should wait on him, care for him, and look after him with all diligence. Hitherto she had nourished him, not without much care and sorrow, and had strenuously defended him among strangers and enemies. Now that he has grown some and she could have her greatest joy and comfort in him, she must suddenly lose him, when she thought he was most secure and her sorrows past, and lose him not only for two hours, nor for a day and night, but three whole days, so that she was compelled to think he was lost forever. Who can think or say how her motherly heart must have been agonized and afflicted during the three whole days she was searching for him? It was marvelous that she lived through this great sorrow.

8. The affliction and suffering she was compelled to endure were not of a nature that they had occurred without her fault, but her conscience forced her to remember how God had entrusted the child to her and that no one else was accountable for him, and hence storms burst and thundered in her heart: Behold, thou hast lost the child. This is no one's fault but thine own; for thou shouldst have waited on him and looked after him, and not permitted him for a moment to go out of thy sight. How wilt thou give an account of this before God, since thou hast failed to watch over him? This is the result of sin and thou art no longer worthy to be his mother; yea, thou hast deserved to be condemned by him before all people, inasmuch as he has conferred on thee the great honor and favor of choosing thee for his mother.

9. Should not her heart have failed and fainted here from anxiety, for two reasons? First, because she lost her son and was unable to find him; secondly, which was the most severe of all and which could not happen to other mothers, making the pain all the more severe, because she must abhor herself before God, the only Father of the child, that he would no longer have or regard her as his mother, and hence she must be more sorrowful and sad at heart than any other woman on earth. In her own heart she regards herself guilty of the same sin as Eve, the first mother, who brought the whole human race to ruin. For what are all sins compared with this one, that she has neglected and lost this child, the Son of God and the Savior of the World? And if he should not be found, or, since he could not be lost, if God should have taken him back to himself, she would be the cause of preventing the completion of the work of the redemption of the world. Such and doubtless many other thoughts filled her heart with great fear, especially since she, as a pious child of God, had a very tender heart and conscience.

10. Here you may see how God dealt with the most holy person, the mother of his Son, even though she had been most highly honored by him and her joy in her Son had been immeasurably great, such as no mother ever had; and yet God so assailed her and she must be so divested of her honor and comfort that she cannot say, I am the mother of the Son. Previously she had been exalted to heaven, now she has been suddenly cast into deepest hell and is in such terror and sorrow that she might have despaired and died, and have wished that she had never seen the child, nor heard of him; and thus she might have committed a more grievous sin than any other person ever committed.

11. Thus you see, that God can deal with his saints in a way to deprive them of happiness and comfort whenever he pleases, and cast them into the greatest fear concerning that in which they have their greatest joy. So, likewise, he can again confer the greatest joy. For this was the greatest joy of this holy Virgin, that she had become the mother of this child, but now she has no greater terror and sorrow than that caused by this Son. Thus, we can have no greater terror than that caused by sin and death; and yet God can comfort us even in this, so that we may glory in the fact, as St. Paul says, Romans 5:20-21, that sin was compelled to serve to the end that grace might be greater and much more abound. And death, overcome by Christ, furnishes the reason why we may desire death and be able to die with gladness.

12. Again, if God has given us a precious faith and we therefore live in strong confidence of the fact that we have a gracious God through Christ, we are in paradise. But before we are aware, it may happen that God may cause our hearts to fail and we may think that he wants to tear Christ cut of our hearts, and Christ may be so hidden from us that we can find no consolation in him, but instead receive only horrible thoughts into our hearts from the devil; so that we may feel as if we had lost Christ and then struggle and tremble as if on account of our sins we had deserved nothing from him but wrath and condemnation.

13. Yea, though it may not be a matter of open sin, the devil can make sin of that which is no sin, and so move and terrify the heart that it will plague itself with the thought: Who knows, if God will accept thee or Christ be favorable to thee? So here; this dear mother doubted whether he would still regard her as his mother and felt in her heart as if she had neglected and lost her Son, although she was innocent in the whole matter, since he was not lost. Thus the heart speaks in temptation: Yea, God has indeed given thee an excellent faith; but perhaps he will no longer give it thee. Thou hast deserved this from some cause or other.

14. And this is the greatest and most severe trial and suffering which God at times visits upon and exercises over his saints, namely, that which we are accustomed to call deserted by grace, on account of which the human heart feels as if the grace of God had been withdrawn, so that no matter where it turns it sees nothing but wrath and terror. But this great trial is not experienced by everyone, and no one can understand its significance unless he has experienced it. A strong spirit is required in order to endure such blows.

15. Yet these examples are held up to us, in order that we may learn from them how to guard and console ourselves in temptation and to prepare ourselves for the time when God may see fit to assail us with similar great trials, in order that we may not be led to despair. For this has not been written for the sake of this Virgin, the mother of Christ, but for our benefit, in order that by it we may be taught and comforted.

16. For the same, reason numerous examples of the great trials of other exalted saints are presented in Scriptures, among whom undoubtedly was that of the patriarch Jacob, of whom Moses writes, Genesis 32:24, that he wrestled the whole night with God; again, of Joshua. Joshua 7:7, to whom God had given the great and powerful promise that he should be able to overcome the heathen that opposed him, admonished him to be comforted and undismayed, for he would be with him, etc. On the strength of this promise Joshua went joyously forward, boldly struck out against his enemies, and gained a great victory. But what happened? Even while he possessed such faith and courage and in the same faith had taken and destroyed Jericho, it came to pass that not more than three thousand men from among all the people of Israel were sent to Ai to conquer and destroy it. They were proud and audacious, because the city was small and the enemy few in number. But when they arrived at the city, they were suddenly seized with fear, turned their backs and fled from the enemy, although not more than thirty six of their number were slain. Joshua himself lost courage, prostrated himself on the ground and lay on his face all day and cried to God: "Alas, O Lord, wherefore hast thou at all brought this people over Jordan, to deliver us into the hand of the Amorites to destroy us? would that we had been content and dwelt beyond Jordan." Behold the great and valiant hero lies there on the ground with his faith, who had received the strong Word of God, and God alone can raise him up again.

Why is he so despondent? Simply because God, in order to try him, had concealed himself and therefore had disheartened him, in order that Joshua might learn to realize what man is and can do without the divine help

17. Sufferings like these are immeasurably heavy and unbearable to human nature; therefore the saints cry and complain woefully and wretchedly under them, many examples of which are found in the Psalms, as Psalm 31:23, "I said in my haste, I am cut off from before thine eyes," that is, "I knew and felt nothing else than that my heart said to me, God does not care for you." And if God would not support them by his power and help them out of their sufferings, they would have to sink into hell. Thus Psalm 94:17 says "Unless the Lord had been my help, my soul had soon dwelt in silence."

18. Therefore, this holy Virgin was a real martyr for three days, and these days were heavier to her than was the external pain of martyrdom to other saints. She had had such anxiety on her Son's account that she could not have suffered any more bitter pain, For that is the greatest torture and woe, when the heart is attacked and tortured. All other sufferings that assail the body are more endurable; yea, amid them the heart can be joyful and can scorn all bodily suffering, as we read concerning St. Agnes and other martyrs. That is only half-suffering when the body alone is afflicted, while the heart and soul remain full of joy; but when the heart alone is compelled to endure suffering only great and noble spirits, and special grace and strength, are able to endure it.

19. Now, why does God permit these afflictions to come upon his loved ones? Certainly not without reason, nor from wrath or lack of grace, but from motives of great grace and mercy, in order to show us how, in all things, he deals with us in a friendly and paternal manner and how faithfully he cares for his own and so guides them that their faith may be more and more exercised and become stronger and stronger. But he does this especially for the following reasons.

20. First, that he may guard his own against presumption, so that great saints, who have received special grace and gifts from God, may not presume and depend on themselves. For if they should at all times be strong in spirit, and experience only joy and sweetness, they might finally fall into the fatal pride of the devil, which despises God and trusts in self. Hence they must be seasoned and tempered so as not always to feel the power of the Spirit; but that their faith may at times tumble and their hearts tremble, in order that they may see what they are and be compelled to confess that they cannot do anything unless God sustains them by his pure grace. Thus God keeps them in humility and the knowledge of themselves, so that they do not become proud nor carnally secure in regard to their faith and holiness, as it happened to St. Peter, when he boasted he was willing to lay down his life for Christ, John 13:37.

21. Thus the prophet David confesses that he was compelled to learn this lesson, Psalm 30:6-7; "I said in my prosperity, I shall never be moved. Thou didst hide thy face, I was troubled." And St. Paul in 2 Corinthians 1:8-9 complains of the great affliction that befell him in Asia, saying: "We would not have you ignorant, brethren, concerning our affliction which befell us in Asia, that we were weighed down exceedingly, beyond our power, insomuch that we despaired even of life; yea, we ourselves have had the answer of death within ourselves, that we should not trust in ourselves, but in God which raiseth the dead." And in 2 Corinthians 12:7-9 he says that there was given him a thorn in the flesh, a messenger of Satan to buffet him, that he should not be too highly exalted, on account of the great revelation which he had received; and that God would not remove this, although he had prayed thrice, but had to cling to the consolation which God afforded him, namely, that he should be satisfied with his grace and by means of it overcome his weakness. Therefore, such a trial of the saints is as necessary or even more necessary than food and drink, in order that they may remain in fear and humility, and learn to adhere alone to the grace of God.

22. Secondly, God permits his saints to suffer these trials as an example for others, both to alarm the carnally secure and to comfort the timid and alarmed. The wicked and impenitent may learn from this how to amend their ways, keep themselves from sin, since they can see that God deals even with the saints in a way to produce anxiety, in order that they may feel nothing but wrath and disfavor, and become alarmed as if they had committed the grossest sins that man can commit. So here, the mother of Christ was forced to contend, even till the third day, with a heavy heart, which accused her as if she had lost the Son of God, a sin the like of which no one else on earth had committed, and she had to fear only the Most High; and yet truly there was no such sin, nor wrath, nor disfavor.

23. If, therefore, the hearts of the godly are overwhelmed with such heavy and unbearable alarm and anxiety, what shall become of others who lie securely and continue impenitent in real sins, and who deserve and heap up the wrath of God? How shall they be able to stand when suddenly seized by fear, which may happen at any moment?

24. Again, such examples are intended to serve as a means of comfort for alarmed and anxious consciences, when they see that God has attacked not only them, but also the most exalted saints and permitted them to suffer the same trials and anxieties. For if we had no examples in Scripture, showing that these things happened to the saints, we would not be able to endure, and timid consciences would be led to cry out: Yea, I alone am compelled to endure these sufferings; when did God permit the pious and holy ones to be thus tempted? Hence, it must be a sign that God will have nothing to do with me. But when we see and hear that God has in like manner dealt with his saints and did not spare even his own mother, we have the knowledge and comfort that we need not despair in our trials, but remain quiet and wait until he helps us, even as he has helped all his saints.

25. In the third place, we note the true reason why God does this, namely, in order that he may teach his saints to seek true comfort and prepare themselves that they may find Christ and keep him. The principal part of this Gospel lesson is to teach us how and where we are to seek and find Christ. So the text says that Mary and Joseph sought the child Jesus for three days without finding him, neither in Jerusalem, nor among their friends and acquaintances, until they came to the temple where he sat among the teachers and where the Scriptures and God's Word are studied. And when they were astonished and began to complain how they had sought him with sorrow, he said to them:

II. The Teaching as to Where We are to Seek Christ

"How is it that ye sought me? Knew ye not that I must be in my Father's house (in the things of my Father)?"

26. What is meant by "I must be in the things of my Father?" Are not all creatures the Father's? All things belong to him; but he gave us the creatures for our use, that we should use them in our earthly life according to our best understanding. But one thing he reserved for himself, which is holy and is called God's own, and which we are in a special manner to receive from him. This is his holy Word, through which he rules the hearts and consciences, and makes holy and saves. Therefore, the temple is also called his holy place or his holy dwelling place, in order that he may there manifest himself and be heard through his Word. Hence Christ is in the things of his Father, when he speaks to us through his Word and by means of it leads us to the Father.

27. Behold, he punishes his parents because they had erred and had sought him among earthly and human affairs, among friends and acquaintances, not thinking that he must be in that which is his Father's. He wishes to indicate by this, that his kingdom and the whole essence of Christianity consists alone in the Word and in faith, not in external things (as the external and hypocritical sanctity of Judaism), nor in temporal and worldly ordinance or government. In a word; he will not permit himself to be found, either among friends and acquaintances, nor in anything outside of his Word. For he does not wish to be worldly, nor in that which is worldly, but in that which is his Father's, even as he always manifested himself from his birth through his entire life. He was, indeed, in the world, but he did not conform to the world, as he also said to Pilate, "My kingdom is not of this world." He was among friends and acquaintances and came to them, but did not identify himself with any of their affairs in the world, except that he sojourned in the world as a guest and used it to satisfy the wants of his body; but he waits alone on that which is his Father's i.e., the Word. There he can be found; there he who wishes truly to find him, must seek him.

28. Hence, as I have already said, God will not tolerate that we depend on anything else and permit our hearts to trust in anything that is not Christ in his Word, be it ever so holy and spiritual. Faith has no other foundation on which it can stand. Hence, it happened that the wisdom, thoughts and hopes of the mother of Christ and of Joseph must fail and everything be lost while they were seeking him in other places. For they did not seek him as they ought, but as flesh and blood do, which always grope after other comfort than that of the Word; for it always wants what it can see and feel, and acquire by meditation and reason.

29. Therefore God permits them to fall and fail, in order that they may learn that all comfort not based on the Word, but on flesh and blood, on men and all other creatures, must inevitably fail. Here everything must be abandoned; friends, acquaintances and the whole city of Jerusalem, all art, wit and everything belonging to these and to men; for all this neither gives nor aids comfort, until the Lord is sought in the temple, since he is in that which is his Father's. There he can truly be found and the heart is made to rejoice, or else it would have to remain without the least comfort.

30. Accordingly, if God permits us to be thus sorely tried, we should learn then not to follow our own opinion, or human counsel, which directs us hither and thither, nor to depend on ourselves and others, but we should consider that we must seek Christ in the things of his Father; that is, that we cling simply and alone to the Word of the Gospel, which directs us Christians in the right way and gives us correct knowledge. Therefore, if you desire to comfort others or yourself, learn in this and all other spiritual trials to say with Christ; Why is it that you run hither and thither and so torment yourself with anxious and sorrowful thoughts, as if God had no more grace for you and as if Christ was not to be found, and that you will not be satisfied unless you find him by your own efforts and can feel yourself holy and without sin? Nothing can result from this; it is merely lost effort and labor. Do you not know that he does not wish to be found, except in that which is his Father's? Not in that which you or all other men are or have. It is not the fault of Christ and his grace; he indeed is not nor does he remain lost, he may always be found. But the fault lies in you, because you do not seek him rightly where he is to be found, since you judge according to your own feelings and think you can lay hold on him through your own thoughts. You must come to this, where neither your work and rule, nor that of any human being, but that of God is, namely, his Word. There you shall meet him, and hear and see that there is neither wrath nor displeasure there, as you feared and dreaded would be, but pure grace and sincere love toward you and as a friendly and dear mediator he entreats the Father most earnestly and effectually for you. Nor does he send such trial upon you in order to cast you off, but that you may the better learn to know and the more closely cling to his Word, to punish your lack of understanding and that you may experience how earnestly and faithfully he cares for you.

31. Behold, here is the precious doctrine of this Gospel, namely, how rightly to seek Christ and how he may be found; and it points out the real comfort that can satisfy troubled consciences, take away all terror and anxiety and again rejoice the heart and at the same time give it a new life. But the heart must become heavy before it can attain and lay hold of this truth; it must first run and experience that everything else is lost and useless in the search for Christ, and finally no counsel is to be had, unless you give yourself, without your own and all human comfort, to the Word alone. In bodily mishaps and straits you may seek comfort in gold, possessions, friends and acquaintances; but in these matters you must have something that is not human but divine, namely, the Word, through which alone Christ deals with us and we can deal with him. This how ever, is especially to be noted, as the Evangelist says: "They understood not the saying, which he spake unto them."

32. This should shut the mouths of vain babblers who exalt the holy Virgin Mary and other saints as if they knew everything and could not err; for you can see here how they err and falter, not only in this that they seek Christ and know not where to find him until they accidentally come to the temple, but also that they could not understand these words with which he censured their ignorance and is compelled to say to them: "Knew ye not, that I must be in the things of my Father.?" The Evangelist has pointed this out with great diligence, in order that men should not give credence to such falsehoods as ignorant, inexperienced and conceited teachers of works-righteousness present in exalting the saints, even setting them up as idols.

33. The holy Virgin is not in need of such falsely invented praise. God led her in such a way that he concealed much from her and daily permitted many things to happen which she had not known beforehand, in order that he might keep her humble, so that she should not regard herself better than others. And this is praise and honor enough for her, that he guided and sustained her by his grace, although he had endowed her with many far greater gifts than others; and yet so that she, like others, was compelled, through manifold temptations and sorrows, to learn daily and grow in grace.

34. Examples like this are useful and necessary to show us that even the saints, who are the children of God and highly favored above others, still have weaknesses so that they frequently err and blunder, yea, retain many faults, at times even commit great sins; yet not intentionally and willfully, but from weakness and ignorance, as we see again and again in the lives of the apostles. This happens in order that we may learn neither to build nor depend on any man; but, as this Gospel teaches, to cling to the Word of God only; and in order that we may find comfort in such examples and be not led to despair, although we may be weak and ignorant; and yet that we should not become bold and carnally secure on account of such grace as the haughty and pretended saints are wont to do.

35. In a word, you have in this Gospel a strong example with which to overthrow the common cry both of the false saints and the great critics, which they still keep up, in order that contrary to the Word of God they may continue in their trifling; to wit, that they may reproach us with the writings and teachings of the fathers and the decrees of the church and councils; for, they say, these had the Holy Spirit, therefore they could not err, etc. In this way they desire to mislead us concerning the Scriptures and the true place to which Christ himself points and where he can surely be found; in order that what happened to Mary the mother, and to Joseph may happen also to us, namely, that we seek Christ everywhere and yet find him nowhere except at the place where he is to be found. The same thing has been carried on with great power in Christendom through the cursed government of the pope, who has striven both by his teachings and actions, threats and punishments to cause men to fail in seeking or finding Christ in the Scriptures.

36. As was stated in the exposition of the Gospel for the preceding Sunday, they filled the world with three kinds of doctrines by which men have been led away from the Word of God. The first was the very gross one written by St. Thomas (of doubtful sanctity) and others by the schoolmen (scholastics) which proceeds from heathen art and natural reason, concerning which they have said: The light of nature is like a beautiful and bright tablet, and Scripture is like the sun shining on this tablet, causing it to shine all the more brightly. So also the divine light shines on the light of nature and illumines it. With this comparison they introduced this heathen doctrine into Christendom. According to this view they have both taught and conducted the high schools in a way to reverse the comparison and thereby attempted, by means of reason and Aristotle, art and teaching, to illumine Scripture, which nevertheless is the only true light, and without which all the light of reason is simply darkness in divine things and in the articles of faith, as we have often said before.

37. In the second place, the world has been filled with the teachings and commands of men and the so-called ordinances and commands of the church concerning fasts, celebrations, prayers, singing, vestments, monkery, etc., with which all the trickeries of the pope and the books of the Summists are filled and by means of these they have held out to the people the false hope of leading them to heaven. This has burst upon men like a flood and drowned the world, ensnared and captured all consciences, so that it is almost impossible to rescue anyone from these jaws of hell. On the basis of this the examples of the saints and the deceived have been so led, and this has been confirmed by the popes and councils, that they were forced to regard them as of equal value with the articles of faith. Therefore they shouted like the insane, without intermission: Aye, the councils have decreed this, the church has commanded it, it has been maintained ever so long, and like statements.

38. In the third place, besides these two doctrines they have abandoned Holy Scripture; yet so as to attach it to some of the writings and expositions of the fathers, nevertheless not any farther than it pleased the pope and would not prove contrary to his law, and that no one should use Scripture except in accordance with the pleasure of the pope, to whom alone pertains the interpretations of Scripture and whose knowledge and judgments everyone is bound to accept. Yet, in spite of this, they so far honor the fathers as to demand that their interpretations and explanations should be followed. All the world accepted this and so received all that the fathers said, as if they could not err, and shouted again: Aye, how could it be possible that so many holy, learned and highly intelligent men should not have understood the Scriptures?

39. To this we should reply as is taught in this Gospel: Be they called holy, learned, fathers, councils, or any other name, even though they were Mary, Joseph and all the saints it does not follow that they could not have erred and made mistakes. For here you learn that the mother of Christ though she possessed great intelligence and enlightenment, showed great ignorance in that she did not know where to find Christ, and in consequence was censured by him because she did not know what she should have known. If she failed and through her ignorance was brought to such anxiety and sorrow that she thought she had lost Christ, is it a wonder that other saints should often have erred and stumbled, when they followed their own notions, without the guidance of Scripture, or put their own notions into Scripture?

40. Hence, it amounts to nothing, if one asserts that men must believe and adhere to the decrees of councils or the teachings and writings of the holy fathers; for all these can and may err. But on the other hand, a definite place must be designated where Christ is and desires to be found, namely, as he here himself points out, when he says: He must be in that which is his Father's.

41. It would be well for us Christians if we always followed the example presented in this Gospel and make it a maxim against all teachings and whatever can be set up against the Word of God, and say: Christ should not be sought among kinsfolk and acquaintances, nor in anything that men may have, no matter how holy, pious, or great they may be; for the mother of Christ herself erred and sinned because she did not know or understand this.

42. Therefore conscience cannot establish itself on any saint or any creature, but on Christ alone. I may regard and honor reason and natural light ever so highly, but this will I reserve, that I dare not depend on it. Whatever the holy fathers and councils may have taught, decreed and ordered, as seemed good to them, I let pass for what it is worth, yet only so, that I am not to be bound by them, as if I were compelled to observe them or depend upon them. In a word, you may allow all these things to remain and stand for their true worth in human affairs, which are regulated as we deem best; but we dare not substitute them for Christ, that is, the comforts of our souls for them, but regard them merely as being concerned about the outward human life before the world.

43. If the papists had been willing to admit this, as the Word of God teaches, we would long ago have been united with them, would have been satisfied that they should order and establish these human affairs as it pleased them, reserving, however, the freedom for ourselves not to be forced to maintain them further than it is our pleasure, not from necessity or as if they had any value before God. They are not indeed willing to do this, but have hung their additions to it so that men are bound to observe their ordinances as if they were necessary to salvation, and call them the commands of the Church of Christ and their non-observance a mortal sin. We neither can nor will do or allow any thing of the kind.

44. Yea, say they, the church, the holy fathers, and the councils have decreed and determined many things in controversial articles against the heretics, that have been received, which each one must believe and observe; therefore what has been decreed by the church and councils concerning other matters must also have authority.

45. Answer: here they must again permit us freedom of judgment, so that we may not be bound, without any exception, by what the councils decreed or the fathers taught; but be allowed to maintain this distinction, namely, if they have determined and established anything in harmony with the Word of God, we accept it, not for their sake, but because of the Word itself, on which they ground themselves and to which they direct us. In this case, they do not act as mere men, but lead us to that which is God's, and are no longer among friends and acquaintances, but sit among those who hear Christ and inquire of him about the things of Scripture. Then we gladly honor them by listening to them. But when they determine anything contrary to and outside of this rule concerning other matters, not according to the Word of God, but according to their own opinion, this does not concern the conscience. Hence, it is to be regarded as a human affair by which we dare not be bound, nor be compelled to regard them as if they contained Christian faith and doctrine, but as St. Augustine has correctly said: *Totum hoc genus habet liberas observationes,* — as to what this thing is, we are free to observe or not.

46. You say further: Yea, the church and the fathers were endowed with the Holy Spirit, who kept them from error. The answer to this is not difficult: The church and councils may have been ever so holy, they did not have the Holy Spirit in greater measure than Mary, the mother of Christ, who was also a member, yea, at the time, the most eminent member of the Church. And although she had been sanctified by the Holy Spirit; yet he permitted her at times to err, even in the important matters of faith. From this it does not follow, that the saints, who were endowed with the Spirit, could on this account not err, nor that everything they said would have to be correct. Great weakness and ignorance may be found to exist even in the most eminent people. and hence we cannot judge concerning doctrines and matters of faith on the basis of personal holiness, for all this can fail. But here you come to the Word of God which is sure and infallible, where you shall certainly find Christ and the Holy Spirit, and can be and remain firmly fortified against sin, death, and the devil.

47. Examples like these, which show that even the saints and the great mass called the church may err, we find elsewhere in the Scripture, especially in Acts 15, where it is shown that only eighteen years after the Ascension of Christ, the apostles and the whole body of Christians came together in Jerusalem. At that time the most eminent and learned of the Pharisees, who had became believers, arose and taught that converts from heathenism would have to be circumcised and be compelled to observe the law of Moses and by this teaching drew nearly the entire body of believers to their views. Then Peter, Paul, Barnabas and James stood alone in opposition to this view and concluded from Scriptures that the Gentiles should not be burdened with the observance of the Law, since God had bestowed on them, without the Law, through the preaching of the Gospel, the Holy Spirit even as upon the Jews. Behold, here were so many Christians who had faith at a time when the church was young and at her best, and yet all of them, except those three or four, fell into the error of thinking that the Law of Moses was necessary to salvation. If these few had not contended against this error, an erroneous article and command against Christ would have been established and confirmed. Again, at a later period St. Peter, who had maintained the true doctrine, stumbled with Barnabas at the same article, in that they dissembled with the Jews who refused to eat with the Gentiles and thereby gave offense to the Gentiles, in the breach of this freedom, so that St. Paul was compelled to reprimand them publicly, as he does in Galatians 2:11. Therefore, let us learn from this example to be prudent in the matters that concern faith and Christ, not allowing ourselves to be led by men, but adhering to the Word and maintaining the rule which St. Paul lays down in Galatians 1:8-9, that, even though an angel should come from heaven and preach another Gospel, he should be accursed; and the fact remains that Christ can be found nowhere else than in that which is God's.

48. The same truth has been previously presented in many figures and examples, as in the Gospel for Christmas, Luke 2:12, where the angels give no other sign to the shepherds by which they might find Christ than the manger and the swaddling clothes. There they should find him lying and wrapped up, not in the bosom of the mother, nor on her lap, which would have seemed credible. That is, God does not wish to direct us to any saint or person of man, but only to the Word or Scripture, in which Christ is wrapped as in swaddling clothes, and in the poor manger (that is the preaching of the Gospel), which is so highly esteemed, and serves merely for the feeding of the cattle. Again, we have also heard from the aged and holy Simeon who, as had been promised him by God, should not die until he had seen Christ, but who does not recognize him until by the instigation of the Holy Spirit he enters the temple. So also the wise men from the east who, when they came to Jerusalem and no longer saw the star, hear of no other sign concerning Christ, as to where he was born and where he could be found, than the Scripture of the prophet Micah. So much may be said concerning the most important teaching and the principal parts of this Gospel. Finally, it is also to be noted that the Evangelist says: "His mother kept all these sayings in her heart."

49. This is also given for our admonition, in order that we may endeavor to keep the Word of God in our hearts, as the blessed Virgin did, who, seeing she had erred and lacked understanding, became all the more diligent to keep in her heart all she heard from Christ. She furnishes another example, that above all things we should adhere to the Word and not permit it to go out of our hearts, but constantly use it, learn to gain strength from it, find comfort in it, and increase in it, as is indeed necessary for all of us. For when we come to the point where we shall be tried and tempted, we are liable to be forgotten or dropped even by those who are diligent.

50. Whatever else might be said concerning this Gospel, as how Christ went home with his parents and was obedient and subject to them, etc., is easy and may readily be ascertained. Again, how we are to understand that Christ increased in wisdom and in favor was presented in the Gospel for a previous Sunday.

Second Sunday after Epiphany. John 2:1-11

Marriage at Cana

Jesus Turns Water into Wine

TEXT: John 2 And the third day there was a marriage in Cana of Galilee; and the mother of Jesus was there: 2 And both Jesus was called, and his disciples, to the marriage. 3 And when they wanted wine, the mother of Jesus saith unto him, They have no wine. 4 Jesus saith unto her, Woman, what have I to do with thee? Mine hour is not yet come. 5 His mother saith unto the servants, Whatsoever he saith unto you, do it. 6 And there were set there six waterpots of stone, after the manner of the purifying of the Jews, containing two or three firkins apiece. 7 Jesus saith unto them, Fill the waterpots with water. And they filled them up to the brim. 8 And he saith unto them, Draw out now, and bear unto the governor of the feast. And they bare it. 9 When the ruler of the feast had tasted the water that was made wine, and knew not whence it was: (but the servants which drew the water knew;) the governor of the feast called the bridegroom, 10 And saith unto him, Every man at the beginning doth set forth good wine; and when men have well drunk, then that which is worse: but thou hast kept the good wine until now. 11 This beginning of miracles did Jesus in Cana of Galilee, and manifested forth his glory; and his disciples believed on him.

1. Enough has been written heretofore on marriage; hence we leave that subject for the present, and treat the following three topics in this Gospel text: first, the consolation this history affords married people by virtue of their marriage; secondly, the faith and love revealed in this Gospel lesson; thirdly, the spiritual significance of this marriage.

2. In the first place, it is indeed a high honor paid to married life for Christ himself to attend this marriage, together with his mother and his disciples. Moreover, his mother is present as the one arranging the wedding, the parties married being apparently her poor relatives or neighbors, and she being compelled to act as the bride's mother; so of course, it was nothing more than a wedding, and in no way a display. For Christ lived up to his doctrine, not going to the rich, but to the poor; or, if he does go to the great and rich, he is sure to rebuke and reprove, coming away with disfavor, earning small thanks at their hands, with no thought of honoring them by a miracle as he does here.

3. Now the second honor is his giving good wine for the poor marriage by means of a great miracle, making himself the bride's chief cup-bearer; it may be too that he had no money or jewel to give as a wedding present. He never did such honor to the life or doings of the Pharisees; for by this miracle he confirms marriage as the work and institution of God, no matter how common or how lowly it appears in the eyes of men, God none the less acknowledges his own work and loves it. Even our Caiaphases themselves have often declared and preached that marriage was the only state instituted by God. Who then instituted the others? Certainly not God, but the devil by means of men; yet they shun, reject and revile this state, and deem themselves so holy that they not only themselves avoid marriage — though they need it and ought to marry — but from excess of holiness they will not even attend a marriage, being much holier than Christ himself, who as an unholy sinner attends a wedding.

4. Since then marriage has the foundation and consolation, that it is instituted by God and that God loves it, and that Christ himself so honors and comforts it, everybody ought to prize and esteem it, and the heart ought to be glad, that it is surely the state God loves and cheerfully endures every burden in it, even though the burdens be ten times heavier than they are. For this is the reason there is so much care and unpleasantness in marriage to the outward man, because everything that is God's Word and work, if it is to be blessed at all, must be distasteful, bitter and burdensome to the outward man. On this account marriage is a state that cultivates and exercises faith in God and love to our neighbor by means of manifold cares, labors, unpleasantnesses, crosses and all kinds of adversities, that are to follow everything that is God's Word and work. All this the chaste whoremongers, saintly effeminates and Sodomites nicely escape, serving God outside of God's ordinance by doings of their own.

5. For this is what Christ also indicates by his readiness to supply any want arising in marriage, bestowing wine where it is needed, and making it of water; as though he would say: Must you drink water, that is, suffer affliction outwardly, and is this distasteful? Very well, I will sweeten it for you and change the water into wine, so that your affliction will be your joy and delight. I will not do this by taking the water away or having it poured out; it shall remain, yea, I will have it poured in and the vessels filled up to the brim. For I will not deprive Christian marriage of its cares and trials, but rather add to it. The thing shall be wondrous, so that none, except they themselves who experience it, shall understand it. It shall be on this wise:

6. God's Word shall do it, by which all things are made, preserved and transformed; that Word which turns your water into wine, and distasteful marriage into delight. That God has instituted marriage (Genesis 2:32) the heathen and unbelievers do not know, therefore their water remains water and never becomes wine; for they feel not God's pleasure and delight in married life, which if they did feel they would experience such delight in my pleasure as not to feel the half of their affliction, feeling it outwardly only, but inwardly not at all. And this would be the way to turn water into wine, mixing my pleasure with your displeasure and placing the one against the other, so that my pleasure would drown your displeasure, and turn it into pleasure; but this pleasure of mine nothing will reveal and give to you except my Word, Genesis 1:31: "God saw everything that he had made, and, behold, it was very good."

7. Here too Christ indicates that he is not displeased with a marriage feast, nor with the things belonging to a wedding such as adornments, cheerfulness, eating and drinking, according to the usage and custom of the country; which appear to be superfluous and needless expense and a worldly matter; only so far as these things are used in moderation and in keeping with a marriage. For the bride and groom must be adorned; so also the guests must eat and drink to be cheerful. And such dining and doing may all be done in good conscience; for the Scriptures occasionally report the like, even the Gospel lessons mentioning bridal adornment, the wedding garment, guests and feastings at weddings. Thus Abraham's servant in Genesis 24:53 presents ornaments of gold and silver to Rebecca, the bride of Isaac, and to her brothers; so that in these things no one need pay attention to the sour-visaged hypocrites and self-constituted saints who are pleased with nothing but what they themselves do and teach, and will not suffer a maid to wear a wreath or to adorn herself at all.

8. God is not concerned about such external things, if only faith and love reign; provided, as already stated, it be in moderation and in accord with each person's station. For this marriage, although it was poor and small, had three tables; which is indicated by the word Architriclinus, showing that the ruler of the feast had three tables to provide for; moreover, the groom did not himself attend to this office, but had servants; then too there was wine to drink; all of which, if poverty were to be urged, might have been dispensed with, as is frequently the case with us. So also the guests did not merely quench their thirst with the wine; for the ruler of the feast speaks of how the good wine ought first to be set on, then, when men have freely drunk, that which is worse. All this Christ allows to pass, and we likewise should let it pass and not make it a matter of conscience. They were not of the devil, even if a few drank of the wine a little beyond what thirst required, and became merry; else you would have to blame Christ for being the cause by means of his presence, and his mother by asking for it; so that both Christ and his mother are sinners in this if the sour-visaged saints are to render judgment.

9. But the excess customary in our times is a different thing, where men do not eat and drink but gorge themselves with food and drink, revel and carouse, and act as though it were a sign of skill or strength to consume overmuch: where, moreover, the intention is not to be merry, but to be full and crazy. But these are swine, not men; to such Christ would not give wine, nor would he visit them. So also in the matter of dress, it is not the marriage that is kept in mind, but display and pomp; as though the most admirable were those most able to wear gold, silver and pearls, and to spoil much silk and broadcloth, which even asses might do and switches.

10. What then is moderation? Reason should teach that, and cite examples from other countries and cities where such pomp and excess are unknown. But to give my opinion, I would say a farmer is well adorned if for his wedding he have clothes twice as fine as he daily wears at his work; a burgher likewise; and a nobleman, if he have garments twice as costly as a townsman; a count, twice as costly as a nobleman; a duke, twice as costly as a count, and so in due order. In like manner food and drink and the entertainment of guests should be governed by their social position, and the purpose of the table should be pleasure not debauchery.

11. Now is it a sin to play and dance at a wedding, inasmuch as some declare great sin is caused by dancing? Whether the Jews had dances I do not know; but since it is the custom of the country, like inviting guests, decorating, eating and drinking and being merry, I see no reason to condemn it, save its excess when it goes beyond decency and moderation. That sin should be committed is not the fault of dancing alone; since at a table or in church that may happen; even as it is not the fault of eating that some while so engaged should turn themselves into swine. Where things are decently conducted I will not interfere with the marriage rites and customs, and dance and never mind. Faith and love cannot be driven away either by dancing or by sitting still, as long as you keep to decency and moderation. Young children certainly dance without sin; do the same also, and be a child, then dancing will not harm you. Otherwise were dancing a sin in itself, children should not be allowed to dance. This is sufficient concerning marriage.

II. The Doctrine and Example of Love and Faith

12. In the second place, to return to. our Gospel lesson, we here see the example of love in Christ and his mother. The mother renders service and takes the part of house-keeper: Christ honors the occasion by his personal presence, by a miracle and a gift. And all this is for the benefit of the groom, the bride and the guests, as is the nature of love and its works. Thus Christ lures all hearts to himself, to rely on him as ever ready to help, even in temporal things, and never willing to forsake any; so that all who believe in him shall not suffer want, be it in spiritual or temporal things; rather must water become wine, and every creature turned into the thing his believer needs. He who believes must have sufficient, and no one can prevent it.

13. But the example of faith is still more wonderful in this Gospel. Christ waits to the very last moment when the want is felt by all present, and there is no counsel or help left. This shows the way of divine grace; it is not imparted to one who still has enough, and has not yet felt his need. For grace does not feed the full and satiated, but the hungry, as we have often said. Whoever still deems himself wise, strong and pious, and finds something good in himself, and is not yet a poor, miserable, sick sinner and fool, the same cannot come to Christ the Lord, nor receive his grace.

14. But whenever the need is felt, he does not at once hasten and bestow what is needed and desired, but delays and tests our faith and trust, even as he does here; yea, what is still more severe, he acts as though he would not help at all, but speaks with harshness and austerity. This you observe in the case of his mother. She feels the need and tells him of it, desiring his help and counsel in a humble and polite request. For she does not say: My dear son, furnish us wine; but: "They have no wine." Thus she merely touches his kindness, of which she is fully assured. As though she would say: He is so good and gracious, there is no need of my asking, I will only tell him what is lacking, and he will of his own accord do more than one could ask. This is the way of faith, it pictures God's goodness to itself in this manner, never doubting but that it is really so; therefore it makes bold to bring its petition and to present its need.

15. But see, how unkindly he turns away the humble request of his mother who addresses him with such great confidence. Now observe the nature of faith. What has it to rely on? Absolutely nothing, all is darkness. It feels its need and sees help nowhere; in addition, God turns against it like a stranger and does not recognize it, so that absolutely nothing is left. It is the same way with our conscience when we feel our sin and the lack of righteousness; or in the agony of death when we feel the lack of life; or in the dread of hell when eternal salvation seems to have left us. Then indeed there is humble longing and knocking, prayer and search, in order to be rid of sin, death and dread. And then he acts as if he had only begun to show us our sins, as if death were to continue, and hell never to cease. Just as he here treats his mother, by his refusal making the need greater and more distressing than it was before she came to him with her request; for now it seems everything is lost, since the one support on which she relied in her need is also gone.

16. This is where faith stands in the heat of battle. Now observe how his mother acts and here becomes our teacher. However harsh his words sound, however unkind he appears, she does not in her heart interpret this as anger, or as the opposite of kindness, but adheres firmly to the conviction that he is kind, refusing to give up this opinion because of the thrust she received, and unwilling to dishonor him in her heart by thinking him to be otherwise than kind and gracious- as they do who are without faith, who fall back at the first shock and think of God merely according to what they feel, like the horse and the mule, Psalm 32:9. For if Christ's mother had allowed those harsh words to frighten her she would have gone away silently and displeased; but in ordering the servants to do what he might tell them she proves that she has overcome the rebuff and still expects of him nothing but kindness.

17. What do you think of the hellish blow, when a man in his distress, especially in the highest distress of conscience, receives the rebuff, that he feels God declaring to him: "What have I to do with thee?" Quid mihi et tibi? He must needs faint and despair, unless he knows and understands the nature of such acts of God, and is experienced in faith. For he will act just as he feels, and will not think of God in a different way and mean the words. Feeling nothing but wrath and hearing nothing but indignation, he will consider God only as his enemy and angry judge. But just as he thinks God to be so will he find him. Thus he will expect nothing good from him. That is to renounce God with all his goodness. The result is that he flees and hates him, and will not have God to be God; and every other blasphemy that is the fruit of unbelief.

18. Hence the highest thought in this Gospel lesson, and it must ever be kept in mind, is, that we honor God as being good and gracious, even if he acts and speaks otherwise, and all our understanding and feeling be otherwise., For in this way feeling is killed, and the old man perishes, so that nothing but faith in God's goodness remains, and no feeling. For here you see how his mother retains a free faith and holds it forth as an example to us. She is certain that he will be gracious, although she does not feel it. She is certain also that she feels otherwise than she believes. Therefore she freely leaves and commends all to his goodness, and fixes for him neither time nor place, neither manner nor measure, neither person nor name. He is to act when it pleases him. If not in the midst of the feast, then at the end of it, or after the feast. My defeat I will swallow, his scorning me, letting me stand in disgrace before all the guests, speaking so unkindly to me, causing us all to blush for shame. He acts tart, but he is sweet I know. Let us proceed in the same way, then we are true Christians.

19. Here note how severely he deals with his own mother, teaching us thereby not only the example of faith mentioned above, but confirming that in things pertaining to God and his service we are to know neither father nor mother, as Moses writes in Deuteronomy 33:9: "He who says of his father and of his mother, I know them not, observes thy Word, Israel." For although there is no higher authority on earth than that of father and mother, still this ends when God's Word and work begin. For in divine things neither father nor mother, still less, a bishop or any other person, only God's Word is to teach and guide. And if father and mother were to order, teach, or even beg you to do anything for God, and in his service that he has not clearly ordered and commanded, you are to reply: Quid mihi et tibi? What have I and you to do with each other? In this same way Chris there refuses absolutely to do God's work when his own mother wants it.

20. For father and mother are in duty bound, yea, God made them father and mother for this very purpose, not to teach and lead their children to God according to their own notions and devotion, but according to God's command; as St. Paul declares in Ephesians 6:4: "Ye fathers; provoke not your children to wrath: but nurture them in the chastening and admonition of the Lord;" i.e. teach them God's command and Word, as you were taught, and not notions of your own.

Thus in this Gospel lesson you see the mother of Christ directing the servants away from herself unto Christ, telling them not: Whatsoever I say unto you, do it; but: "Whatsoever he saith unto you, do it." To this Word alone you must direct everyone, if you would direct aright; so that this word of Mary (whatsoever he saith, do it) is, and ought to be, a daily saying in Christendom, destroying all doctrines of men and everything not really Christ's Word. And we ought firmly to believe that what is imposed upon us over and above God's Word is not, as they boast and lie, the commandment of the church. For Mary says: Whatsoever he saith that, that, that do, and that alone; for in it there will be enough to do.

21. Here also you see, how faith does not fail, God does not permit that, but gives more abundantly and gloriously than we ask. For here not merely wine is given, but excellent and good wine, and a great quantity of it. By this he again entices and allures us to believe confidently in him, though he delay. For he is truthful and cannot deny himself; he is good and gracious, that he must of himself confess and in addition prove it, unless we hinder him and refuse him time and place and the means to do so. At last he cannot forsake his work, as little as he can forsake himself — if only we can hold out until his hour comes.

III. The Significance of this Marriage

22. In the third place, we must briefly touch upon the spiritual significance of the text. This marriage and every marriage signifies Christ, the true bridegroom, and Christendom, the bride; as the Gospel lesson of Matthew 22:1-14 sufficiently shows.

23. This marriage took place in Cana of Galilee; that is, Christendom began in the days of Christ among the Jewish people, and continues still among all who are like the Jews. The Jewish nation is called Cana, which signifies, zeal, because it diligently practiced the Law and zealously clung to the works of the Law, so that even the Gospel lessons always call the Jews zealots, and especially St. Paul in Romans 9 and Romans 10. It is natural too that wherever Law and good works are, there zeal will be and contention, one claiming to be better than the other, first of all, however, opposing faith which cares naught for works and boasts only of God's grace. Now wherever Christ is there such zealots will always be, and his marriage must be at Zeal City, for you always find by the side of the Gospel and faith work-righteous people and Jewish zealots who quarrel with faith.

24. Galilee signifies border or the edge of the country, where you pass from one country into another. This signifies the same people in Zeal City who dwell between the Law and the Gospel, and ought to emigrate and pass from works to faith, from the Law into the Christian liberty; as some also have done, and now still do. But the greater part remains in their works and dwell on the border, achieving neither good works nor faith, shielding themselves behind the shine and glitter of works.

25. Christ's being bidden to the marriage signifies that he was promised long ago in the Law and the prophets and is earnestly expected and invoked to turn water into wine, fulfill the Law and establish faith, and make true Galileans of us.

26. His disciples are bidden with him; for he is expected to be a great King, hence to need apostles and disciples in order to have his Word freely and fully preached everywhere. Likewise, his mother is the Christian church, taken from the Jews, who herself most of all belongs to the marriage, for Christ was really promised to the Jewish nation.

27. The six waterpots of stone, for the purification of the Jews, are the books of the Old Testament which by law and commandment made the Jewish people only outwardly pious and pure; for which reason the Evangelist says, they were set there after the Jews' manner of purifying, as if to say: This signifies the purification by works without faith, which never purifies the heart, but only makes it more impure; which is a Jewish, not a Christian or spiritual purification.

28. There being six waterpots signifies the labor and toil which they who deal in works undergo in such purification; for the heart finds no rest in them, since the Sabbath, the seventh day, is wanting, in which we rest from our works and let God work in us. For there are six work days, in which God created heaven and earth, and commanded us to labor. The seventh day is the day of rest, in which we are not to toil in the works of the Law, but to let God work in us by faith, while we remain quiet and enjoy a holiday from the labors of the Law.

29. The water in the pots is the contents and substance of the Law by which conscience is governed, and is graven in letters as in the waterpots of stone.

30. And they are of stone, as were the tables of Moses, signifying the stiff-necked people of the Jews. For as their heart is set against the Law, so the Law appears outwardly to be against them. It seems hard and difficult to them, and therefore it is hard and difficult; the reason is that their heart is hard and averse to the Law; we all find, feel and discover by experience that we are hard and averse to what is good, and soft and prone to what is evil. This the wicked do not feel, but those who long to be pious and labor exceedingly with their works. This is the significance of the two or three firkins apiece.

31. To turn water into wine is to render the interpretation of the Law delightful. This is done as follows: Before the Gospel arrives everyone understands the Law as demanding our works, that we must fulfill it with works of our own. This interpretation begets either hardened, presumptuous dissemblers and hypocrites, harder than any pot of stone, or timid, restless consciences. There remains nothing but water in the pot, fear and dread of God's Judgment. This is the water interpretation, not intended for drinking, neither filling any with delight; on the contrary, there is nothing to it but washing and purification, and yet no true inner cleansing. But the Gospel explains the Law, showing that it requires more than we can render, and that it demands a person different from ourselves to fulfill it; that is, it demands Christ and brings us unto him, so that first of all by his grace we are made in true faith a different people like unto Christ, and that then we do truly good works. Thus the right interpretation and significance of the Law is to lead us to the knowledge of our helplessness, to drive us from ourselves to another, namely to Christ, to seek grace and help of him.

32. Therefore, when Christ wanted to make wine he had them pour in still more water, up to the very brim. For the Gospel comes and renders the interpretation of the Law perfectly clear (as already stated), showing that what belongs to us is nothing but sin; wherefore by the law we cannot escape sinning. When now the two or three firkins hear this, namely the good hearts who have labored according to the law in good works, and are already timid at heart and troubled in conscience, this interpretation adds greatly to their fear and terror; and the water now threatens to rise above the lid and brim. Before this, while they felt disinclined and averse to what is good, they still imagined they might yet succeed by their good works; now they hear that they are altogether unfit and helpless: and that it is impossible to gain their end by good works. That overfills the pot with water, it cannot hold more. This is to interpret the Law in the highest manner, leaving nothing but despair.

33. Then comes the consoling Gospel and turns the water into wine. For when the heart hears that Christ fulfills the Law for us and takes our sin upon himself, it no longer cares that impossible things are demanded by the Law, that we must despair of rendering them, and must give up our good works. Yea, it is an excellent thing, and delectable, that the Law is so deep and high, so holy and righteous and good, and demands things so great; and it is loved and lauded for making so many and such great demands. This is because the heart now has in Christ all that the Law demands, and it would be sorry indeed if it demanded less. Behold, thus the Law is delightful now and easy which before was disagreeable, difficult and impossible; for it lives in the heart by the Spirit. Water no longer is in the pots, it has turned to wine, it is passed to the guest, it is consumed, and has made the heart glad.

34. And these servants are all preachers of the New Testament like the apostles and their successors.

35. The drawing and passing to the guests is, to take this interpretation from the Scriptures, and to preach it to all the world, which is bidden to Christ's marriage.

36. And these servants knew (the Evangelist tells us) whence the wine was, how it had been water. For the apostles and their successors alone understand how the law becomes delightful and pleasant through Christ, and how the Gospel by faith does not fulfill the Law by works, every thing being unchanged from what it formerly was in good works.

37. But the ruler of the feast does indeed taste that the wine is good, yet he knows not whence it is. This ruler of the feast is the old priesthood among the Jews who knew of naught but works, of whom Nicodemus was one, John 3:9; he indeed feels how fine this cause of Christ would be, but knows not how it can be, and why it is so, clinging still to works. For they who teach works cannot understand and apprehend the Gospel and the actions of faith.

38. He calleth the bridegroom and reproacheth him for setting on the good wine last, whereas every man setteth on last that which is worse. To this very day it is the surprise of the Jews that the preaching of the Gospel should have been delayed so long, coming first of all now to the Gentiles, while they are said to have been drinking the worse wine for so long a time, bearing so long the burden and heat of the day under the Law; as is set forth in another Gospel lesson. Matthew 20:12.

39. Observe, God and men proceed in contrary ways. Men set on first that which is best, afterward that which is worse. God first gives the cross and affliction, then honor and blessedness. This is because men seek to preserve the old man; on which account they instruct us to keep the Law by works, and offer promises great and sweet. But the outcome is stale, the result has a vile taste; for the longer it goes on the worse is the condition of conscience, although, being intoxicated with great promises, it does not feel its wretchedness; yet at last when the wine is digested, and the false promises gone, the wretchedness appears. But God first of all terrifies the conscience, sets on miserable wine, in fact nothing but water; then, however, he consoles us with the promises of the Gospel which endure forever.

Third Sunday after Epiphany. Matthew 8:1-13

Christ heals the Centurion's Servant, or Two Examples of Faith and Love. The Faith and Baptism of Children

The Thankful Leper

TEXT: Matthew 8 When he was come down from the mountain, great multitudes followed him. 2 And, behold, there came a leper and worshipped him, saying, Lord, if thou wilt, thou canst make me clean. 3 And Jesus put forth his hand, and touched him, saying, I will; be thou clean. And immediately his leprosy was cleansed. 4 And Jesus saith unto him, See thou tell no man; but go thy way, shew thyself to the priest, and offer the gift that Moses commanded, for a testimony unto them. 5 And when Jesus was entered into Capernaum, there came unto him a centurion, beseeching him, 6 And saying, Lord, my servant lieth at home sick of the palsy, grievously tormented. 7 And Jesus saith unto him, I will come and heal him. 8 The centurion answered and said, Lord, I am not worthy that thou shouldest come under my roof: but speak the word only, and my servant shall be healed. 9 For I am a man under authority, having soldiers under me: and I say to this man, Go, and he goeth; and to another, Come, and he cometh; and to my servant, Do this, and he doeth it.

10 When Jesus heard it, he marvelled, and said to them that followed, Verily I say unto you, I have not found so great faith, no, not in Israel. 11 And I say unto you, That many shall come from the east and west, and shall sit down with Abraham, and Isaac, and Jacob, in the kingdom of heaven. 12 But the children of the kingdom shall be cast out into outer darkness: there shall be weeping and gnashing of teeth. 13 And Jesus said unto the centurion, Go thy way; and as thou hast believed, so be it done unto thee. And his servant was healed in the selfsame hour.

1. Two examples of faith and love are taught in this Gospel: one by the leper, the other by the centurion. Let us first consider the leper. This leper would not have been so bold as to go to the Lord and ask to be cleansed, if he had not trusted and expected with his whole heart, that Christ would be kind and gracious and would cleanse him. For because he was a leper, he had reason to be timid. Moreover the law forbids lepers to mingle with the people. Nevertheless he approaches, regardless of law and people, and of how pure and holy Christ is.

2. Here behold the attitude of faith toward Christ: it sets before itself absolutely nothing but the pure goodness and free grace of Christ, without seeking and bringing any merit. For here it certainly cannot be said, that the leper merited by his purity to approach Christ, to speak to him and to invoke his help. Nay, just because he feels his impurity and unworthiness, he approaches all the more and looks only upon the goodness of Christ. This is true faith, a living confidence in the goodness of God. The heart that does this, has true faith; the heart that does it not, has not true faith; as they do who keep not the goodness of God and that alone in sight, but first look around for their own good works, in order to be worthy of God's grace and to merit it. These never become bold to call upon God earnestly or to draw near to him.

3. Now this confidence of faith or knowledge of the goodness of Christ would never have originated in this leper by virtue of his own reason, if he had not first heard a good report about Christ, namely, how kind, gracious and merciful he is, ready to help and befriend, comfort and counsel everyone that comes to him. Such a report must undoubtedly have come to his ears, and from this fame he derived courage, and turned and interpreted the report to his own advantage. He applied this goodness to his own need and concluded with all confidence: To me also he will be as kind as his fame and good report declare. His faith therefore did not grow out of his reason, but out of the report he heard of Christ, as St. Paul says: "Belief cometh of hearing, and hearing by the Word (or report) of Christ." Romans 10:17.

4. This is the Gospel that is the beginning, middle and end of everything good and of all salvation. For we have often heard that we must first hear the Gospel, and after that believe and love and do good works; not first do good works and so reverse the order, as the teachers of works do. But the Gospel is a good report, saying or fame of Christ, how he is all goodness, love and grace, as can be said of no other man or saint. For even if other saints have a good report and reputation, it is nevertheless not the Gospel, unless it tells alone of the goodness and grace of Christ; and if it should include other saints also, it is no longer the Gospel. For the Gospel builds faith and confidence alone upon the rock, Jesus Christ.

5. You see therefore that this example of the leper fights for faith and against works. For as Christ helps him out of pure grace through faith without any works or merits of his own, so he does for every man, and would have all to think thus of him and expect from him like aid. And if this leper had said: "Behold, Lord, I have prayed and fasted so much; I beg you to look upon this and on account of it make me clean" – if he had come in this manner, Christ would never have cleansed him. For such a person does not rest upon God's grace, but upon his own merit. In this way God's grace is not praised, loved, magnified nor desired; but one's own works deprive God of his honor and rob him of that which is his. This is to kiss the hand and to deny God, as Job 31:27-28 says: "If my mouth hath kissed my hand; this also were an iniquity to be punished by the judges; for I should have denied God that is above;" and Isaiah 2:8: "They worship the work of their own hands," that is, the honor and confidence they ought to give to God, they attribute to their own work.

6. Furthermore the example of love is presented here in the love of Christ to the leper. For you see here, how love makes a servant of Christ, so that he helps the poor man freely without any reward, and seeks neither advantage, favor nor honor thereby, but only the good of the poor man and the honor of God the Father. For this reason he also forbids him to tell anyone, in order that it may be a pure, sincere work of free and gracious love.

7. This is what I have often said, that faith makes of us lords, and love makes of us servants,. Indeed, by faith we become gods and partakers of the divine nature and name, as is said in Psalm 82:6: "I said, Ye are gods, and all of you sons of the Most High." But through love we become equal to the poorest. According to faith we are in need of nothing, and have an abundance; according to love we are servants of all. By faith we receive blessings from above, from God; through love we give them out below, to our neighbor. Even as Christ in his divinity stood in need of nothing, but in his humanity served everybody who had need of him. Of this we have spoken often enough, namely, that we also must by faith be born God's sons and gods, lords and kings, even as Christ is born true God of the Father in eternity; and again, come out of ourselves by love and help our neighbors with kind deeds, even as Christ became man to help us all.

And as Christ is not God, because he first merited divinity by his works or attained to it through his incarnation, but has it by birth, without any works, even before he became man; so we also have not merited by works or love sonship with God, so that our sins are forgiven, and death and hell cannot injure us; but without works and before our love, we have received it in the Gospel by grace through faith. And as Christ first became man to serve us after being God from eternity; so we also do good and exercise love to our neighbor, after we have become pious, free from sin, alive, saved, and sons of God by faith. Let this suffice concerning the first example, the leper.

8. The other example is like it in respect to faith and love. For this centurion also has a heartfelt confidence in Christ, and sets before his eyes nothing but the goodness and grace of Christ; otherwise he would not have come to him, or he would not have sent to him, as Luke 7:3 says. Likewise he would not have had this bold confidence, if he had not first heard of the goodness and grace of Christ. In this instance also the Gospel is the beginning and incentive of his confidence and faith.

9. Here we learn again, that we must begin with the Gospel and believe it and not look upon any merit or work of our own as this centurion also advanced no merit or work, but only his confidence in the goodness of Christ. So we see that all the works of Christ exhibit examples of the Gospel, of faith and of love.

10. We also observe the example of love, how Christ freely shows him kindness, without any request or reward, as was said above. Moreover, the centurion also shows an example of love, in that he took pity upon his servant as upon himself, even as Christ also has had compassion upon us, and did the good deed freely, solely for the benefit of the servant, as Luke 7:2 says, he did it because the servant was dear to him; just as if he said: The love and affection, which he bore to him, impelled him to consider his need and to do this. Let us also do likewise, and see to it that we do not deceive ourselves and rest satisfied in that we now have the Gospel, and yet have no regard for our neighbor in his need. This having been said of these two examples, we will now also examine some details of the text.

II. The Explanation of Two Thoughts in This Gospel

11. When the leper here limits his prayer and says: "Lord, if thou wilt, thou canst make me clean." it is not to be understood as if he doubted the goodness and grace of Christ. For such a faith would be of no value, even if he believed that Christ was almighty, and was able to do and know all things. For that is living faith, which does not doubt that God is also good to us and is graciously willing to do what we ask. But it is to be understood in this way: faith does not doubt the good will God has toward a person, by which he wishes him every good; but it is not known to us, whether what faith asks and presents, is good and useful for us; God alone knows this. Therefore faith prays in a way that it submits all to the gracious will of God, whether it is for his honor and our good, and yet it does not doubt that God will grant it, or, if it cannot be granted, that his divine will withholds it in great grace, because he sees it is better not to bestow it. But in all this faith nevertheless remains certain and sure of God's gracious will, whether he gives or withholds, as St. Paul also says in Romans 8:26, we know not how to pray as we ought, and as the Lord's Prayer bids us to prefer his will and to pray for it.

12. This is what we have often said: we ought to believe without doubting and without limiting the divine goodness; but we ought to pray with the limitation, that it may be his honor, his kingdom and will, in order that we may not limit his will to time, place, measure or name, but leave all that freely to him. For this reason the prayer of the leper pleased the Lord so well and was soon heard. For where we submit to his will, and seek what is acceptable to him, he cannot refrain from doing in return what is acceptable to us. Faith inclines his favor to us, and submissive prayer inclines him to grant us what we pray for. As to the sending of the leper to the priests, why it was done and what it signified, enough has been said in the Postil of the ten lepers.

13. However, the saying of Christ: "I have not found so great faith, no, not in Israel," has been discussed with solicitude, lest it should imply that Christ did not speak truly or that the Mother of God and the apostles were inferior to this centurion. Although I might say here that Christ is speaking of the people of Israel, among whom he had preached and to whom he had come, and that therefore his mother and disciples were excluded, because they traveled with him and came with him to the people of Israel in his preaching, nevertheless I will abide by the words of the Lord and take them as they stand; and for the following reasons. First, it is contrary to no article of belief that this faith of the centurion was without a parallel among the apostles or in the Mother of God. But whenever no article of faith openly contradicts the words of Christ, they are to be taken literally, and are not to be adapted and bent by our interpretation, neither for the sake of any saint, or angel, nor of God himself. For his Word is the truth itself, above all saints and angels.

14. Secondly, such interpretation and adaptation spring from a carnal mind and intention, namely to estimate the saints of God not according to God's grace, but according to their person, worth and greatness; which is contrary to God, who estimates quite differently, according to his gifts alone. For he never granted to John the Baptist to perform miracles, John 10:41, as many inferior saints did. In short, he frequently does through inferior saints what he does not do through great saints. He concealed himself from his mother, when he was twelve years old, and suffered her to be in ignorance and error, Luke 2:43. On Easter Sunday he showed himself to Mary Magdalene, before he showed himself to his mother and the apostles, John 20:14. He spoke to the Samaritan woman, John 4:7, and to the woman taken in adultery, more kindly than he ever spoke to his own mother. John 8:10. And when Peter fell and denied him, the murderer on the cross stood firm in his faith.

15. By these and similar wonders he shows that he will not have his Spirit in his saints limited by us, and that we are not to judge according to the person. He wills to bestow his gifts freely, according to his pleasure and not according to our opinion, as St. Paul says in 1 Corinthians 12:11. Indeed even of himself he says in John 14:12: "He that believeth on me, the works that I do shall he do also; and greater works than these shall he do." The purpose of all this is to prevent men from being presumptuous toward others and from elevating one saint above another and creating divisions. All are to be equal in the grace of God, however unequal they are in his gifts. It is his will to do through St. Stephen what he does not do through St. Peter, and through St. Peter what he does not do through his mother; so that it may be he alone who does all in all without distinction of person according to his will.

16. In this sense also is it to be understood that at the time of his preaching he found not such faith either in his mother or in the apostles, whether or not he found then or afterward greater faith in his mother and the apostles, or in many others. For it may easily be possible that at the time of his conception and birth he granted great faith to his mother, and afterwards never or seldom like great faith. At times he may have permitted it to decline, as he did when for three days she had lost him, Luke 2:48. He deals thus with all his saints; and if he did not, the saints would doubtless fall into presumption and make idols of themselves or we would make idols of them, and look more upon their worthiness and persons than upon God's grace.

17. Now learn from this how foolish and void of understanding we are in regard to God's works and wonders, when we despise the plain Christian man and think that only the "men with pointed mitres" and the learned know and understand God's truth; whereas Christ here exalts this heathen with his faith above all his disciples. This is because we hold to persons and dignities, and not to God's Word and grace. Therefore with persons and dignities we also plunge into every error, and then say, the Christian church and the councils have declared so; they cannot err, because they have the Holy Spirit. Meanwhile Christ is with those despised ones and gives dignitaries and councils over to the devil. Therefore note well, how Christ exalts this heathen. He surpasses Annas, Caiaphas and all the priests, scholars and saints, all of whom ought by right to be the pupils of this heathen, not to say that they ought never to be above him in their opinions and judgments. God sometimes grants to a great saint no faith and to a small saint great faith, in order that one may always esteem another better than himself. Romans 12:10.

III. The Discussion of the Doctrine of Person Faith and the Faith of Others; Also, of Faith and the Baptism of Children "Lord, I am not worthy."

18. Herein is the great faith of this heathen, that he knows salvation does not depend upon the bodily presence of Christ, for this does not avail, but upon the Word and faith. But the apostles did not yet know this, neither perhaps did his mother, but they clung to his bodily presence and were not willing to let it go, John 16:6. They did not cling to his Word alone. But this heathen is so fully satisfied with his Word, that he does not even desire his presence nor does he deem himself worthy of it. Moreover, he proves his strong faith by a comparison and says: I am a man and can do what I wish with mine own by a word; should not you be able to do what you wish by a word, because I am sure, and you also prove, that health and sickness, death and life are subject to you as my servants are to me?

Therefore also his servant was healed in that hour by the power of his faith.

19. Now since the occasion is offered and this Gospel requires it, we must say a little about alien faith and its power. For many are interested in this subject, especially on account of the little children, who are baptized and are saved not by their own, but by the faith of others; just as this servant was healed not by his own faith, but by the faith of his master. We have never yet treated of this matter; therefore we must treat of it now in order to anticipate, as much as in us lies, future danger and error.

20. First we must let the foundation stand firm and sure, that nobody will be saved by the faith or righteousness of another, but only by his own; and on the other hand nobody will be condemned for the unbelief or sins of another, but for his own unbelief; as the Gospel says clearly and distinctly in Mark 16:16: "He that believeth and is baptized shall be saved; but he that disbelieveth shall be condemned." And Romans 1:17: "The righteous shall live by faith." And John 3:16-18: "Whosoever believeth on him should not perish, but have eternal life. He that believeth on him is not judged: he that believeth not hath been judged already." These are clear, public words, that everyone must believe for himself, and nobody can help himself by the faith of others., without his own faith. From these passages we dare not depart and we must not deny them, let them strike where they may, and we ought rather let the world perish than change this divine truth. And if any plausible argument is made against it, that you are not able to refute, you must confess that you do not understand the matter and commit it to God, rather than admit anything contrary to these clear statements. Whatever may become of the heathen, Jews, Turks, little children and everything that exists, these words must be right and true.

21. Now the question is, what becomes of the young children, seeing that they have not yet reason and are not able to believe for themselves, because it is written in Romans 10:17: "Belief cometh of hearing, and hearing by the word of Christ." Little children neither hear nor understand the Word of God, and therefore they can have no faith of their own.

22. The sophists in the universities and the sects of the pope have invented the following answer to the question: Little children are baptized without their own faith, and on the faith of the Church, which the sponsors confess at the baptism; thereupon the infant receives in baptism the forgiveness of sins by the power and virtue of the baptism, and faith of its own is infused with grace, so that it becomes a newborn child through the water and the Holy Spirit.

23. But if you ask them for the proof of this answer and where this is found in the Scriptures, it is found up the dark chimney, or they will point to their doctor's hat and say: We are the highly learned doctors and we say so; therefore it is true, and you must not inquire any farther. For almost all their doctrine has no other foundation than their own dreams and imaginations. And when they prepare themselves most carefully, they drag in some quotation from St. Augustine or another holy father. But this is not enough in the things that concern the salvation of souls; for they themselves are, and all the holy fathers were, men. Who will be surety and guarantee that they speak the truth? Who will rely upon it and die by it?

For they say so without Scripture and the Word of God. Saints hither, and saints thither; if my soul is at stake, either to be lost or to be saved eternally, I cannot depend upon all the angels and saints put together, much less upon one or two saints, where they show us no Word of God.

24. From this falsehood they have gone farther and have even come to the point, where they have taught and still teach, that the sacraments have such power, that even if you have no faith and receive the sacrament (provided you have no intention to sin), you shall still receive the grace and the forgiveness of sins without faith. This they have inferred from the former opinion, that little children receive grace in this way without faith, solely by the virtue and power of the sacrament, as they dream. Therefore they also ascribe the same thing to adults and to all men, and utter such things from their own mind, and thereby they have in a masterly way eradicated and made void and unnecessary the Christian faith, and have set up human works alone by virtue of the power of the sacraments. On this subject I have said enough in what I wrote concerning the articles of the bull of Leo.

25. The holy ancient fathers have spoken somewhat better, although not clearly enough. They say nothing about this imaginary power of the sacraments, but they teach that little children are baptized in the faith of the Christian church. But since they do not explain thoroughly, how this Christian faith benefits the children, whether they thereby receive a faith of their own, or are baptized only upon the Christian faith, without faith of their own: the sophists rush in and interpret the language of the holy fathers to the effect, that children are baptized without faith of their own and receive grace solely by reason of the faith of the church. For they are enemies of faith; if only they can exalt works, faith must allow them to do so. They do not think for a moment, whether the holy fathers erred or they themselves understood the fathers aright.

26. Beware of this poison and error, even if it were the expressed opinion of all the fathers and councils; for it will not stand; it has no Scripture for its foundation, but only the imaginations and dreams of men. Moreover it is directly and manifestly opposed to the chief texts already mentioned, where Christ says: "He that believeth and is baptized shall be saved." The conclusion from this is in short, baptism avails for nobody and is to be administered to nobody, unless he believes for himself; and without faith nobody is to be baptized, as St. Augustine himself says: Non sacramentum justficat, sed fides sacramenti (Not the sacrament justifies, but the faith of the sacrament).

27. Besides these there are others, like the brethren called Waldensians.

They teach that everyone must believe for himself, and receive baptism or the Lord's supper with his own faith; otherwise neither baptism nor the Lord's supper is of any benefit to him. So far they speak and teach correctly. But it is a mockery of holy baptism, when they go on and baptize little children, although they teach that they have no faith of their own.

They thus sin against the second commandment, in that they consciously and deliberately take the name and Word of God in vain. Nor does the excuse help them which they plead, that children are baptized upon their future faith, when they come to the age of reason. For the faith must be present before or at least in the baptism; otherwise the child will not be delivered from the devil and sins.

28. Therefore if their opinion were correct, all that is done with the child in baptism is necessarily falsehood and mockery. For the baptizer asks whether the child believes, and the answer for the child is: Yes. And he asks whether it desires to be baptized, and the answer for the child is again: Yes, Now nobody is baptized for the child, but it is baptized itself.

Therefore it must also believe itself, or the sponsors must speak a falsehood, when for it they say: I believe. Furthermore, the baptizer declares that it is born anew, has forgiveness of sins, is freed from the devil, and as a sign of this he puts on it a white garment, and deals with it in every way as with a new, holy child of God: all of which would necessarily be untrue, if the child had not its own faith. Indeed, it would be better never to baptize a child, than to trifle and juggle with God's Word and sacrament, as if he were an idol or a fool.

29. Nor is it of any use that they make a threefold distinction in the kingdom of God: first, it is the Christian church; secondly, eternal life; thirdly, the Gospel; and then say children are baptized for the kingdom of heaven in the third and first sense. That is, they are baptized, not to be saved thereby and to receive forgiveness of sins; but they are received into the church and brought to the Gospel. All this amounts to nothing and is only an invention of their imagination. For it is not entering the kingdom of heaven, if I get among Christians and hear the Gospel. The heathen can also do that without baptism. This is not entering the kingdom of heaven, however, you may talk of the first, second and third sense of the kingdom of heaven. But being in the kingdom of heaven means to be a living member of the church, and not only to hear, but also to believe the Gospel.

Otherwise a man would be in the kingdom of heaven, just as if I threw a stick or stone among Christians, or as the devil is among them. All this is worth nothing.

30. It also follows from this, that the Christian church has two kinds of baptism, and that children have not the same baptism as adults. Nevertheless St. Paul says there is only "one baptism, one Lord, one faith." Ephesians 4:5: For if the baptism of children does not effect and bestow, what the baptism of adults effects and bestows, it is not the same baptism: it is indeed no baptism at all, but a sport and mockery of baptism, inasmuch as there is no baptism but that which saves. If one knows or believes that it does not save, he ought not to administer it. But if it is administered, it is not Christian baptism; for one does not believe, that it effects what baptism is to effect. Therefore it is another and foreign baptism. For this reason it were almost necessary, that the Waldensian brethren should have themselves baptized again, as they baptize our people again; because they not only receive baptism without faith, but even contrary to faith, and in mockery and dishonor of God administer another, foreign, unchristian baptism.

31. If now we cannot give a better answer to this question and prove that the little children themselves believe and have their own faith, my sincere counsel and judgment is, that we abstain altogether and the sooner the better, and never baptize a child, so that we may not mock and blaspheme the adorable majesty of God by such trifling and juggling with nothing in it. Therefore we here conclude and declare that in baptism the children themselves believe and have their own faith, which God effects in them through the sponsors, when in the faith of the Christian church they intercede for them and bring them to baptism. And this is what we call the power of alien faith: not that anybody can be saved by it, but that through it as an intercession and aid he can obtain from God himself his own faith, by which he is saved. It may be compared to my natural life and death. If I am to live, I myself must be born, and nobody can be born for me to enable me to live; but mother and midwife can by their life aid me in birth and enable me to live. In the same way I myself must suffer death, if I am to die; but one can help to bring about my death, if he frightens me, or falls upon me, or chokes, crushes or suffocates me. In like manner, nobody can go to hell for me; but he can seduce me by false doctrine and life, so that I go thither by my own error, into which his error has led me. So nobody can go to heaven for me: but he can assist me, can preach, teach, govern, pray and obtain faith from God, through which I can go to heaven. This centurion was not healed of the palsy of his servant; but yet he brought it about that his servant was restored to health.

32. So here we also say, that children are not baptized in the faith of the sponsors or of the church; but the faith of sponsors and of the church prays and gains faith for them, in which they are baptized and believe for themselves. For this we have strong and firm Scripture proof, Matthew 19:13-15; Mark 10:13-16; Luke 18:15-16. When some brought little children to the Lord Jesus that he should touch them, and the disciples forbade them, he rebuked the disciples, and embraced the children, and laid his hands upon them and blessed them, and said: "To such belongeth the kingdom of God" etc. These passages nobody will take from us, nor refute with good proof. For here is written: Christ will permit no one to forbid that little children should be brought to him; nay, he bid them to be brought to him, and blesses them and gives to them the kingdom of heaven. Let us give due heed to this Scripture.

33. This is undoubtedly written of natural children. The interpretation of Christ's words, as if he had meant only spiritual children, who are small in humility, will not stand. For they were small children as to their bodies, which Luke calls infants. His blessing is placed upon these, and of these he says that the kingdom of heaven is theirs. Will we say they were without faith of their own? Then the passages quoted above are untrue: "He that disbelieveth shall be condemned." Then Christ also speaks falsely or feigns, when he says the kingdom of heaven is theirs, and is not really speaking of the true kingdom of heaven. Interpret these words of Christ as you please, we have it that children are to be brought to Christ and not to be forbidden to be brought: and when they are brought to Christ, he here compels us to believe that he blesses them and gives to them the kingdom of heaven, as he does with these children. And it is in no way proper for us to act and believe otherwise as long as the words stand: "Suffer the little children to come unto me, and forbid them not." Not less is it proper for us to believe that when they are brought to him he embraces them, blesses them, and bestows upon them heaven, as long as the text stands that he blessed the children which were brought to him and gave heaven to them. Who can ignore this text? Who will be so bold as not to suffer little children to come to baptism, or not to believe that Christ blesses them when they come ?

34. He is just as present in baptism now as he was then: this we Christians know for certain. Therefore we dare not forbid baptism to children. Nor dare we doubt that he blesses all who come thither, as he did those children. So then there is nothing left here but the piety and faith of those who brought the little children to him. By bringing them, they effect and aid that the little children are blessed and obtain the kingdom of heaven; which cannot be the case unless they themselves have their own faith, as has been said. So we also say here, that children are brought to baptism by the faith and work of others; but when they get there and the pastor or baptizer deals with them in Christ's stead, he blesses them and grants to them the faith and the kingdom of heaven: for the word and deed of the pastor are the word and work of Christ himself.

35. With this agrees also what St. John says in his first Epistle, 1 John 2:13: "I write unto you, fathers; I write unto you, young men; I have written unto you, little children." He is not satisfied to write to the young men; he also writes to the children, and writes that they may know the Father. From this it follows that the apostles baptized children also, and held that they believe and know the Father, just as if they had attained to reason and could read. Although somebody might here interpret the word "children" as adults, as Christ designates his disciples sometimes: yet it is certain that here they are meant who are younger than the young men; so that it is evident he is speaking of young people who are under fifteen or eighteen years of age, and excludes nobody down to the first year: for these all are called children.

36. But let us examine their reason why they do not think children believe.

They say, because they have not attained to reason they cannot hear God's Word; but where God's Word is not heard there can be no faith. Romans 10:17: "Belief cometh of hearing, and hearing by the word of Christ." Tell me is this Christian to judge of God's works by our thinking, and say, Children have not attained to reason, therefore they cannot believe? How if through this very reason you have already departed from faith, and the children come to faith through their unreason? Dear friend, what good does reason do for faith and the Word of God? Is it not reason which resists in the highest degree faith and the Word of God, so that nobody can come to faith by means of reason? Reason will not endure God's Word unless it is first blinded and disgraced. Man must first die to reason and become, as it were, a fool, and even as unreasonable and unintelligent as a little child, if he is to become a believer and receive the grace of God; as Christ says in Matthew 18:3: "Except ye turn, and become as little children, ye shall in no wise enter into the kingdom of heaven." How often does Christ hold before us that we must become children and fools, and condemn reason?

37. Tell me also, what kind of reason had the little children whom Christ embraced and blessed, and upon whom he bestowed the kingdom of heaven? Were they not still without reason? Why does he command to bring them to him and then bless them? Where did they get the faith which makes them children of the kingdom of heaven? Nay, just because they are without reason and foolish, they are better prepared to believe than adults and those possessed of reason, because reason is always in the way and with its large head is not willing to push through the narrow door. One must not look upon reason or its works when faith and God's work are under consideration. Here God alone works and reason is dead, blind and, compared to this work, an unreasonable block, in order that the Scripture may stand, which says: "God is wonderful in his saints;" and: "As the heavens are higher than the earth, so are my ways higher than your ways," Isaiah 55:9.

38. But since they stick so fast in reason, we must assail them with their own wisdom. Tell me, why do you baptize a man when he has come to the age of reason? You answer: He hears God's Word and believes. I ask: How do you know that? You answer: He professes it with his mouth. What shall I say? How, if he lies and deceives? You cannot see his heart.

Very well, then you baptize for no other reason than for what the man shows himself to be externally, and you are uncertain of his faith, and must believe that if he has not more within in his heart than you perceive without, neither his hearing, nor his profession, nor his faith will help him; for it may all be a delusion and no true faith. Who then are you, that you say external hearing and profession are necessary to baptism; where these are wanting one must not baptize? You yourself must confess that such hearing and profession are uncertain, and not enough for one to receive baptism. Now upon what do you baptize? How will you justify your actions when you thus bungle baptism and bring it into doubt? Is it not the fact that you must come and say that it is not becoming for you to know or do more than that he whom you are to baptize be brought to you and ask baptism from you; and you must believe or commit the matter to God, whether he inwardly truly believes or not? In this way you are excused and baptize aright. Why then will you not do the same for the children, whom Christ commands to be brought to him and promises to bless? But you wish first to have the outward hearing and profession, which you yourself acknowledge is uncertain and not sufficient for baptism on the part of the one to be baptized. And you let go the sure word of Christ: in which he bids the little children to be brought unto him, on account of your uncertain external hearing.

39. Moreover tell me, where is the reason of a Christian while he is asleep, since his faith and the grace of God never leave him? If faith can thus continue without the aid of reason, so that the latter is not conscious of it, why should it not also begin in children before reason knows anything about it? In the same way I would like to say of every hour in which a Christian lives and is busy and occupied, that he is not conscious of his faith and reason, and yet his faith does not on that account cease. God's works are mysterious and wonderful, where and when he wills: and again manifest enough, where and when he wills. Judgment upon them is too high and too deep for us.

40. Since it is commanded here, not to forbid little children to come unto him in order to receive his blessing, and it is not demanded of us to know the exact state of faith within, and the external hearing and profession are not sufficient for the one baptized, we are to be content that it is enough for us, the baptizers, to hear the profession of the one to be baptized, who comes to us of himself. And this for the reason that we may not administer the sacrament against our conscience, as giving it to those in whom no fruit is to be hoped for. But if they assure our conscience of their desire and profession, so that we can administer it as a sacrament that imparts grace, we are excused. If his faith is not true, let that rest with God; we have not given the sacrament as a useless thing, but with the consciousness that it is beneficial.

41. All this I say in order that one may not baptize recklessly, as they do who even administer it with the deliberate knowledge that it will be of no effect or benefit to the person receiving it. For therein the baptizers sin. because they knowingly use God's sacrament and Word in vain, or at least have the consciousness that it is neither intended nor able to effect anything; which is an altogether unworthy use of the sacrament and a temptation and blasphemy of God. For that is not administering the sacrament, but making a mockery of it. But if the person baptized denies and does not believe, you have done right anyhow, and have administered the true sacrament with the good consciousness that it ought to be beneficial.

42. However, those who do not come of themselves, but are brought, as Christ bids us to bring little children, the faith of these commit to him who bids them to be brought, and baptize them by his command, and say: Lord, thou dost bring them and command to baptize them. Thou wilt answer for them. On this I rely. I dare not drive them away nor forbid them. If they have not heard the Word, by which faith comes, as adults; hear it, they nevertheless hear it like little children. Adults take it up with their ears and reason, often without faith; but they hear it with their ears, without reason and with faith. And faith is nearer in proportion as reason is less, and he is stronger who brings them than the will of adults who come of themselves.

43. These inventive spirits stumble mostly because in adults there is reason, which acts as if it believed the Word it hears. This then they call faith.

Again they see that in children there is as yet no reason; for they act as if they did not believe. But they do not observe that faith in God's Word is quite a different and deeper thing than what reason does with the Word of God. For it is the work of God alone above all reason, to which the child is just as near as the adult, yes, much nearer, and from which the adult is just as far as the child, yea, much farther.

44. But this that is contrived by reason is a human work. I think, if any baptism is certain, the baptism of children is most certain, because of the Word of Christ, where he commands to bring them, whereas the adults come of themselves. In adults there may be deception because of the reason that is manifest; but in children there can be no deception, because of their hidden reason, in whom Christ works his blessing, even as he has bidden them to be brought to himself. It is a glorious word and not to be treated lightly, that he commands us to bring the children to him, and rebukes those who forbid it.

45. But hereby we do not mean to weaken or destroy the office of preaching. For God indeed does not cause his Word to be preached for the sake of the rational hearing, since no fruit results from that; but for the sake of the spiritual hearing, which, as I have said, children also have as well and even better than adults; for they also hear the Word. For what else is baptism but the Gospel to which they are brought? However, they hear it only once, but they hear it more effectively, because Christ, who has commanded to bring them, receives them. For adults have the advantage that they frequently hear and can think of it again. Yet even in the case of adults it is a fact that the spiritual hearing is not affected by many sermons. But it may occur once during one sermon, and then he has enough forever. What he hears afterwards, he hears either to improve the first hearing or to destroy it again.

46. In short, the baptism and consolation of children lie in the word: "Suffer the little children to come unto me; forbid them not; for to such belongeth the kingdom of God." He has spoken this and he does not lie. Therefore it must be right and Christian to bring little children to him. This can only be done in baptism. So also it must be certain that he blesses them, and bestows the kingdom of heaven upon all who come to him, according to the words: "To such belongeth the kingdom of God." Let this be enough for this time.

47. Finally it would be in order here to treat of the spiritual meaning of leprosy and the palsy. But of leprosy much has been said in the Postil of the ten lepers. Therefore it need not be treated at length here.

Fourth Sunday after Epiphany. Matthew 8:23-27

Christ stilling the Tempest, or Faith and Unbelief, and Love

Jesus Asleep in the Storm

TEXT: Matthew 8:23 Then he got into the boat and his disciples followed him. 24 Suddenly a furious storm came up on the lake, so that the waves swept over the boat. But Jesus was sleeping. 25 The disciples went and woke him, saying, "Lord, save us! We're going to drown!" 26 He replied, "You of little faith, why are you so afraid?" Then he got up and rebuked the winds and the waves, and it was completely calm. 27 The men were amazed and asked, "What kind of man is this? Even the winds and the waves obey him!"

1. This Gospel, as a narrative, gives us an example of faith and unbelief, in order that we may learn how mighty the power of faith is, and that it of necessity has to do with great and terrible things and that it accomplishes nothing but wonders; and that on the other hand unbelief is so fainthearted, shamefaced and trembling with fear that it can do nothing whatever. An illustration of this we see in this experience of the disciples, which shows the real state of their hearts. First, as they in company with Christ entered the ship, all was calm and they experienced nothing unusual, and had anyone asked them then if they believed, they would have answered, Yes. But they were not conscious of how their hearts trusted in the calm sea and the signs for fair weather, and that thus their faith was founded upon what their natural eyes saw. But when the tempest comes and the waves fill the boat, their faith vanishes; because the calm and peace in which they trusted took wings and flew away, therefore they fly with the calm and peace, and nothing is left but unbelief.

2. But what is this unbelief able to do? It sees nothing but what it experiences. It does not experience life, salvation and safety; but instead the waves coming into the boat and the sea threatening them with death and every danger. And because they experience these things and give heed to them and turn not their fear from them, trembling and despair cannot be suppressed. Yea, the more they see and experience it the harder death and despair torment them and every moment threatens to devour them. But unbelief cannot avoid such experiences and cannot think otherwise even for a second. For it has nothing besides to which it can hold and comfort itself, and therefore it has no peace or rest for a single minute. And thus will it also be in perdition, where there will be nothing but despair, trembling and fear, and that without end.

3. But had they had faith, it would have driven the wind and the waves of the sea out of their minds, and pictured before their eyes in place of the wind and tempest the power and grace of God, promised in his Word; and it would have relied upon that Word, as though anchored to an immovable rock and would not float on the water, and as though the sun shined brightly and all was calm and no storm was raging. For it is the great characteristic and power of faith to see what is not visible, and not to see what is visible, yea, that which at the time drives and oppresses us; just as unbelief can see only what is visible and cannot in the least cleave to what is invisible.

4. Therefore God bestows faith to the end that it should deal not with ordinary things, but with things no human being can master as death, sin, the world and Satan. For the whole world united is unable to stand before death, but flees from and is terrified by it, and is also conquered by it; but faith stands firm, opposes death that devours everything, and triumphs over it and even swallows the insatiable devourer of life. In like manner, no one can control or subdue the flesh, but it reigns everywhere in the world, and what it wills must be done, so that the whole world thereby is carnal; but faith lays hold of the flesh and subdues and bridles it, so that it must become a servant. And in like manner no one can endure the rage, persecution, and blasphemy, infamy, hatred and envy of the world; everyone retreats and falls back exhausted before it, it gets the upper hand over all and triumphs; and if they are without faith, it mocks them besides and treads all under its feet, and takes pleasure and delight in doing so.

5. Further, who could conquer Satan with his innumerable, subtle suggestions and temptations, by which he hinders the truth and God's Word, faith and hope, and starts so many false doctrines, sects, seductions, heresies, doubts, superstitions and innumerable abominations? The whole world compared with him is like a spark of fire compared with a fountain of water. All must be here subject to him; as we also see, hear and understand. But it is faith that keeps him busy, and it not only stands before him invulnerable, but also reveals his roguery and puts him to shame, so that his deception fails and he faints and falls; as now takes place with his indulgences and his papacy. Just so no one can allay and quiet the least sin, but it bites and devours the conscience, so that nothing avails, even if the whole world were to comfort and support such a person, he must be cast down into perdition. Here faith is a hero, it appeases all sins, even if they were as many as the whole world had committed.

6. Is there now not something almighty and inexpressible about faith that it can withstand all our powerful enemies and gain the victory, so that St.John says in his first Epistle 1 John 5:4: "This is the victory that hath overcome the world, even our faith?" Not that this is done in peace and by quietly resting; for it is a battle that is carried on not without wounds and shedding of blood. Yea, the heart so severely experiences in this battle sin and death, the flesh, Satan and the world, that it has no other thought than that it is lost, that sin and death have triumphed, and that Satan holds the field of battle. The power of faith however experiences but little of that. This is set forth in our narrative, when the waves not only dashed into the boat, but even covered it, so that it was about to go under and sink, and Christ was lying asleep. Just then there was no hope of life, death had the upper hand and had triumphed; life was lying prostrate and was lost.

7. As it went here, so it goes and must go in all other temptations of sin, Satan, etc. We must experience how sin has taken captive the conscience and nothing but wrath and perdition wish to reign, and how we must be eternally lost. Satan must start so many things by his error and false teaching that it appears God's Word must fall to the ground, and the world must glory in falsehood. Likewise the world must rage and persecute to such an extent that it appears no one can stand or be saved, or even confess his faith; but Cain will rule alone and will not rest until his brother is dead, so that he may never be in his way. But we must not judge and act according to appearance and our experience, but according to our faith.

8. Therefore this Gospel is a comforting example and doctrine, how we should conduct ourselves, so that we may not despair in the agony of sin, in the peril of death, and in the tumult of the world; but be assured that we are not lost, although the waves at once overwhelm our little boat; that we will not perish, although we experience in our evil conscience sin, wrath, and the lack of grace; that we will not die, although the whole world hates and persecutes us, although it opens its jaws as wide as the rosy dawn of the morning. These are all waves that fall over your little bark, cause to despair, and force you to cry out: "Save, Lord; we perish". Thus you have here the first part of this Gospel, faith, how it should thrive and succeed, and besides, how incapable and fainthearted unbelief is.

II. Of Love

9. The second part of our text, treating of love, shows forth Christ in that he rises, breaks his sleep for their sake, takes to heart their need as though it were his own, and ministers to them help out of free love, without any merit on their part. He neither receives nor seeks any reward for his help, but permits them to enjoy and use his power and resources. For as we have often heard, it is characteristic of Christian love to do all freely and gratuitously, to the praise and honor of God, that a Christian lives upon the earth for the sake of such love, just as Christ lived solely for the purpose of doing good; as he himself says: "The Son of man came not to be ministered unto, but to minister." Matthew 20:28.

III. The Spiritual Meaning of the Narrative

10. Christ pictured to us in this narrative the Christian life, especially the office of the ministry. The ship signifies Christendom; the sea, the world; the wind, Satan; his disciples are the preachers and pious Christians; Christ is the truth, the Gospel, and faith.

11. Now, before Christ entered the ship with his disciples the sea and the wind were calm; but when Christ with his disciples entered, then the storm began, as he himself says, Matthew 10:34: "Think not that I came to send peace on the earth: I came not to send peace but a sword." So, if Christ had left the world in peace and never punished its works, then it would indeed have been quiet. But since he preaches that the wise are fools, the saints are sinners and the rich are lost, they become wild and raging; just as at present some critics think it would be fine if we merely preached the Gospel and allowed the office of the ministry to continue in its old way. This they would indeed tolerate; but that all their doings should be rebuked and avail nothing, that they call preaching discontent and revolution, and is not Christian teaching.

12. But what does this Gospel say? There was a violent tempest on the lake when Christ and his disciples were in the ship. The sea and the wind allowed the other ships to sail in calm weather; but this ship had to suffer distress because of Christ being in it. The world can indeed tolerate all kinds of preaching except the preaching of Christ. Hence whenever he comes and wherever he is, there he preaches that he only is right and reproves all others; as he says in Matthew 12:30: "He that is not with me is against me", and again, John 16:8: "The spirit will convict the world in respect of sin, and of righteousness and of judgment;" he says that he will not only preach, but that he will convict the whole world and what is in the world. But it is this convicting that causes such tempests and dangers to this ship. Should he preach that he would allow the world to go unpunished and to continue in its old ways, he would have kept quiet before and never have entered the world; for if the world is good and is not to be convicted then there would never have been any need of him coming into the world.

13. Now it is the consolation of Christians, and especially of preachers, to be sure and ponder well that when they present and preach Christ, that they must suffer persecution, and nothing can prevent it; and that it is a very good sign of the preaching being truly Christian, when they are thus persecuted, especially by the great, the saintly, the learned and the wise. And on the other hand that their preaching is not right, when it is praised and honored, as Christ says in Luke 6:22-26: "Woe unto you, when all men shall speak well of you; for in the same manner did their fathers to the false prophets. Blessed are ye, when men shall hate you, and when they shall separate you from their company, and reproach you, and cast out your name as evil, for the Son of Man's sake; in the same manner did their fathers to the prophets." Behold our preachers, how their teachings are esteemed; the wealth, honor and power of the world have them fully under their control, and still they wish to be Christian teachers, and whosoever praises and preaches their ideas, lives in honor and luxury.

14. Hence, people have here an example where they are to seek their comfort and help, not in the world; they are not to guard the wisdom and power of men, but Christ himself and him alone; they are to cleave to him and depend on him in every need with all faithfulness and confidence as the disciples, do in our text. For had they not believed that he would help them, they would not have awakened him and called upon him. True their faith was weak and was mingled with much unbelief, so that they did not perfectly and freely surrender themselves to Christ and risk their life with him, nor did they believe he could rescue them in the midst of the sea and save them from death. Thus it is ordained that the Word of God has no master nor judge, no protector or patron can be given it besides God himself. It is his Word. Therefore, as he let it go forth without any merit or counsel of men, so will he himself without any human help and strength administer and defend it. And whoever seeks protection and comfort in these things among men, will both fall and fail, and be forsaken by both God and man.

15. That Jesus slept indicates the condition of their hearts, namely, that they had a weak, sleepy faith, but especially that at the time of persecution, Christ withdraws and acts as though he were asleep, and gives neither strength nor power, neither peace nor rest, but lets us worry and labor in our weakness, and permits us to experience that we are nothing at all, and that all depends upon his grace and power, as Paul confesses in Corinthians 1:9, that he had to suffer great affliction, so as to learn to trust not in himself but in God, who raised the dead. Such a sleeping on the part of God David often experienced and refers to it in many places, as when he says in Psalm 44:23: "Awake, why sleepest thou, O Lord? Arise, cast us not off forever."

16. The summary of this Gospel is this, it gives us two comforting, defying proverbs, that when persecution for the sake of God's Word arises, we may say: I indeed thought Christ was in the ship, therefore the sea and wind rage, and the waves dash over us and threaten to sink us; but let them rage, it is ordained that the wind and sea obey his will. The persecutions will not continue longer than is his pleasure; and although they overwhelm us, yet they must be subject to him; he is Lord over all, therefore nothing will harm us. May he only give us his help that we may not despair in unbelief. Amen.

17. That the people marveled and praised the Lord that the wind and sea were subject to him, signifies that the Gospel, God's Word, spreads farther through persecution, it thus becomes stronger and faith increases; and this is also a paradoxical characteristic of the Gospel compared with all worldly things which decrease through every misfortune and opposition, and increase through prosperity and peace. Christ's kingdom grows through tribulations and declines in times of peace, ease and luxury, as St. Paul says in 2 Corinthians 12:9: "My power is made perfect in weakness, etc." To this end help us God! Amen.

Fifth Sunday after Epiphany. Matthew 13:24-30

The Parable of the Tares

Matthew 13:24 Another parable put he forth unto them, saying, The kingdom of heaven is likened unto a man which sowed good seed in his field: 25 But while men slept, his enemy came and sowed tares among the wheat, and went his way. 26 But when the blade was sprung up, and brought forth fruit, then appeared the tares also. 27 So the servants of the householder came and said unto him, Sir, didst not thou sow good seed in thy field? from whence then hath it tares? 28 He said unto them, An enemy hath done this. The servants said unto him, Wilt thou then that we go and gather them up? 29 But he said, Nay; lest while ye gather up the tares, ye root up also the wheat with them. 30 Let both grow together until the harvest: and in the time of harvest I will say to the reapers, Gather ye together first the tares, and bind them in bundles to burn them: but gather the wheat into my barn.

1. The Savior himself explained this parable in the same chapter upon the request of his disciples and says: He that soweth the good seed is the Son of man; and the field is the world; and the good seed, these are the children of the kingdom; and the tares are the sons of the evil one; and the enemy that sowed them is the devil; and the harvest is the end of the world; and the reapers are the angels. These seven points of explanation comprehend and clearly set forth what Christ meant by this parable. But who could have discovered such an interpretation, seeing that in this parable he calls people the seed and the world, the field; although in the parable preceding this one he defines the seed to be the Word of God and the field the people or the hearts of the people. If Christ himself had not here interpreted this parable everyone would have imitated his explanation of the preceding parable and considered the seed to be the Word of God, and thus the Savior's object and understanding of it would have been lost.

2. Permit me to make an observation here for the benefit of the wise and learned who study the Scriptures. Imitating or guessing is not to be allowed in the explanation of Scripture; but one should and must be sure and firm. Just like Joseph in Genesis 40:12f. interpreted the two dreams of the butler and baker so differently, although they resembled each other, and he did not make the one a copy of the other. True, the danger would not have been great if the seed had been interpreted to be the Word of God; still had this been the case the parable would not have been thus understood correctly.

3. Now this Gospel teaches us how the kingdom of God or Christianity fares in the world, especially on account of its teaching, namely, that we are not to think that only true Christians and the pure doctrine of God are to dwell upon the earth; but that there must be also false Christians and heretics in order that the true Christians may be approved, as St. Paul says in 1 Corinthians 11:19. For this parable treats not of false Christians, who are so only outwardly in their lives, but of those who are unchristian in their doctrine and faith under the name Christian, who beautifully play the hypocrite and work harm. It is a matter of the conscience and not of the hand. And they must be very spiritual servants to be able to identify the tares among the wheat. And the sum of all is that we should not marvel nor be terrified if there spring up among us many different false teachings and false faiths. Satan is constantly among the children of God. Job 1:6.

4. Again this Gospel teaches how we should conduct ourselves toward these heretics and false teachers. We are not to uproot nor destroy them.

Here he says publicly let both grow together. We have to do here with God's Word alone; for in this matter he who errs today may find the truth to-morrow. Who knows when the Word of God may touch his heart? But if he be burned at the stake, or otherwise destroyed, it is thereby assured that he can never find the truth; and thus the Word of God is snatched from him, and he must be lost, who otherwise might have been saved. Hence the Lord says here, that the wheat also will be uprooted if we weed out the tares. That is something awful in the eyes of God and never to be justified.

5. From this observe what raging and furious people we have been these many years, in that we desired to force others to believe; the Turks with the sword, heretics with fire, the Jews with death, and thus outroot the tares by our own power, as if we were the ones who could reign over hearts and spirits, and make them pious and right, which God's Word alone must do. But by murder we separate the people from the Word, so that it cannot possibly work upon them and we bring thus with one stroke a double murder upon ourselves, as far as it lies in our power, namely, in that we murder the body for time and the soul for eternity, and afterwards say we did God a service by our actions, and wish to merit something special in heaven.

6. Therefore this passage should in all reason terrify the grand inquisitors and murderers of the people, where they are not brazened faced, even if they have to deal with true heretics. But at present they burn the true saints and are themselves heretics. What is that but uprooting the wheat, and pretending to exterminate the tares, like insane people?

7. Today's Gospel also teaches by this parable that our free will amounts to nothing, since the good seed is sowed only by Christ, and Satan can sow nothing but evil seed; as we also see that the field of itself yields nothing but tares, which the cattle eat, although the field receives them and they make the field green as if they were wheat. In the same way the false Christians among the true Christians are of no use but to feed the world and be food for Satan, and they are so beautifully green and hypocritical, as if they alone were the saints, and hold the place in Christendom as if they were lords there, and the government and highest places belonged to them; and for no other reason than that they glory that they are Christians and are among Christians in the church of Christ, although they see and confess that they live unchristian lives.

8. In that the Savior pictures here also Satan scattering his seed while the people sleep and no one sees who did it, he shows how Satan adorns and disguises himself so that he cannot be taken for Satan. As we experienced when Christianity was planted in the world Satan thrust into its midst false teachers. People securely think here God is enthroned without a rival and Satan is a thousand miles away, and no one sees anything except how they parade the Word, name and work of God. That course proves beautifully effective. But when the wheat springs up, then we see the tares, that is, if we are conscientious with God's Word and teach faith, we see that it brings forth fruit, then they go about and antagonize it, and wish to be masters of the field and fear lest only wheat grows in the field, and their interests be overlooked.

9. Then the church and pastor marvel; but they are not allowed to pass judgment, and eagerly wish to interpret all for the best, since such persons bear the Christian name. But it is apparent they are tares and evil seed, have strayed from the faith and fallen to trust in works, and think of rooting out the tares. They lament because of it before the Lord, in the heartfelt prayer of their spirit. For the sower of the good seed says again, they should not uproot it, that is, they should have patience, and suffer such blasphemy, and commend all to God; for although the tares hinder the wheat, yet they make it the more beautiful to behold, compared with the tares, as St. Paul also says in 1 Corinthians 11:19: "For there must be false factions among you, that they that are approved may be made manifest among you." This is sufficient on today's text.

Septuagesima Sunday. Matthew 20:1-16

The Labourers in the Vineyard

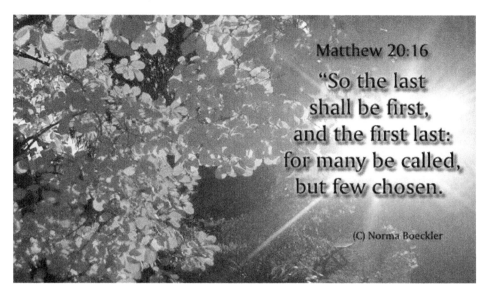

TEXT: Matthew 20 For the kingdom of heaven is like unto a man that is an householder, which went out early in the morning to hire labourers into his vineyard. 2 And when he had agreed with the labourers for a penny a day, he sent them into his vineyard. 3 And he went out about the third hour, and saw others standing idle in the marketplace, 4 And said unto them; Go ye also into the vineyard, and whatsoever is right I will give you. And they went their way. 5 Again he went out about the sixth and ninth hour, and did likewise. 6 And about the eleventh hour he went out, and found others standing idle, and saith unto them, Why stand ye here all the day idle? 7 They say unto him, Because no man hath hired us. He saith unto them, Go ye also into the vineyard; and whatsoever is right, that shall ye receive. 8 So when even was come, the lord of the vineyard saith unto his steward, Call the labourers, and give them their hire, beginning from the last unto the first. 9 And when they came that were hired about the eleventh hour, they received every man a penny. 10 But when the first came, they supposed that they should have received more; and they likewise received every man a penny. 11 And when they had received it, they murmured against the goodman of the house, 12 Saying, These last have wrought but one hour, and thou hast made them equal unto us, which have borne the burden and heat of the day. 13 But he answered one of them, and said, Friend, I do thee no wrong: didst not thou agree with me for a penny? 14 Take that thine is, and go thy way: I will give unto this last, even as unto thee. 15 Is it not lawful for me to do what I will with mine own? Is thine eye evil, because I am good? 16 So the last shall be first, and the first last: for many be called, but few chosen.

1. Some church fathers applied this Gospel to all the preachers from the beginning to the end of the world, and taught the first hour was the time of Adam, the third that of Noah, the sixth that of Abraham, the ninth that of Moses, and the eleventh hour that of Christ and his apostles. Such talk is all right for pastime, if there is nothing else to preach. For it does not harmonize with Scripture to say that the shilling signifies eternal life, with which the first, or Adam and the holy patriarchs, were dissatisfied, and that such holy characters should murmur in the kingdom of heaven, and be rebuked by the householder and made the last, that is, be condemned.

2. Therefore we will let such fables pass and abide by the simple teaching and meaning of Christ, who wishes to show by this parable how it actually is in the kingdom of heaven, or in Christendom upon the earth; that God here directs and works wonderfully by making the first last and the last first. And all is spoken to humble those who are great that they should trust in nothing but the goodness and mercy of God. And on the other hand that those who are nothing should not despair, but trust in the goodness of God just as the others do.

3. Therefore we must not consider this parable in every detail, but confine ourselves to the leading thought, that which Christ designs to teach by it.

We should not consider what the penny or shilling means, not what the first or the last hour signifies; but what the householder had in mind and what he aims to teach, how he desires to have his goodness esteemed higher than all human works and merit, yea, that his mercy alone must have all the praise. Like in the parable of the unrighteous steward, Luke 16:5f., the whole parable in its details is not held before our eyes, that we should also defraud our Lord; but it sets forth the wisdom of the steward in that he provided so well and wisely for himself and planned in the very best way, although at the injury of his Lord. Now whoever would investigate and preach long on that parable about the doctors, what the book of accounts, the oil, the wheat and the measure signify, would miss the true meaning and be led by his own ideas which would never be of any benefit to anyone.

For such parables are never spoken for the purpose of being interpreted in all their minutia. For Paul compared Christ to Adam in Romans 5:18, and says, Adam was a figure of Christ; this Paul did because we inherited from Adam sin and death, and from Christ life and righteousness. But the lesson of the parable does not consist in the inheritance, but in the consequence of the inheritance. That just like sin and death cling to those who are born of Adam and descend by heredity, so do life and righteousness cling to those who are born of Christ, they are inherited. Just as one might take an unchaste woman who adorns herself to please the world and commit sin, as a figure of a Christian soul that adorns itself also to please God, but not to commit sin as the woman does.

4. Hence the substance of the parable in today's Gospel consists not in the penny, what it is, nor in the different hours; but in earning and acquiring, or how one can earn the penny; that as here the first presumed to obtain the penny and even more by their own merit, and yet the last received the same amount because of the goodness of the householder. Thus God will show it is nothing but mercy that he gives, and no one is to arrogate to himself more than another. Therefore he says I do thee no wrong, is not the money mine and not thine; if I had given away thy property, then thou wouldest have reason to murmur; is it not lawful for me to do what I will with mine own?

5. Now in this way Christ strikes a blow first against the presumption (as he also does in today's Epistle) of those who would storm their way into heaven by their good works; as the Jews did and wished to be next to God; as hitherto our own clergy have also done. These all labor for definite wages, that is, they take the law of God in no other sense than that they should fulfill it by certain defined works for a specified reward, and they never understand it correctly, and know not that before God all is pure grace. This signifies that they hire themselves out for wages, and agree with the householder for a penny a day; consequently their lives are bitter, and they lead a career that is indeed hard.

6. Now when the Gospel comes and makes all alike, as Paul teaches in Romans 3:23, so that they who have done great works are no more than public sinners, and must also become sinners and tolerate the saying: "All have sinned", Romans 3:23, and that no one is justified before God by his works; then they look around and despise those who have done nothing at all, while their great worry and labor avail no more than such idleness and reckless living. Then they murmur against the householder, they imagine it is not right; they blaspheme the Gospel, and become hardened in their ways; then they lose the favor and grace of God, and are obliged to take their temporal reward and trot from him with their penny and be condemned; for they served not for the sake of mercy but for the sake of reward, and they will receive that and nothing more, the others however must confess that they have merited neither the penny nor the grace, but more is given to them than they had ever thought was promised to them. These remained in grace and besides were saved, and besides this, here in time they had enough; for all depended upon the good pleasure of the householder.

7. Therefore if one were to interpret it critically, the penny would have to signify temporal good, and the favor of the householder, eternal life. But the day and the heat we transfer from temporal things to the conscience, so that workrighteous persons do labor long and hard, that is, they do all with a heavy conscience and an unwilling heart, forced and coerced by the law; but the short time or last hours are the light consciences that live blessed lives, led by grace, and that willingly and without being driven by the law.

8. Thus they have now each a penny, that is, a temporal reward is given to both. But the last did not seek it, it was added to them because they sought first the kingdom of heaven, Matthew 6:33, and consequently they have the grace to everlasting life and are happy. The first however seek the temporal reward, bargain for it and serve for it; and hence they fail to secure grace and by means of a hard life they merit perdition. For the last do not think of earning the penny, nor do they thus blunder, but they receive all. When the first saw this, by a miscalculation they thought they would receive more, and lost all. Therefore we clearly see, if we look into their hearts, that the last had no regard for their own merit, but enjoyed the goodness of the householder. The first however did not esteem the goodness of the householder, but looked to their own merits, and thought it was theirs by right and murmured about it.

9. We must now look at these two words "last" and "first," from two view points. Let us see what they mean before God, then what they mean before men. Thus, those who are the first in the eyes of man, that is, those who consider themselves, or let themselves be considered, as the nearest to or the first before God, they are just the opposite before God, they are the last in his eyes and the farthest from him. On the other hand, those who are the last in the eyes of man, those who consider themselves, or let themselves be considered, the farthest from God and the last before him, they also are just the opposite, in that they are the nearest and the first before God. Now whoever desires to be secure, let him conduct himself according to the saying: "Whosoever exalteth himself, shall be humbled." For it is here written: The first before men are the last before God; the last in the eyes of men are first in the eye of God. On the other hand, the first before God are the last before men; and those God esteems as the last are considered by men to be the first.

10. But since this Gospel does not speak of first and last in a common, ordinary sense, as the exalted of the world are nothing before God, like heathen who know nothing of God; but it means those who imagine they are the first or the last in the eyes of God, the words ascend very high and apply to the better classes of people; yea, they terrify the greatest of the saints. Therefore it holds up Christ before the apostles themselves. For here it happens that one who in the eyes of the world is truly poor, weak, despised, yea, who indeed suffers for God's sake, in whom there is no sign that he is anything, and yet in his heart he is so discouraged and bashful as to think he is the last, is secretly full of his own pleasure and delight, so that he thinks he is the first before God, and just because of that he is the last. On the contrary should one indeed be so discouraged and bashful as to think he is the last before God, although he at the time has money, honor and property in the eyes of the world, he is just because of this the first.

11. One sees here also how the greatest saints have feared, how many also have fallen from high spiritual callings. David complains in Psalm 131:2: "Surely I have stilled and quieted my soul; like a weaned child with his mother." Likewise in another place, Psalm 36:11: "Let not the foot of pride come against me". How often he chastises the impudent, and haughty, Psalm 119:21. So Paul in 2 Corinthians 12:7 says: "That I should not be exalted overmuch there was given to me a thorn in the flesh," etc. And as we have heard in today's Epistle, what honorable men have fallen. To all of whom without doubt the sad secret ill turn came because they became secure, and thought, we are now near to God, there is no need. we know God, we have done this and that; they did not see how they made themselves the first before God. Behold, how Saul fell! How God permitted David to fall! How Peter had to fall! How some disciples of Paul fell!

12. Therefore it is indeed necessary to preach this Gospel in our times to those who now know the Gospel as myself and those like me, who imagine they can teach and govern the whole world, and therefore imagine they are the nearest to God and have devoured the Holy Spirit, bones and feathers.

For why is it that so many sects have already gone forth, this one making a hobby of one thing in the Gospel and that one of another? No doubt, because none of them considered that the saying, "the first are last," meant and concerned them; or if applied to them, they were secure and without fear, considering themselves as the first. Therefore according to this saying, it must come to pass that they be the last, and hence rush ahead and spread shameful doctrines and blasphemies against God and his Word.

13. Was not this the fate of the pope when he and his followers imagined they were the vice-regents and representatives of and the nearest to God, and persuaded the world to believe it? In that very act they were the vicegerents of Satan and the farthest from God, so that no mortals under the sun ever raged and foamed against God and his Word like they have done. And yet they did not see the horrible deceiver, because they were secure and feared not this keen, sharp, high and excellent judgment, "The first shall be the last." For it strikes into the lowest depths of the heart, the real spiritual darkness, that considers itself as the first, even in the midst of poverty, dishonor and misfortune, yea, most of all then.

14. Hence the substance of this Gospel is that no mortal is so high, nor will ever ascend so high, who will not have occasion to fear that he may become the very lowest. On the other hand, no mortal lies so low or can fall so low, to whom the hope is not extended that he may become the highest; because here all human merit is abolished and God's goodness alone is praised, and it is decreed as on a festive occasion that the first shall be last and the last first. In that he says, "the first shall be last" he strips thee of all thy presumption and forbids thee to exalt thyself above the lowest outcast, even if thou wert like Abraham, David, Peter or Paul. However, in that he also says, "the last shall be first," he checks thee against all doubting, and forbids thee to humble thyself below any saint, even if thou wert Pilate, Herod, Sodom and Gomorrah.

15. For just as we have no reason to be presumptuous, so we have also no cause to doubt; but the golden mean is confirmed and fortified by this Gospel, so that we regard not the penny but the goodness of the householder, which is alike and the same to high and low, to the first and the last, to saints and sinners, and no one can boast nor comfort himself nor presume more than another; for he is God, not only of the Jews, but also of the Gentiles, yea, especially of all, and it matters not who they are or what they are called.

Sexagesima Sunday. Luke 8:415

Parable of the Sower

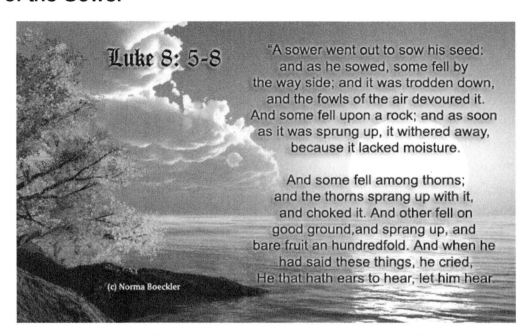

Luke 8: 5-8

"A sower went out to sow his seed: and as he sowed, some fell by the way side; and it was trodden down, and the fowls of the air devoured it. And some fell upon a rock; and as soon as it was sprung up, it withered away, because it lacked moisture.

And some fell among thorns; and the thorns sprang up with it, and choked it. And other fell on good ground,and sprang up, and bare fruit an hundredfold. And when he had said these things, he cried, He that hath ears to hear, let him hear.

(c) Norma Boeckler

TEXT: Luke 8:4 And when much people were gathered together, and were come to him out of every city, he spake by a parable: 5 A sower went out to sow his seed: and as he sowed, some fell by the way side; and it was trodden down, and the fowls of the air devoured it. 6 And some fell upon a rock; and as soon as it was sprung up, it withered away, because it lacked moisture. 7 And some fell among thorns; and the thorns sprang up with it, and choked it. 8 And other fell on good ground, and sprang up, and bare fruit an hundredfold. And when he had said these things, he cried, He that hath ears to hear, let him hear. 9 And his disciples asked him, saying, What might this parable be? 10 And he said, Unto you it is given to know the mysteries of the kingdom of God: but to others in parables; that seeing they might not see, and hearing they might not understand.11 Now the parable is this: The seed is the word of God. 12 Those by the way side are they that hear; then cometh the devil, and taketh away the word out of their hearts, lest they should believe and be saved. 13 They on the rock are they, which, when they hear, receive the word with joy; and these have no root, which for a while believe, and in time of temptation fall away. 14 And that which fell among thorns are they, which, when they have heard, go forth, and are choked with cares and riches and pleasures of this life, and bring no fruit to perfection. 15 But that on the good ground are they, which in an honest and good heart, having heard the word, keep it, and bring forth fruit with patience.

1. This Gospel treats of the disciples and the fruits, which the Word of God develops in the world. It does not speak of the law nor of human institutions; but, as Christ himself says, of the Word of God, which he himself the sower preaches, for the law bears no fruit, just as little as do the institutions of men. Christ however sets forth here four kinds of disciples of the divine Word.

2. The first class of disciples are those who hear the Word but neither understand nor esteem it. And these are not the mean people in the world, but the greatest, wisest and the most saintly, in short they are the greatest part of mankind; for Christ does not speak here of those who persecute the Word nor of those who fail to give their ear to it, but of those who hear it and are students of it, who also wish to be called true Christians and to live in Christian fellowship with Christians and are partakers of baptism and the Lord's Supper. But they are of a carnal heart, and remain so, failing to appropriate the Word of God to themselves, it goes in one ear and out the other. Just like the seed along the wayside did not fall into the earth, but remained lying on the ground in the wayside, because the road was tramped hard by the feet of man and beast and it could not take root.

3. Therefore Christ says the devil cometh and taketh away the Word from their heart, that they may not believe and be saved. What power of Satan this alone reveals, that hearts, hardened through a worldly mind and life, lose the Word and let it go, so that they never understand or confess it; but instead of the Word of God, Satan sends false teachers to tread it under foot by the doctrines of men. For it stands here written both that it was trodden under foot, and the birds of the heaven devoured it. The birds Christ himself interprets as the messengers of the devil, who snatch away the Word and devour it, which is done when he turns and blinds their hearts so that they neither understand nor esteem it, as St. Paul says in 2 Timothy 4:4: "They will turn away their ears from the truth, and turn aside unto fables." By the treading under foot of men, Christ means the teachings of men, that rule in our hearts, as he says in Matthew 5:13 also of the salt that has lost its savor, it is cast out and trodden under foot of men; that is, as St. Paul says in 2 Thessalonians 2:11, they must believe a lie because they have not been obedient to the truth.

4. Thus all heretics, fanatics and sects belong to this number, who understand the Gospel in a carnal way and explain it as they please, to suit their own ideas, all of whom hear the Gospel and yet they bear no fruit, yea, more, they are governed by Satan and are harder oppressed by human institutions than they were before they heard the Word. For it is a dreadful utterance that Christ here gives that the devil taketh away the Word from their hearts, by which he clearly proves that the devil rules mightily in their hearts, notwithstanding they are called Christians and hear the Word. Likewise it sounds terrible that they are to be trodden under foot, and must be subject unto men and to their ruinous teachings, by which under the appearance and name of the Gospel, the devil takes the Word from them, so that they may never believe and be saved, but must be lost forever; as the fanatical spirits of our day do in all lands. For where this Word is not, there is no salvation, and great works or holy lives avail nothing, for with this, that he says: "They shall not be saved," since they have not the Word, he shows forcibly enough, that not their works but their faith in the Word alone saves, as Paul says to the Romans: "It is the power of God unto salvation to everyone that believeth." Romans 1:16.

5. The second class of hearers are those who receive the Word with joy, but they do not persevere. These are also a large multitude who understand the Word correctly and lay hold of it in its purity without any spirit of sect, division or fanaticism, they rejoice also in that they know the real truth, and are able to know how they may be saved without works through faith. They also know that they are free from the bondage of the law, of their conscience and of human teachings; but when it comes to the test that they must suffer harm, disgrace and loss of life or property, then they fall and deny it; for they have not root enough, and are not planted deep enough in the soil. Hence they are like the growth on a rock, which springs forth fresh and green, that it is a pleasure to behold it and it awakens bright hopes. But when the sun shines hot, it withers, because it has no soil and moisture, and only rock is there. So these do; in times of persecution they deny or keep silence about the Word, and work, speak and suffer all that their persecutors mention or wish, who formerly went forth and spoke, and confessed with a fresh and joyful spirit the same, while there was still peace and no heat, so that there was hope they would bear much fruit and serve the people. For these fruits are not only the works, but more the confession, preaching and spreading of the Word, so that many others may thereby be converted and the kingdom of God be developed.

6. The third class are those who hear and understand the Word, but still it falls on the other side of the road, among the pleasures and cares of this life, so that they also do nothing with the Word. And there is quite a large multitude of these; for although they do not start heresies, like the first, but always possess the absolutely pure Word, they are also not attacked on the left as the others with opposition and persecution; yet they fall on the right side, and it is their ruin that they enjoy peace and good days. Therefore they do not earnestly give themselves to the Word, but become indifferent and sink in the cares, riches and pleasures of this life, so that they are of no benefit to anyone. Therefore they are like the seed that fell among the thorns. Although it is not rocky but good soil; not wayside but deeply plowed soil; yet, the thorns will not let it spring up, they choke it. Thus these have all in the Word that is needed for their salvation, but they do not make any use of it, and they rot in this life in carnal pleasures. To these belong those who hear the Word but do not bring under subjection their flesh. They know their duty but do it not, they teach but do not practice what they teach, and are this year as they were last.

7. The fourth class are those who lay hold of and keep the Word in a good and honest heart, and bring forth fruit with patience, those who hear the Word and steadfastly retain it, meditate upon it and act in harmony with it.

The devil does not snatch it away, nor are they thereby led astray, moreover the heat of persecution does not rob them of it, and the thorns of pleasure and the avarice of the times do not hinder its growth; but they bear fruit by teaching others and by developing the kingdom of God, hence they also do good to their neighbor in love; and therefore Christ adds, "they bring forth fruit with patience." For these must suffer much on account of the Word, shame and disgrace from fanatics and heretics, hatred and jealousy with injury to body and property from their persecutors, not to mention what the thorns and the temptations of their own flesh do, so that it may well be called the Word of the cross; for he who would keep it must bear the cross and misfortune, and triumph.

8. He says: "In honest and good hearts." Like a field, that is without a thorn or brush, cleared and spacious, as a beautiful clean place: so a heart is also cleared and clean, broad and spacious, that is without cares and avarice as to temporal needs, so that the Word of God truly finds lodgment there. But the field is good, not only when it lies there cleared and level, but when it is also rich and fruitful, possesses soil and is productive, and not like a stony and gravelly field. Just so is the heart that has good soil and with a full spirit is strong, fertile and good to keep the Word and bring forth fruit with patience.

9. Here we see why it is no wonder there are so few true Christians, for all the seed does not fall into good ground, but only the fourth and small part; and that they are not to be trusted who boast they are Christians and praise the teaching of the Gospel; like Demas, a disciple of St. Paul, who forsook him at last, 2 Timothy 4:10; like the disciples of Jesus, who turned their backs to him. John 6:66. For Christ himself cries out here: "He that hath ears to hear, let him hear," as if he should say: O, how few true Christians there are; one dare not believe all to be Christians who are called Christians and hear the Gospel, more is required than that.

10. All this is spoken for our instruction, that we may not go astray, since so many misuse the Gospel and few lay hold of it aright. True it is unpleasant to preach to those who treat the Gospel so shamefully and even oppose it. For preaching is to become so universal that the Gospel is to be proclaimed to all creatures, as Christ says in Mark 16:15: "Preach the Gospel to the whole creation;" and Psalm 19:4: "Their line is gone out through all the earth, and their words to the end of the world." What business is it of mine that many do not esteem it? It must be that many are called but few are chosen. For the sake of the good ground that brings forth fruit with patience, the seed must also fall fruitless by the wayside, on the rock and among the thorns; inasmuch as we are assured that the Word of God does not go forth without bearing some fruit, but it always finds also good ground; as Christ says here, some seed of the sower falls also into good ground, and not only by the wayside, among the thorns and on stony ground. For where-ever the Gospel goes you will find Christians. "My word shall not return unto me void." Isaiah 55:11.

III. The Fruit of this Word

11. Here observe that Mark 4:8 and Matthew 13:8 say the seed yielded fruit some thirty, some sixty and some a hundredfold, which according to all interpretations is understood of three kinds of chastity, that of virgins, married persons and widows; and virgins are credited with a hundredfold of fruit, wedded persons with thirtyfold, the least of all, and widows with sixtyfold. But this is such coarse and corrupt talk that it is a sin and a shame that this interpretation has continued so long in Christendom and has been advocated by so many noted teachers, and criticized by none of them. In this one perceives how many wide-awake, well-armed and faithful teachers the church has had heretofore, and how one blindly believed another, and how God allowed many noted saints and people to play the fool so completely in these important matters pertaining to the soul that he warned us to believe no teacher, however saintly and great he may be, unless he comes with the pure Word of God.

12. First, it would be doing the Word of God injustice to hold that it brings forth no other fruit than chastity, since St. Paul boasts quite differently in Galatians 5:22. In brief, the Word of God accomplishes all good, it makes us wise, sensible, prudent, cautious, pious, kind, patient, faithful, discreet, chaste, etc. Hence this comment referring only to three kinds of chastity is wholly unchristian. The heathen and wicked people, who neither possess the Gospel nor persecute it, have also virgins, widows and married persons. Doubtless Anna and Caiaphas had been properly married. Thus there were virgins, widows and consorts before the Word of God; for virgins were born, and when the Gospel comes it finds virgins, widows and wives; the Gospel did not first make them virgins, widows or wives.

13. Secondly, thus marriage, virginity and widowhood are not fruits, nor virtues, nor good works; but three stations or states in life created and ordained by God, and are not creatures of our power. They are divine works and creations like all other creatures. For if it should be valid to interpret a station or state in life as good fruit, one would have to say the state of a lord, a servant, a man, a child and of officers was only fruit of the Gospel; in this way there would be no fruit at all left for the Gospel, since such states or callings are found everywhere regardless of the Gospel. But the chastity of virgins is paraded thus for the sake of a show, to the great danger and injury of immortal souls; just as if no virtue adorns a Christian but virginity.

14. I will say further, that chastity is a different and a far higher thing than virginity, and is nothing more than that a woman has never been under any obligation to a man. Besides, however, it is possible that a virgin has not only a desire and a passion for man, in harmony with the character and nature of her female body; but she must also be full of blood and life in order to bear children and multiply the race, for which God created her, and that creation is not her work but God's alone. Therefore that woman may not hinder God's work, nature as created by God must take its course, whether children be born or not. But chastity must indeed be a state of a woman's mind that has no or little desire for man, and has in her body also little or no seed to bear fruit or children.

15. Now it is generally the case that a married woman does not so often experience such desire and lust, such a flow of love or life; for she will be relieved of the same by or through her husband; and besides, where a virgin has only passion in the thoughts of her heart and in the seed of her body, a married woman has much displeasure mingled with the pleasure of her husband, so that to speak in common terms, the high and best chastity is in the married state, because in it is the least lust and passion, while the least chastity is in the state of virgins, because in it there is much more lust and passion. Therefore chastity is a virtue far above virginity; for we call a bride still a virgin, although she is indeed full of desire, passion and love for her bridegroom. Chastity waves high over all three states, over marriage, over widowhood and over virginity. But when God does not work wonders it sinks low and exists most in the married state and least in the state of virgins, and there are not three kinds of chastity, but three states of chastity.

16. True, when we consider virginity according to its outward appearance, it seems great that a woman restrains herself and never satisfies her desires with a man. But what does it help if persons restrain their passions longer without a man or a woman and then satisfy them more than with a man or woman? Is there not more unchastity where there is greater lust, love, lewdness and sensation than where there is less? Therefore to calculate according to the amount of lust and sensation, as unchastity should be considered, virginity is more unchaste than the state of marriage. This is very apparent among prostitutes, who are virgins and yet are very forward and obscene, and cherish greater thoughts of the sin than the sin itself is. In short, I wonder if there is a virgin twenty years of age, who has a healthy, perfect female body.

17. This is enough concerning chastity, that we know how the fruits of the Word must be understood differently and in a wider sense than pertaining to chastity, and be applied especially to the fruits, by which many are converted and come to the knowledge of the truth. For although works are also called fruits, yet Christ speaks here especially of the fruits the seed of the Word brings forth in hearts that become enlightened, believing, happy and wise in Christ, as St. Paul says in Romans 1:13: "That I might have some fruit in you also, even as in the rest of the Gentiles;" and Colossians 1:6: "Even as the Gospel is also in all the world bearing fruit and increasing, as it doth in you also;" that is, many will be made alive through the Gospel, delivered from their sins and be saved; for it is the characteristic work of the Gospel, as the Word of life, grace and salvation to release from sin, death and Satan. In harmony with this fruit follow the fruits of the Spirit, the good works of patience, love, faithfulness, etc.

18. Now that some seed brings forth thirty, some sixty, and some a hundredfold, means that more people will be converted in some places than in others, and one apostle and minister may preach farther and more than another; for the people are not everywhere alike numerous and do not report the same number of Christians, and one minister may not preach as many sermons or cover as great a territory as another, which God foresaw and ordained. To the words of St. Paul, who preached the farthest and the most, we may indeed ascribe the hundredfold of fruit; although he was not a virgin.

IV. Why Christ Calls the Doctrine Concerning the Disciples and the Fruits of the Word a Mystery

19. But what does it mean when he says: "Unto you it is given to know the mysteries of the kingdom of Gad", etc.? What are the mysteries? Shall one not know them, why then are they preached? A "mystery" is a hidden secret, that is not known: and the "mysteries of the kingdom of God" are the things in the kingdom of God, as for example Christ with all his grace, which he manifests to us, as Paul describes him; for he who knows Christ aright understands what God's kingdom is and what is in it. And it is called a mystery because it is spiritual and secret, and indeed it remains so, where the Spirit does not reveal it. For although there are many who see and hear it, yet they do not understand it. Just as there are many who preach and hear Christ, how he offered himself for us; but all that is only upon their tongue and not in their heart; for they themselves do not believe it, they do not experience it, as Paul in 1 Corinthians 2:14 says: "The natural man receiveth not the things of the Spirit of God." Therefore Christ says here: "Unto you it is given", the Spirit gives it to you that you not only hear and see it, but acknowledge and believe it with your heart. Therefore it is now no longer a mystery to you. But to the others who hear it as well as you, and have no faith in their heart, they see and understand it not; to them it is a mystery and it will continue unknown to them, and all that they hear is only like one hearing a parable or a dark saying. This is also proved by the fanatics of our day, who know so much to preach about Christ; but as they themselves do not experience it in their heart, they rush ahead and pass by the true foundation of the mystery and tramp around with questions and rare foundlings, and when it comes to the test they do not know the least thing about trusting in God and finding in Christ the forgiveness of their sins.

20. But Mark says, Mark 4:33, Christ spake therefore to the people with parables, that they might understand, each according to his ability. How does that agree with what Matthew says, Matthew 13:13-14: He spake therefore unto them in parables, because they did not understand? It must surely be that Mark wishes to say that parables serve to the end that they may get a hold of coarse, rough people, although they do not indeed understand them, yet later, they may be taught and then they know: for parables are naturally pleasing to the common people, and they easily remember them since they are taken from common every day affairs, in the midst of which the people live. But Matthew means to say that these parables are of the nature that no one can understand them, they may grasp and hear them as often as they will, unless the Spirit makes them known and reveals them. Not that they should preach that we shall not understand them; but it naturally follows that wherever the Spirit does not reveal them, no one understands them. However, Christ took these words from Isaiah 6:9-10, where the high meaning of the divine foreknowledge is referred to, that God conceals and reveals to whom he will and whom he had in mind from eternity.

Quinquagesima Sunday. Luke 18:31-43

Christ's Passion and the Faith and Love of the Blind Man

The Blind Man Received his Sight

TEXT: Luke 18:31 Then he took unto him the twelve, and said unto them, Behold, we go up to Jerusalem, and all things that are written by the prophets concerning the Son of man shall be accomplished. 32 For he shall be delivered unto the Gentiles, and shall be mocked, and spitefully entreated, and spitted on: 33 And they shall scourge him, and put him to death: and the third day he shall rise again. 34 And they understood none of these things: and this saying was hid from them, neither knew they the things which were spoken. 35 And it came to pass, that as he was come nigh unto Jericho, a certain blind man sat by the way side begging: 36 And hearing the multitude pass by, he asked what it meant. 37 And they told him, that Jesus of Nazareth passeth by. 38 And he cried, saying, Jesus, thou son of David, have mercy on me. 39 And they which went before rebuked him, that he should hold his peace: but he cried so much the more, Thou son of David, have mercy on me. 40 And Jesus stood, and commanded him to be brought unto him: and when he was come near, he asked him, 41 Saying, What wilt thou that I shall do unto thee? And he said, Lord, that I may receive my sight.

42 And Jesus said unto him, Receive thy sight: thy faith hath saved thee. 43 And immediately he received his sight, and followed him, glorifying God: and all the people, when they saw it, gave praise unto God.

1. This Gospel presents to us again the two thoughts of faith and love, both in that Christ says he must go up to Jerusalem and suffer crucifixion; and in that Christ serves and helps the blind man. By the first thought, that of faith, it is proved that the Scriptures are not fulfilled except by Christ's sufferings; also that the Scriptures speak of no other theme than of Christ, and they treat only of Christ, who must fulfill the Scriptures by his death.

But if his death must do this, then our death will add nothing to that end; for our death is a sinful and a cursed death. However, if our death be sin and cursed, which is the highest and severest suffering and misfortune, what can our suffering and death merit? And since our sufferings are nothing and are lost, what can our good works do, in view of the fact that suffering is always nobler and better than doing good works? Christ alone must be supreme here and faith must firmly lay hold of him.

2. But Christ spoke these words before he finished his passion, when on his way to go up to Jerusalem at the time of the Easter festivities, when the disciples least expected to witness his sufferings, and instead anticipated a joyful occasion at the Feast of the Passover. These words Christ spoke for the purpose that his disciples might later grow stronger in their faith, when they recalled that he had before told them, that he had voluntarily offered himself as a sacrifice, and that he was not crucified by the power or strategy of his enemies, the Jews. Long before Isaiah also had prophesied that Christ would voluntarily and cheerfully give himself as a sacrifice, Isaiah 5:3-7; and the angel also on Easter morning, Luke 26:6, admonishes the women to call to mind what he here utters, in order that they might be assured and the firmer believe how he suffered thus willingly in our behalf.

3. And this is the true foundation, thoroughly to know Christ's passion, when we not only understand and lay hold of Christ's sufferings, but also of his heart and will in those sufferings, for whoever views his sufferings in a way that they do not see his will and heart in them, must be more terrified before them than they are made to rejoice on account of them. But if one sees Christ's will and heart in his passion, they cause true comfort, assurance and pleasure in Christ. Therefore Psalm 40:7-8 also praises this will of God and of Christ: " In the roll of the book it is written of me: I delight to do thy will, O, my God." The Epistle to the Hebrews says on this point: "By which will we have been sanctified;" Hebrews 10:10; it does not say: Through the suffering and blood of Christ, which is also true, but through the will of God and of Christ, that they both were of one will, to sanctify us through the blood of Christ.

This will to suffer he shows here in this Gospel when he first announced that he would go up to Jerusalem and allow them to crucify him; as if he had said, look into my heart and see that I do all willingly, freely and cheerfully, in order that it may not terrify nor shock you when you shall now soon see it, and you think I do it reluctantly, I must do it, I am forsaken, and the power of the Jews force me to it.

4. "But the disciples understood none of these things," says Christ, "And this saying was hid from them." That is as much as to say: Reason, flesh and blood, cannot understand it nor grasp that the Scriptures should say how the Son of man must be crucified; much less does reason understand that this is Christ's will and he does it cheerfully; for it does not believe it is necessary for him to suffer for us, it will deal directly with God through its own good works. But God must reveal it in their hearts by his Spirit more than is proclaimed by words into their ears; yea, even those to whom the Spirit reveals it in their hearts believe it with difficulty and must struggle with it. Such a great and wonderful thing it is that the Son of man died the death of the cross willingly and cheerfully to fulfill the Scriptures, that is, for our welfare; it is a mystery and it remains a mystery.

5. From this it now follows how foolish they act who teach that people should patiently bear their sufferings and death in order to atone for their sins and obtain grace; and especially those who comfort such, who should be put out of the way by the civil law and the sentence of death, or who are to die in other ways; and pretend that if they suffer willingly all their sins will consequently be forgiven them. Such persons only mislead the people for they bury out of sight Christ and his death upon whom our comfort is founded, and bring the people to a false confidence in their own suffering and death. This is the worst of all things a man can experience at the end of his life, and by it he is led direct into perdition. But you learn and say.

Whose death! Whose patience! My death is nothing; will not have it nor hear of it for my consolation. Christ's suffering and death are my consolation, upon it I rely for the forgiveness of my sins; but my own death I will suffer, to the praise and honor of my God, freely and gratuitously, and for the advantage and profit of my neighbor, and in no way whatever depend upon it to avail anything in my own behalf before God.

6. It is indeed one thing to die boldly and fearlessly, or to suffer death patiently, or to bear other pain willingly; and another thing to atone for sin by such death and sufferings, and thus obtain grace from God. The first the heathen have done, and many reckless villains and rough people still do; but the other is a poisonous addition, devised by Satan, like all other lies, by which he founds our trust and consolation upon our own doings, and works, against which we are to guard. For as firmly as I should resist one, who teaches me to enter a monastery, when I wish to be saved; so firmly should I also oppose any who would in my last hour point me to my own death and suffering for consolation and hope, as if they would help to wash away my sins. For both deny God and his Christ, blaspheme his grace and pervert his Gospel. They, however, do much better who hold a crucifix before the dying and admonish them of Christ's death and sufferings.

7. I must relate an example and experience that is in point here and is not to be despised. There was once a good hermit, reared in this faith of human merit, who was called upon to comfort a man of prominence upon his death bed, and he approached the sick man dauntlessly and consoled him thus: My dear friend, only suffer death patiently and willingly and I will pledge you my soul you will be a child of eternal life. Well, he promised him he would do so, and he passed away by death with this comfort. But three days later the hermit himself became sick unto death, when the true teacher, Rev. Reuling, came and opened his eyes so that he saw what he had done and taught, and he lay until he died and lamented that he had given such counsel and consolation: O, woe is me, what have I advised!

Frivolous people laughed at him that he failed to do as he had taught others to do; he offered another the pledge of his own soul that he might die in peace and he himself now sinks in despair not only before death, but also at the advice he so confidently had given and now so publicly rebuked and recalled. But God surely said to him that which is written in Luke 4:23: "Physician, heal thyself;" and another passage, Luke 12:21; "So is he that layeth up treasures for himself, and is not rich toward God." For here surely the blind led the blind and both fell into the ditch, and both were condemned. Luke 6:39. The first, because he died trusting in his own patient suffering and death, the other, because he despaired of God's grace and had not acknowledged it, and besides he also thought, had he not committed sin, he would have departed this life saved; and in both Christ remained unknown and was denied. On this point some books are misleading, in which the sayings also of St. Augustine and others are sounded forth, how death is only a door to life and a medicine against sin; for they do not see that these words are to be understood as referring to Christ's death and sufferings. But simple and plain as this example is, it teaches us in a masterly manner how no work, no human suffering, no death can help us or stand before God. For one cannot indeed deny here that the first did the highest work, namely, suffered death with patience, in which free will did its best; and yet he was lost as the other who confessed and clearly proved by his despair. And whoever will not believe these two examples must find it out by experience for himself.

8. The above is said concerning faith in the sufferings of Christ. As he now offered himself for us, we should also follow the same example of love, and offer ourselves for the welfare of our neighbor, with all we have. We have spoken sufficiently on other occasions that Christ is to be preached in these two ways; but it is talk that no one desires to understand; the Word is hid from them; for "the natural man receiveth not the things of the Spirit of God." 1 Corinthians 2:14.

II. The Faith and Love of the Blind Man

9. The second part of our Gospel treats of the blind man, in which we see beautifully and clearly illustrated both the love in Christ to the blind man and the faith of the blind man in Christ. At present we will briefly consider the faith of the blind man.

10. First, he hears that Christ was passing by, he had also heard of him before, that Jesus of Nazareth was a kind man, and that he helps everyone who only calls upon him. His faith and confidence in Christ grew out of his hearing; so he did not doubt but that Christ would also help him. But such faith in his heart he would not have been able to possess had he not heard and known of Christ; for faith does not come except by hearing.

11. Secondly, he firmly believes and doubts not but that it was true what he heard of Christ, as the following proves. Although he does not yet see nor know Christ, and although he at once knew him, yet he is not able to see or know whether Christ had a heart and will to help him; but he immediately believed, when he heard of him; upon such a noise and report he founded his confidence, and therefore he did not make a mistake.

12. Thirdly, in harmony with his faith, he calls on Christ and prays, as St. Paul in Romans 10:13-14 wrote: "How then shall they call on him in whom they have not believed." Also, "Whoever shall call upon the name of the Lord shall be saved."

13. Fourthly, he also freely confesses Christ and fears no one; his need constrains him to the point that he inquires for no one else. For it is the nature of true faith to confess Christ to be the only one who can and will help, while others are ashamed and afraid to do this before the world.

14. Fifthly, he struggles not only with his conscience, which doubtless moves him to think he is not worthy of such favor, but he also struggles, with those who threatened him and urged him to keep quiet. They wished thereby to terrify his conscience and make him bashful, so that he should see his own unworthiness, and then despair. For wherever faith begins, there begin also war and conflict.

15. Sixthly, the blind man stands firm, presses through all obstacles and triumphs, he would not let the whole world sever him from his confidence, and not even his own conscience to do it. Therefore he obtained the answer of his prayer and received Christ, so that Christ stood and commanded him to be brought unto him, and he offered to do for him whatever he wished. So it goes with all who hold firmly only to the Word of God, close their eyes and ears against the devil, the world and themselves, and act just as if they and God were the only ones in heaven and on earth.

16. Seventhly he follows Christ, that is he enters upon the road of love and of the cross, where Christ is walking, does righteous works, and is of a good character and calling, refrains from going about with foolish works as workrighteous persons do.

17. Eighthly, he thanks and praises God, and offers a true sacrifice that is pleasing to God, Psalm 50:23: "Whoso offereth the sacrifice of thanksgiving glorifieth me; and to him that ordereth his way aright will I show the salvation of God."

18. Ninthly, he was the occasion that many others praised God, in that they saw what he did, for every Christian is helpful and a blessing to everybody, and besides he praises and honors God upon earth.

19. Finally, we see here how Christ encourages us both by his works and words. In the first place by his works, in that he sympathizes so strongly with the blind man and makes it clear, how pleasing faith is to him, so that Christ is at once absorbed with interest in the man, stops and does what the blind man desires in his faith. In the second place, that Christ praises his faith in words, and says: "Thy faith hath made thee whole;" he casts the honor of the miracle from himself and attributes it to the faith of the blind man. The summary is: to faith is vouchsafed what it asks, and it is moreover our great honor before God.

20. This blind man represents the spiritually blind, the state of every man born of Adam, who neither sees nor knows the kingdom of God; but it is of grace that he feels and knows his blindness and would gladly be delivered from it. They are saintly sinners who feel their faults and sigh for grace. But he sits by the wayside and begs, that is, he sits among the teachers of the law and desires help; but it is begging, with works he must appear blue and help himself. The people pass him by and let him sit, that is the people of the law make a great noise and are heard among the teachers of good works, they go before Christ and Christ follows them. But when he heard Christ, that is, when a heart hears the Gospel of faith, it calls and cries, and has no rest until it comes to Christ. Those, however, who would silence and scold him are the teachers of works, who wish to quiet and suppress the doctrine and cry of faith; but they stir the heart the more. For the nature of the Gospel is, the more it is restrained the more progress it makes. Afterwards he received his sight, all his work and life are nothing but the praise and honor of God, and he follows Christ with joy, so that the whole world wonders and is thereby made better.

Invocavit First Sunday in Lent. Matthew 4:1-11

The Fast and the Temptation of Christ

Temptation by the Devil

Matthew 4:1 Then was Jesus led up of the Spirit into the wilderness to be tempted of the devil. 2 And when he had fasted forty days and forty nights, he was afterward an hungred. 3 And when the tempter came to him, he said, If thou be the Son of God, command that these stones be made bread. 4 But he answered and said, It is written, Man shall not live by bread alone, but by every word that proceedeth out of the mouth of God. 5 Then the devil taketh him up into the holy city, and setteth him on a pinnacle of the temple, 6 And saith unto him, If thou be the Son of God, cast thyself down: for it is written, He shall give his angels charge concerning thee: and in their hands they shall bear thee up, lest at any time thou dash thy foot against a stone. 7 Jesus said unto him, It is written again, Thou shalt not tempt the Lord thy God. 8 Again, the devil taketh him up into an exceeding high mountain, and sheweth him all the kingdoms of the world, and the glory of them; 9 And saith unto him, All these things will I give thee, if thou wilt fall down and worship me. 10 Then saith Jesus unto him, Get thee hence, Satan: for it is written, Thou shalt worship the Lord thy God, and him only shalt thou serve.11 Then the devil leaveth him, and, behold, angels came and ministered unto him.

1. This Gospel is read today at the beginning of Lent in order to picture before Christians the example of Christ, that they may rightly observe Lent, which has become mere mockery: first, because no one can follow this example and fast forty days and nights as Christ did without eating any food. Christ rather followed the example of Moses, who fasted also forty days and nights, when he received the law of God on mount Sinai. Thus Christ also wished to fast when he was about to bring to us, and give expression to, the new law. In the second place, Lent has become mere mockery because our fasting is a perversion and an institution of man. For although Christ did fast forty days, yet there is no word of his that he requires us to do the same and fast as he did. Indeed he did many other things, which he wishes us not to do; but whatever he calls us to do or leave undone, we should see to it that we have his Word to support our actions.

2. But the worst of all is that we have adopted and practiced fasting as a good work: not to bring our flesh into subjection; but, as a meritorious work before God, to atone for our sins and obtain grace. And it is this that has made our fasting a stench and so blasphemous and shameful, so that no drinking and eating, no gluttony and drunkenness, could have been as bad and foul. It would have been better had people been drunk day and night than to fast thus. Moreover, even if all had gone well and right, so that their fasting had been applied to the mortification of the flesh; but since it was not voluntary, and it was not left to each to do according to their own free will, but was compulsory by virtue of human commandment, and they did it unwillingly, it was all lost and to no purpose. I will not mention the many other evils as the consequences, as that pregnant mothers and their offspring, the sick and the weak, were thereby ruined, so that it might be called a fasting of Satan instead of a fasting unto holiness. Therefore we will carefully consider how this Gospel teaches us by the example of Christ what true fasting is.

3. The Scriptures present to us two kinds of true fasting: one, by which we try to bring the flesh into subjection to the spirit, of which St. Paul speaks in 2 Corinthians 6:5: "In labors, in watchings, in fastings." The other is that which we must bear patiently, and yet receive willingly because of our need and poverty, of which St. Paul speaks in 1 Corinthians 4:11: "Even unto this present hour we both hunger, and thirst," and Christ in Matthew 9:15: "When the bridegroom shall be taken away from them, then will they fast." This kind of fasting Christ teaches us here while in the wilderness alone without anything to eat, and while he suffers his penury without murmuring. The first kind of fasting, one can end whenever he wills, and can satisfy it by food; but the other kind we must observe and bear until God himself changes it and satisfies us. Hence it is much more precious than the first, because it moves in greater faith.

4. This is also the reason that the Evangelist with great care places it first: Then was Jesus led up of the Spirit into the wilderness, that he might there fast and be tempted, so that no one might imitate his example of their own choice and make of it a selfish, arbitrary, and pleasant fasting; but instead wait for the Spirit, who will send him enough fastings and temptations. For whoever, without being led by the Spirit, wantonly resorts to the danger of hunger or to any temptation, when it is truly a blessing of God that he can eat and drink and have other comforts, tempts God. We should not seek want and temptation, they will surely come of themselves; we ought then do our best and act honestly. The text reads: Jesus was led up of the Spirit into the wilderness; and not: Jesus himself chose to go into the wilderness. "For as many as are led by the Spirit of God, these are sons of God." Romans 8:14. God gives his blessings for the purpose that we may use them with thanksgiving, and not that we may let them lie idle, and thus tempt him; for he wishes it, and forces us to fast by the Spirit or by a need which we cannot avoid.

5. This narrative, however, is written both for our instruction and admonition. First, for instruction, that we should know how Christ has served and helped us by his fasting, hunger, temptation and victory; also that whoever believes on Christ shall never suffer need, and that temptation shall never harm him; but we shall have enough in the midst of want and be safe in the midst of temptation; because his Lord and Head triumphed over these all in his behalf, and of this he is assured, as Christ says in John 16:33: "Be of good cheer; I have overcome the world." God, who was able to nourish Christ forty days without any food, can nourish also his Christians.

6. Secondly, this is written for our admonition, that we may in the light of this example also cheerfully suffer want and temptation for the service of God and the good of our neighbor, like Christ did for us, as often as necessity requires it; which is surely accomplished if we learn and confess God's Word. Therefore this Gospel is sweet consolation and power against the unbelief and infamy of the stomach, to awaken and strengthen the conscience, that we may not be anxious about the nourishment of our bodies, but be assured that he can and will give us our daily bread.

II. The Temptation of Christ

7. But as to how temptation takes place and how it is overcome, is all very beautifully pictured to us here in Christ. First, that he is led up into the wilderness, that is, he is left solitary and alone by God, angels and men, by all creatures. What kind of a temptation would it be, if we were not forsaken and stood not alone? It is, however, painful when we do not feel anything that presents its back to us; as for example, that I should support myself and have not a nickel, not a thread, not a twig, and I experience no help from others, and no advice is offered. That means to be led into the desert and to be left alone. There I am in the true school, and I learn what I am, how weak my faith is, how great and rare true faith is, and how deeply unbelief is entrenched in the hearts of all men. But whoever has his purse, cellar and fields full, is not yet led into the desert, neither is he left alone; therefore he is not conscious of temptation.

8. Secondly, the tempter came forward and attacked Christ with these very same cares of food for the body and with the unbelief in the goodness of God, and said: "If thou art the Son of God, command that these stones become bread," as if he should say: Yes, trust thou in God and bake and cook nothing; only wait patiently until a roasted fowl flies into your mouth; do you now say that you have a God who cares for you; where is now your heavenly Father, who has charge of you? Yea, it seems to me he lets you in a fine condition; eat now and drink from your faith, let us see how you will satisfy your hunger; yea, when you have stones for bread. What a fine Son of God you are! How fatherly he is disposed toward you in that he fails to send you a slice of bread and permits you to be so poor and needy; do you now continue to believe that you are his son and he is your father? With like thoughts, he truly attacks all the children of God. And Christ surely felt this temptation, for he was no stock nor stone; although he was and remained pure and without sin, as we cannot do.

9. That Satan attacked Christ with the cares for daily food or with unbelief and avarice, Christ's answer proves, in that he says: "Man shall not live by bread alone;" that sounds as if he said: thou wilt direct me to bread alone and dost treat me as though I thought of nothing but the sustenance of my body. This temptation is very common also among pious people, and they especially feel it keenly who have children and a family, and have nothing to eat. Therefore St. Paul says in 1 Timothy 6:10 that avarice is a root of all kind of evil; for it is a fruit of unbelief. Do you not think that unbelief, care and avarice are the reasons people are afraid to enter married life? Why do people avoid it and live in unchastity, unless it be the fear that they must die of hunger and suffer want? But here we should consider Christ's work and example, who suffered want forty days and nights, and finally was not forsaken, but was ministered to even by angels.

10. Thirdly, behold how Christ resists this temptation of bread, and overcomes; he sees nothing but stones and what is uneatable, then he approaches and clings to the Word of God, strengthens himself by it and strikes the devil to the ground with it. This saying all Christians should lay hold of when they see that there is lack and want and everything has become stones, so that courage trembles, and they should say: What were it if the whole world were full of bread, still man does not live by bread alone, but more belongs to life, namely, the Word of God. The words, however, are so beautiful and powerful that we must not pass over them lightly, but carefully explain them.

11. These words Christ quotes from Deuteronomy 8:3, where Moses says: "Thy God humbled thee, and suffered thee to hunger, and fed thee with manna, which thou knewest not, neither did thy fathers know; that he might make thee know that man doth not live by bread only, but by everything that proceedeth out of the mouth of Jehovah doth man live." That is as much as to say: Since God permits you to hunger and you still continue to live, you ought indeed to grasp the thought that God nourishes you without bread through his Word; for if you should live and sustain yourself by bread alone then you must continually be full of bread. But the Word, that nourishes us is, that he promises us and causes it to be published that he is our God and desires to be our God.

12. Thus now the meaning of Moses and of Christ is: Whoever has here God's Word and believes, has both blessings; the first, where he is in want and has nothing, but must suffer hunger, that Word will sustain him, so that he will not die of hunger nor perish, just as well as if he had abundance to eat; for the Word he has in his heart nourishes and sustains him without eating and drinking. But has he little to eat, then a bite or slice of bread will feed and nourish him like a kingly meal; for not only bread but the Word of God also nourishes the body naturally, as it creates and upholds all things, Hebrews 1:3. The other blessing he will also enjoy, namely, that finally bread will surely be at hand, come whence it will, and should it rain from heaven like manna where none grows and none can grow. In these two thoughts every person can freely trust, namely, that he must in time of hunger receive bread or something to eat, or if not, then his hunger must become so moderate and bearable that it will nourish him even as well as bread does.

13. What has been said of eating and feeding the body should be understood also of drinking, clothing, house, and all our needs: namely that although he still permits us to become naked and suffer want for clothing, house etc., clothing must finally be at hand, and before it fails the leaves of the trees must become coats and mantles; or if not, then the coats and garments that we wear must never grow old; just as happened to the Children of Israel in the desert Deuteronomy 8:2-4, whose clothing and shoes never wore out. Likewise the wild wilderness must become their houses, and there must be a way where there is no way; and water, where there is no water; stones must become water. For here stands God's Word, which says: "He cares for you;" and St. Paul in 1 Timothy 6:17: "God giveth us richly all things to enjoy;" and Matthew 6:33-34: "But seek ye first the kingdom of God and his righteousness; and all these things shall be added unto you. Be not therefore anxious for the morrow." These and like words must continue true and stand forever firm.

14. All this one may indeed learn from his own daily experiences. For it is held, and I almost believe it, that there are not as many sheaves of wheat grown as there are people living on the earth; but God daily blesses and increases the wheat in the sack, the flour in the tray, the bread on the table and in the mouth, as Christ did. John 6:12 f. It is also noticeable that as a rule, poor people and their children are fatter and their food reaches farther and agrees with them better than is the case among the rich with all their provisions. However, that the godless at times suffer need, or in times of famine many die of hunger, is caused by a special plague as pestilence, war etc. In other ways, we see that in all things it is not the food, but the Word of God that nourishes every human being.

15. Now that God sustains all mankind by bread, and not by the Word alone, without bread, is done to the end, that he conceals his work in the world in order to exercise believers; just as he commanded the children of Israel to arm themselves and to fight, and yet it was not his pleasure that victory should come through their own sword and deeds; but he himself was to slay their enemies and triumph with their swords and through their deeds. Here it might also be said: The warrior was not victorious through his sword alone, but by every word that proceeded out of the mouth of God, as David sings, Psalm 44:6: "For I will not trust in my bow, neither shall my sword save me." Also Psalm 147:10 and Psalm 33:16-17: "He taketh no pleasure in the legs of a man. A mighty man is not delivered by great strength. A horse is a vain thing for safety." Yet he uses man and the horse, the sword and bow: but not because of the strength and power of man and of the horse, but under the veil and covering of man and the horse he fights and does all. This he proves in that he often did and daily does the same without man and the horse, where there is need and he is not tempted.

16. Thus he does also with the bread; since it is at hand, he nourishes us through it and by means of it, so that we do not see it and we think the bread does it; but where it is not at hand, there he nourishes us without the bread, only through the Word, as he does by means of the bread; so that thus bread is God's helper, as Paul says in 1 Corinthians 3:9: "We are God's fellow workers," that is, through and under our outward ministerial office he gives inwardly his grace, which he also could give and does give indeed without our office; but since the office is at hand, one should not despise it nor tempt God. Thus God sustains us outwardly by bread; but only inwardly he gives that growth and permanency, which the bread cannot give. And the summary is: All creatures are God's larva and mummery, which he permits to work with him and to help to do everything that he can do and does do otherwise without their cooperation, in order that we may cleave alone to his Word. Thus, if bread is at hand, that we do not therefore trust the more; or if there is no bread present, that we do not therefore despair the more; but use it when it is at hand, and do without it, when there is none; being assured that we shall still live and be sustained at both times by God's Word, whether there be bread or no bread. With such faith one overcomes avarice and temporal care for daily bread in the right way.

17. Christ's second temptation is opposed to the first and is repugnant to common sense. Its substance is that the devil teaches us to tempt God; as he here calls to Christ to cast himself down from the pinnacle of the temple, which was not at all necessary, since there were surely good steps upon which he could descend. And that this temptation was for the purpose of tempting or making trial of God, the answer of Christ also clearly proves, when he says: "Thou shalt not make trial of the Lord thy God." By this he shows that the devil wished to lead him into temptation.

18. And this very appropriately follows the first temptation. For where the devil feels a heart trusts God in times of want and need, he soon ceases his temptation of bread and avarice and thinks: Wait, wilt thou be very spiritual and believing, I will assist you: He approaches and attacks on the other side, that we might believe where God has not commanded us to believe, nor wills that we should believe. For example, if God gave you bread in your homes, as he does yearly everywhere in the world, and you would not use it, but instead you would cause need and want yourselves, and say: Why, we are to believe God; I will not eat the bread, but will patiently wait until God sends me manna from heaven. See, that would be tempting God; for that is not believing where all is at hand that we need and should have. How can one believe that he will receive what he already has ?

19. Thus you see here that Satan held before Christ want and need where there was neither want nor need; but where there was already good means by which to descend from the temple without such a newly devised and unnecessary way of descending. For this purpose Satan led Christ to the top of the temple, in the holy city, says the Evangelist, and placed him in a holy place. For he creates such precious thoughts in man that he thinks he is filled with faith and is on the true way of holiness; and yet he does not stand in the temple, but is only on the outside of the temple, that is, he is not in the true holy mind or life of faith; and yet he is in the holy city; that is, such persons are found only in Christendom and among true Christians, who hear a great deal of preaching about faith. To these persons he applies the sayings of Scripture. For such persons learn Scripture also by daily hearing it; but not farther than they can apply it to their erroneous opinions and their false faith. For Satan here quotes from the Psalter, Psalm 91:11-12, that God commanded the angels that they should protect the children of God and carry them on their hands. But Satan like a rogue and cheat fails to quote what follows, namely, that the angels shall protect the children of God in all their ways. For the Psalm reads thus: "For he will give his angels charge over thee to keep thee in all thy ways. They shall bear thee up in their hands, lest thou dash thy foot against a stone;" hence the protection of the angels does not reach farther, according to the command of God, than the ways in which God has commanded us to walk.

When we walk in these ways of God, his angels take care of us. But the devil omits to quote "the ways of God" and interprets and applies the protection of the angels to all things, also to that which God has not commanded; then it fails and we tempt God.

20. Now, this temptation seldom takes place in outward material things as bread, clothing, house, etc. For we find many foolhardy people, who risk and endanger their body and life, their property and honor, with out any need of doing so; as those do who willfully enter into battle or jump into the water, or gamble for money, or in other ways venture into danger, of whom the wise man says in Sirach 3:27: "Whoever takes pleasure in danger, will thereby be overcome;" for in the degree one struggles to get a thing, will he succeed in obtaining it; and good swimmers are likely to drown and good climbers likely to fall. Yet it is seldom that those of false faith in God abstain from bread, clothing and other necessities of life, when they are at hand. As we read of two hermits, who would not accept bread from the people, but thought God should send it to them directly from heaven; so the consequence was that one died and went to his father, the devil, who taught him such faith and left him fall from the pinnacle.

21. But in spiritual matters this temptation is powerful when one has to do with the nourishment not of the body but of the soul. Here God has held before us the person and way, by which the soul can be forever nourished in the richest manner possible without any want, namely Christ, our Savior. But this way, this treasure, this provision no one desires. Everybody seeks another way, other provisions to help their souls. The real guilty ones are those who would be saved through their own work; these the devil sets conspicuously on the top of the temple. They follow him and go down where there is no stairway; they believe and trust in their own work where there is no faith nor trust, no way nor bridge, and break their necks. But Satan makes use of and persuades them through the Scriptures to believe that the angels will protect them, and that their way, works and faith are pleasing to God, and who called them through the Scriptures to do good works; but they do not care how falsely they explain the Scriptures.

22. Who these are, we have identified often enough and very fully, namely, work-righteous persons and unbelieving hypocrites under the name of being Christians and among the congregation of Christian people. For the temptation must take place in the holy city and one temptation is seldom against another. In the first temptation want and hunger are the reasons that we should not believe; and by which we become anxious to have a full sufficiency, so that there is no chance for us to believe. In the second temptation, however, the abundance and the full sufficiency are the reasons that we do not believe, by which we become tired of the common treasure, and everyone tries to do something through his own powers to provide for his soul. So we do; if we have nothing, then we doubt God and believe not; if we have abundance, then we become tired of it and wish to have something different, and again we fail to believe. There we flee and turn against want and seek abundance: here we seek want and flee from the abundance we have. No, whatever God does for us, is never right. Such is the bottomless wickedness of our unbelief.

23. Christ's third temptation consists in temporal honor and power; as the words of the devil clearly teach, when Satan shows and offers Christ all the kingdoms of the world if he would worship him. To this class those belong who fall from their faith for the sake of honor and power, that they may enjoy good days, or not believe further than their honor and power extend. Such are also the heretics who start sects and factions in matters of faith among Christians, that they may make a great parade before the world and soar aloft in their own honor. Hence one may place this third temptation on the right, and the first on the left side. The first is the temptation of misfortune, by which man is stirred to anger, impatience and unbelief; the third and last, the temptation of prosperity, by which man is enticed to lust, honor, joy, and whatever is high. The second or middle temptation is spiritual and deals with the blind tricks and errors that mislead reason from faith.

24. For whom the devil cannot overcome with poverty, want, need and misery, he attacks with riches, favor, honor, pleasure, power and the like, and contends on both sides against us; yea, "he walketh about," says St. Peter in 1 Peter 5:8, so that if he cannot overthrow us either with suffering or love, that is, with the first temptation on the left or the third on the right, he retires to a higher and different method and attacks us with error, blindness and a false understanding of the Scripture. If he wins there, we fare ill on all sides and in all things; and whether one suffers poverty or has abundance, whether he fights or surrenders, all is lost. For when one is in error, neither patience in misfortune nor firmness in prosperity helps him; seeing that in both heretics are often powerful and the devil deliberately acts as if he were overcome in the first and last temptations, although he is not, if he has only won in the middle or second temptation. For he lets his own children suffer much and be patient, even at times to spurn the world; but never with a true and honest heart.

25. Now these three temptations taken together are heavy and hard; but the middle one is the greatest; for it attacks the doctrine of faith itself in the soul, and is spiritual and in spiritual matters. The other two attack faith in outward things, in fortune and misfortune, in pleasure and pain etc., although both severely try us. For it is sad that one should lay hold of heaven and ever be in want and eat stones where there is no bread. Again, it is sad to despise favors, honor and possessions, friends and associates, and let go what one already has. But faith, rooted in God's Word, is able to do all things; is faith strong, then it is also easy for the believer to do this.

26. The order of these temptations, as they met Christ, one cannot absolutely determine; for the Evangelists give them in different order. The temptation Matthew places as the middle one, Luke places last, Luke 4, 4f.; and again, the temptation Luke places in the middle, Matthew places last, as if little depended on the order. But if one wished to preach or speak of them, the order of Luke would be the better. For it is a fine opportunity to repeat and relate that the devil began with want and misfortune; when that did not work, then he began with prosperity and honor; and last, when all fails, that he wantonly and wickedly springs forth and strikes people with terror, lies and other spiritual tricks. And since they have no order in practice and experience, but as it happens that a Christian may be attacked at one time with the last, and another time with the first etc., Matthew gave little attention to the order for a preacher to observe in speaking of this theme. And perhaps it was also the same with Christ through the forty days that the devil held to no order, but today attacked him with this and tomorrow with another temptation, and again in ten days with the first and so on, just as occasion was given.

27. At last angels approached and served him. This must have taken place in a literal sense, that they appeared in a bodily form and gave him to eat and drink, and just as at a table, they ministered to all his wants. For the service is offered outwardly to his body, just like, no doubt, the devil, his tempter, also appeared in a bodily form, perhaps like an angel. For, seeing that he places him on the pinnacle of the temple and shows him all the kingdoms of the world in a moment, he must have been a higher being than a man, since he represents himself as a higher being, in that he offers him all the kingdoms of the world and permits himself to be worshiped. But he surely did not bear the form of the devil, for he desires to be beautiful when he lies and deceives, as St. Paul says of him in 2 Corinthians 11:14: "For even Satan fashioneth himself into an angel of light."

28. This however is written for our comfort, that we may know that many angels minister also to us, where one devil attacks us; if we fight with a knightly spirit and firmly stand, God will not let us suffer want, the angels of heaven would sooner appear and be our bakers, waiters and cooks and minister to all our wants. This is not written for Christ's sake for he does not need it. Did the angels serve him, then they may also serve us.

Reminiscere. Second Sunday in Lent. Matthew 15:21-28

The Faith of the Syrophenician Woman

Woman at the Well

Matthew 15:21 Then Jesus went thence, and departed into the coasts of Tyre and Sidon. 22 And, behold, a woman of Canaan came out of the same coasts, and cried unto him, saying, Have mercy on me, O Lord, thou son of David; my daughter is grievously vexed with a devil. 23 But he answered her not a word. And his disciples came and besought him, saying, Send her away; for she crieth after us. 24 But he answered and said, I am not sent but unto the lost sheep of the house of Israel. 25 Then came she and worshipped him, saying, Lord, help me. 26 But he answered and said, It is not meet to take the children's bread, and to cast it to dogs. 27 And she said, Truth, Lord: yet the dogs eat of the crumbs which fall from their masters' table. 28 Then Jesus answered and said unto her, O woman, great is thy faith: be it unto thee even as thou wilt. And her daughter was made whole from that very hour.

1. This Gospel presents to us a true example of firm and perfect faith. For this woman endures and overcomes in three great and hard battles, and teaches us in a beautiful manner the true way and virtue of faith, namely, that it is a hearty trust in the grace and goodness of God as experienced and revealed through his Word. For St. Mark says, she heard some news about Jesus, Mark 7:25. What kind of news? Without doubt good news, and the good report that Christ was a pious man and cheerfully helped everybody. Such news about God is a true Gospel and a word of grace, out of which sprang the faith of this woman; for had she not believed, she would not have thus run after Christ etc. In like manner we have often heard how St. Paul in Romans 10:17 says that faith cometh by hearing, that the Word must go in advance and be the beginning of our salvation.

2. But how is it that many more have heard this good news concerning Christ, who have not followed him, and did not esteem it as good news?

Answer: The physician is helpful and welcome to the sick; the healthy have no use for him. But this woman felt her need, hence she followed the sweet scent, as is written in the Song of Solomon 1:3. In like manner Moses must precede and teach people to feel their sins in order that grace may be sweet and welcome to them. Therefore all is in vain, however friendly and lovely Christ may be pictured, if man is not first humbled by a knowledge of himself, and he possesses no longing for Christ, as Mary's Song says, "The hungry he hath filled with good things; and the rich he hath sent empty away," Luke 1:53. All this is spoken and written for the comfort of the distressed, the poor, the needy, the sinful, the despised, so that they may know in all times of need to whom to flee and where to seek comfort and help.

3. But see in this example how Christ like a hunter exercises and chases faith in his followers in order that it may become strong and firm. First when the woman follows him upon hearing of his fame and cries with assured confidence that he would according to his reputation deal mercifully with her, Christ certainly acts differently, as if to let her faith and good confidence be in vain and turn his good reputation into a lie, so that she could have thought: Is this the gracious, friendly man? or: Are these the good words, that I have heard spoken about him, upon which I have depended? It must not be true; he is my enemy and will not receive me; nevertheless he might speak a word and tell me that he will have nothing to do with me. Now he is as silent as a stone. Behold, this is a very hard rebuff, when God appears so earnest and angry and conceals his grace so high and deep; as those know so well, who feel and experience it in their hearts. Therefore she imagines he will not fulfill what he has spoken, and will let his Word be false; as it happened to the children of Israel at the Red Sea and to many other saints.

4. Now, what does the poor woman do? She turns her eyes from all this unfriendly treatment of Christ; all this does not lead her astray, neither does she take it to heart, but she continues immediately and firmly to cling in her confidence to the good news she had heard and embraced concerning him, and never gives up. We must also do the same and learn firmly to cling to the Word, even though God with all his creatures appears different than his Word teaches. But, oh, how painful it is to nature and reason, that this woman should strip herself of self and forsake all that she experienced, and cling alone to God's bare Word, until she experienced the contrary. May God help us in time of need and of death to possess like courage and faith!

5. Secondly, since her cry and faith avail nothing, the disciples approach with their faith, and pray for her, and imagine they will surely be heard. But while they thought he should be more tenderhearted, he became only the more indifferent, as we see and think. For now he is silent no more nor leaves them in doubt; he declines their prayer and says: "I was not sent but unto the lost sheep of the house of Israel." This rebuff is still harder since not only our own person is rejected, but the only comfort that remains to us, namely, the comfort and prayers of pious and holy persons, are rejected. For our last resort, when we feel that God is ungracious or we are in need, is that we go to pious, spiritual persons and there seek counsel and help, and they are willing to help as love demands; and yet, that may amount to nothing, even they may not be heard and our condition becomes only worse.

6. Here one might upbraid Christ with all the words in which he promised to hear his saints, as Matthew 18:19: "If two of you shall agree on earth as touching anything that they shall ask, it shall be done for them." Likewise, Mark 11:24: "All things whatsoever ye pray and ask for, believe that ye receive them, and ye shall have them;" and many more like passages. What becomes of such promises in this woman's case? Christ, however, promptly answers and says: Yes, it is true, I hear all prayers, but I gave these promises only to the house of Israel. What do you think? Is not that a thunderbolt that dashes both heart and faith into a thousand pieces, when one feels that God's Word, upon which one trusts, was not spoken for him, but applies only to others? Here all saints and prayers must be speechless, yea, here the heart must let go of the Word, to which it would gladly hold, if it would consult its own feelings.

7. But what does the poor woman do? She does not give up, she clings to the Word although it be torn out of her heart by force, is not turned away by this stern answer, still firmly believes his goodness is yet concealed in that answer, and still she will not pass judgment that Christ is or may be ungracious. That is persevering steadfastness.

8. Thirdly, she follows Christ into the house, as Mark 7:24-25 informs us, perseveres, falls down at his feet, and says: "Lord, help me!" There she received her last mortal blow, in that Christ said in her face, as the words tell, that she was a dog, and not worthy to partake of the children's bread. What will she say to this! Here he presents her in a bad light, she is a condemned and an outcast person, who is not to be reckoned among God's chosen ones.

9. That is an eternally unanswerable reply, to which no one can give a satisfactory answer. Yet she does not despair, but agrees with his judgment and concedes she is a dog, and desires also no more than a dog is entitled to, namely, that she may eat the crumbs that fall from the table of the Lord. Is not that a masterly stroke as a reply? She catches Christ with his own words. He compares her to a dog, she concedes it, and asks nothing more than that he let her be a dog, as he himself judged her to be. Where will Christ now take refuge? He is caught. Truly, people let the dog have the crumbs under the table; it is entitled to that. Therefore Christ now completely opens his heart to her and yields to her will, so that she is now no dog, but even a child of Israel.

10. All this, however, is written for our comfort and instruction, that we may know how deeply God conceals his grace before our face, and that we may not estimate him according to our feelings and thinking, but strictly according to his Word. For here you see, though Christ appears to be even hardhearted, yet he gives no final decision by saying "No." All his answers indeed sound like no, but they are not no, they remain undecided and pending. For he does not say: I will not hear thee; but is silent and passive, and says neither yes nor no. In like manner he does not say she is not of the house of Israel; but he is sent only to the house of Israel; he leaves it undecided and pending between yes and no. So he does not say, Thou art a dog, one should not give thee of the children's bread; but it is not meet to take the children's bread and cast it to the dogs; leaving it undecided whether she is a dog or not. Yet all those trials of her faith sounded more like no than yes; but there was more yea in them than nay; ay, there is only yes in them, but it is very deep and very concealed, while there appears to be nothing but no.

11. By this is set forth the condition of our heart in times of temptation; Christ here represents how it feels. It thinks there is nothing but no and yet that is not true. Therefore it must turn from this feeling and lay hold of and retain the deep spiritual yes under and above the no with a firm faith in God's Word, as this poor woman does, and say God is right in his judgment which he visits upon us; then we have triumphed and caught Christ in his own words. As for example when we feel in our conscience that God rebukes us as sinners and judges us unworthy of the kingdom of heaven, then we experience hell, and we think we are lost forever. Now whoever understands here the actions of this poor woman and catches God in his own judgment, and says: Lord, it is true, I am a sinner and not worthy of thy grace; but still thou hast promised sinners forgiveness, and thou art come not to call the righteous, but, as St. Paul says in 1 Timothy 1:15, "to save sinners." Behold, then must God according to his own judgment have mercy upon us.

12. King Manasseh did likewise in his penitence as his prayer proves; he conceded that God was right in his judgment and accused himself as a great sinner and yet he laid hold of the promised forgiveness of sins. David also does likewise in Psalm 51:4 and says: "Against thee, thee only, have I sinned, and done that which is evil in thy sight; that thou mayest be justified when thou speakest, and be clear when thou judgest." For God's disfavor in every way visits us when we cannot agree with his judgment nor say yea and amen, when he considers and judges us to be sinners. If the condemned could do this, they would that very moment be saved. We say indeed with our mouth that we are sinners; but when God himself says it in our hearts, then we are not sinners, and eagerly wish to be considered pious and free from that judgment. But it must be so; if God is to be righteous in his words that teach you are a sinner, then you may claim the rights of all sinners that God has given them, namely, the forgiveness of sins. Then you eat not only the crumbs under the table as the little dogs do; but you are also a child and have God as your portion according to the pleasure of your will.

13. This is the spiritual meaning of our Gospel and the scriptural explanation of it. For what this poor woman experienced in the bodily affliction of her daughter, whom she miraculously caused to be restored to health again by her faith, that we also experience when we wish to be healed of our sins and of our spiritual diseases, which is truly a wicked devil possessing us; here she must become a dog and we become sinners and brands of hell, and then we have already recovered from our sickness and are saved.

14. Whatever more there is in this Gospel worthy of notice, as that one can obtain grace and help through the faith of another without his own personal faith, as took place here in the daughter of this poor woman, has been sufficiently treated elsewhere. Furthermore, that Christ and his disciples along with the woman in this Gospel exhibit to us an example of love, in that no one acts, prays and cares for himself but each for others, is also clear enough and worthy of consideration.

Oculi. Third Sunday in Lent. Luke 11:14-23

Jesus Casts out a Demon, or Christ's Defense against his Blasphemers

"But the fruit of the Spirit is, love, joy, peace, longsuffering, gentleness, goodness, faith, Meekness, temperance: against such there is no law." Galatians 5:22-23

(c) Norma Boeckler

The Gospel

TEXT: Luke 11:14 And he was casting out a devil, and it was dumb. And it came to pass, when the devil was gone out, the dumb spake; and the people wondered. 15 But some of them said, He casteth out devils through Beelzebub the chief of the devils.16 And others, tempting him, sought of him a sign from heaven.17 But he, knowing their thoughts, said unto them, Every kingdom divided against itself is brought to desolation; and a house divided against a house falleth. 18 If Satan also be divided against himself, how shall his kingdom stand? because ye say that I cast out devils through Beelzebub. 19 And if I by Beelzebub cast out devils, by whom do your sons cast them out? therefore shall they be your judges. 20 But if I with the finger of God cast out devils, no doubt the kingdom of God is come upon you. 21 When a strong man armed keepeth his palace, his goods are in peace:22 But when a stronger than he shall come upon him, and overcome him, he taketh from him all his armour wherein he trusted, and divideth his spoils. 23 He that is not with me is against me: and he that gathereth not with me scattereth.

1. This is a beautiful Gospel from which we learn many different things, and in which nearly everything is set forth as to what Christ, his kingdom and his Gospel are: what they accomplish and how they fare in the world. In the first place, like all the Gospels this one teaches us faith and love; for it presents Christ to us as a most loving Savior and Helper in every need and tells us that he who believes this is saved. For we see here that Christ had nothing to do with people who were healthy, but with a poor man who was greatly afflicted with many ills. He was blind, as Matthew says; also dumb and possessed with a demon, as Luke tells us here. Now all mutes are also deaf, so that in the Greek language deaf and dumb are one word. By this act Christ draws us to himself, leads us to look to him for every blessing, and to go to him in every time of need. He does this that we also, according to the nature of love, should do unto others as he does unto us. This is the universal and the most precious doctrine of this Gospel and of all the Gospels throughout the church year. This poor man, however, did not come to Christ without the Word; for those who brought him to Christ must have heard his love preached and were moved thereby to trust in him. We learn therefore that faith comes through the Word; but more of this elsewhere.

2. Secondly, it is here demonstrated how Christ and his Gospel fare in the world, namely, that there are three kinds of hearers. Some marvel at him; these are pious and true Christians, who consider this deed so great that they are amazed at it. Some blaspheme the Gospel; these are the Pharisees and scribes, who were vexed because they could not do the like, and were worried lest the people should hold Christ in higher esteem than themselves. Some tempt him, like Herod desired a sign after his own heart, that they may make sport of it. But he answers both parties; at first, the blasphemers in this Gospel, and later on the tempters, saying that no sign shall be given this wicked generation except the sign of the prophet Jonah, of which we read in the verses following. He answers the blasphemers in a friendly way and argues five points with them.

3. In the first place, with honest and reasonable arguments he concludes from two comparisons that one devil cannot cast out another; for if that were so, the devils would be divided among themselves and Satan's kingdom would indeed not stand. For nature teaches that if a kingdom is divided against itself and its citizens drive out each other, it is not necessary to go to war against it, for it will come to ruin soon enough of itself. Likewise, a house divided against itself needs no other destruction. Even the heathen author Sallust, teaching only from the light of nature and experience, says: "Great wealth passes away through discord, but through concord small means become large." If now the devils were divided among themselves to such a degree that one should drive out the other, Satan's dominion would be at an end, and we would have rest from his attacks.

4. What then were these blasphemers able to say to such clear arguments? They were put to silence, but their hearts were hardened, so that they did not heed his words. A hardened heart will not be instructed, no matter how plainly and clearly the truth is presented; but the faith of the righteous is strengthened when they see that the ground of their faith is right and good. And for the sake of such we must answer those whose hearts are hardened, and put them to silence. Even though they will not be converted nor keep silence, still it serves to reveal their hardened hearts, for the longer they talk, the more foolish they become, and they are caught in their folly, and their cause is robbed of the appearance of being right and good, as Solomon also says in Proverbs 26:5: "Answer a fool according to his folly, lest he be wise in his own conceit." That is, answer him according to his folly that his folly may be put to shame for the sake of others, that they may not follow him and be deceived, thinking that he is right. Otherwise, where no such condition exists, it is better to keep silent, as Solomon also says in the same chapter, verse 4 "Answer not a fool according to his folly, lest thou also be like unto him."

5. Nor could they say here that the devils only pretended to be divided among themselves and to yield to one another, in order to deceive the people, for it is publicly seen how they resist and contend, cry and rave, tear and rage, when they see that Christ means to expel them. It is then clearly seen that they are opposed to Christ and his Spirit, and they are not united with him, to whom they must yield so unwillingly. Therefore it is only a flagrant blasphemous lie, in which they are caught and put to shame, by which they try in venomous hate to give the devil credit for a work of God. From this we learn not to be surprised when our doctrine and life are blasphemed and stubborn hearts will not be convinced nor converted, although they are overwhelmed, as it were, with tangible truth and completely put to silence. It is enough that through our arguments their obstinate folly is revealed, acknowledged and made harmless to pious people, so that the latter may not be misled by its fine pretension. They may then go whither they will, they have condemned themselves as St. Paul says, Titus 3:11.

6. In the second place, he replies with a public example and a similar work, when he says: "By whom do your sons cast them out?" As if he would say: "Is this not simple idiocy? Just what you praise in your sons, you condemn in me. Because your sons do it, it is of God; but because I do it, it must be of the devil." So it is in this world. What Christ does, is of the devil; if someone else did it, it would be all right. Thus the tyrants and enemies of the Gospel do now, when they condemn in us what they themselves do, confess and teach; but they must proceed thus in order that their judgment may be publicly approved, when they are condemned by all justice. The sons, of whom Christ here says that they drive out devils, were, I think, certain exorcists among the people, for God, from the beginning, had given this people manifold spiritual gifts and he calls them their "sons," as though to say: I am the Son of God and must be called a child of the devil, while those who are your sons, begotten by you, do the same things and are not to be considered children of the devil.

7. "Therefore shall they be your judges," that is, I appeal to them. They will be forced to decide that you wrongfully blaspheme me, and thus condemn yourselves. For if one devil does not drive out another then some other power must do it that is neither satanic nor human, but divine. Hence the words: "But if I by the finger of God cast out demons, then is the kingdom of God come upon you." This finger of God is called in Matthew 12:28 the Holy Ghost, for the words read thus: "But if I by the Spirit of God cast out demons," etc. In short, Christ means to say: If the kingdom of God is to come unto you, the devil must be driven out, for his kingdom is against God's kingdom, as you yourselves must confess. But demon is not driven out by demon, much less by men or the power of men, but alone by the Spirit and power of God.

8. From this follows that where the finger of God does not cast out the devil, there the devil's kingdom still exists; where Satan's kingdom still exists, there the kingdom of God cannot be. The unavoidable conclusion then is that, as long as the Holy Spirit does not enter our hearts, we are not only incapable of any good, but are of necessity in the kingdom of Satan. And if we are in his kingdom, then we can do nothing but that which pleases him, else it could not be called his kingdom. As St. Paul says to Timothy: "The people are taken captive in the snares of the devil unto his will" 2 Timothy 2:26. How could Satan suffer one of his people to take a notion to do something against, and not for, his kingdom? Oh, it is a striking, terrible and powerful statement that Christ here admits such a dominion, which we cannot escape except by the power of God; and that the kingdom of God cannot come to us until that kingdom is driven out by divine, heavenly power.

9. This truth is proved in the case of this poor man, who was bodily possessed of the devil. Tell me, what could he and all mankind do to free him from the devil? Without a doubt, nothing. He had to do and suffer just as his master the devil willed, until Christ came, with the power of God. Now then, if he could not free himself from the devil as to his body, how could he, by his own power, deliver his soul from Satan's spiritual dominion? Especially is this the case since the soul, because possessed of sin, is the cause of all bodily possession as a punishment, and sins are more difficult to remove than the punishment of them, and the soul is always more firmly possessed than the body. This is proved by the fact that the devil permits the body to have its natural powers and functions; but he robs the soul of reason, judgment, sense, understanding, and all its powers, as you readily see in the case of this possessed man.

10. He answers them in the third place, by a comparison taken from life, namely that of a strong man overcome by one stronger, and robbed of all his armor and goods etc. By this he testifies also that no one but God can overcome the devil, so that again no man can boast of being able of himself to drive out either sin or the devil. Notice how he pictures the devil! He calls him a mighty giant who guards his court and home, that is, the devil not only possesses the world as his own domain, but he has garrisoned and fortified it, so that no one can take it from him. He rules it also with undisputed sway, so that it does whatever he commands. Just as little as a house or court may withstand or contend against the tyrant who is its master, can man's free will and natural powers oppose sin and Satan, that is, not at all; but they are subject to them. And as that house must be conquered by a stronger man and thus wrested from the tyrant, so must man also be ransomed through Christ and wrested from Satan. We see again, therefore, that our works and righteousness contribute absolutely nothing toward our salvation; it is effected alone by the grace of God.

11. He answers them fourthly, with pointed proverbs and teachings, as: "He that is not with me is against me," and, "He that gathereth not with me, scattereth." "The devil is not with me for I drive him out, hence he must of necessity be against me." But this saying does not apply to the devil alone, but also to the blasphemers whom he here convicts and condemns, as being against him since they are not for him. "To be with Christ" is to have the same mind and purpose as Christ, that is, to believe in Christ that his works save us and not our own, for this is what Christ holds and teaches. But "to gather with Christ" is to do good out of love to him, and to become rich in good works. He that does not believe is, by his own free will, not with Christ but against him, because he depends upon his own works. Therefore, he that does not love, does not gather with Christ, but by fruitless works becomes only more sinful and drifts farther and farther from the faith.

12. In the fifth place, he answers with a threat, namely, that the last state always is worse than the first. Therefore we should take heed that we not only refrain from blaspheming the Gospel and Christ, who does such great things for us and drives the devil out of us; but with zeal and fear hold fast to them, in order that we may not become possessed of seven worse devils whereas one possessed us before. For thus it was with the Jews, who had never been so wicked as while the Gospel was being preached to them. So also under the papacy, we have become seven times, (that is, many times) worse heathen under the name of Christ than we ever had been before as St. Peter says: "The last state is become worse with them than the first." 2 Peter 2:20. And if we neglect the great light which we now have, it will come to pass in our case also, that we shall become worse than we were before, for the devil does not slumber. This should be sufficient warning.

13. Finally, when the woman cries out to Christ and praises him, saying, "Blessed is the mother that bore such a son," etc., he opposes her carnal worship and takes occasion to teach all of us the substance of this Gospel, namely, that we should not go gaping after the works or merits of the saints but rather see to it that we hear and keep the Word of God. For it does not concern or profit us in the least to know how holy and honorable the mother of this child might be, nor how noble this Son of hers may be; but rather what this Son has done for us, namely that, by grace, without any merit or worthiness on our part, he has redeemed us from the devil. This fact is proclaimed to us through the Word of God, and this we are to hear and hold in firm faith; then shall we too be blessed like this mother and her child. Although such a Word and work will be blasphemed, we should suffer it and give an answer with meekness, as St. Peter teaches, for the improvement of others.

II. The Allegorical or Spiritual Meaning of the Gospel

14. This dumb, deaf, blind, and demon-possessed man represents all the children of Adam, who through the flesh are possessed of Satan in original sin, so that they must be his slaves and do according to his will. Hence they are also blind, that is, they do not see God. They are deaf, for they do not hear God's Word, and are not obedient or submissive to it. They are also dumb, for they do not give him one word of thanks or praise, nor do they preach and proclaim Christ and the grace of God. But they are all too talkative about the teachings of the devil and the opinions of men. In these things they see only too well and are wiser than the children of light in their undertakings, opinions, and desires. In these things they hear with both ears and readily adopt the suggestions of flesh and blood. So then, whatever we do, in word and deed, as to both body and soul, is of the devil, whether it be externally good or bad, and must be redeemed through the work of God. We are in his kingdom and therefore we acknowledge him, see, hear, and follow him and praise and proclaim his name. All this takes place through the Spirit of God in his Word, which casts out the devil and his kingdom.

15. The Jews called the chief of the devils Beelzebub. The Hebrew word "sebub" means a fly; "baal" or "beel," a man or ruler, as a householder. When the two words form a combination, they mean an arch-fly or chief-fly, or, in plain German "Fliegenkoenig oder grosse Hummel," that is, king-fly or the great drone. They gave Satan this contemptuous epithet as though they were entirely free from him, secure against him, and lords over him. That is the way all conceited, corrupt hypocrites do; they imagine they are so pure and holy, that the devil is a helpless, feeble fly compared with them, and that they do not need the grace of Christ nor the Word of God. Still they think he is strong enough for others, yet, that whatever god-fearing people teach and do must be the devil's own work, and they consider it such a trifling thing as though it were a dead fly. The devil can well endure such contempt, for by it he is placed above the true God in their hearts.

16. The tyrant in the court or palace is the devil, as I said before. He is in peace, however, as long as God's Word and finger do not oppose him, and just like this deaf-mute, his people do whatever he wishes, for they know no better. His weapons and armor are the carnal conceit, doctrines and traditions of men, by which he terrifies the conscience and protects himself.

17. But when the stronger man, the Gospel, comes, peace flees, and he rages like a madman, for he resents being condemned, unmasked, punished, and publicly branded. Then he gathers up his armor, the powerful, wise, rich and holy people, and sets them all to attacking God's Word, as we see in the persecution of the teachers of the Gospel. Such rage and persecution signify that the devil retires very unwillingly and raves in his whole body; for as he acts in the body and its members when he must depart, so he also behaves in the whole world, resisting with all his power when he is to give place to the Gospel; but it is all in vain, he must be expelled.

18. For a Stronger One, that is, Christ, comes and overpowers him and takes away his whole armor, that is, he converts some of those same persecutors, and to that extent makes him weaker, and his own kingdom stronger. He divides the spoils too, that is, those he converts he uses for various offices, graces, and works in Christendom, of which Paul writes in Romans 12:6. He is also in the court yard or ante-room of the palace, for the devil's kingdom consists in outward appearances and pretenses of wisdom, holiness, and strength; but when it is captured by the Gospel it is found to consist of pure folly, sin and weakness.

19. The text continues, "When the unclean spirit has gone out, he wanders through dry places, seeking rest," etc. This means as much as the saying, "The devil never takes a vacation" and "The devil never sleeps," for he is seeking how he may devour man. "Dry places" are not the hearts of the ungodly, for in such he rests and dwells like a mighty tyrant, as the Gospel here says; but there are dry and waste places here and there in the country where no people live, as forests and wildernesses. To these he flees in wicked rage because he is driven out. You will remember that the devil found Christ in the wilderness. Now, in Judea, there is not much water, hence we read that it contains many arid wastes. In other countries, however, as in our own, which are well watered, the devils stay in rivers and lakes, and there they sometimes drown those who bathe or sail upon them. Furthermore, at some places there are water spirits, who entice the children from the shores into the water and drown them. These are all devils.

20. That he comes again and finds the house swept and garnished (Matthew adds "empty") signifies that the man is sanctified and adorned with beautiful spiritual gifts, and that the evil spirit clearly sees that he can do nothing there with his familiar tricks, for he is too well known. Thus when the worship of idols was driven from the heathen, he never attacked the world with that device again. But what did he do then? He tried something else, went out, took with him seven spirits, more evil than himself, and entered in with them and dwelt there, and the last state of that man was worse than the first. So he has dealt with us. When Christ had become known in the world and the devil's former kingdom with its idol worship had been destroyed, he adopted another plan and attacked us with heresy and introduced and established the papacy, in which Christ was entirely forgotten, and men became worse heathen under the name of Christ than before he was preached, as we can see now with our own eyes. Such also was the lot of the Jews after the destruction of Jerusalem, and of the Greeks under the Turks. And so all will fare, who at first hear the Word of God and afterwards become secure and weary of it. St. Matthew says, in Matthew 12:14, that Satan finds the house empty. And in Matthew 13:25, he sowed tares among the wheat, by night, while men slept. Therefore it is necessary for us to watch as the apostles always admonish us, especially St. Peter in 1 Peter 5:3: "Brethren, be sober, be watchful: your adversary the devil, as a roaring lion, walketh about, seeking whom he may devour"; for wherever he overthrows faith, he easily restores again all former vices.

Laetare. Fourth Sunday in Lent. John 6:1-5

Jesus Feeds 5000 People

Feeding the Five Thousand

TEXT: John 6:1 After these things Jesus went over the sea of Galilee, which is the sea of Tiberias. 2 And a great multitude followed him, because they saw his miracles which he did on them that were diseased. 3 And Jesus went up into a mountain, and there he sat with his disciples. 4 And the passover, a feast of the Jews, was nigh. 5 When Jesus then lifted up his eyes, and saw a great company come unto him, he saith unto Philip, Whence shall we buy bread, that these may eat? 6 And this he said to prove him: for he himself knew what he would do. 7 Philip answered him, Two hundred pennyworth of bread is not sufficient for them, that every one of them may take a little. 8 One of his disciples, Andrew, Simon Peter's brother, saith unto him, 9 There is a lad here, which hath five barley loaves, and two small fishes: but what are they among so many? 10 And Jesus said, Make the men sit down. Now there was much grass in the place. So the men sat down, in number about five thousand. 11 And Jesus took the loaves; and when he had given thanks, he distributed to the disciples, and the disciples to them that were set down; and likewise of the fishes as much as they would. 12 When they were filled, he said unto his disciples, Gather up the fragments that remain, that nothing be lost. 13 Therefore they gathered them together, and filled twelve baskets with the fragments of the five barley loaves, which remained over and above unto them that had eaten. 14 Then those men, when they had seen the miracle that Jesus did, said, This is of a truth that prophet that should come into the world. 15 When Jesus therefore perceived that they would come and take him by force, to make him a king, he departed again into a mountain himself alone.

1. In today's Gospel Christ gives us another lesson in faith, that we should not be overanxious about our daily bread and our temporal existence, and stirs us up by means of a miracle; as though to say by his act what he says by his words in Matthew 6:33: "Seek ye first the Kingdom of God, and his righteousness, and all these things shall be added unto you." For here we see, since the people followed Christ for the sake of God's Word and the signs, and thus sought the Kingdom of God, he did not forsake them but richly fed them. He hereby also shows that, rather than those who seek the Kingdom of God should suffer need, the grass in the desert would become wheat, or a crumb of bread would be turned into a thousand loaves; or a morsel of bread would feed as many people and just as satisfactorily as a thousand loaves; in order that the words in Matthew 4:4 might stand firm, that "Man shall not live by bread alone, but by every word that proceedeth out of the mouth of God." And to confirm these words Christ is the first to be concerned about the people, as to what they should eat, and asks Philip, before they complain or ask him; so that we may indeed let him care for us, remembering that he cares more and sooner for us than we do for ourselves.

2. Secondly, he gives an example of great love, and he does this in many ways. First, in that he lets not only the pious, who followed him because of the signs and the Word, enjoy the food; but also the slaves of appetite, who only eat and drink, and seek in him temporal honor; as follows later when they disputed with him at Capernaum about the food, and he said to them in John 6:26: "Ye seek me, not because ye saw signs, but because ye ate of the loaves," etc., also because they desired to make him king; thus here also he lets his sun shine on the evil and the good, Matthew 5:45. Secondly, in that he bears with the rudeness and weak faith of his disciples in such a friendly manner. For that he tests Philip, who thus comes with his reason, and Andrew speaks so childishly on the subject, all is done to bring to light the imperfections of the disciples, and on the contrary to set forth his love and dealings with them in a more beautiful and loving light, to encourage us to believe in him, and to give us an example to do likewise; as the members of our body and all God's creatures in their relation to one another teach us. For these are full of love, so that one bears with the other, helps and preserves what God has created.

3. That he now takes the five loaves and gives thanks etc., teaches that nothing is too small and insignificant for him to do for his followers, and he can indeed so bless their pittance that they have an abundance, whereas even the rich have not enough with all their riches; as Psalm 34:11 says: "They that seek Jehovah shall not want any good thing; but the rich must suffer hunger." And Mary in her song of praise says: "The hungry he hath filled with good things; and the rich he hath sent empty away." Luke 1:53.

4. Again, that he tells them so faithfully to gather up the fragments, teaches us to be frugal and to preserve and use his gifts, in order that we may not tempt God. For just as it is God's will that we should believe when we have nothing and be assured that he will provide; so he does not desire to be tempted, nor to allow the blessings he has bestowed to be despised, or lie unused and spoil, while we expect other blessings from heaven by means of miracles. Whatever he gives, we should receive and use, and what he does not give, we should believe and expect he will bestow.

II. The Allegorical Interpretation

5. That Christ by the miraculous feeding of the five thousand has encouraged us to partake of a spiritual food, and taught that we should seek and expect from him nourishment for the soul, is clearly proved by the whole sixth chapter of John, in which he calls himself the bread from heaven and the true food, and says: "Verily, verily, I say unto you, ye seek me, not because ye saw signs, but because ye ate of the loaves, and were filled. Work not for the food which perisheth, but for the food which abideth unto eternal life, which the Son of man shall give unto you." John 6:26-27. In harmony with these words we will, explain also this evangelical history in its spiritual meaning and significance.

6. First, there was much hay or grass in the place. The Evangelist could not fail to mention that, although it appears to be unnecessary; however it signifies the Jewish people, who flourished and blossomed like the grass through their outward holiness, wisdom, honor, riches etc., as Isaiah 40:6-7, says: "All flesh is grass, and all the goodliness thereof is as the flower of the field. The grass withereth, the flower fadeth, because the breath of Jehovah bloweth upon it; surely the people is grass." From the Jewish people the Word of God went forth and the true food was given to us; for salvation is of the Jews, John 4:22. Now, as grass is not food for man, but for cattle; so is all the holiness of the outward Jewish righteousness nothing but food for animals, for fleshly hearts, who know and possess nothing of the Spirit.

7. The very same is taught by the people sitting on the grass; for the true saints despise outward holiness, as Paul does in Philippians 3:8, in that he counted his former righteousness to be filth and even a hindrance. Only common and hungry people receive the Word of God and are nourished by it. For here you see that neither Caiaphas nor Anna, neither the Pharisees nor the Scribes follow Christ and see Christ's Signs; but they disregard them, they are grass and feed on grass. This miracle was also performed near the festive time of the Jewish passover; for the true Easter festival, when Christ should be offered as a sacrifice, was near, when he began to feed them with the Word of God.

8. The five loaves signify the outward, natural word formed by the voice and understood by man's senses; for the number five signifies outward things pertaining to the five senses of man by which he lives; as also the five and five virgins illustrate in Matthew 25:1. These loaves are in the basket, that is, locked up in the Scriptures. And a lad carries them, that means the servant class and the priesthood among the Jews, who possessed the sayings of God, which were placed in their charge and entrusted to them, Romans 3:2, although they did not enjoy them. But that Christ took these into his own hands, and they were thereby blessed and increased, signifies that by Christ's works and deeds, and not by our deeds or reason, are the Scriptures explained, rightly understood and preached.

This he gives to his disciples, and the disciples to the people. For Christ takes the Word out of the Scriptures; so all teachers receive it from Christ and give it to the people, by which is confirmed what Matthew 23:10 says: "For one is your master, even the Christ," who sits in heaven, and he teaches all only through the mouth and the word of preachers by his Spirit, that is, against false teachers, who teach their own wisdom.

9. The two fishes are the example and witness of the patriarchs and prophets, who are also in the basket; for by them the Apostles confirm and strengthen their doctrine and the believers like St. Paul does in Romans 4:2-6, where he cites Abraham and David etc. But there are two, because the examples of the saints are full of love, which cannot be alone, as faith can, but must go out in exercise to its neighbor. Furthermore the fishes were prepared and cooked; for such examples are indeed put to death by many sufferings and martyrdoms, so that we find nothing carnal in them, and they comfort none by a false faith in his own works, but always point to faith and put to death works and their assurance.

10. The twelve baskets of fragments are all the writings and books the Apostles and Evangelists bequeathed to us; therefore they are twelve, like the Apostles, and these books are nothing but that which remains from and has been developed out of the Old Testament. The fishes are also signified by the number five (Moses' books); as John 21:25 says: "Even the world itself would not contain the books that should be written" concerning Christ, all which nevertheless was written and proclaimed before in the Old Testament concerning Christ.

11. That Philip gives counsel as how to feed the people with his few shillings, and yet doubts, signifies human teachers, who would gladly aid the soul with their teachings; but their conscience feels it helps nothing. For the discussion Christ here holds with his disciples takes place in order that we may see and understand that it is naturally impossible to feed so many people through our own counsel, and that this sign might be the more public. Thus he lets us also disgrace ourselves and labor with human doctrines, that we may see and understand how necessary and precious God's Word is and how doctrines do not help the least without God's Word.

12. That Andrew pointed out the lad and the loaves, and yet doubted still more than Philip, signifies the teachers who wish to make the people pious and to quiet them with God's laws; but their conscience has no satisfaction or peace in them; but only becomes continually worse, until Christ comes with his Word of grace. He is the one, and he alone, who makes satisfaction, delivers from sin and death, gives peace and fullness of joy, and does it all of his own free will, gratuitously, against and above all hope and presumption, that we may know that the Gospel is devised and bestowed, not through our own merit, but out of pure grace.

13. Finally, you see in this Gospel that Christ, though he held Gospel poverty in the highest esteem and was not anxious about the morrow, as he teaches in Matthew 6:34, had still some provisions, as the two hundred shillings, the five loaves and the two fishes; in order that we may learn how such poverty and freedom from care consist not in having nothing at all, as the barefooted fanatics and monks profess, and yet they themselves do not hold to it; but it consists in a free heart and a poor spirit. For even Abraham and Isaac had great possessions, and yet they lived without worry and in poverty, like the best Christians do.

Judica. Fifth Sunday in Lent. John 8:46-59

The Jews Try to Stone Jesus, or Christ Defends Himself Against His Enemies

John 8:46 Which of you convinceth me of sin? And if I say the truth, why do ye not believe me? 47 He that is of God heareth God's words: ye therefore hear them not, because ye are not of God. 48 Then answered the Jews, and said unto him, Say we not well that thou art a Samaritan, and hast a devil? 49 Jesus answered, I have not a devil; but I honour my Father, and ye do dishonour me. 50 And I seek not mine own glory: there is one that seeketh and judgeth. 51 Verily, verily, I say unto you, If a man keep my saying, he shall never see death. 52 Then said the Jews unto him, Now we know that thou hast a devil. Abraham is dead, and the prophets; and thou sayest, If a man keep my saying, he shall never taste of death. 53 Art thou greater than our father Abraham, which is dead? and the prophets are dead: whom makest thou thyself? 54 Jesus answered, If I honour myself, my honour is nothing: it is my Father that honoureth me; of whom ye say, that he is your God: 55 Yet ye have not known him; but I know him: and if I should say, I know him not, I shall be a liar like unto you: but I know him, and keep his saying. 56 Your father Abraham rejoiced to see my day: and he saw it, and was glad. 57 Then said the Jews unto him, Thou art not yet fifty years old, and hast thou seen Abraham? 58 Jesus said unto them, Verily, verily, I say unto you, Before Abraham was, I am. 59 Then took they up stones to cast at him: but Jesus hid himself, and went out of the temple, going through the midst of them, and so passed by.

1. This Gospel teaches how hardened persons become the more furious, the more one teaches them and lovingly stirs them to do their duty. For Christ asks them here in a very loving way for a reason why they still disbelieve, since they can find fault neither with his life nor with his teaching. His life is blameless; for he defies them and says: "Which of you convicteth me of sin?" His teaching also is blameless; for he adds: "If I say truth, why do ye not believe me?" Thus Christ lives, as he teaches.

2. And every preacher should prove that he possesses both: first a blameless life, by which he can defy his enemies, and no one may have occasion to slander his teachings; secondly, that he possesses the pure doctrine, so that he may not mislead those who follow him. And thus he will be right and firm on both sides: with his good life against his enemies, who look much more at life than at his doctrine, and despise the doctrine for the sake of the life; with his doctrine then for the kind of life he leads and will bear with his life for the sake of his teaching.

3. For it is indeed true that no one lives so perfect a life as to be without sin before God. Therefore it is sufficient that he be blameless in the eyes of the people. But his doctrine must be so good and pure as to stand not only before man but also before God. Therefore every pious pastor may well ask: Who among you can find fault with my life? Among you, I say who are man; but before God I am a sinner. This Moses also boast in Numbers 16:15 that he took nothing from the people and he did them no injustice. Samuel did likewise in 1 Samuel 12:3 also Jeremiah and Hezekiah, who rightly boasted of their blameless life before the people, in order to stop the mouths of blasphemers. But Christ does not speak thus of his doctrine, he says not: "Who among you can find fault with my doctrine"; but "If I tell you the truth." For one must be assured that his doctrine is right before God and that it is the truth, and accordingly care not how it is judged by the people.

4. Hence the Jews have no ground for their unbelief than that they are not the children of God; therefore he passes judgment upon them and says: "He that is of God heareth the words of God; for this cause ye hear them not, because ye are not of God," that cannot mean anything else than that you are of the devil.

5. The Jews could not stand this, for they wished to be God's children and people; therefore they are now raging and slander both Christ's life and his doctrine; his doctrine, in that they say: "Thou hast a devil," that is, thou speakest moved by the devil and thy doctrine is his lie; and they slander his life, in that they say, "Thou art a Samaritan," which sounds among the Jews worse than any other crime. In this way Christ teaches us here the fate that awaits us Christians and his Word; both our life and our doctrine must be condemned and reviled, and that by the foremost, wisest and greatest of earth. Thus one knows the corrupt tree by its fruits, as they, under the pretense of being good, are so bitter, angry, impatient, cruel and mad as to condemn and pass sentence, when one touches them at their tender spot and rejects their ideas and ways.

6. What does Christ do here? His life he abandons to shame and dishonor, is silent and suffers them to call him a Samaritan; while he takes pains to defend his doctrine. For the doctrine is not ours, but God's, and God dare not suffer in the least, here patience is at an end; but I should stake all that I have and suffer, all that they do, in order that the honor of God and of his Word may not be injured. For if I perish, no great harm is done; but if I let God's Word perish, and I remain silent, then I do harm to God and to the whole world. Although I cannot now close their mouth nor prevent their wickedness, I shall nevertheless not keep silent, nor act as if they are right, as I do about my good life, so that they retain their right. Although they do me injustice at the time, yet it remains right before God. Further, Christ excuses himself, and says: "I have not a demon," that is, my doctrine is not of the devil's lies; "but I honor my father," that is, I preach in my doctrine the grace of God, through which he is to be praised, loved and honored by believers. For the evangelical office of the ministry is nothing but glorifying God, Psalm 19:2: "The heavens declare the glory of God" etc. "But you dishonor me," that is, you call me the devil's liar, who reviles and dishonors God.

7. Why does he not say: I honor my father, and ye dishonor him; but says: "Ye dishonor me?" Impliedly he proves by this, that the father's and his honor are alike and the same, as he and the Father are one God; yet along with this he also wishes to teach that if the office of the ministry, which God honors, is to be duly praised, then it must suffer disgrace. In like manner we will also do to our princes and priests; when they attack our manner of life, we should suffer it and show love for hatred, good for evil; but when they attack our doctrine, God's honor is attacked, then love and patience should cease and we should not keep silent, but also say: I honor my Father, and you dishonor me; yet I do not inquire whether you dishonor me, for I do not seek my own honor. But nevertheless be on your guard, there is one who seeks it and judges, that is, the Father will require it of you, and judge you and never let you go unpunished. He seeks not only his honor, but also mine, because I seek his honor, as he says in 1 Samuel 2:30: "Them that honor me I will honor." And it is our consolation that we are happy; although the whole world reviles and dishonors us, we are assured that God will advance our honor, and therefore will punish, judge and revenge. If one could only believe it and persevere, he will surely come. "Verily, verily, I say unto you, if a man keep my word, he shall never see death."

8. By these words he spoils it entirely, in that he does not only defend his doctrine as right and good, which they attribute to the devil; but also ascribes such virtue to his teaching that it becomes a powerful emperor over Satan, death and sin, to give and sustain eternal life. Behold here, how divine wisdom and human reason conflict with one another. How can a human being grasp the thought, that a corporeal, an oral word should redeem forever from death? But let blindness run its course; we shall consider this beautiful saying. Christ is speaking here not of the word of the law, but of the Gospel, which is a discourse about Christ, who died for our sins etc. For God did not wish to impart Christ to the world in any other way; he had to embody him in the Word and thus distribute him, and present him to everybody; otherwise Christ would have existed for himself alone and remained unknown to us; he would have thus died for himself. But since the Word places before us Christ, it thus places us before him who has triumphed over death, sin and Satan. Therefore he who grasps and retains Christ, has thus also eternal deliverance from death. Consequently, it is a Word of life, and it is true, that whoever keeps the Word shall never see death.

9. And from this we may well understand what Christ meant by the word "keep;" it does not refer to such keeping as one keeps the law by good works; for this word of Christ must be kept in the heart by faith and not with the fist or by good works, as the Jews in this case understand it; they fearfully rage against Christ, that Abraham and the prophets are dead; they know nothing of what it is "to keep," "to die" or "to live." And it is not called "to keep" in vain; for there is a conflict and battle when sin bites, death presses and hell faces us; then we are to be in earnest in holding firmly to the Word and let nothing separate us from it. Thus see now how Christ answers the Jews and praises his own teachings. You say, my Word is of the devil and wish to sink it to the bottom of perdition; on the contrary I say to you that it has divine power in it, and I exalt it higher than the heaven of heavens, and above all creatures.

10. How does it then come to pass that man does not see nor taste death, and yet Abraham and all the prophets are dead, who notwithstanding had the Word of God as the Jews say? Here we must give attention to the words of Christ, who makes the distinction that death is a different thing than to see or taste death. We all must face death and die; but a Christian neither tastes nor sees it, that is, he does not feel it, he is not terrified before it, and he enters death calmly and quietly, as though falling asleep, and yet he does not die. But a godless person feels and experiences death, and is terrified before it forever. Thus to taste death may well be called the power and reign or the bitterness of death, yea, it is the eternal death and hell. The Word of God makes this difference. A Christian has that Word and clings firmly to it in death; therefore he does not see death, but his eyes are filled with the life and the Christ in that Word; therefore he never feels death. But the godless possess not that Word, therefore they see no life, but only death; and they must also feel death; that is then the bitter and eternal death.

11. Now Christ means here that whoever clings to his Word will in the midst of death neither feel nor see death, as he also says in John 11:25: "I am the resurrection, and the life: he that believeth in me though he die, yet shall he live," that is, he will not experience real death. Here we see now what a glorious estate it is to be a Christian, who is already released from death forever and can never die. For his death or dying seems outwardly indeed like the dying of the godless, but inwardly there is a difference as great as between heaven and earth. For the Christian sleeps in death and in that way enters into life, but the godless departs from life and experiences death forever; thus we may see how some tremble, doubt and despair, and become senseless and raging in the midst of the perils of death. Hence death is also called in the Scriptures a sleep. For just as he who falls asleep does not know how it happens, and he greets the morning when he awakes; so shall we suddenly arise on the last day, and never know how we entered and passed through death.

12. Let us take another example. When Israel marched out of Egypt and came to the Red Sea, they were free and experienced no death, but only life. However when King Pharaoh arrived behind them with all his forces, then they stood in the midst of death, then no life was in sight. For before them was the sea, through which they could not pass, behind them King Pharaoh, and on both sides of them high mountains; on all sides they were seized and enclosed by death, so that they said to Moses: "Because there were no graves in Egypt, hast thou taken us away to die in the wilderness?" Exodus 14:11, so completely and wholly did they despair of life. Just then Moses came and brought them God's Word that comforted them in the midst of death and preserved them alive, when he said in verse 13: "Fear not, stand still, and see the salvation of Jehovah, which he will work for you today: for the Egyptians whom ye have seen today, ye shall see them again no more for ever." They clung to this Word and held out until victory came; through it life appeared in the presence of death, because they believed the Word, that it would come to pass, and relying upon it they marched into the midst of the Red Sea, which stood on both sides of them like two walls. Then it came to pass that nothing but life and safety were in the sea, where before there were only death and danger.

For they would have never become so bold as to go into the sea, had it divided a hundred times, if God's Word had not been present, which comforted them and promised life. Thus man triumphs over death through the Word of Life, if he cleaves to it and believes, and marches into death with it.

13. Likewise Christ also says here in replying to the Jews, that Abraham and the prophets still live and they never died, but have life in the midst of death; they however only lie and sleep in death. For "Abraham," he says, "rejoiced to see my day; and he saw it, and was glad." Thus, the prophets also saw it. Where and when did Abraham see it? Not with his bodily eyes, as the Jews interpret it, but with the sight of faith in the heart; that is, he recognized Christ when he was told in Genesis 22:18: "In thy seed shall all the nations of the earth be blessed." Then he saw and understood that Christ, born of his seed through a pure virgin, so as not to be cursed with Adam's children but to remain blessed, should suffer for the whole world, cause this to be preached, and thus overwhelm the whole world with blessing etc. This is the day of Christ, the dispensation of the Gospel, that is the light of this day, which radiates from Christ as from the sun of righteousness, and shines and enlightens the whole world. This is a spiritual day, yet it arose at the time Christ was on the earth in the flesh, a day like Abraham saw. But the Jews understood nothing about such a day because of their carnal minds, and hence they reviled Christ as a liar.

14. Therefore Christ proceeds farther and gives the ground and reason why it is just his Word and not the word of anyone else, that giveth life, and says it is because he was before Abraham, or in other words, because he was the one true God. For if the person who offered himself as a sacrifice for us were not God, it would not help or avail anything, even if he were born of the Virgin Mary and suffered a thousand deaths. But the fact that the Seed of Abraham, who gave himself for us, is also true God, secures blessing and victory for all sinners. Therefore Christ speaks, not of his human nature that they saw and experienced; for they could easily see he was not yet fifty years of age, and did not live before Abraham. But with that nature by which he existed long before the time of Abraham, by which he existed also before all creatures and before the whole world. Just as he was man according to his spiritual nature before Abraham, that is. in his Word and in the knowledge of faith was he in the saints; for they all knew and believed that Christ, as God and man, should suffer for us, as is written in Hebrews 13:8: "Jesus Christ is the same yesterday and today, yea and for ever;" and in the Revelation of John, 13:8: "The Lamb of God that hath been slain from the foundation of the world." Yet now he is speaking here especially of his divine nature.

15. But here reason is terribly offended and becomes mad and furious because God should become man; this reason cannot harmonize and understand. And this is the article of faith to which the Jews still in our day cannot reconcile themselves, hence they cannot cease their throwing stones and their blasphemy. But Christ also continues on the other hand to hide himself from them and to go out of their temple, so that they cannot see nor find him in the Scriptures, in which they search daily. Again, this narrative is not a little terror to all who are so foolhardy about the Scriptures and never approach them with a humble spirit. For even in our day it happens that many read and study in the Scriptures and yet they cannot find Christ, he is hid and has gone out of the temple. And how many there are who say with their mouth that God is become man, and yet they are without the Spirit in their hearts; who whenever tested, prove that they were never in real earnest. This is sufficient on this subject.

Palm Sunday

Christ Entry into Jerusalem

TEXT: Matthew 21: 1 And when they drew nigh unto Jerusalem, and were come to Bethphage, unto the mount of Olives, then sent Jesus two disciples, 2 Saying unto them, Go into the village over against you, and straightway ye shall find an ass tied, and a colt with her: loose them, and bring them unto me. 3 And if any man say ought unto you, ye shall say, The Lord hath need of them; and straightway he will send them. 4 All this was done, that it might be fulfilled which was spoken by the prophet, saying, 5 Tell ye the daughter of Sion, Behold, thy King cometh unto thee, meek, and sitting upon an ass, and a colt the foal of an ass. 6 And the disciples went, and did as Jesus commanded them, 7 And brought the ass, and the colt, and put on them their clothes, and they set him thereon. 8 And a very great multitude spread their garments in the way; others cut down branches from the trees, and strewed them in the way. 9 And the multitudes that went before, and that followed, cried, saying, Hosanna to the son of David: Blessed is he that cometh in the name of the Lord; Hosanna in the highest.

This Gospel with its Postil is found on the First Sunday in Advent, Volume I.

Following that we wish to speak a little of Christ's Passion and of the Lord's Supper, as is becoming in this week.

Good Friday

How To Contemplate Christ's Sufferings

1. In the first place, some reflect upon the sufferings of Christ in a way that they become angry at the Jews, sing and lament about poor Judas, and are then satisfied; just like by habit they complain of other persons, and condemn and spend their time with their enemies. Such an exercise may truly be called a meditation not on the sufferings of Christ, but on the wickedness of Judas and the Jews.

2. In the second place, others have pointed out the different benefits and fruits springing from a consideration of Christ's Passion. Here the saying ascribed to Albertus is misleading, that to think once superficially on the sufferings of Christ is better than to fast a whole year or to pray the Psalter every day, etc. The people thus blindly follow him and act contrary to the true fruits of Christ's Passion; for they seek therein their own selfish interests. Therefore they decorate themselves with pictures and booklets, with letters and crucifixes, and some go so far as to imagine that they thus protect themselves against the perils of water, of fire, and of the sword, and all other dangers. In this way the suffering of Christ is to work in them an absence of suffering, which is contrary to its nature and character.

3. A third class so sympathize with Christ as to weep and lament for him because he was so innocent, like the women who followed Christ from Jerusalem, whom he rebuked, in that they should better weep for themselves and for their children. Such are they who run far away in the midst of the Passion season, and are greatly benefited by the departure of Christ from Bethany and by the pains and sorrows of the Virgin Mary, but they never get farther. Hence they postpone the Passion many hours, and God only knows whether it is devised more for sleeping than for watching.

And among these fanatics are those who taught what great blessings come from the holy mass, and in their simple way they think it is enough if they attend mass. To this we are led through the sayings of certain teachers, that the mass opere operati, non opere operantis, is acceptable of itself, even without our merit and worthiness, just as if that were enough. Nevertheless the mass was not instituted for the sake of its own worthiness, but to prove us, especially for the purpose of meditating upon the sufferings of Christ.

For where this is not done, we make a temporal, unfruitful work out of the mass, however good it may be in itself. For what help is it to you, that God is God, if he is not God to you? What benefit is it that eating and drinking are in themselves healthful and good, if they are not healthful for you, and there is fear that we never grow better by reason of our many masses, if we fail to seek the true fruit in them?

II. The True View of Christ's Sufferings

4. Fourthly, they meditate on the Passion of Christ aright, who so view Christ that they become terror-stricken in heart at the sight, and their conscience at once sinks in despair. This terror-stricken feeling should spring forth, so that you see the severe wrath and the unchangeable earnestness of God in regard to sin and sinners, in that he was unwilling that his only and dearly beloved Son should set sinners free unless he paid the costly ransom for them as is mentioned in Isaiah 53:8: "For the transgression of my people was he stricken." What happens to the sinner, when the dear child is thus stricken? An earnestness must be present that is inexpressible and unbearable, which a person so immeasurably great goes to meet, and suffers and dies for it; and if you reflect upon it real deeply, that God's Son, the eternal wisdom of the Father, himself suffers, you will indeed be terror-stricken; and the more you reflect the deeper will be the impression.

5. Fifthly, that you deeply believe and never doubt the least, that you are the one who thus martyred Christ. For your sins most surely did it. Thus St. Peter struck and terrified the Jews as with a thunderbolt in Acts 2:36-37, when he spoke to them all in common: "Him have ye crucified," so that three thousand were terror-stricken the same day and tremblingly cried to the apostles: "O beloved brethren what shall we do?" Therefore, when you view the nails piercing through his hands, firmly believe it is your work. Do you behold his crown of thorns, believe the thorns are your wicked thoughts, etc.

6. Sixthly, now see, where one thorn pierces Christ, there more than a thousand thorns should pierce thee, yea, eternally should they thus and even more painfully pierce thee. Where one nail is driven through his hands and feet, thou shouldest eternally suffer such and even more painful nails; as will be also visited upon those who let Christ's sufferings be lost and fruitless as far as they are concerned. For this earnest mirror, Christ, will neither lie nor mock; whatever he says must be fully realized.

7. Seventhly, St. Bernard was so terror-stricken by Christ's sufferings that he said: I imagined I was secure and I knew nothing of the eternal judgment passed upon me in heaven, until I saw the eternal Son of God took mercy upon me, stepped forward and offered himself on my behalf in the same judgment. Ah, it does not become me still to play and remain secure when such earnestness. is behind those sufferings. Hence he commanded the women: "Weep not for me, but weep for yourselves, and for your children." Luke 23:28; and gives in the 31st verse the reason: "For if they do these things in the green tree, what shall be done in the dry?" As if to say: Learn from my martyrdom what you have merited and how you should be rewarded. For here it is true that a little dog was slain in order to terrorize a big one. Likewise the prophet also said: "All generations shall lament and bewail themselves more than him"; it is not said they shall lament him, but themselves rather than him. Likewise were also the apostles terror-stricken in Acts 2:27, as mentioned before, so that they said to the apostles: "O, brethren, what shall we do?" So the church also sings: I will diligently meditate thereon, and thus my soul in me will exhaust itself.

8. Eighthly, one must skillfully exercise himself in this point, for the benefit of Christ's sufferings depends almost entirely upon man coming to a true knowledge of himself, and becoming terror-stricken and slain before himself. And where man does not come to this point, the sufferings of Christ have become of no true benefit to him. For the characteristic, natural work of Christ's sufferings is that they make all men equal and alike, so that as Christ was horribly martyred as to body and soul in our sins, we must also like him be martyred in our consciences by our sins. This does not take place by means of many words, but by means of deep thoughts and a profound realization of our sins. Take an illustration: If an evildoer were judged because he had slain the child of a prince or king, and you were in safety, and sang and played, as if you were entirely innocent, until one seized you in a horrible manner and convinced you that you had enabled the wicked person to do the act; behold, then you would be in the greatest straits, especially if your conscience also revolted against you.

Thus much more anxious you should be, when you consider Christ's sufferings. For the evil doers, the Jews, although they have now judged and banished God, they have still been the servants of your sins, and you are truly the one who strangled and crucified the Son of God through your sins, as has been said.

9. Ninthly, whoever perceives himself to be so hard and sterile that he is not terror-stricken by Christ's sufferings and led to a knowledge of him, he should fear and tremble. For it cannot be otherwise; you must become like the picture and sufferings of Christ, be it realized in life or in hell; you must at the time of death, if not sooner, fall into terror, tremble, quake and experience all Christ suffered on the cross. It is truly terrible to attend to this on your deathbed; therefore you should pray God to soften your heart and permit you fruitfully to meditate upon Christ's Passion. For it is impossible for us profoundly to meditate upon the sufferings of Christ of ourselves, unless God sink them into our hearts. Further, neither this meditation nor any other doctrine is given to you to the end that you should fall fresh upon it of yourself, to accomplish the same; but you are first to seek and long for the grace of God, that you may accomplish it through God's grace and not through your own power. For in this way it happens that those referred to above never treat the sufferings of Christ aright; for they never call upon God to that end, but devise out of their own ability their own way, and treat those sufferings entirely in a human and an unfruitful manner.

10. Tenthly, whoever meditates thus upon God's sufferings for a day, an hour, yea, for a quarter of an hour, we wish to say freely and publicly, that it is better than if he fasts a whole year, prays the Psalter every day, yea, than if he hears a hundred masses. For such a meditation changes a man's character and almost as in baptism he is born again, anew. Then Christ's suffering accomplishes its true, natural and noble work, it slays the old Adam, banishes all lust, pleasure and security that one may obtain from God's creatures; just like Christ was forsaken by all, even by God.

11. Eleventhly, since then such a work is not in our hands, it happens that sometimes we pray and do not receive it at the time; in spite of this one should not despair nor cease to pray. At times it comes when we are not praying for it, as God knows and wills; for it will be free and unbound: then man is distressed in conscience and is wickedly displeased with his own life, and it may easily happen that he does not know that Christ's Passion is working this very thing in him, of which perhaps he was not aware, just like the others so exclusively meditated on Christ's Passion that in their knowledge of self they could not extricate themselves out of that state of meditation. Among the first the sufferings of Christ are quite and true, among the others a show and false, and according to its nature God often turns the leaf, so that those who do not meditate on the Passion, really do meditate on it; and those who hear the mass, do not hear it; and those who hear it not, do hear it.

III. The Comfort of Christ's Sufferings

12. Until the present we have been in the Passion week and have celebrated Good Friday in the right way: now we come to Easter and Christ's resurrection. When man perceives his sins in this light and is completely terror-stricken in his conscience, he must be on his guard that his sins do not thus remain in his conscience, and nothing but pure doubt certainly come out of it; but just as the sins flowed out of Christ and we became conscious of them, so should we pour them again upon him and set our conscience free. Therefore see well to it that you act not like perverted people, who bite and devour themselves with their sins in their heart, and run here and there with their good works or their own satisfaction, or even work themselves out of this condition by means of indulgences and become rid of their sins; which is impossible, and, alas, such a false refuge of satisfaction and pilgrimages has spread far and wide.

13. Thirteenthly. Then cast your sins from yourself upon Christ, believe with a festive spirit that your sins are his wounds and sufferings, that he carries them and makes satisfaction for them, as Isaiah 53:6 says: "Jehovah hath laid on him the iniquity of us all;" and St. Peter in his first Epistle 1 Peter 2:24: "Who his own self bare our sins in his body upon the tree" of the cross; and St. Paul in 2 Corinthians 5:21: "Him who knew no sin was made to be sin on our behalf; that we might become the righteousness of God in him." Upon these and like passages you must rely with all your weight, and so much the more the harder your conscience martyrs you. For if you do not take this course, but miss the opportunity of stilling your heart, then you will never secure peace, and must yet finally despair in doubt. For if we deal with our sins in our conscience and let them continue within us and be cherished in our hearts, they become much too strong for us to manage and they will live forever. But when we see that they are laid on Christ and he has triumphed over them by his resurrection and we fearlessly believe it, then they are dead and have become as nothing. For upon Christ they cannot rest, there they are swallowed up by his resurrection, and you see now no wound, no pain, in him, that is, no sign of sin. Thus St. Paul speaks in Romans 4:25, that he was delivered up for our trespasses and was raised for our justification; that is, in his sufferings he made known our sins and also crucified them; but by his resurrection he makes us righteous and free from all sin, even if we believe the same differently.

14. Fourteenthly. Now if you are not able to believe, then, as I said before, you should pray to God for faith. For this is a matter in the hands of God that is entirely free, and is also bestowed alike at times knowingly, at times secretly, as was just said on the subject of suffering.

15. But now bestir yourself to the end: first, not to behold Christ's sufferings any longer; for they have already done their work and terrified you; but press through all difficulties and behold his friendly heart, how full of love it is toward you, which love constrained him to bear the heavy load of your conscience and your sin. Thus will your heart be loving and sweet toward him, and the assurance of your faith be strengthened. Then ascend higher through the heart of Christ to the heart of God, and see that Christ would not have been able to love you if God had not willed it in eternal love, to which Christ is obedient in his love toward you; there you will find the divine, good father heart, and, as Christ says, be thus drawn to the Father through Christ. Then will you understand the saying of Christ in John 3:16: "God so loved the world that he gave his only begotten Son," etc. That means to know God aright, if we apprehend him not by his power and wisdom, which terrify us, but by his goodness and love; there our faith and confidence can then stand unmovable and man is truly thus born anew in God.

16. Sixteenthly. When your heart is thus established in Christ, and you are an enemy of sin, out of love and not out of fear of punishment, Christ's sufferings should also be an example for your whole life, and you should meditate on the same in a different way. For hitherto we have considered Christ's Passion as a sacrament that works in us and we suffer; now we consider it, that we also work, namely thus: if a day of sorrow or sickness weighs you down, think, how trifling that is compared with the thorns and nails of Christ. If you must do or leave undone what is distasteful to you: think, how Christ was led hither and thither, bound and a captive. Does pride attack you: behold, how your Lord was mocked and disgraced with murderers. Do unchastity and lust thrust themselves against you: think, how bitter it was for Christ to have his tender flesh torn, pierced and beaten again and again. Do hatred and envy war against you, or do you seek vengeance: remember how Christ with many tears and cries prayed for you and all his enemies, who indeed had more reason to seek revenge. If trouble or whatever adversity of body or soul afflict you, strengthen your heart and say: Ah, why then should I not also suffer a little since my Lord sweat blood in the garden because of anxiety and grief? That would be a lazy, disgraceful servant who would wish to lie in his bed while his lord was compelled to battle with the pangs of death.

17. Behold, one can thus find in Christ strength and comfort against all vice and bad habits. That is the right observance of Christ's Passion, and that is the fruit of his suffering, and he who exercises himself thus in the same does better than by hearing the whole Passion or reading all masses. And they are called true Christians who incorporate the life and name of Christ into their own life, as St. Paul says in Galatians 5:24: "And they that are of Christ Jesus have crucified the flesh with the passions and the lusts thereof." For Christ's Passion must be dealt with not in words and a show, but in our lives and in truth. Thus St. Paul admonishes us in Hebrews 12:3: "For consider him that hath endured such gainsaying of sinners against himself, that ye wax not weary, fainting in your souls;" and St. Peter in his 1 Epistle 1 Peter 4:1: "As Christ suffered in the flesh, arm ye yourselves also with the same mind." But this kind of meditation is now out of use and very rare, although the Epistles of St. Paul and St. Peter are full of it. We have changed the essence into a mere show, and painted the meditation of Christ's sufferings only in letters and on walls.

Confession and the Lord's Supper

The Lord's Supper

1. Although I have often preached and written on the Lord's Supper and Confession, yet annually the time appointed for the consideration of these subjects, for the sake of those who desire to commune, returns, and so we must review them in a summary and speak of them once more.

2. In the first place, I have often enough said that Christians are not obliged to commune on this particular festive day, but that they have the right and authority to come whenever they desire; for God established the office of the ministers for the purpose that they might at all times serve the people and provide them with God's Word and the Sacraments. Therefore it is unchristian to force people under pain of committing mortal sin to commune just at this time; as has been done heretofore, and is still done in many places. For it is not and cannot be in keeping with the Lord's Supper to force or compel anyone to partake of it; on the contrary, it is intended only for a hungry soul that compels itself and rejoices in being permitted to come; those who must be driven are not desired.

3. Therefore, until the present the devil has ruled with unrestrained power and authority through the pope, compelling him to drive and force the whole world to commune; and in fact, everybody did come running, like swine, because of the pope's command. In this way so much dishonor and shame have been brought upon the Lord's Supper, and the world has been so filled with sin that one is moved with compassion to think of it. But since we know these things we ought to let no command bind us, but to hold fast the liberty wherewith Christ has made us free. I say this for the sake of those who will not commune except at this time of the year, and who come only because of the custom and the common practice. There is, to be sure, no harm in coming at this Easter festival, if only the conscience be free and not bound to the time, and is properly prepared to receive the Lord's Supper.

II. of Confession

4. In the second place, we must say the same thing concerning Confession. First of all we know that the Scriptures speak of three kinds of confession. The first is that which is made to God, of which the prophet David speaks in Psalm 32:5: "I acknowledged my sin unto thee, and my iniquity did I not hide: I said, I will confess my transgressions unto Jehovah; and thou forgavest the iniquity of my sin." Likewise, in the preceding third verse David says: "When I kept silence, my bones wasted away as with the drought of summer ;" that is, before God no one is able to stand unless he come with this confession, as Psalm 130:4 declares: "But there is forgiveness with thee, that thou mayest be feared ;" that is, whoever would deal with thee must deal so that this confession proceeds from his heart, which says: Lord, if thou be not merciful all is lost, no matter how pious I may be. Every saint must make this confession, as again we read in the Psalm mentioned, verse 6, "For this let everyone that is godly pray unto thee." Therefore, this kind of confession teaches us that we are all alike wicked and sinners, as the saying is, If one of us is good, all of us are good. If anyone have special grace, let him thank God and refrain from boasting. Has anyone fallen into sin, it is because of his flesh and blood; nor has any fallen so low but that another who now stands may fall even lower. Therefore, as far as we are concerned, there is no difference among us, the grace of God alone is dividing us.

5. This kind of confession is so highly necessary that it dare not cease for a moment, but must constitute the entire life of a Christian, so that without ceasing he praise the grace of God and reproach his own life in the eyes of God. Otherwise, if he dare to plead some good work or a good life before God, his judgment, which can tolerate nothing of the kind, would follow; and no one is able to stand before it. Therefore, this kind of confession must be made, that you may condemn yourself as worthy of death and the fire of hell; thus you will anticipate God so that he will not be able to judge and condemn you, but must show you mercy. Concerning this kind of confession, however, we will not speak at this time.

6. The second kind of confession is that made to our neighbor, and is called the confession springing from love, as the other is called the confession springing from faith. Concerning this kind of confession we read in James 5:16: "Confess therefore your sins one to another." In this confession, whenever we have wronged our neighbor, we are to acknowledge our fault to him, as Christ declares in Matthew 5:23-25: "If therefore thou art offering thy gift at the altar, and there rememberest that thy brother hath aught against thee, leave there thy gift before the altar, and go thy way, first be reconciled to thy brother, and then come and offer thy gift. Agree with thine adversary quickly, while thou art with him in the way etc." God here requires of both parties that he who hath offended the other ask forgiveness, and that he who is asked grant it. This kind of confession, like the former, is necessary and commanded; for God will be merciful to no one, nor forgive his sins, unless he also forgive his neighbor. In like manner, faith cannot be true unless it produce this fruit, that you forgive your neighbor, and that you ask for forgiveness; otherwise a man dare not appear before God. If this fruit is absent, faith and the first kind of confession are not honest.

7. The third kind of confession is that ordered by the pope, which is privately spoken into the ears of the priest when sins are enumerated. This confession is not commanded by God; the pope, however, has forced the people to it and, in addition, has invented so many kinds and varieties of sin that no one is able to keep them in mind; thus consciences have been troubled and tortured in a manner that is pitiful and distressing. Concerning this, however, we will say that God does not force you to confess by faith to him, or by love to your neighbor, when you have no desire to be saved and to receive his grace. Neither does he want you to make confession against your will and desire; on the contrary, he wants you to confess of your own accord, heartily, with love and pleasure. In like manner, he does not compel you to make a private confession to the priest when you have no desire of your own to do so, and do not long for absolution.

This the pope disregarded, and proceeded as though it were a part of the civil government requiring that force be employed; he did not inquire whether a person felt willing or not, but he simply issued the order, that whosoever does not confess at this time shall not have burial in the cemetery. But God cares not whether a thing is done or not, as long as it is not done with pleasure. It is better, therefore, to postpone a duty than to perform it unwillingly. For no one can come to God unless he come gladly and of his own free will; hence, no one can compel you to come. If you come because of the command and in order to show obedience to the pope, you do wrong. Yet it is the custom in the whole world that everybody runs to the Lord's Supper solely because it is commanded; hence this is very properly called the week of torture, since in it the consciences of the people are tortured and tormented so that they are really to be pitied, besides the injury and destruction of souls. Moreover, Christ himself is also tortured far more shamefully than when he hung upon the cross. Therefore, we may well lift up our hands and thank God for giving us such light. For although we do not bear much fruit and amend, still we have the right knowledge. Hence, it is much better to stay away from confession and communion than to go unwillingly: then at least our consciences remain untortured.

8. Hence we say of private confession, that no one is compelled to observe it. Still it is for this reason a commendable and good thing. Wherever and whenever you are able to hear God's Word you ought not to despise it, but receive it with heartfelt desire. Now, God has caused his Word to go forth through all the world, so that it fills every nook and corner, and wherever you go you find God's Word. If I preach the forgiveness of sins, I preach the true Gospel. For the sum of the Gospel is: Whosoever believeth in Christ shall receive the forgiveness of his sins. Thus a Christian preacher cannot open his mouth unless he pronounces an absolution. Christ also does the same in the Gospel lesson when he says, "Pax vobiscum," Peace be unto you. That is, I proclaim unto you, as of God, that you have peace and forgiveness of sins; this is even the Gospel itself, and absolution. So also the words of the Lord's Supper, "This is my body which is given for you; this is my blood which is shed for you for the remission of sins etc." If I were to say, I will not go to confession because I have the Word in the Lord's Supper, I will be like him who declares, Neither am I going to hear the preaching. The Gospel must ring and echo without ceasing in every Christian's mouth. Therefore we are to accept it with joy wherever and whenever we can hear it, lift up our hands, and thank God that we can hear it everywhere.

9. Therefore, when you go to private confession give more heed to the priest's word than to your own confessing; and make this distinction, What you say is one thing, and what he says who hears you is another. Do not place much value on what you do, but give heed to what he says, to wit, that in God's stead he proclaims to you the forgiveness of sins. It makes no difference whatever whether he be a priest, called to preach, or merely a Christian. The word which he speaks is not his, but God's Word; and God will keep it as surely as if he had spoken it. This is the way he has placed his holy Word into every corner of the world. Since, therefore, we find it everywhere, we ought to receive it with great thankfulness, and not cast it to the winds.

10. For in Confession as in the Lord's Supper you have the additional advantage, that the Word is applied to your person alone. For in preaching, it flies out into the whole congregation, and although it strikes you also, yet you are not so sure of it; but here it does not apply to anyone except to you. Ought it not to fill your heart with joy to know a place where God is ready to speak to you personally? Yea, if we had a chance to hear an angel speak, we would surely run to the ends of the earth. Are we not then foolish, wretched and ungrateful people not to listen to what is told us? Here the Scriptures stand, and testify that God speaks through us, and that this is as valid as though he were to speak it with his own mouth; even as Christ declares in Matthew 18:20, "Where two or three are gathered together in my name, there am I in the midst of them;" again in John 20:23, "Whose soever sins ye forgive, they are forgiven unto them; whose soever sins ye retain, they are retained." Here God himself pronounces the absolution, just as he himself baptizes the child; and do you say we don't need Confession? For although you hear the same thing in the Lord's Supper you ought not on that account to reject it, especially since it applies to you, as already stated, personally.

11. Besides this you have another advantage, in Confession you are enabled to disclose all your failings and to obtain counsel regarding them. And if there were no other reason, and God did not himself speak in Confession, I would not willingly give it up for this one reason, that here I am permitted to open my heart to my brother and tell him what troubles me. For it is a deplorable thing to have the conscience burdened and prostrate with fear, and to know neither counsel nor consolation.

This is why it is such an excellent and comforting thing for two to come together, and the one to offer advice, help and consolation to the other, proceeding in a fine brotherly and affectionate manner. The one reveals his ailment; whereupon the other heals his wounds. Therefore I would not give Confession up for all the treasure of the world. Still it dare not be made a command, lest it be turned into a matter of conscience, as though a person would not dare to commune without first making confession; nevertheless, we ought never to despise Confession, you cannot hear God's Word too frequently, nor impress it so deeply upon your heart that it could not be done still better.

12. Therefore I said that confession and absolution must be carefully distinguished from each other, that you give attention chiefly to the absolution, and that you attend confession not because of the command, or in order to do a good work by your confessing, thinking that because of this good work your sins are forgiven; on the contrary, we are to go only because we there hear God's Word and by it receive consolation. To this incline your ears, and be persuaded that God speaks through men and forgives you your sins; this, of course, requires faith. Hitherto the manner of our Confession was as follows: when people were absolved so many works were required of them as to render satisfaction for their sins. This was called absolving, whereas in truth it meant binding worse than ever. Sins ought to be completely removed by the absolution; but they first imposed the task of rendering satisfaction for them, and thus force people away from faith and absolution, and induce them to rely upon their own works. They should be taught thus, Behold, this word which I speak to you in God's stead you must embrace in true faith. If you have not this faith postpone your confession; yet this does not mean that when your faith is too weak you are not to come and demand consolation and strength. If you cannot believe, tell the brother to whom you would confess of it, and say to him, I do indeed feel that I have need of confession and absolution, but I find I am too cold and too weak in faith. For to whom are you going to confide your weakness if not to God? And where can you find him except in your brother? He can strengthen and help you by his words. This is confessing in the right way; and would to God the whole world were brought far enough at least for everyone to confess that he cannot believe.

13. Let it be said now concerning Confession that everything ought to be free, so that each person attends without constraint, of his own accord. But what ought one to confess? Here is where our preachers in the past have pounded a great deal into us by means of the five senses, the seven deadly sins, the ten commandments, etc., thereby perplexing our consciences. But it should be, that you first of all feel that which weighs you down, and the sins that pain you most and burden your conscience you ought to declare and confess to your brother. Then you need not search long nor seek all kinds of sins; just take the ones that come to your mind, and say, This is how frail I am and how I have fallen; this is where I crave consolation and counsel. For confession ought to be brief. If you recall something that you have forgotten, it is not to trouble you; for you confessed not in order to do a good work, or because you were compelled, but in order to be comforted by the word of absolution. Moreover, you can easily confess to God in secret what was forgotten, or you can hear the absolution for it during the communion service. We are therefore not to worry even if sins have been forgotten; though forgotten they are still forgiven; for God looks, not to the excellence or completeness of your confession, but to his Word and how you believe it. So also the absolution does not state that some sins are forgiven and others not; on the contrary, it is a free proclamation declaring that God is merciful to you. But if God is merciful to you all your sins must be blotted out.

Therefore, hold fast to the absolution alone and not to your confession; whether or not you have forgotten anything makes no difference; as much as you believe so much are you forgiven. This is the way we must ever trust in God's Word in spite of sin and an evil conscience.

III. Of the Lord's Supper

14. In the third place we must speak of the Lord's Supper. We said above that no one should be compelled to commune at any special time, but that this should be left free. It remains for us to speak of the two elements in the Lord's Supper. I have already said that among us one element alone is not to be offered to the communicant; he who wants the Lord's Supper should receive the whole of it. For we have preached and practiced this long enough and cannot assume that there should be anyone unable to understand it; yet if there be one so dense, or claiming to be so weak that he cannot grasp the true meaning of it, we will excuse him; it is just as well that he remains away. For anyone to hear God's Word so long, to have himself coddled like a child, and after all to continue saying, I do not understand, is no good sign. For it is impossible for you to hear so long and still be unenlightened; since then you remain blind it is better for you not to receive the Lord's Supper. If you cannot grasp the Word that is bright, clear and certain, you need not grasp the sacrament; for the sacrament would be nothing if there were no Word.

Moreover, this Word has now resounded again and again throughout the whole world, so that even they who oppose it know it. These, however, are not weak but obdurate and hardened; they set their heads against the doctrine they hear us prove from the Scriptures with such clearness that they are unable to reply or establish the contrary; yet they simply remain in the Romish Church and try to force us to follow them. Therefore, it is out of the question for us any longer to yield or to endure them, since they defy us and maintain as their right what they teach and practice. Hence we wish to receive both elements in the Lord's Supper, just because they wish to prevent us from having them. The thought of causing offense no longer applies to those people. But if there were a locality where the Gospel had not been heard, it would be proper and Christian to adapt one's self for a time to those who are weak; as also we did in the beginning when our cause was entirely new. Now, however, since so much opposition is offered, and so many efforts at violent suppression are made, forbearance is out of the question.

15. It is, moreover, a fine example of God's providential ruling and guidance that the Lord's Supper is not devoid of persecution, for in instituting it he intended it to be a token and mark whereby we might be identified as Christians. For if we were without it, it would be impossible to tell where to find Christians, and who are Christians, and where the Gospel has borne fruit. But when we go to the Lord's Supper people can see who they are that have heard the Gospel; moreover, they can observe whether we lead Christian lives. So this is a distinctive mark whereby we are recognized, whereby we also confess the name of God and show that we are not ashamed of his Word.

When now the pope sees me going to the Lord's Supper and receiving both elements, the bread and the wine, according to the Gospel, it is a testimony that I am determined to cling to the Gospel. If then he grows angry and endeavors to slay me, it is just as it was in the early days of Christianity when the Christians confessed God in the same way by this token of the Lord's Supper. Our bishops have forbidden both elements as contrary to God's ordinance and command. If now we mean to confess Christ we must receive both elements, so that people may know that we are Christians and abide by the Word of God. If for this cause they slay us we ought to bear it, knowing that God will abundantly restore life to us again. Hence it is proper for us to suffer persecution on this account; otherwise, if everything were to go smoothly, there would be no real confession. In this way we remain in the right state, always expecting shame and disgrace, yea, even death for the Lord's sake, as it was in the ancient church.

16. Furthermore, I said it is not enough to go to the Lord's Supper, unless you are assured and know a defense to which you can refer as the foundation and reason that you do right in going; in order that you may be armed when attacked, and able to defend yourself with the Word of God against the devil and the world. On this account you dare not commune on the strength of another's faith; for you must believe for yourself, even as I must, just as you must defend yourself as well as I must defend myself. Therefore, above all you must know the words Christ used in instituting the Lord's Supper. They are these: "Our Lord Jesus Christ, the same night in which he was betrayed, took bread; and when he had given thanks, he broke it and gave it to his disciples and said, Take, eat; this is my body which is given for you: this do in remembrance of me." "After the same manner also he took the cup, when he had supped, gave thanks and gave it to them, saying: Take, drink ye all of it; this cup is the New Testament in my blood, which is shed for you for the remission of sins: this do ye, as oft as ye drink it, in remembrance of me."

17. These are the words which neither our opponents nor Satan are able to deny, on them we must stand. Let them make whatever comments they please; we have the clear Word of God, saying, the bread is Christ's body given for us; and the cup his blood shed for us. This he bids us do in remembrance of him; but the pope commands that it be not done. Well, they say, we are only erring laymen, we do not understand, nor are we able to explain the words. But we reply: it is for us to explain just as much as it is for them; for we are commanded to believe in Christ, to confess our faith, and to keep all the commandments of God, just as well as they are. For we have the same God they claim to have. How then are we to believe without knowing and understanding his Word? Since I am commanded to believe I must know the words I am to believe; for how can I believe without the words? Moreover, it is my duty to stand firm, and I must know how to defend myself and how to refute the arguments to the contrary. This is how you can stop their mouths and bring them to silence. My faith must be as good as yours, therefore I must have and must know the Word as well as you. For example the Evangelist here says, "Jesus took the cup and gave it to his disciples, saying, Drink ye all of it; this is my blood of the New Testament which is shed for you," etc. These words are certainly clear enough; and there is no one so stupid that he cannot understand what is meant by, "Take, drink ye all of it; this is the cup of the New Testament in my blood" etc. Therefore we reply, Unless they prove to us that drinking here signifies something different from what all the world understands by the term, we shall stick to the interpretation, that we are all to drink of the cup. Let them bring forward what they please, custom or councils, we reply, God is older and greater than all things.

18. Likewise, the words are clear, "This do in remembrance of me." Tell me, who is to remember the Lord? Is this said to the priests alone, and not to all Christians? And to remember the Lord, what is that but to preach him and to confess him? Now if we are all to remember the Lord in his Supper we must certainly be permitted to receive both elements, to eat the bread and to drink the cup; this surely no one can deny. Therefore, there is no use for you to cover up these words and tell us that we are not to know them. If we are not to know them, what are you here for? You claim to be a shepherd, and therefore you ought to be here to teach these words and preach them to me, and now by your own rotten defense you are forced to confess your own shame and bite your own tongue, having so shamefully spoken in contradiction of the truth.

19. Thus you see how we are to understand the words of the institution of the Lord's Supper and firmly hold to them; for in them all the virtue is centered, we all must know them, understand them, and cling to them in faith, so as to be able to defend ourselves and to repulse the foe. When you wish to go to the Lord's Supper listen to the words spoken, and be assured that they contain the whole treasure on which you are to stand and rely, for they are really spoken to you. My body is given, my blood is shed, Christ declares. Why? Just for you to eat and drink? No; but for the remission of sins. This is what strikes you; and everything else that is done and said has no other purpose than that your sins may be forgiven.

But if it is to serve for the forgiveness of sins, it must be able also to overcome death. For where sin is gone, there death is gone, and hell besides; where these are gone, all sorrow is gone and all blessedness has come.

20. Here, here the great treasure lies; on this keep your eyes and dismiss the follies which occupy and trouble the great schools when they inquire how the body of Christ can be present and concealed in so small a space. Be not puzzled about the marvel, but cleave to the Word, and endeavor to obtain the benefit and fruit of the Lord's Supper, namely that your sins be forgiven. Therefore, you must act so that the words mean you. This will be when you feel the sting and terror of your sin, the assault of the flesh, the world, and the devil. At one time you are angry and impatient; at another you are assailed by the love of money and the cares of life etc.; so that you are constantly attacked, and at times even gross sins arise, and you fall and injure your soul. Thus you are a poor and wretched creature, afraid of death, despondent, and unable to be happy. Then it is time, and you have reason enough to go, make confession, and confide your distress to God, saying, Lord, thou hast instituted and left us the sacrament of thy body and blood that in it we may find the forgiveness of sin. I now feel that I need it. I have fallen into sin. I am full of fear and despair. I am not bold to confess thy Word. I have all these failings, and these. Therefore, I come now that thou mayest heal, comfort, and strengthen me etc.

21. For this reason I made the statement that the Lord's Supper is to be given only to him who is able to say that this is his condition; that is, he must state what troubles him, and must long to obtain strength and consolation by means of the Word and the symbol. Let him who is unable to use the Lord's Supper in this way remain away, nor let him do like those who wretchedly torture themselves at this time, when they come to the sacrament, and have no idea what they are doing. Now when you have received the Lord's Supper, go forth and exercise your faith. The sacrament serves to the end that you may be able to say, I have the public declaration that my sins are forgiven; besides, my mouth has received the public symbol, this I can testify, as also I have testified before the devil and all the world. When death now and an evil conscience assail you, you can rely on this and defy the devil and sin, and thus strengthen your faith and gladden your conscience towards God, and amend your life day by day, where otherwise you would be slothful and cold, and the longer you remained away the more unfit you would be. But if you feel that you are unfit, weak and lacking in faith, where will you obtain strength but here? Do you mean to wait until you have grown pure and strong, then indeed you will never come and you will never obtain any benefit from the holy communion.

22. This is the right use of the Lord's Supper, serving not to torture, but to comfort and gladden the conscience. For by instituting it for us, God did not intend it to be poison and torture to frighten us; this is what we made of it by our false doctrine, when we imagined we were to bring the offering of our piety to God, and hid the words that were to give comfort and salvation, strengthen our consciences, refresh, gladden and free them from every distress. This is the meaning of the Lord's Supper, and we are to look upon it only as containing sweet grace, consolation, and life. It is poison and death to those who approach it with insolence, who feel no weakness, frailty, or distress to impel them, who act as if they were pure and pious from the start. The Lord's Supper welcomes those who perceive their frailties and feel that they are not pious, yet would like to be. Thus it all depends on this feeling, for we are all frail and sinful, only we do not all confess it.

23. Let this suffice on how we ought to prepare ourselves to receive the communion and conduct ourselves toward it, namely, that we are to exercise and strengthen our faith by the words of the institution of the Supper which say that Christ's body and blood are given and shed for the remission of sins. These words sufficiently show the benefit, fruit and use of the Lord's Supper as far as partaking of it for ourselves is concerned. But the second thought springing from the first is Christian love, and this also deserves attention. It is our duty to let the benefit and fruit of the Lord's Supper become manifest, and we ought to show that we have received it with profit. We at present see it received throughout all the world in so many celebrations of the mass, but where do you see the least fruit following from it?

24. Now this is the fruit, that even as we have eaten and drunk the body and blood of Christ the Lord, we in turn permit ourselves to be eaten and drunk, and say the same words to our neighbor, Take, eat and drink; and this by no means in jest, but in all seriousness, meaning to offer yourself with all your life, even as Christ did with all that he had, in the sacramental words. As if to say, Here am I myself, given for you, and this treasure do I give to you; what I have you shall have; when you are in want, then will I also be in want; here, take my righteousness, life, and salvation, that neither sin, nor death, nor hell, nor any sorrow may overcome you; as long as I am righteous and alive, so long shall you also be righteous and alive. These are the words he speaks to us; these we must take, and repeat them to our neighbor, not by the mouth alone, but by our actions, saying, Behold, my dear brother, I have received my Lord; he is mine, and I have more than enough and great abundance. Now you take what I have, it shall be yours, and I place it at your disposal. Is it necessary for me to die for you, I will even do that. The goal placed before us in the Lord's Supper is that the attainment of such conduct toward our neighbor may appear in us.

25. Of course, it is true, we will not become so perfect that one places his soul and body, goods and honor at the disposal of the other. We still live in the flesh, and this is so deeply rooted in us that we are unable to furnish this symbol and evidence as perfectly as we should. On account of these our shortcomings Christ has instituted the Lord's Supper for our training, that here we may obtain what we lack. For what will you do when you miss in yourself what we have described? You must even come and tell him, Behold, this is what I need. Thou dost give thyself to me so richly and abundantly, but I am unable to do likewise toward my neighbor; this I lament before thee, and I pray thee, let me grow rich and strong enough to accomplish it. Though it is impossible for us to reach such perfection, we are nevertheless to sigh for it, and not to despair when we fall short, only so the desire to obtain it continue in our hearts.

26. Yet the least part of love and devotion is not the sacrifice of my pride. I can indeed give my neighbor temporal goods and bodily service by my efforts and labor; I can also render him service by offering instruction and intercession; likewise I can visit and comfort him when he is sick and in sorrow, feed him when hungry, loose him when bound, etc. But to bear my neighbor's weakness is far greater than all these. Yet with us the trouble will always be that we will not be able to do it as perfectly as Christ did. He is the bright, radiant sun without a single shadow, whereas our light, compared with this sun, is only a gleaming bit of lighted straw. Yonder a glowing oven full of fire and perfect love; and he is satisfied if we light only a little taper and endeavor somewhat to let love shine forth and burn.

This is the shortcoming we all see and feel in each other. But never let anyone conclude and say, This is not Christ. On the contrary, see what he did in the Gospel story when so often he suffered his disciples to stray and stumble, making his wisdom yield and serve their folly. He condemns them not, but endures their weakness and tells them in John 13:7-33: "Whither I go, ye cannot come." Likewise, to Peter, "What I do, thou knowest not now." By such love he abandons his righteousness, judgment, power, vengeance, and punishment, and his authority over us and our sins. He could indeed condemn us for our folly, but all he does is to say, You do wrong, you do not know; yet casts us not away, but comforts us. Therefore I said, it is no small evidence of love to be able to bear with one's neighbor when he is weak in faith or in love.

27. On the other hand, Christ dealing so kindly with his disciples is no permission for us to approve of human weaknesses or of sin. For later he tells Peter, "What I do thou shalt understand hereafter." Here he merely gives his weakness time and bears with it. It is as though he said, I will bear with your ignorance and weak faith for your sake and will spare you as long as you understand that you must do better, and intend to later on; not that you may grow idle and secure.

28. Therefore, when we have received the Lord's Supper we must not allow ourselves to become indolent, but must be diligent and attentive to increase in love, aid our neighbor in distress, and lend him a helping hand when he suffers affliction and requires assistance. When you fail to do this you are not a Christian, or only a weak Christian, though you boast of having received the Lord and all that he is, in the Lord's Supper.

29. If, however, you would be sure of partaking profitably of the Lord's Supper, there is no better way than to observe your conduct toward your neighbor. You need not reflect on the great devoutness you experienced, or on the sweetness of the words in your heart. These indeed are good thoughts, but they will not give you assurance, they may deceive you. However, you will be sure as to whether the sacrament is efficacious in your heart, if you watch your conduct toward your neighbor. If you discover that the words and the symbol soften and move you to be friendly to your enemy, to take an interest in your neighbor's welfare, and to help him bear his suffering and affliction, then it is well. On the other hand, if you do not find it so, you continue uncertain even if you were to commune a hundred times a day with devotions so great as to move you to tears for very joy; for wonderful devotions like this, very sweet to experience, yet as dangerous as sweet, amount to nothing before God. Therefore we must above all be certain for ourselves, as Peter writes in 2 Peter 1:10, "Give the more diligence to make your calling and election sure." The Word and the sacrament are indeed certain in themselves; for God himself, together with all the angels and saints, testify to this; the question is in regard to yourself whether you furnish the same testimony. Therefore, even if all the angels and the whole world were to testify that you had received the Lord's Supper profitably, it would be weaker testimony than that furnished by yourself. This you cannot reach unless you consider your conduct, whether it shines forth, works in you, and bears fruit.

30. Now when fruit fails to appear, when you feel that constantly you remain just as you were, and when you care nothing for your neighbor, then you have reason to take a different attitude in these things; for this is no good sign. Even Peter had to hear the same who was godly and ready to die and to do wonderful deeds for Christ. What then will you do? If you still experience evil desires, anger, impatience etc., you are again in trouble and that should urge and impel you to go to Christ and lay it before him, saying. I partake of the Lord's Supper, still I remain as I was, without fruit.

I have received the great treasure, yet it remains inactive and dormant within me: This I lament before thee. As thou hast bestowed this treasure upon me, grant now that it may also produce fruit and a new life within me, manifesting themselves toward my neighbor. Now when you begin a little to prove this, you will continually grow stronger and break forth in good deeds to your neighbor more from day to day.

31. For this life is nothing more than a life of faith, of love, and of sanctified affliction. But these three will never be perfect in us while we live here on earth, and no one possesses them in perfection except Christ. He is the sun and is set for our example, which we must imitate. For this reason there will always be found among us some that are weak, others that are strong, and again some that are stronger; these are able to suffer less, those more; and so they must all continue in the imitation of Christ. For this life is a constant progress from faith to faith, from love to love, from patience to patience, and from affliction to affliction. It is not righteousness, but justification; not purity, but purification; we have not yet arrived at our destination, but we are all on the road, and some are farther advanced than others. God is satisfied to find us busy at work and full of determination. When he is ready he will come quickly, strengthen faith and love, and in an instant take us from this life to heaven. But while we live on earth we must bear with one another, as Christ also bore with us, seeing that none of us is perfect.

32. Christ has shown this to us not only by his own example and by his Word, but he has also pictured it to us in the form of the Sacrament of the Altar, namely, by means of the bread and the wine. We believe that the true body and blood of Christ is under the bread and wine, even as it is. Here we see one thing and believe another, which describes faith. For when we hear the Word and receive the Lord's Supper we have merely a word and an act, yet by it we embrace life and every treasure, even God himself.,Likewise love is pictured in these signs and elements. First of all in the bread. For as long as the grains of wheat are in a pile before they are ground, each is a body separate for itself, and is not mingled with the others; but when they are ground they all become one body. The same thing takes place with the wine. As long as the berries are not crushed each retains its own form, but when they are crushed they all flow together and become one drink. You cannot say, this is the flour from this grain, or this is a drop from that berry; for each has entered the form of the other, and thus was formed one bread and one drink. This is the interpretation of St. Paul in 1 Corinthians 10:17: "Seeing that we, who are many, are one bread, one body: for we all partake of the one bread." We eat the Lord by the faith of the Word which the soul consumes and enjoys. In this way my neighbor also eats me: I give him my goods, body, and life and all that I have, and let him consume and use it in his want. Likewise, I also need my neighbor; I too am poor and afflicted, and suffer him to help and serve me in turn. Thus we are woven one into the other, helping one another even as Christ helped us. This is what it means spiritually to eat and drink one another.

33. Let me say now in conclusion in regard to the Lord's Supper that when we have received it we ought to give heed to love, and in this way assure ourselves that we have received the sacrament profitably, and at the same time furnish evidence to others; so that we may not always come and still continue unchanged. Therefore, as I said, we must turn from our devotions and thoughts to our conduct toward our neighbor, and examine ourselves in this mirror with all seriousness. The sacrament is to act upon us so that we may be transformed and become different people. For God's word and work do not intend to be idle, but are bound to produce great things, to wit, set us free from sin, death, and the devil, and every kind of fear, and make us servants even of the least among men on earth, and this without the slightest complaint on our part, rejoicing rather to find someone in need of our help, and fearing only lest after receiving so much we may not apply it all.

34. Whenever the Lord's Supper fails to produce this result there is reason to fear it has wrought injury. Nevertheless, even if the result is not great, we are not to reject those that are imperfect and weak, but those that are indolent and insolent, who imagine they have done enough when they have partaken of the sacrament. A change must take place in you, and there must be evidence of it, then you will be able to perceive through the symbol that God is with you, and your faith will grow sure and strong. For you can easily feel whether you have grown more joyous and bold than you were before. Formerly the world seemed too narrow for us when we heard of death and thought of sin. If now we feel different it is not because of our own strength, for in the past we could not get so far, although we put forth greater exertions and endeavored to help ourselves by means of works.

Likewise, you can feel whether you are kind to him who injured you, and whether you are merciful to him who is sick. Thus you can discover, whether the Lord's Supper is producing any fruit through your own life. If you experience nothing, go to God and tell him of your shortcomings and troubles; we all must do the same thing as long as we live, for, as we have said, not one of us is perfect. For the present let this suffice on this subject.

Easter Sunday. Mark 16:1-8

The Fruit and Power of Christ's Resurrection... A Fine Sermon on the Reception of the Lord's Supper

The Resurrection

TEXT: Mark 16:1 And when the sabbath was past, Mary Magdalene, and Mary the mother of James, and Salome, had bought sweet spices, that they might come and anoint him. 2 And very early in the morning the first day of the week, they came unto the sepulchre at the rising of the sun. 3 And they said among themselves, Who shall roll us away the stone from the door of the sepulchre? 4 And when they looked, they saw that the stone was rolled away: for it was very great. 5 And entering into the sepulchre, they saw a young man sitting on the right side, clothed in a long white garment; and they were affrighted. 6 And he saith unto them, Be not affrighted: Ye seek Jesus of Nazareth, which was crucified: he is risen; he is not here: behold the place where they laid him. 7 But go your way, tell his disciples and Peter that he goeth before you into Galilee: there shall ye see him, as he said unto you. 8 And they went out quickly, and fled from the sepulchre; for they trembled and were amazed: neither said they any thing to any man; for they were afraid.

1. As we heard while explaining the meaning of Christ's passion, that it was not enough to know its mere narrative and history; so it is not enough to learn only how and when Christ our Lord arose from the dead; we must also preach and understand the benefit and use both of the sufferings and the resurrection of Christ, namely, what he thereby acquired for us. For if we preach only its history, it is an unprofitable sermon, which Satan and the godless know, read and understand as well as true Christians; but when we preach to what end it serves, it becomes profitable, wholesome and comforting.

2. Christ himself pointed out the benefit of his sufferings and resurrection when he said to the women in Matthew 28:10: "Fear not: go tell my brethren that they depart into Galilee, and there shall they see me." These are the very first words they heard from Christ after his resurrection from the dead, by which he confirmed all the former utterances and loving deeds he showed them, namely, that his resurrection avails in our behalf who believe, so that he therefore anticipates and calls Christians his brethren, who believe it, and yet they do not, like the apostles, witness his resurrection.

3. The risen Christ waits not until we ask or call on him to become his brethren. Do we here speak of merit, by which we deserve anything? What did the apostles merit? Peter denied his Lord three times; the other disciples all fled from him; they tarried with him like a rabbit does with its young. He should have called them deserters, yea, betrayers, reprobates, anything but brethren. Therefore this word is sent to them through the women out of pure grace and mercy, as the apostles at the time keenly experienced, and we experience also, when we are mired fast in our sins, temptations and condemnation.

4. These are words, full of all comfort that Christ receives desperate villains as you and I are and calls us his brethren. Is Christ really our brother, then I would like to know what we can be in need of? Just as it is among natural brothers, so is it also here. Brothers according to the flesh enjoy the same possessions, have the same father, the one inheritance, otherwise they would not be brothers: so we enjoy with Christ the same possessions, and have in common with him one Father and one inheritance, which never decreases by being distributed, as other inheritances do; but it ever grows larger and larger; for it is a spiritual inheritance. But an earthly inheritance decreases when distributed among many persons. He who has a part of this spiritual inheritance, has it all.

5. However, what is Christ's inheritance? His heritage is life and death, sin and grace, all that is in heaven and earth, eternal truth, power, wisdom, righteousness; he governs and rules over all, over hunger and thirst, over fortune and misfortune, over everything imaginable, whether in heaven or on earth, not only spiritual but also secular affairs; and the sum total of all is, he has all things in his hand, be they eternal or temporal. Now if I believe on him, I become partaker with him of all his possessions, and obtain not only a part or a piece; but, like him, I obtain all, eternal righteousness, eternal wisdom, eternal strength, and become a lord and reign over all. The stomach will not hunger, sins will not oppress, I will no more fear death, nor be terror-stricken by Satan, and I will never be in want, but will be like Christ the Lord himself.

6. In the light of this we now easily understand the sayings here and there in the prophets and especially in the Psalms; as when David in Psalm 34:10 says: "The young lions (the rich) do lack, and suffer hunger; but they that seek Jehovah shall not want any good thing." And in another Psalm: "Jehovah knoweth the days of the perfect; and their inheritance shall be forever. They shall not be put to shame in the time of evil; and in the days of famine they shall be satisfied." Psalm 37:18-19. And immediately following in verse 25: "I have been young, and now am old; yet have I not seen the righteous forsaken, nor his seed begging bread." All this comes of itself from the fact that we are and are called Christ's brethren; not because of our worthiness, but because of God's pure grace. Yes, if God gave us this in our heart, so that we experience it, then we would be saved; but it goes in one ear and out the other. And this it is that Paul praises so highly and strongly to the Romans when he says: "For as many as are led by the Spirit of God, these are sons of God. For ye received not the spirit of bondage again unto fear; but ye received the spirit of adoption, whereby we cry, Abba, Father. The Spirit himself beareth witness with our spirit, that we are children of God: and if children, then heirs; heirs of God, and joint-heirs with Christ; if so be that we suffer with him, that we may be also glorified with him." Romans 8:14-17.

7. The title of being Christ's brothers is so high that the heart of man cannot understand it. If the Holy Spirit bestows not this grace, none can say: Christ is my brother. For reason is not bold enough to say so; although one may say it with the tongue, as the spirits of modern times do. It is not uttered in this way, it is necessary for the heart to experience it; otherwise it is pure hypocrisy. If you truly experience it in your heart it will be such a great thing that you will much prefer to keep silence than to speak about it, yea, in the presence of the magnitude of this inheritance you easily doubt and waver as to whether it is really true or not. Those who only cry: Christ is my brother! Christ is my brother! are not true Christians. A Christian acts quite differently, and it is very wonderful, so that the flesh shudders at it and dares indeed neither speak of it nor confess it.

8. We should bestir ourselves to hear this, not only with the natural ear, but also to experience it in our hearts, for then we would not be so forward and impudent, but would be surprised and amazed over it. True and godly Christians go along in life in contempt of themselves and in fear; they think thus: Ah, shall I, a poor, miserable person, who am steeped in sin, be now so exalted that God's Son becomes my brother? Ay, how is it that I, a miserable poor creature, am thus honored? I am at once confounded before it and feed upon it; for it truly requires a great effort to believe it; yea, when one experiences it thus, how it is in truth, he must from that hour die; for man, since he is flesh and blood, cannot understand it. Here in this life man's heart is in too great straits to lay hold of it; but after death, when the heart becomes larger and broader, we experience what we have heard through the Word.

9. In the Gospel of John, Christ tells Mary Magdalene of the benefit and use of his death and resurrection still more plainly, when he says: "But go unto my brethren, and say to them, I ascend unto my Father and your Father, and my God and your God." John 20:17. This is one of the great and comforting passages upon which we can venture, and of which we dare boast. As if Christ had said: Go hence, Mary, and say to my disciples who have deserted me on the field of battle, and who have well merited punishment and eternal condemnation, that my resurrection has taken place for their benefit; that is, by my resurrection I have brought it to pass that my Father is their Father, and my God is their God. These are few words and very short; but they contain a great thought, namely, that we have as great a confidence and refuge in God as Christ his Son himself has. Who can grasp such exceeding joy, unless one speaks of himself when he says a poor, corrupt sinner can and may call God his Father and his God, just like Christ himself does?

10. The author of the Epistle to the Hebrews has grasped the words of Psalm 22:23 and taken them well to heart, when he says of Christ: "For which cause he is not ashamed to call them brethren, saying, I will declare thy name unto my brethren, in the midst of the congregation will I sing thy praise." Hebrews 2:11-12. If any worldly lord were to condescend so low as to say to a thief, or a murderer or to a low French character, Thou art my brother; that would be a great thing and everyone would be amazed at it; but that this King, who in his glory sits at the right hand of God, his Father, says to a poor sinner: Thou art my brother, that no one takes to heart, no one receives it in earnest, and yet on that hangs our highest comfort and courage against sin, death, Satan, hell, law, and against all misfortune, both of the body and of the soul.

11. Since we are flesh and blood, and subject to all kinds of affliction, it follows that it must be thus also with our brother; or he would not be like us in all respects. Therefore, in that he becomes like us, he tastes of all that we do, in order to be our true brother and save us, so that we on the other hand may become like him. This the Epistle to the Hebrews paints and brings out very beautifully when it says: "Since then the children are sharers in flesh and blood, he also himself in like manner partook of the same; that through death he might bring to naught him that had the power of death, that is, the devil; and might deliver all them who through fear of death were all their lifetime subject to bondage. For verily not to angels doth he give help, but he giveth help to the seed of Abraham. Therefore it behooveth him in all things to be made like unto his brethren, that he might become a merciful and faithful high priest in things pertaining to God, to make propitiation for the sins of the people. For in that he himself hath suffered being tempted, he is able to succor them that are tempted." Hebrews 2:14-18.

12. St. Paul in a very beautiful way condensed the benefit and use both of Christ's sufferings and his resurrection in one short passage, as in a nutshell, when he says to the Romans: "Who was delivered up for our trespasses, and was raised for our justification." Romans 4:25.

But on this theme enough has been said for the present; whoever desires may with profit meditate on it; more is written about it in the Postil; whoever desires to have it let him get it and read. We will now discuss another subject. Since people in many localities still cling to the papal abuses, so that they flock to the Sacrament of the Lord's Supper on Easter, and this custom is so deeply drilled into them, that it is very difficult to root it out everywhere, we wish to give some instruction to the single-minded and plain people, how they should at the present time partake of the Sacrament of the Lord's Supper. (Rodt's Ed., 1525.)Of this the following sermon plainly speaks.

The Reception of the Holy Sacrament

Sacraments

I. The Holy Sacrament of the Lord's Supper

1. You, beloved, have often before heard how we should prepare for the time when we receive the most worthy Sacrament of the body and blood of Christ. But since this is the time appointed for the consideration of this subject, we must again speak of it, especially those features of it that are needed to be touched upon; for if I mistake not there are some who do not understand it. However, I hold that we cannot better grasp and understand it than by comparing the misuse of the Sacrament with the right Christian, evangelical use of it, which Christ instituted and prescribes.

2. In the first place, hitherto we have taught that we should be of good cheer and firmly believe that under the bread is the true body of Christ and under the wine the true blood of Christ. This is the first thing that has been most emphasized, and when we planted this in the people, we thought we were very successful preachers. Afterwards however, we proceeded farther and asked the people whether they had a desire to receive the Sacrament, and thus freely gave it to them and then never concerned ourselves further.

Thus it rested upon two thoughts, that we thus believe and that we desired the Sacrament; but to what end we should desire it and what more belongs to it, no one cared for that and no one saw that such faith might be, and is, in Satan and all unchristians; for we are easily persuaded to believe this much. For, if I can believe that Christ rose from the dead; likewise that he went through the stone at the mouth of the grave and made no hole in it; and if I can believe that he went through closed doors without breaking or damaging anything, thus that wood and his body were in one place, and yet true flesh and blood were there; then can I also readily believe that the body and blood of Christ are present in the bread and wine.

3. Hence it is an unimportant matter if we let it rest there and believe only that much, although the communicants thought they thereby did a precious work. Such faith and desire are still not enough for the Sacrament, and all, who know no more about and have not higher faith and desire for it, should remain away; for giving the Holy Sacrament to such persons is not much different than when you thrust it down the throat of a pig. It is mockery and a dishonoring of the Sacrament. Therefore remember you must be different, or not approach the Lord's Supper.

4. Therefore hereafter it shall be ordered that no one is to be admitted to the Sacrament unless he be asked first and it be learned from him what is the state of his heart, whether he knows what it is and why he goes to the communion. We have looked through our fingers at this long enough and tolerated the old misuse of it; but since the Gospel has now been working farther into the world, we must give attention to this matter and improve the imperfections. We should here act, as we do with a child or any other person we baptize. When one brings him to baptism, it is not enough for him to believe that that is baptism and a sacrament instituted by Christ. It is also not enough for one to inquire whether he wishes to be baptized, which is the last thing to be asked; but first one asks him: Dost thou renounce the devil, and all his works and ways? Then: Dost thou believe in God the Father, the Son, and the Holy Ghost? When the one baptizing inquires whether he has true faith and knows what he is seeking and why he is there and for what purpose he makes use of the Sacrament. Much more then should one do thus in the Lord's Supper, so that no one goes to the communion unless we first hear whether he is a vessel that can contain it, so that it is not thrust as it were into the throat of an unclean animal. For those who go to the Lord's Supper only with such a faith, think no farther than that they may only receive it, they hold it to be a meritorious work and think that is enough. They do it only because it is instituted and it is the custom to do so, just as when you ask one, why he desired to be baptized and he answers: I do not know; it is thus instituted, therefore I will also do like other people. I think it is a good thing to do.

5. Now, one can in no way abuse and dishonor the most worthy Sacrament of the Lord's Supper more than by regarding it only as a good work. For a good work is that which I can do to another and it must be my work; but the Lord's Supper is not my work but God's work, with which I permit myself to be served, and I receive a blessing, therefore, as far as God's work and my work are different from one another, so far are the thoughts separated from one another which hold the Sacrament to be God's and at the same time our own work. Hence it is now clear that it is a great abuse of the Sacrament and blasphemy, if you do not esteem it to be the work of God.

6. Therefore the people should be asked when anyone desires to go to the Sacrament: first, what is the Sacrament? Then the answer should be: The words which Christ spoke at his Last Supper are the Sacrament: "Take ye, this is my body, which is given for you; this is my blood that is shed for you, for the remission of sins." Therefore Christ instituted by these words the bread and wine, under which are his flesh and blood, for a token and a seal that his words are true. Then ask further: To what end are these words a blessing which Christ here speaks and attaches to them a token? Answer: They are a blessing to the end that I believe in them, not that I make a good work out of them, thus that my faith clings to them with my heart, and I doubt not but that it is as the words read. How then do the words read? Thus: "This is my body, which is given for you." These words Christ says to all who receive the Lord's Supper, therefore you must cleave to them by faith, and say, I come and desire the Sacrament because I believe his body was given for me and his blood was shed for me, in order that thereby my faith may be strengthened, for this reason I desire to receive the token of bread and wine. Whoever cannot do this, or does not believe, should by no means go to the communion; for where this faith is not in the heart all is lost.

7. Behold now how far that and this faith are from one another. For if you do even believe that the Sacrament is the body and blood of Christ, how are you made better? To what end does that profit you? The devil believes that too; but what does it help him? By it you do nothing but a good work, and you have no more benefit of it than the box in which the wafer is kept, or the cloth that is spread over it; for you are not a vessel prepared, in which true faith works. But when the faith comes that lays hold of the Word, and .says: These words Christ spoke and I believe they are true, and I am ready to die trusting in them, and I am certain and sure that he is there present, that he has given himself to me and he is mine, also that I appropriate him to myself, as if it were my own possession which God has bestowed upon me. This is far different from the other faith; for that gives you nothing, but this gives you and brings you, as you believe, all the treasures of which the words speak.

8. Therefore until the present time we have shown enough forbearance; but hereafter no one shall be given the Sacrament until it is known how he believes and that he is a vessel that can hold it, and knows how to give information concerning his faith. Moreover it is very necessary to do this, because the Sacrament is instituted in an outward form to the end that people may confess and prove their faith, in order that it may become manifest before the world. For before God it is enough that we believe in the Gospel, but now he wants us to remain upon the earth to serve the people and to confess before the world the faith we have in our hearts by means of certain tokens, that is, by means of baptism and the Lord's Supper. With the mouth we must confess the Gospel and then receive the Lord's Supper as a token that the world may know that we are Christians. And in this way I then become certain, as for my own person, that I have a gracious God, besides I have done enough before the world. If you do not do this, what do you accomplish then at the Lord's Supper? What will you do if it should cost you your life and you approach a cross? Likewise, when it comes to the point that you should die and the devil tests you? If you will then say: Yes, I believe that I received the Sacrament; I believe that it is the true body and blood of Christ; then the devil will reply: yes, that I also believe. Thus your faith will not help you, and the devil has triumphed and will remove you where there will never be any help for you.

9. But if you say: Behold, thou tyrant, or thou devil and death, I have received the Sacrament, in which my Lord Christ confidently promised through his Word that his body and blood are mine, and this I believe: not only so far as you do, that it is his flesh and blood; but that all is given to me that the words imply. The words will not lie to me, for they are God's words and God's token. In this way you must be armed when you die; there neither I nor any other man can help you, even if all priests stood by your side with the Sacrament; like they heretofore did and accomplished no more than made a good work out of it and imagined it should help. Yes, indeed it should have helped them.

10. We read in the books of the Kings, 1 Samuel 4:3 f., when the Israel warred against the Philistines and were defeated and put to flight, the elders of Israel said to the people: The reason God permitted us to suffer defeat was because we have not the ark of the covenant with us. Then they went and brought the ark; when they had now returned they cried in a hostile, triumphant way, so that their enemies almost feared and thought they had now been defeated; but when they met one another, the Israelites were nevertheless again slain. What then was the cause? The ark or chest was in their midst, where God was, as surely as he is in the Lord's Supper; why would he not help them? Because they also made of it a work of merit. For they clung to it alone and had no faith; therefore God punished them and they were slain worse than before. We also do likewise, we cling only to our work, that we have received the Sacrament, and go ahead without any faith. Thus will also Satan, when the test comes, smite us worse than any time before.

11. I know very well that this misuse of the Sacrament is, alas, a deeply spread evil; therefore we must indeed bestir ourselves to root out the error and give the alarm to those who think it is enough for one to believe that the body and blood of Christ are present in the Lord's Supper. True it is, the food is indeed there; but you do not eat and enjoy it. Christ does not say in his words: Behold, there it is, there it lies; but he says: "Take ye," it shall be yours. It is therefore not the nature of the Sacrament that we should have Christ lying there; but that we should make use of him and his.

12. Then there is no right use of the Lord's Supper unless thou believest that this body was offered for thee and this blood was poured out for thee; then thou hast, what thou believest. When thy conscience troubles thee and says: There and there thou hast sinned and thou art anxious to be free from thy trouble, then go to the Sacrament, and say: Have I sinned, then this body has not sinned, it is without guilt; this body is offered for me, and this blood is shed for me for the remission of sins, this I do believe, and as a token of it I will receive the Sacrament. When thou dost this, then thy sins are taken away and can cause thee no more distress. For who then can do thee any harm? Everything must here close its mouth and remain speechless, in spite of Satan and all misfortune; for I am one bread (*ein Kuchen*) with Christ, and no suffering can befall me, of that I am certain; and there I have then triumphed.

13. It is now necessary for every Christian to know this, so that he can also tell, when asked, that he knows why he takes the Sacrament. Therefore I say again, although heretofore indeed according to the old custom, everyone who came was allowed to go to the Sacrament; yet from now on it shall not continue so, but be so ordered that whoever wishes to receive the Sacrament must be asked what the Lord's Supper is and what he seeks there; and that he answers as I just mentioned: First, that the words of Christ and the token of Christ's body and blood are the Lord's Supper. Secondly, that he seeks these to strengthen his faith and to console his conscience, so that we get out of ourselves and come to Christ. In this you must prepare yourself so that you may know how to make the right use of the Sacrament; can you not do this, then the Lord's Supper should not be administered to you.

14. Besides, be on your guard not to make a false faith, even if you do believe that Christ is there given and is thine; and if your faith is only a human thought, that you have originated, then remain away from this Sacrament. For it must be a faith that God makes, you must know and feel that God works this in you, that this Word and token are given to you, and that you are so bold as to think you would be willing to die for it. And if you still waver and doubt, then kneel down and pray God to impart to you grace that you may forsake self and come to the true faith. Then you would see how few Christians there are and how few of them would go to the Sacrament.

15. However we should plan and accomplish it, as I have earnestly wished, that we might gather into one place those who truly believe, and acknowledge our faith before others. I earnestly desired to have this done long ago, but circumstances did not permit; for this truth has not been preached and urged enough. That is the way Christ did; he delivered his sermons to the multitude for everybody as the apostles later did, so, that every person heard them, believers and unbelievers; whoever caught it, caught it. We must do the same. But we are not to cast the Sacrament among the people in a crowd, as the pope has done. When I preach the Gospel, I do not know to whom it applies; but here I should take it for granted that it applies to those who come to the Sacrament. Here I must not act in doubt, but be sure that the one to whom I give the Sacrament has laid hold of the Gospel and has true faith, just like when I baptize anyone; neither the one who receives the Sacrament should doubt, nor the one that is baptized. Thus you have now the right way and the Christian use of receiving the Lord's Supper. In addition we will speak of the fruits that follow when one makes the right use of the Sacrament. We will now consider this thought.

The Fruits of the Holy Spirit

16. We have two blessings or fruits from the holy Sacrament. The one is that it makes us brethren and fellow-heirs with our Lord Jesus Christ, that thus he and we become one bread, (*ein Kuchen*, one cake). The second is that we become like, and one with, all other believers, wherever they are upon the earth, and all are thus one bread, one cake. St. Paul pathetically touches upon these two fruits in his first Epistle to the Corinthians: "Seeing that we, who are many, are one bread, one body; for we all partake of the one bread," 1 Corinthians 10:17. Likewise in the same connection Paul says in verse 16: "The cup of blessing which we bless, is it not a communion of the blood of Christ? The bread which we break, is it not a communion of the body of Christ?" These words should be very familiar and constantly repeated in Christendom and thoroughly understood, since so much is embodied in them. When we eat the bread, he says, then we all have the same food, you have just what I have, and there is no difference, whether you be a man or a woman; and in that we all receive it in common in the Sacrament. We receive all that Christ has and is. When I believe that his body and blood are mine, then I have the whole Christ, my Lord, and all he can do is to make my heart happy and bold, because I do not trust in my own goodness, but in the innocent blood and in the pure body, which I receive at the Communion.

17. Now, what has our Lord Jesus Christ and what is he able to do? His body and blood are without sin, full of grace, yea, the bodily dwelling place of the divine majesty. In brief, all that the Lord God has is Christ's, and all these possessions become here mine. But in order to have a token and the assurance that such precious and indescribable treasures are mine, I appropriate to myself the body and blood of Christ. Therefore no sin will ever be blotted out by a work of mine, as the poor, raging multitude under the papacy has falsely taught; but through my fully and truly believing that the body and blood of Christ are given to me. Therefore I am fully assured and conscious that Christ, my Lord, bestows upon me all the treasures he has, and all his strength and authority. Thus his wisdom, truth and godliness take away and blot out all my sins; his eternal life swallows up death for me; through his strength and influence I conquer Satan. Then will the Christian be an heir of eternal life and lord over all things, so that nothing can do him any harm.

18. Such vast possessions you cannot acquire even if you held a thousand masses every day. Christ is a person who gives himself for you, so that it is impossible for sin, death, hell and Satan to stand before him, not to mention that they should gain a victory over the Divine Majesty. Now where his flesh and blood are, there he will always. without a doubt. have his eyes open and never permit them to be trodden under foot; you have all power that God himself has; that is, we become one bread, one cake, with Christ, our Lord, so that we enter into the fellowship of his treasures and he into the fellowship of our misfortune. For here his innocence and my sins, my weakness and his strength are thrust together, and all thus become one. What is mine is his, and what is his that I also have. This is high, inexpressible grace, because of which the heart must be happy and of good courage. If you are now one cake, as it were, with Christ, what more do you wish? You have all in superabundance whatever your heart desires; and you are now sitting in paradise.

19. This is what we should have heretofore urged had we really treated of the Lord's Supper. But it has been so completely lost that not a word has been heard about it. When we wished to prove what kind of fruit and benefits the Lord's Supper brought, we taught whoever hears a mass on any day no harm would befall him that day (and like monkeyism, "Affenspiel," Ed. 1531): and they thus applied it to all outward fortune and misfortune. Besides this, they have done more, and so cancelled and covered up the words that no one should hear or speak them in Christendom except the priests only, because they were the holiest words in the mass. Who but the worst devil in hell has spoken and originated it, that we should keep that covered up and concealed which we are to tell forth and advocate above everything else in Christendom, and which should be the best known of all things? If that is governing Christendom, then may God have mercy. This is now the first fruit of the Lord's Supper.

20. The other fruit or blessing of the Lord's Supper is, that we become also one bread and one drink among one another, as Paul says. These are marvelous words and out of the ordinary way of speaking, so that we do not understand them; and the only reason of this is that we make a meritorious work out of the Sacrament. How is it then that we are all one bread and eat one another. It is done in this way. When I eat the Sacrament, then it eats me again: outwardly I eat the Sacrament; but inwardly and spiritually I receive all the treasures of Christ and even himself, just as when I eat my temporal bread it strengthens me inwardly as to my physical existence. So when I receive the Sacrament, then Christ receives me and consumes me also, and devours me and my sins, and I enjoy his righteousness. Thus his godliness and riches swallow up my sins and misery, so that afterwards I am nothing but righteousness (and nothing but riches, "reichthum," Ed. 1531).

21. Just so is it also among us, we all become one bread, one cake, and eat one another. You know when we make bread all the grains of wheat are crushed and ground, so that each grain becomes the flour of the others, they are then mixed together so that we see in a sack of flour all the grains joined together, and that each has become the flour of the other, and no grain of wheat retains its own form, but each gives the other its flour, and each loses its body, in order that the body of the many grains may become the body of one bread. The same way is it when we make wine, each grape mixes its juice with the juice of the other grapes, and each loses its form, so that there comes from it one drink. So should it also be with us. When I become a public servant and serve you so that you enjoy my service whenever you need me, then I am thus your food; even as you enjoy your daily bread when you are hungry so that it helps and gives strength to your weak body and your hungry stomach. Therefore when I help and serve you in every time of need, then I am thus your bread. Again, art thou also a Christian, then thou dost in return act so that thou dost serve me with all thou hast, that all may be benefited and that I may enjoy' the same as my meat or drink. For example, am I a sinner and thou art pious through God's grace, then thou approachest me and sharest thy piety with me, thou prayest for me, intercedest in my behalf before God, and dost interest thyself in me as if thou wast in my place. Thus thou dost swallow by thy godliness my sins, as Christ devoured our sins. Thus thou eatest me; then I in return eat you.

22. Here you see what an exceedingly great thing this Sacrament is when a person uses it aright, that man would be terrified to death because of its greatness, if he fully experienced it; for reason can never grasp it. Is it not great that the High Majesty intercedes for me and even gives himself as my own? Afterwards, that all the saints step before me and stand there, are interested in and care for me, and serve and help me? Thus God places us in fellowship with Christ and his elect; there we have great comfort upon which we can depend. Am I a sinner, Christ stands there and says: The sinner belongs to me, I will lay hold of him with my holy fingers, who will murmur against it? Thus my sins drop out of sight and I enjoy his righteousness. And we Christians do the same thing among one another, one becomes interested in the other, so that one bears the other's sins and infirmities and serves him with his piety. This we do not understand; and even if we did hear and understand it, we could not believe it; therefore we continually rush ahead and never experience any fruit or change for the better.

23. These are the fruits of the wafer of the Sacrament and this is its true Christian use, and in brief it consists in this (we must soon conclude) that we believe the words to be true that belong to the Sacrament, and then go forth (receive the Sacrament, Ed. 1531) and confess that we are Christians. Later we can feel and see whether those who received the Lord's Supper also prove thus that the fruits follow and whether they show love for others; where they will not do as they thus profess, we can excommunicate them from the congregation. Thus may it come into use again, so that it may be known who are faithful Christians and who are not.

II. Confession and Absolution

24. This we have said for the present on the reception of the Lord's Supper; we will now speak a little on Confession and soon conclude. In confession certain words are also spoken, by which the minister absolves you as the representative of God; these same words we ought not to despise here. We will force no one to enumerate all his sins; still no one should go to the Lord's Supper who does not esteem the confession. But we have often preached on this; yet we wish now to say and admonish you: When you desire to confess, then be on your guard that you look to, and think about, your future more than your past life; and do not, as persons formerly did, go to confession because you were commanded to go once a year, by which the conscience was sorely oppressed, and especially, in that you were forced to relate all the details and the circumstances, when, how and where.

The people only thought of going through the form of confession and never cared how they might live better lives in the future. Therefore, we should turn this around, so that you be wholly concerned about your future; for all the sins you committed before are now forgiven. Therefore you are to see to it, how you may begin a different life, and that you grieve over, and are tired of, your former life.

25. Then be on your guard that you be thus disposed. If you are not, then it will not help you, even if you confessed all your life. For when you go and confess it should serve to the end that you be absolved and think about beginning to live another life; so that you may now say that your sins are forgiven, and God is gracious to you. The pope commanded and by law forced people to go to confession every year at the time of the Easter festival when they went to the Sacrament, and all there confessed the sins they did during the entire year, and every year the same was to be repeated; when it should have been left free, only for the benefit of those who are prepared to begin a new life; then each may confess whenever he will. The papists thought it was in our power and free will to be penitent over our sins and begin a different life; therefore they urged it with laws. But here they bring the people to the point that they must lie and say they are sorry for their sins when it is not true. Therefore see to it that you thoroughly grasp this part.

26. The other part that belongs in this connection is, that you hear with true faith the absolution, and doubt not that the words he speaks, to whom you confess, are spoken by God himself. For God thus humbled himself and condescended to lay his holy, divine Word in the mouth of man, so that the one confessing should in no way doubt that God himself said it. Therefore we should receive it as if God himself did it. He did it for your good; for perhaps you might not stand it, if he spake to you directly. How you would run, yes, to the end of the world, if you heard that God himself was announced to speak there. This you have at home at your door. Why do you not then see it? And it is as sure here as there, yea, even surer. For here I have his promise, there I have it not. Therefore prepare yourself to the end that you may believe and think how to lead a different life; otherwise it is better for you to remain away from the Confession and the Lord's Supper. We will let it rest at this for the present and call upon God for grace.

Easter Sunday. Second Sermon. Mark 16:1-8

The Story of Christ's Resurrection

The Empty Tomb

TEXT: Mark 16:1 And when the sabbath was past, Mary Magdalene, and Mary the mother of James, and Salome, had bought sweet spices, that they might come and anoint him.2 And very early in the morning the first day of the week, they came unto the sepulchre at the rising of the sun. 3 And they said among themselves, Who shall roll us away the stone from the door of the sepulchre? 4 And when they looked, they saw that the stone was rolled away: for it was very great. 5 And entering into the sepulchre, they saw a young man sitting on the right side, clothed in a long white garment; and they were affrighted. 6 And he saith unto them, Be not affrighted: Ye seek Jesus of Nazareth, which was crucified: he is risen; he is not here: behold the place where they laid him. 7 But go your way, tell his disciples and Peter that he goeth before you into Galilee: there shall ye see him, as he said unto you. 8 And they went out quickly, and fled from the sepulchre; for they trembled and were amazed: neither said they anything to any man; for they were afraid.

1. In the first place we shall briefly examine the text of this narrative, and afterwards speak of the benefits of the resurrection of Christ, and how we should build upon it. The text reads: "And when the sabbath was past." Here we must remember Mark writes of the sabbath according to the custom of the Hebrews, for according to the Jewish reckoning, the day began in the evening and lasted until the evening of the next day, as the first chapter of Genesis says: "And there was evening and there was morning, one day," "a second day," "a third day," and so forth. Thus the first and greatest sabbath began on the evening of the day when Christ was crucified, that is to say at the time of sunset on the evening of Friday. Our reckoning conveys the wrong sense. Yesterday was the great sabbath, when Christ lay in the grave; in addition to this the Jews had seven full days which they celebrated and all of which they called sabbaths, counting them from the first holiday after the great sabbath and calling it *prima sabbathorum* (first of the sabbaths), and the third holiday *secundam sabbathorum* (second of the sabbaths), and so forth. On these days they ate only wafers and unleavened bread, for which reason they are also called by the Evangelist the days of unleavened bread. From this we must conclude that Christ rose before sunrise and before the angel descended in the earthquake. Afterwards the angel only came to open the empty grave, etc., as has been clearly described by the Evangelists.

2. The question now arises: How can we say that he rose on the third day, since he lay in the grave only one day and two nights? According to the Jewish calculation it was only a day and a half; how shall we then persist in believing there were three days? To this we reply that he was in the state of death for at least a part of all three days. For he died at about two o'clock on Friday and consequently was dead for about two hours on the first day. After that night he lay in the grave all day, which is the true sabbath. On the third day, which we commemorate now, he rose from the dead and so remained in the state of death a part of this day, just as if we say that something occurred on Easter-day, although it happens in the evening, only a portion of the day. In this sense Paul and the Evangelists say that he rose on the third day.

3. For this period and no longer Christ was to lie in the grave, so that we might suppose that his body remained naturally uncorrupted and that decomposition had not yet set in. He came forth from the grave so soon that we might presume that corruption had not yet taken place according to the course of nature; for a corpse can lie no longer than three days before it begins to decompose. Therefore Christ was to rise on the third day, before he saw corruption.

4. The great longing and love of the women for the Lord must also be particularly noted here, so that unadvised and alone they go early to the grave, not thinking of the great stone which was rolled before the tomb. They might have thought of this and taken a man with them. But they act like timid and sorrowing persons, and therefore they go on their way without even thinking of the most necessary things. They do not even think of the watchers who were clad in armor, nor of the wrath of Pilate and the Jews, but boldly they freely risk it and alone they venture on their way. What urged these good women to hazard life and body? It was nothing but the great love they bore to the Lord, which had sunk so deeply into their hearts that for his sake they would have risked a thousand lives. Such courage they had not of themselves, but here the power of the resurrection of Christ was revealed, whose Spirit makes these women, who by nature are timid, so bold and courageous that they venture to do things which might have daunted a man.

5. These women also show us a beautiful example of a spiritual heart that undertakes an impossible task, of which the whole world would despair.

Yet a heart like this stands firm and accomplishes it, not thinking the task impossible. So much we say for the present on this narrative, and now let us see what are the fruits and benefits of the resurrection of Christ.

II. The Fruits and Benefits of the Resurrection of Christ

6. St. Paul writes in Romans 4:25 as follows: "Christ was delivered up for our trespasses, and was raised for our justification." Paul is indeed the man who extols Christ in a masterly manner, telling us exactly why and for what purpose he suffered and how we should conform ourselves to his sufferings, namely, that he died for our sins. This is a correct interpretation of the sufferings of Christ, by which we may profit. And as it is not sufficient to know and believe that Christ has died, so it will not suffice to know and believe that he rose with a transfigured body and is now in a state of joy and blessedness, no longer subject to mortality, for all this would profit me nothing or very little. But when I come to understand the fact that all the works God does in Christ are done for me, nay, they are bestowed upon and given to me, the effect of his resurrection being that I also will arise and live with him; that will cause me to rejoice. This must be brought home to our hearts, and we must not merely hear it with the ears of our body nor merely confess it with our mouth.

7. You have heard in the story of the Passion how Christ is portrayed as our exemplar and helper, and that he who follows him and clings to him receives the Spirit, who will enable him also to suffer. But the words of Paul are more Christian and should come closer home to our hearts and comfort us more, when he says: "Christ was raised for our justification." Here the Lamb is truly revealed, of whom John the Baptist testifies, when he says in John 1:29: "Behold, the Lamb of God, that taketh away the sin of the world." Here is fulfilled that which was spoken to the serpent: "I will put enmity between thee and the woman, and between thy seed and her seed: he shall bruise thy head," which means that for all those who believe in him, hell, death, and the devil and sin have been destroyed. In the same manner the promise is fulfilled today which God gave to Abraham, when he said in Genesis 22:18: "In thy seed shall all the nations of the earth be blessed." Here Christ is meant, who takes away our curse and the power of sin, death and the devil.

8. All this is done, I say, by faith. For if you believe that by this seed the serpent has been slain, then it is slain for you; and if you believe that in this seed all nations are to be blessed, then you are also blessed. For each one individually should have crushed the serpent under foot and redeemed himself from the curse, which would have been too difficult, nay impossible for us. But now it has been done easily, namely, by Christ, who has crushed the serpent once, who alone is given as a blessing and benediction, and who has caused this Gospel to be published throughout the world, so that he who believes, accepts it and clings to it, is also in possession of it, and is assured that it is as he believes. For in the heart of such a man the Word becomes so powerful that he will conquer death, the devil, sin and all adversity, like Christ himself did. So mighty is the Word that God himself would sooner be vanquished than that his Word should be conquered.

9. This is the meaning of the words by St. Paul: "Christ was raised for our justification." Here Paul turns my eyes away from my sins and directs them to Christ, for if I look at my sins, they will destroy me. Therefore I must look unto Christ who has taken my sins upon himself, crushed the head of the serpent and become the blessing. Now they no longer burden my conscience, but rest upon Christ, whom they desire to destroy. Let us see how they treat him. They hurl him to the ground and kill him. O God; where is now my Christ and my Savior? But then God appears, delivers Christ and makes him alive; and not only does he make him alive, but he translates him into heaven and lets him rule over all. What has now become of sin. There it lies under his feet. If I then cling to this, I have a cheerful conscience like Christ, because I am without sin. Now I can defy death, the devil, sin and hell to do me any harm. As I am a child of Adam, they can indeed accomplish it that I must die. But since Christ has taken my sins upon himself, has died for them, has suffered himself to be slain on account of my sins, they can no longer harm me; for Christ is too strong for them, they cannot keep him, he breaks forth and overpowers them, ascends into heaven (takes sin and sorrow captive, Ed. 1531), and rules there over all throughout eternity.

Now I have a clear conscience, am joyful and happy and am no longer afraid of this tyrant, for Christ has taken my sins away from me and made them his own. But they cannot remain upon him; what then becomes of them? They must disappear and be destroyed. This then is the effect of faith. He who believes that Christ has taken away our sin, is without sin, like Christ himself, and death, the devil and hell are vanquished as far as he is concerned and they can no longer harm him.

10. Here we also refer to the passage in Hosea 13:14, which Paul quotes in reference to the victory that Christ has won by his resurrection and by which he has conquered sin, death, hell and all our enemies. Paul says that death is swallowed up in this victory, and he defies death with these words: "O death, where is thy victory? O death, where is thy sting?" Just as if Paul would say: O death, where are thy teeth? Come, bite off one of my fingers. Thou formerly hadst a spear, what has become of it now? Christ has taken it from thee. Death, where is now thy spear, etc.? Sin, where is now the edge of thy sword and thy power? Paul says that the power of sin is the law. The more clearly we understand the law, the more sin oppresses and stings us. For this reason Paul says that Christ has completely destroyed and annihilated the spear and whetstone of death. Now, this Gospel he has not taken with him into heaven, but he caused it to be preached throughout the world, so that for him who believes in Christ, spear and whetstone, nay, sin and death, should be destroyed. This is the true Gospel, which bestows life, strength, power and marrow, and of which all the passages of Scripture speak.

11. Therefore seek and learn to know Christ aright, for the whole Scriptures confer upon us the righteousness of the true knowledge of Christ. But this must be brought about by the Holy Spirit. Let us therefore pray God that his Gospel may prosper, that we all may truly learn to know Christ and thus rise with him and be honored by God as he was honored.

12. The question now arises: If Christ has taken away death and our sins by his resurrection and has justified us, why do we then still feel death and sin within us? For our sins torment us still, we are stung by our conscience, and this evil conscience creates the fear of hell.

13. To this I reply: I have often said before that feeling and faith are two different things. It is the nature of faith not to feel, to lay aside reason and close the eyes, to submit absolutely to the Word, and follow it in life and death. Feeling however does not extend beyond that which may be apprehended by reason and the senses, which may be heard, seen, felt and known by the outward senses. For this cause feeling is opposed to faith and faith is opposed to feeling. Therefore the author of the Epistle to the Hebrews writes of faith: "Now faith is assurance of things hoped for, a conviction of things not seen." For if we would see Christ visibly in heaven, like the visible sun, we would not need to believe it. But since Christ died for our sins and was raised for our justification, we cannot see it nor feel it, neither can we comprehend it with our reason.

Therefore we must disregard our feeling and accept only the Word, write it into our heart and cling to it, even though it seems as if my sins were not taken from me, and even though I still feel them within me. Our feelings must not be considered, but we must constantly insist that death, sin and hell have been conquered, although I feel that I am still under the power of death, sin and hell. For although we feel that sin is still in us, it is only permitted that our faith may be developed and strengthened, that in spite of all our feelings we accept the Word, and that we unite our hearts and consciences more and more to Christ. Thus faith leads us quietly, contrary to all feeling and comprehension of reason, through sin, through death and through hell. Then we shall see salvation before our eyes, and then we shall know perfectly what we have believed, namely, that death and all sorrow have been conquered.

14. Take as an illustration the fish in the water. When they are caught in the net, you lead it quietly along, so that they imagine they are still in the water; but when you draw them to the shore, they are exposed and begin to struggle, and then they first feel they are caught. Thus it also happens with souls that are caught with the Gospel, which Christ compares with a net, Matthew 13:47. When the heart has been conquered, the Word unites this poor heart to Christ and leads it gently and quietly from hell and from sin, although the soul still feels sin and imagines to be still under its power. Then a conflict begins, the feelings struggling against the Spirit and faith, and the Spirit and faith against our feelings; and the more faith increases, the more our feelings diminish, and vice versa. We have still sins within us, as for instance pride, avarice, anger and so forth, but only in order to lead us to faith, so that faith may increase from day to day, and the man become finally a thorough Christian and keep the true sabbath, consecrating himself to Christ entirely. Then the conscience must become calm and satisfied and all the surging waves of sin subside. For as upon the sea one billow follows and buffets the other, as though they would destroy the shore, yet they must disappear and destroy themselves, so also our sins strive against us and would fain bring us to despair, but finally they must desist, grow weary and disappear.

15. In the second place, death is still at our elbow. It also is to exercise the faith of him who believes that death has been killed and all his power taken away. Now, reason feels that death is still at our elbow and is continually troubling us. He who follows his feelings will perish, but he who clings to the Word with his heart will be delivered. Now, if the heart clings to the Word, reason will also follow; but if reason follows, everything will follow, desire and love and all that is in man. Yea, we desire that all may come to the point when they may consider death to be dead and powerless. But this cannot come to pass until the old man, that is the old Adam, be entirely destroyed, and meanwhile that process has been going on of which Christ speaks in Matthew 13:33, where he compares the kingdom of God to leaven, which a woman took and hid in three measures of meal. For even if the kneading has begun, the meal is not yet thoroughly leavened. So, it is here.

Although the heart clings to the belief that death and hell are destroyed, yet the leaven has not yet worked through it entirely. For it must penetrate and impregnate all the members of the body, until everything becomes leavened and pure, and there remains nothing but a pure faith. This will not be brought about before the old man is entirely destroyed; then all that is in man is Christlike from center to circumference.

16. These two things, sin and death, therefore remain with us to the end that we might cultivate and exercise our faith, in order that it may become more perfect in our heart from day to day and finally break forth, and all that we are, body and soul, become more Christlike. For when the heart clings to the Word, feelings and reasoning must fail. Then in the course of time the will also clings to the Word, and with the will everything else, our desire and love, till we surrender ourselves entirely to the Gospel, are renewed and leave the old sin behind. Then there comes a different light, different feelings, different seeing, different hearing, acting and speaking, and also a different outflow of good works. Now, our scholastics and papists have taught an external piety; they would command the eyes not to see, and the ears not to hear, and would put piety into our hearts from the outside. Ah, how far this is from the truth! But it comes in this way: When the heart and conscience cling to the Word in faith, they overflow in works, so that, when the heart is holy, all the members become holy, and good works follow naturally.

17. This is signified by the sabbath that was to be hallowed and on which the Lord lay quietly in the grave. It signifies that we should rest from all our works, should not stir, nay, should not allow any sin to stir within us, but we should firmly believe that death, hell, sin and the devil are destroyed by the death of Christ, and we are righteous, pious, holy and therefore contented, experiencing no longer any sin. Then all the members are calm and quiet, being convinced that sin and death are vanquished and prostrated. But this cannot be brought about, as I have said, until this impotent, wretched body and the old Adam are destroyed. Therefore it is indeed necessary that we are required to keep this sabbath. For as Christ lies in the grave on the sabbath, never feels nor moves, so it must be with us, as we have heard: Our feelings and actions must cease. And I say again that this cannot be accomplished before the old Adam is annihilated. Nevertheless we still experience sin and death within us, wrestle with them and fight against them. You may tie a hog ever so well, but you cannot prevent it from grunting (until it is strangled and killed Ed. 1531). Thus it is with the sins in our flesh. As they are not yet entirely conquered and killed, they are still active, but when death comes, they must also die, and then we are perfect Christians and pure, but not before. This is the reason why we must die, namely, that we may be entirely freed from sin and death.

These words on the fruits of the resurrection of Christ may suffice for the present, and with them we will close. Let us pray God for grace that we may understand them and learn to know Christ aright.

Easter Sunday. Third Sermon: Mark 16:1-8

The Benefits and Comfort of Christ's Resurrection

Mark 16:1 And when the sabbath was past, Mary Magdalene, and Mary the mother of James, and Salome, had bought sweet spices, that they might come and anoint him.2 And very early in the morning the first day of the week, they came unto the sepulchre at the rising of the sun. 3 And they said among themselves, Who shall roll us away the stone from the door of the sepulchre? 4 And when they looked, they saw that the stone was rolled away: for it was very great. 5 And entering into the sepulchre, they saw a young man sitting on the right side, clothed in a long white garment; and they were affrighted. 6 And he saith unto them, Be not affrighted: Ye seek Jesus of Nazareth, which was crucified: he is risen; he is not here: behold the place where they laid him. 7 But go your way, tell his disciples and Peter that he goeth before you into Galilee: there shall ye see him, as he said unto you. 8 And they went out quickly, and fled from the sepulchre; for they trembled and were amazed: neither said they anything to any man; for they were afraid.

1. This Gospel lesson is part of the general account and the first announcement of the resurrection of Christ, which was made by the angel to the women who went early to the tomb to anoint the dead body of the Lord, before Christ showed himself to them and talked with them; inasmuch as he wanted to reveal his resurrection through the Word, even before they should see him and experience the power of his resurrection.

2. And as we said there are two ways of considering Christ's passion and death and the other doctrines of Christ, so there are also two things concerning the Lord's resurrection that we ought to know and understand. First, the history which relates the events as they occurred, together with the different circumstances and how he revealed himself alive in various manifestations; so that we might have a sure record and testimony of everything as a foundation and support of our faith, inasmuch as this article of faith on the resurrection is the chief one upon which our salvation is finally based, and without which all others would be useless and altogether fruitless. Now, what a person ought to know about the historical events, namely in what order these two events, the appearance of the angel — which is reported in part in this Gospel — and the manifestation of the Lord occurred, that should be discussed in connection with the full account, compiled and arranged in order from all the Evangelists; therefore, we will treat the part mentioned in this Gospel in connection with that account.

II. The Benefit and Comfort of Christ's Resurrection

.3. The second point, that is more important and necessary, and on account of which the narrative has been recorded and is preached, is the power, benefit and comfort of the joyous resurrection of the Lord; and the use we are to make of the same faith. Concerning this Paul and all the apostles and the entire Scriptures teach and preach gloriously and richly; but most gloriously of all did Christ the Lord himself preach, when he manifested himself first of all to the women. Therefore, in order that we too may hear and gather something useful from it, let us consider the words Christ spoke unto Mary Magdalene, as recorded in the Gospel according to John 20:17: "Touch me not; for I am not yet ascended unto the Father; but go unto my brethren, and say to them, I ascend unto my Father and your Father, and my God and your God."

4. This is the first sermon our Lord delivered after his resurrection and, without doubt, also the most comforting; although in words very brief, but exceedingly kind and tender, and spoken first of all to his beloved Mary Magdalene, and through her also to his disciples after their deep woe, grief and sorrow, caused by his departure and death, that he might comfort and gladden them by his resurrection. And since this Mary is far more deeply and tenderly concerned about the Lord than the others, and is first at the grave to anoint the body of Christ with costly spices; and especially because, when she fails to find him, she is frightened and bewildered, deeply troubled and in tears, supposing him to have been taken away; therefore, he permits her to enjoy this evidence of his love, in that he appears first of all to her, comforting her in her fears, and preaching this beautiful sermon, which we will now consider.

5. In the first place, when Jesus manifests himself to her not far from the tomb, before he speaks to her, she mistakes him for the gardener; but when he calls her by name and says "Mary," she immediately recognizes the voice, and at once turns with that name upon her lips by which she as well as the other disciples had been accustomed to address him in their language, namely "Rabboni," that is: O dear Master, or dear Lord, for they would say Master, whereas we generally say, My Lord, and immediately, as she was accustomed to do, she falls at his feet to touch him. But he restrains her and says: "Touch me not," as though he meant to say: I know indeed that thou lovest me, but thou canst not yet rightly look upon nor touch me, as thou shouldest look upon and touch me. For her joy is no higher or greater than the mere bodily, fleshly pleasure of having her Lord alive again as she had him before; clinging thus only to the fact of his return, and thinking that he will again be with them as he had been before, to eat and drink with them, to preach and do miracles; intending therefore, by her service and by touching his feet, to show him that love she had shown him before, when she anointed him both in life and in death.

6. He does not permit himself to be touched in this manner now, however, because he wants her to stand still and listen, and learn what as yet she knows not; namely, that he refuses to be touched and anointed or to be served and waited upon, as she had done heretofore; but he says ' I will tell thee something different and new' I am not risen in order to walk and remain with you bodily and temporally, but that I may ascend to my Father; hence I do not need or desire such service and attention, nor will it do to look upon me as you look upon Lazarus and others, still living in the body. For it is not here that I intend to dwell and abide; but I would have you believe that I go to the Father, where I will rule and reign with him eternally, and whither I will also bring you out of your death and sorrow.

There you shall have me visibly and tangibly with you indeed, and you shall rejoice forever in eternal communion with me and the Father. Therefore, he wishes to say: Refrain henceforth from all such bodily service and reverence, and go rather and become a messenger, and proclaim what I tell thee unto my dear brethren, that I will no more be and abide here in bodily form, but that I have left this mortal state to enter upon a different existence, where ye may no more handle and touch me, but shall know and possess me only in faith.

7. Here he uses language entirely new, when he says: "Go and tell my brethren," taken from Psalm 22:22, which treats entirely of Christ, and in which he speaks both of his passion and resurrection, saying: "I will declare thy name unto my brethren, etc." Never had he spoken in this manner to his apostles before. For at the celebration of the Lord's Supper, he indeed calls them his "dear children" and his "friends," John 13:33; John 15:14; but now he employs the most affectionate and glorious name possible and calls them his "brethren." And it is of great importance to him; for he does not delay, but as soon as he is risen, his first concern is to have them told what he intends to do and why he is risen from the dead.

8. And, indeed, this is said in a manner that is lovely and sweet beyond all measure, so that whoever desires to believe, has reason enough to believe, all his life and as long as the world endures, that these things are true indeed; even as the dear apostles themselves had found in them encouragement enough, and more than enough, to believe. For the comfort is too great and the joy too glorious, and the heart of man too small and narrow to have attained it.

9. The Apostles crouched behind barred doors, not only discouraged and cowed, as sheep that are scattered without a shepherd, but also troubled in conscience. Peter had denied and renounced his Lord with an oath, and cursed himself; and the others had all fled and proved themselves to be disloyal. That was indeed a fall so deep and terrible that they might well think they would never be forgiven for denying the Son of God, and so shamefully forsaking their dear Lord and faithful Savior. How could it have ever entered their hearts that Christ would send such an affectionate greeting and such a kind good-morning to them who had been so disloyal and denied him, and would not only forgive everything, but also call them his dear brethren? Or who can believe and grasp it today? I myself would like to believe it at times, but I cannot get it into my heart so completely that I dare rely upon it wholly, and dare count it to be really true. Yea, if we only could, we would be in heavenly bliss already in this life, and would fear neither death, nor the devil, nor the world, but our hearts would constantly bound for joy, and sing to God an eternal Te Deum Laudamus, i.e. We praise thee, O God.

10. But alas, this is not the case upon earth; our miserable beggar's bag, this old hide of ours, is too cramped. Therefore, the Holy Spirit must come to our rescue, not only to preach the Word to us, but also to enlarge and impel us from within, yea, even to employ the devil, the world and all kinds of afflictions and persecutions to this end. Just as a pig's bladder must be rubbed with salt and thoroughly worked to distend it, so this old hide of ours must be well salted and plagued until we call for help and cry aloud, and so stretch and expand ourselves, both through internal and through external suffering, that we may finally succeed and attain this heart and cheer, joy and consolation, from Christ's resurrection.

11. For, let us consider for a moment what manner of words these are, which Christ here uses; and let us not pass lightly over them, as has been done heretofore, and is still done in all popedom, where we have read, heard and sung them until we are weary; and nevertheless we have passed over them, as a cow walks by a sanctuary; so that it is a sin and a shame to have heard and known such words, and still to let them lie, cold and dead, outside of the heart, as if they were spoken and written altogether for naught; and that even Christians themselves, though they do not despise them as others do but use them daily, neither appreciate them as highly nor believe them as firmly as they would like to do.

12. For consider, I say, what these words contain and offer: Go my dear sister, for thus he would undoubtedly address these women, since he appeared unto them first, and tell the denying and disloyal disciples that they are called, and shall be, my dear brethren. Is not this, in a word, including and placing us with Christ into the complete tenure and inheritance of heaven and of everything Christ has? Rich and blessed indeed must be the brethren and sisters who can boast of this Brother, not hanging now upon the cross, nor lying in the grave under the power of death, but a mighty Lord over sin, death, hell and the devil.

13. But how have these poor, frightened and discouraged disciples come to such honor and grace, and wherein have they deserved such brotherhood? Was it by Peter's shameful denial of Christ, and by the disloyalty of all the others to him? And how have I and others deserved it to apply this also to ourselves? I, who have read the idolatrous mass for fifteen years blaspheming God and helping daily to crucify Christ afresh? Fine merit this, forsooth, riding to hell in the devil's service and looking to other brotherhoods, — those of the devil and his clique, bearing the names of dead saints, St. Anthony, St. Francis, St. Sebastian, St. Christopher, St. George, St. Ann, St. Barbara, concerning some of whom it is not known whether they were saintly, yea, whether they ever lived at all. Fie! what a sin and shame for us, who are called Christians, to have had this brotherhood of Christ the Lord, so graciously offered us, and then to despise and reject it, and fall into such deep blindness as to have ourselves inscribed in the rascally brotherhood of the shameful monks and of the whole herd of the pope, and to preach about and praise this as though it were a precious thing indeed! But that is what the world deserves. Why did we not appreciate the Word of God that was written, painted, played, sung and rung before our eyes and ears? And even now, that the Word of God itself points this out, and rebukes us, we cease not to blaspheme and to persecute; whereas we ought to thank and praise God for having so graciously delivered us, without, and contrary to, any merit of our own from such blindness and blasphemy, and for having vouchsafed unto us grace to recognize it.

14. Now let him who can, believe it. For whether we believe it or not, it is the truth none the less. This brotherhood is founded among us, and is not such a brotherhood as our loose Kaland, and the brotherhood of the monks, but it is that of Christ, wherein God is our Father and his own Son our brother, and where such inheritance is bestowed upon us as assures not merely a hundred thousand dollars, one or more kingdoms, but in which we are redeemed from the fellowship of the devil, from sin and death, and obtain the inheritance and possession of eternal life and eternal righteousness; and though we were once in sin, worthy of death and eternal damnation, and are so even now, we should know that this brotherhood is greater, mightier, stronger and superior to. the devil, sin and all things. We are not fallen so deeply', and things are not so bad and ruined that this brotherhood cannot arrange and fully restore everything again, inasmuch as it is eternal, infinite and inexhaustible.

15. For who is he that has instituted this brotherhood? The only Son of God and almighty Lord of all creatures, so that on his own account he did not need to endure suffering or death. But I have done all this, he tells us, for your sake, as your dear Brother, who could not bear to see, that you, eternally separated from God by the devil, sin and death, should so miserably perish; hence I stepped into your place and took your misery upon myself, gave my body and life for you that you might be delivered; and I have risen again to proclaim and impart this deliverance and victory to you, and receive you into my brotherhood, that you might possess and enjoy with me all that I have and hold.

16. Thus you see, it is not enough for Christ that the historical fact has occurred, and that as far as he is concerned everything is accomplished; he infuses it into us and creates a brotherhood from it, so that it may become the common possession and inheritance of us all; he does not place it in *praedicamento absoluto*, but *relationis*, namely, he has done this, not for himself personally nor for his own sake, but as our Brother and alone for our good. And he does not want to be considered and known otherwise than as being ours with all these blessings, and that we, on the other hand, are his; and that we are therefore so closely united that we could not be more intimately related, having a common Father, enjoying an equal, common and undivided estate, and authorized to use all his power, honor and estate, to boast of it, and to comfort ourselves with it, as though it were our own.

17. Who can fully, comprehend this? and what heart can sufficiently believe that the Lord is so completely ours? For indeed, it is a thing too great and unspeakable, that we poor, miserable children of Adam, born and grown old in sin, are to be the real brethren of supreme Majesty, joint-heirs and joint-rulers in eternal life; as St. Paul so gloriously declares, Romans 8:17; Galatians 4:7: "And if children then heirs, heirs of God, and joint-heirs with Christ, etc." For all this follows in order: if we are called the children of God, then we must truly be also his heirs, and brethren and joint-heirs of Christ the Lord, who is the only essential Son of God.

18. Hence, let him who can learn rightly to begin to pray the Lord's Prayer; and to know what it signifies for me to call God my Father, and for me most truly and fully to regard and consider myself his dear child and the brother of Christ the Lord, who has shared with me everything that he has and placed me in possession of his eternal treasures. Here examine and ask your own heart, whether without doubt and wavering you can thus say from the bottom of your heart: "Our Father;" whether you are firmly grounded upon and can be assured before God: I consider myself thy dear child, and thee my dear Father, not because I have merited it, or could ever merit it, but because my dear Lord wants to be my Brother, and of his own accord has proclaimed it and invited me to regard him as my Brother, and has said that he would also regard me as such. Only begin this, I say, and see how you will succeed in the task; and you will soon discover what an unbelieving knave is hidden in your bosom, and that your heart is too dull to believe it. O, I am such a poor sinner, nature exclaims, how dare I exalt myself so highly, seat myself in heaven and boast that Christ is mine, and I am his brother! For this greatness and glory is so exceedingly high, beyond all human sense, heart and thought, that we cannot comprehend it; even as Paul himself also confesses in Philippians 3:12, that he is pressing on to. lay hold of it, but has not yet attained it. Yea, man is astounded and terrified at himself for presuming to receive and boast of such honor and glory.

19. But, what shall we do? We must indeed say, and it is true, that we are poor sinners, and with St. Peter, we have denied our Lord (I especially above others). But what shall we do about it? It is enough and more than enough that which I did against him in falling away from him and making myself a knave. Should I, in addition, make him a liar and a knave, and deny this comforting proclamation, and blaspheme? God forbid!

20. Yea, says the devil, through my flesh thou art not worthy of this. Alas, it is true; but if I would not believe and accept it, I would have to, make my Lord a liar, and declare that it is not true when he tells me that he is my Brother. God forbid that I should do this, for that would be rejecting my God and all my salvation and eternal blessedness, and to trample it under foot.

21. This, therefore, will I say: I know very well that I am an unworthy being, worthy to be the brother of the devil, not of Christ and his saints; but now Christ has said that I, for whom he died and rose again, as well as for St. Peter, who like myself was a sinner, am his brother; and he earnestly would have me to believe him, without doubt and wavering, and would not have me consider that I am unworthy and full of sin, because he himself will not so consider nor remember it, as indeed he well might do, having abundant cause to repay his followers and visit upon them what they committed against him. But it is all forgotten and blotted out of his heart; yea, he has slain, covered and buried it; and he knows nothing to say of them now but that which is kind and good, and he greets them and addresses them affectionately as his faithful, dearest friends and pious children, as though they had not done any wrong, nor grieved him, but had done only good to him; so that their hearts may not be uneasy or worried with the thought that he would remember it and charge it against or visit it upon them. Since then he does not want it remembered, but wants it slain and buried, why should not I leave it at that, and thank, praise and love my dear Lord with my whole heart, for being so gracious and merciful? Even though I am laden with sin, why should I go on and brand as a falsehood this gracious Word, which I hear himself speak; and willfully reject the proffered brotherhood? If I do not believe it, I will not receive its benefits; but that neither renders it false nor proves that anything is lacking in Christ.

22. If anyone now desires to load himself down with new sins, and does not want forgotten what he has forgotten, let him then so sin that it never will be forgotten, and he never can be helped; as we read in the Epistle to the Hebrews, Hebrews 4:4-6, and Hebrews 10:26, concerning those who have sinned by falling away from God's Word and rebuking it as a lie. This is the sin against the Holy Ghost and is described as crucifying the Son of God afresh and putting the Spirit of grace to an open shame. From this may God protect all who desire to be Christians! Alas, there is too much of the old blindness and folly, in which we have been enveloped hitherto. This ought to perish and be forgotten, now that we have become his brethren, if we only accept it. If we cannot believe as firmly as we ought, let us begin, like young children, to drink at least a little spoonful of this milk, until we become stronger, and not thrust it from us altogether.

23. Therefore, though your own unworthiness rebukes you, when you engage in prayer, and though you think: Alas, my sins are too many, and I am afraid that I cannot be Christ's brother, strike out about you and defend yourself as best you can, that such thoughts may find no room in your mind. For here you are in great danger of committing the sin against the Holy Ghost. With all confidence and boldness reply to such thoughts of the devil: I know very well what I am, and you need not tell nor teach me, for it is not your business to judge this case; therefore, away, thou lying spirit! I will not and must not listen to thee. Here is my Lord Jesus Christ, God's only Son, who died for me and rose again from the dead; he tells me that all my sins are forgotten, and that he will be my Brother, and that I likewise am to be his brother; and it is his will that I should believe this from my heart without wavering.

24. A knave and a villain, yea, a brother of the wretched devil himself must he be who would not accept this. Though I be not worthy of it, yet am I in great need of it; and even if that were not so, God at least is worthy that I should honor him and judge him to be the true God. But should I not believe, I would, in addition to all other sins, in this worst possible way heap dishonor upon him in violation of the first commandment, in making him a liar and a vain God. What greater wickedness and blasphemy has any man ever heard or proclaimed? Much rather do thus: When you feel that it is too hard for you to believe, fall down upon your knees and complain to God of your inability; and say with the apostles: "O, Lord, increase our faith." Luke 17:57. I would at heart gladly count thee my dearest Father, and Christ my Brother, but my flesh, alas, will not submit; therefore help my unbelief that I may honor thy name and hold thy Word to be true.

25. See, in this way you will yourself experience what a great conflict it requires to believe God's Word and to pray the Lord's Prayer aright; not as though this Word in itself were not sure, steadfast and strong enough, but that we are so weak, yea, so much like wretched, unstable mercury that we cannot hold fast that which is well worthy of being held with hands and hearts of steel and adamant.

26. Formerly, when we were led astray and cheated with lies and false worship, we could hold fast and comfort ourselves with firm, though false, faith in all the saints and the brotherhoods of the monks; and joyfully said: Help, dear lord St. George, or St. Anthony, and St. Francis, and let me enjoy the benefit of thy intercessions! There was no doubting or opposition then; this occupation was agreeable to us, and we had fists and strength of iron to believe. But here where Christ, the Truth itself, offers us his fellowship, even invites and urges us in the most affectionate manner, saying: Beloved, receive me as your Brother, he cannot succeed in leading us to believe and accept it. So mightily do the flesh and the devil resist and oppose it

.27. Therefore, I say, it is best for each one, when he goes into his closet and begins to pray, to make an effort to understand what he is saying, and properly to weigh two words, "Our Father." For example: My friend, what are you praying? How does your heart respond? Do you truly regard God as your Father, and yourself as his dear child? No, indeed, says the heart, I do not know; how can I presume to ascribe a thing so great and glorious to myself? Then why do you not refrain from prayer, when with your lips you call God your Father, while your heart gives the lie to yourself and to him as he has revealed himself in his Word? Rather, confess your weakness and say: I indeed call thee my Father, and ought to call thee so, according to thy Word and command; but I am afraid that my heart is lying like a knave. And the worst of it is, not that I myself alone am lying; but that I accuse thee also of falsehood. Help me, dear Lord and Father, that I may not make thee a liar; for I cannot become a liar myself without first having made thee one.

28. Therefore, though I realize and experience, alas, that I cannot say "Our Father" with my whole heart, as indeed no man on earth fully can, else we would already be in heavenly blessedness, yet will I make an attempt and begin, as a little child begins to nurse at its mother's breast. If I cannot believe it fully, yet will not I count it a falsehood, nor say, nay. Though I cannot play the game as is proper, I will beware lest I play in opposition as the monks and the despairing hearts do, who fail to regard Christ as their Brother, but as an enemy and a taskmaster; for that would be turning him into the very devil. But I would daily spell at the letters, until I am able to repeat "Our Father" and this Sermon of Christ as well or as poorly as I may. God grant that though I stammer and stutter or lisp, I may to some degree at least accomplish it.

29. For, as already stated, this is the sin of all sins, that when God is gracious and wants all our sins forgiven, man by his unbelief rejects God's truth and grace, and casts it away from him, and will not let the death and resurrection of Christ the Lord avail. For, indeed, I cannot say that this brotherhood, which brings us forgiveness of sins and every blessing, is my work and doings, or that of any man, or that anybody labored or sought for it. For this resurrection occurred and was accomplished before any man knew aught about it; and that it is proclaimed and preached to us is likewise not done through the word of man, but by that of God; wherefore it cannot fail or lie. Since then it is solely the truth and work of God, it behooves us, under penalty of God's extreme wrath and displeasure, to accept it as coming from God, and to hold it fast by faith, so that we may not fall into the sin that is unpardonable.

30. For whatever other sins there are, contrary to God's command and Law, which consist of all that we are to do and that God demands of us, these are all covered by forgiveness, since we are never entirely free from them during our whole life; and if God were to reckon with us according to our life and conduct, we could never be saved. But he who will not believe the Word of Christ nor accept his work, sins a hundred thousand times more; for he strives against grace, and robs himself of forgiveness. For it is grace that saith: The law shall not hurt nor condemn thee, although thou hast sinned against it exceedingly, but these sins shall all be forgiven and taken away by Christ; since that is why he died for thee and rose again, and now presents all this to thee, through this proclamation of his brotherhood.

Now if you will not believe nor accept this, but stubbornly set your head against it, and say: I want no grace, what will then help you? Or what will you seek further, to obtain forgiveness and be saved? Yea, I will be a Carthusian friar, go barefooted to Rome and buy an indulgence, etc. Very well, go ahead as you will, not in God's, but in the wretched devil's name; for by this you have denied not only grace, but also the law, and are fallen from God completely, inasmuch as you seek such works and holiness as are not commanded by God, yea, are even forbidden.

31. Should not God be angry and punish us for daily babbling, singing and reading the Lord's Prayer and the Creed without understanding, faith and heart, and for thinking nothing not only of Christ, but also of God's Law; boasting instead and bringing before God only our own efforts and false spirituality, over and above and opposed to his grace and command, expecting thereby to reconcile him and earn heaven from him? This is what we deserve for despising God's Word and this glorious, comforting proclamation of Christ; to. be shamefully blinded and cheated by the devil, and punished and plagued by the pope; as though God thereby said: Very well, if you will not have my Son as your Brother, and me for your dear Father, then take the pope with his monks, who point you away from the Gospel, the Creed and the Ten Commandments, to their shabby, stinking cowls and the devil's brotherhood.

32. For since they did not want Christ to be and remain our Brother without our merit and worthiness, and to bring us God's grace and forgiveness of sin; what is this but really and actually denying faith in God and his Son, as St. Paul says, Titus 1:16, even though they confess him with their lips? Just as I too did in my former blindness, when I helped to sing and read these words with others, and yet thought far more highly of my monkery and my own works. For if I had accepted as true and certain what St. Paul says in Romans 4:25 that Christ died for our sins and was raised again for our justification, in order that we might become his brethren, then I would thereby have learned that my own works and my monk's hood could not obtain this for me. Otherwise what need would there have been for Christ to go and take my sins and the wrath of God upon himself in his cross and death, and by his resurrection to place me into the inheritance of the forgiveness of sins, of eternal salvation and glory?

33. But now, inasmuch as they cling to their monkery, and seek God's grace by their own merits, desiring thereby to get rid of and atone for their sins, they bear witness against themselves that they do not believe what they say with their lips: I believe in Jesus Christ who died for me and rose again, etc.; but they believe, on the contrary, in the cowl and cord of the barefooted monks, in St. Ann, St. Anthony, and in the devil (pardon me), in his rump. Because it is impossible for one who knows Christ in this brotherhood to be engaged in such follies as are taught and observed not only without faith and contrary to it, but also contrary to the commandments, and which are real diabolical sins, the sins of all sins.

34. Therefore, in opposition to all this, a Christian ought to acquire the custom of praying the Lord's Prayer, firmly crossing himself and saying in thought: Keep me, dear Lord, from the sin against the Holy Ghost, that I may not fall from faith and thy Word, and may not become a Turk, a Jew or a monk and a papal saint, who believe and live contrary to this brotherhood; but that I may hold fast to a little fringe of the garment of this brotherhood. Let it be sufficient that we have believed and lived contrary to it so long; now it is time to pray God to make this faith sure and steadfast in us. For if we have this faith, then are we healed and delivered from sin, death and hell, and are able to try all other spirits, to discern and reject all error, deception, and false faith, and to pronounce the sentence: He who dons the cowl and shaves his head in order to become holy, or joins the brotherhood of monks, is a mad, senseless fool, yea, a blind, miserable, unhappy and despairing creature; he who tortures himself with much fasting and castigation, like the Carthusian friars or Turkish saints, is already separated from God and Christ and condemned to hell. For all this is nothing but blasphemy and contradiction of the blessed heavenly brotherhood of Christ. They may indeed pray and read a great deal about it, as Isaiah 29:13 says: "This people draweth nigh to me with their lips," cometh before my face in the churches: with singing and ringing, "but their hearts are far from me." What pleasure, think you, can he have in such saints, who outwardly act as though they were real children of God, reading and singing the Gospel, employing the most beautiful words and celebrating a glorious Easter festival in processions, with banners and candles, and yet, do not try to understand or believe it, but rather oppose it by their doctrine and life?

35. For if they understood and believed it, they would not cling to their mockery and vanities, but would forthwith trample their cowls and cords under foot, and say: Fie upon this shameful brotherhood! To the wretched devil with it, for opposing the brotherhood taught me by the Creed and the Lord's Prayer! For it is not worthy of notice or attention. Thus Paul in Philippians 3:5, pronounces judgment upon his own holy life in Judaism: I was, says he, a pious, blameless man, not only in my own vain estimation, but according to the law of Moses; but when I learned to know Christ, I counted all my righteousness under the law loss, yea, not only loss, but I counted it refuse and filth. I indeed thought I was a great saint, that I had kept the law strictly and with all diligence, and counted this my highest treasure and greatest gain; but when I heard of this brotherhood and inheritance of the Lord Jesus Christ, O how my pride and the boast of my own righteousness left me so completely that I now shudder at it, and do not even want to think of it.

36. See, he extols the righteousness this brotherhood brings us in such a way that he belittles and thoroughly despises the life and the holiness of all men even when it is at its best according to the law of God, which law must indeed be kept, and than which there is verily nothing more praiseworthy and better on earth. And yet, because it still is our own effort and life, it cannot and shall not have the honor and glory of making us God's children, and of acquiring the forgiveness of sins and eternal life; but this is effected when you hear the word of Christ, saying: Good-morning, my dear brother; in me thy sin and death are overcome, for all I have done, I have done for thee, etc.

37. This is the ground of St. Paul's defiance of sin and death: "O death, where is thy victory? O death, where is thy sting?" 1 Corinthians 15:55 and Hosea 13:14. As though he wished to say: In times past you were mighty, terrible foes, before whom all men, no matter how holy and pious, had to tremble and despair; but where are you now? How did I lose you so completely? Why, he replies, everything is swallowed up and completely drowned in a victory. But where is the victory, or whose is the victory? "Thanks be to God", he replies in verse 51, "who giveth us the victory through our Lord Jesus Christ."

38. This indeed is glorious and great boldness, possible, however, for such faith alone as that of St. Paul; yet which, as he himself laments, was not as strong as he desired it to be; still, he certainly had it, and was able to maintain it against the wrath and power of the devil. That we are not able to do likewise and are still so fearful and terrified at death and hell, is an evidence that we still have too little faith. Therefore we have the more reason to impel us to call upon God and pray and also to ask the supplications of our brethren to that end, and daily to work the Word into our hearts, until we too, in some degree, obtain this assurance.

39. Let our adversaries laugh us to scorn and derisively say that we know how to teach nothing but faith, and let them cry that we must rise far higher and do far more. But if we only had faith enough, we would soon attend to everything else. For the chief and most necessary thing, of which they know nothing, is, how to get rid of the terror of sin, death and hell, and how to acquire a peaceful conscience before God, so that we may be able truly and heartily to pray "Our Father." Where this has not been found everything else is in vain, though we should torture ourselves to death with our works. But since everybody comes short in this respect, we need not be ashamed of learning and being concerned about these things daily, as we are about our daily bread, and in addition we should ask God to give us power and strength. Amen.

Easter Monday, or Second Easter Day. Emmaus.
Luke 24:13-35

Explanation of this Gospel and the Lord's Supper

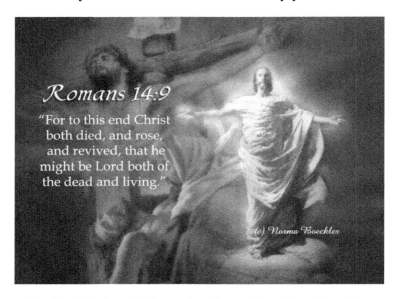

Christ Died and Rose Again to Pay For Our Sins

Luke 24:13 And, behold, two of them went that same day to a village called Emmaus, which was from Jerusalem about threescore furlongs. 14 And they talked together of all these things which had happened. 15 And it came to pass, that, while they communed together and reasoned, Jesus himself drew near, and went with them. 16 But their eyes were holden that they should not know him. 17 And he said unto them, What manner of communications are these that ye have one to another, as ye walk, and are sad? 18 And the one of them, whose name was Cleopas, answering said unto him, Art thou only a stranger in Jerusalem, and hast not known the things which are come to pass there in these days? 19 And he said unto them, What things? And they said unto him, Concerning Jesus of Nazareth, which was a prophet mighty in deed and word before God and all the people: 20 And how the chief priests and our rulers delivered him to be condemned to death, and have crucified him. 21 But we trusted that it had been he which should have redeemed Israel: and beside all this, to day is the third day since these things were done. 22 Yea, and certain women also of our company made us astonished, which were early at the sepulchre; 23 And when they found not his body, they came, saying, that they had also seen a vision of angels, which said that he was alive. 24 And certain of them which were with us went to the sepulchre, and found it even so as the women had said: but him they saw not.

25 Then he said unto them, O fools, and slow of heart to believe all that the prophets have spoken: 26 Ought not Christ to have suffered these things, and to enter into his glory? 27 And beginning at Moses and all the prophets, he expounded unto them in all the scriptures the things concerning himself. 28 And they drew nigh unto the village, whither they went: and he made as though he would have gone further. 29 But they constrained him, saying, Abide with us: for it is toward evening, and the day is far spent. And he went in to tarry with them. 30 And it came to pass, as he sat at meat with them, he took bread, and blessed it, and brake, and gave to them. 31 And their eyes were opened, and they knew him; and he vanished out of their sight. 32 And they said one to another, Did not our heart burn within us, while he talked with us by the way, and while he opened to us the scriptures? 33 And they rose up the same hour, and returned to Jerusalem, and found the eleven gathered together, and them that were with them, 34 Saying, The Lord is risen indeed, and hath appeared to Simon. 35 And they told what things were done in the way, and how he was known of them in breaking of bread.

I. The Preparation for Partaking of the Lord's Supper

1. This Gospel, in one part, teaches and urges us to take pleasure in speaking and working for our Lord Jesus Christ. It does so by showing what fruit follows from such a course, although that fruit is not understood; and grasped so clearly as it ought to be. You see here that the two disciples are still full of unbelief; yet, as they are speaking about Jesus, and seemingly in vain, he cannot remain absent from them; but draws near, opens their eyes and interprets to them the Scriptures. You ought to faithfully lay hold of this and retain it, for it is a precious thing. However, before I treat further of the Gospel, which is easy as to its history, I must first, for the sake of the simple and plain people, say a few things about the sacrament of the Lord's Supper.

2. Beloved, you have heard that we preached who are worthy to receive the Lord's Supper, namely, those who by the Word of God are moved in their hearts to believe, and that those who are not thus prepared ought to refrain from it. And it is right to deter everyone from rushing to it or going in one's own preparation, as was formerly common. That is the right way to preach, and I would to God that many might be thus terrified. But again I notice in many, and in myself also, that the devil spirit presses the other side also too much, so as to cause hearts to be weary and backward in partaking of the communion, so that they never approach it unless they feel for a certainty that they are fervid in faith. This is also dangerous, since thereby we would do away with the preparation which was formerly customary, but would establish a new preparation that would also not be right.

3. We have rejected those who prepare to receive the sacrament by their own works, a thing that God abhors. But by so doing we may easily cause people to become slow, so as always to wait until God comes and gives us perfect faith, so that they may go. Hence we can never preach enough about faith, even if we preach long and earnestly about it, for our reason can never understand it. Hence, to meet this evil, we will treat it more at length and must divide it into two parts, or rather, into the two classes of persons who prepare to go to the Lord's Supper.

4. In the first place we have taught that it did not profit anyone to prepare for the sacrament by his own strength, as those did who endeavored by their confession and other works to make themselves worthy to receive it. This is a terrible error and abuse, and the only true advice we can give those who undertake such things is to refrain from them and to keep far from the sacrament.

5. The other preparation, that is made in faith, and of which we have said enough before, is right, as it comes and proceeds from God. It is not done in such a way that one always feels confident he is worthy. Where would faith be if that were the case? But it takes place thus: Without any of my preparing and doing, God's Word comes to me. I may indeed go and hear it, or read and preach it, so that it thus enters my heart. And that is the right preparation, which is not made by the power and cunning of man, but by the strength of God. Hence there is no better preparation for all the sacraments than to permit and suffer God to prepare us. This is a brief talk about the preparation. And now we will consider the communicants.

II. Persons for Whom the Holy Supper is not and for Whom it Is

6. The Gospel and Word of God, which is a speech or discourse about Christ, sometimes falls upon the ears of those who do not accept it or even despise it; and, as Christ says in Luke 8:5, it falls by the wayside, that is, into hard, unprepared hearts.

7. Then there are others who are vile rascals and live in open vice. Matthew 13:22. Even though they hear the Gospel and never really oppose it, they are not much concerned about it. As you see our fanatics do now, who can greatly talk and spit about it, especially when they are full, and make light of it. They have grasped nothing of it, except a glibness in talking about it. They are all wicked hearts. Of this class are also those who live in deep avarice, so materialistic that they feel it. And thus they live in other gross sins and have little reverence for the holy Gospel, even if they are able to talk glibly about it. But we never care to preach to them, for all is lost on them and the Gospel makes them neither humble nor hungry.

8. Thirdly, the very worst are those who besides persecute the Gospel. Of them Christ says in Matthew 7:6: "Give not that which is holy unto the dogs, neither cast your pearls before the swine." These three sects do not belong to the Gospel Church, and we are not preaching to them. And I wish the law were enforced and they were punished, — these rude swine, — who talk so foolishly about the Gospel as if it were a story of Theodocius of Bern, or some other tale. If anyone will be a pig let him know what is becoming a pig. I really wish I could exclude them from my preaching, that they might never hear it, and be far away from it. They can do nothing but misuse the Gospel to their own injury, and disgrace us, so that for their own sake the Word of God must suffer dishonor and abuse. Out with the dirty swine!

9. Finally, there are some who are like the people here in this Gospel. Behold, how they still lack in faith, for they speak in this wise: "We hoped he would redeem Israel." As if they meant to say: We do not know what the result will be. It is clearly evident that it will amount to nothing. He is dead now and even if he came to life again and arose from the dead, he surely cannot redeem the people and become a king. And so they thought redemption was a failure. Therefore the two disciples here are the multitude that taste the Gospel in their hearts and dislike to have it despised and disobeyed; but still they are so timid that they hesitate to draw near because they feel they are neither strong nor fervid enough. They draw back and do not want to approach near until they feel and experience that they are strong in faith. These are persons to whom the Gospel belongs, even though they stumble at times, so that they become disgusted with themselves, feel their disease and wish to get rid of it, and are not hard of heart. These should be urged and drawn to Christ. We have never yet preached to any but such people.

10. For it is the nature of faith that a man knows his faults and earnestly desires to be free from them. No one dare wait until God performs a miraculous sign for him, and treats him differently from other people to whom he gives the signs in the Gospel and in the sacraments. God gave us the treasure and revealed it for the purpose alone that we should go and get it. Hence, when you feel your weakness, you ought to go and say: My Lord, I have fallen. I want to be strong. Now thou hast instituted the Lord's Supper for us to kindle and strengthen our faith thereby and that we might be thus helped. So here I am and wish to receive it. This should be our comfort and we ought joyfully to use the Word and the sacraments when we feel our lack of faith, and rejoice to receive aid to seek help and strength. There our souls find it within us.

11. For you must not make Christ a tyrant, but accept him for what he in truth is and let him be unto you nothing but rich, abounding grace. However, if you feel in your heart you have not reached this point and do not believe, and yet would like to believe, you must after all not despair and shun the communion, but seek your help right there, so that your faith may be kindled and increased. For, though some have been terribly punished for partaking of the sacrament unworthily and without faith, they are only those whom we described above, namely, the hardened, wicked hearts. You must do and think thus: Lord, see, that is thy Word and this is my sickness and failing. Thou thyself hast said, "Come unto me all ye that are weary and heavy laden and I will give you rest." Matthew 11:28. Do you think he said that to those who are already fervid and strong in faith? His kingdom is not established to the end of furthering the righteous, Matthew 9:3, but of helping sinners and making them righteous. 1 Timothy 1:15. Hence, whoever is weak and experiences it, should go to the communion and let God help him.

12. But there is another herd not on the right track. We have prophets abroad in the land who teach the people too freely to be bold and defiant, who speak with the divine Majesty as they would with a cobbler's apprentice. These impudent and proud spirits are by no means to be followed. It is well for you to be backward and timid, and to fear and tremble. I like such fear. You just abide in it and go and have your conscience calmed. But such proud minds and unbroken hearts that act so defiantly and deal with God as if he must be afraid of them, he cannot tolerate.

13. Therefore you must humble yourself, and abide in fear so as to feel your struggles and weaknesses, and desire faith. If you experience that, then thank God, for that is a sure sign the Word has struck and moved you, and exercises, constrains and impels you. What sort of faith would that be if I went and had no fear and anguish of heart to exercise my faith? For it is the very nature of faith, that it proves its strength in fear, in death and sins, and in all things that make a human being afraid and timid. Therefore if you feel thus, it is the proper time for you to go, for then your faith will find something to do. And to this end private confession is helpful. It is well to go to a pious man, and point out your need to him and ask advice, whether he thinks you are worthy to go to the Lord's Supper, and then follow his advice. That is the real' purpose of confession and of the sacrament. They are of no other use and are instituted for the purpose of assisting weak consciences that are burdened by their sins.

14. But you say: How then, if I am so inert and cold that I have no desire for it, still I feel that I need it; yet the Gospel and the sacrament do not satisfy me so that almost every spark in my heart is extinguished? Answer: You must not desist. For as long as you feel that you are not yet lost and not yet so wicked as those described above; for you always wish to burn with zeal. Therefore you must do as follows: Take to yourself the Word of God, go and hear it preached, read it, write it or even sing it, only so you live it and keep busy with it, then you will experience something. Then go to the Lord's Supper and say: Lord, I am a lazy character; but I come that thou shouldst help me and kindle my heart. Add to it whatever words and thought you can think and say. You must not stop to think how to prepare yourself to be worthy for the communion; you are already prepared if you feel that you would gladly be helped, and your need constrains you to go.

15. It has often happened to me that I hesitated and thus departed farther from it, until I saw nothing helped me and I had to go. Thus you also will find that it is the devil's spectre that draws people away so that the more they are afraid and wait until they experience faith in their hearts, the farther they drift from it. And at last, if they continue in this state, all desire and impulse, both toward the Word and the sacrament, dies out in them, and they never come. Hence you must put aside such thoughts and fear, and go and ask God to help you. If you do so often, you will experience that you will gain more and more desire for it, a thing you would not have gained otherwise. Therefore I wish you would do this, and that there were many to go to the sacrament in such a frame of mind and would gain more and more pleasure in it, and become stronger and stronger. But if you do not go, you will always remain cold and will ever grow colder and colder.

16. This ought to comfort you, and you will experience it if you try it. For it is impossible for God's Word not to produce fruit and be a blessing. God spake as follows: "For as the rain cometh down and the snow from heaven and returneth not thither but watereth the earth and maketh it bring forth and bud, and giveth seed to the sower and bread to the eater; so shall my Word be that goeth forth out of my mouth; it shall not return unto me void, but it shall accomplish that which I please and it shall prosper in the thing whereto I sent it." Isaiah 55:10-11. This Scripture ought to make us very bold and happy, if we have already grown cold. By the grace of God we have God's Word and we ought to raise our hands and thank him for it. How many are there in the world who do not possess it? How could you otherwise have obtained it? There you have the whole supply and the preparation that serves it, and yet you have knavery enough to contend with it. Therefore, as God says that his Word will not return without fruit and if you use it not to make a mockery of it, but are in earnest about it, you will undoubtedly feel and experience something, and the more you use it, the more you will have this experience. You cannot have evil thoughts in your heart if you take a portion of the Scriptures before you and read it, or you meet another person and converse with him about it. If you do this, evil lusts will succumb and the flesh will be subdued. I have often tried it, and if you try it you will also find the fruits and experience that it is as God says. What more do you wish prepared for you?

17. Isaiah it not enough that you possess God's Word that draws you, and besides that you feel your distress driving you to it? And then Christ is there and waits to help you. What more shall he do? And there is nobody excluded but proud, insolent persons and the castaways that are not in earnest. Therefore you must go and remember that Christ looks more deeply into your heart than you do yourself, as you see in this Gospel. These two poor men would not have dared to wish for what meets them. Yet such grace is bestowed upon them that Christ himself comes to them, while speaking of him, and reveals himself so that they know him. This fills their hearts with joy that they could not tarry there but ran and told the other disciples how the Lord manifested himself to them. Then they are full of joy, as they would not have dared to wish; but still it was so deep in their hearts that they themselves did not perceive that they desired it, although their hearts were so set upon it that they would have loved to see nothing better than for the Lord Jesus Christ to rise from the dead and be king. Therefore God looks more deeply into the depths of the heart than we ourselves, and he also gives us more than we desire. Thus he does also here. If you feel that you are not so fervent as you would like to be, he looks more deeply into your heart than you do, since you are anxious to be fully set on fire and become a burning light. Therefore you ought not to flee from him, but approach boldly.

18. To this end many passages in Paul's writings serve. For example, he says to the Ephesians: "The Lord is able to do exceeding abundantly above all that we ask or think." Ephesians 3:20. Now we clearly see what he gives us when we receive it and we feel that we receive it with joy. Therefore St. Paul says that we do not see nor even think of it while we desire it; but the Lord, who searcheth the hearts, sees and understands our desire, and therefore he bestows upon us his grace abundantly. Thus we read of St. Monica, the mother of St. Augustine, that she wept for her son during nine long years. It was her heart's desire for him to become a Christian, and she devised many plans by which to bring him to Christ. She wanted him to marry a Christian woman who should make a plain Christian husband of him. But she did not dare to hope or expect him to become the man he did later, although she would have gladly seen it.

19. Then look at the examples all through the Gospel. St. Peter was too timid when the Lord wished to wash his feet and said, "Shouldest thou wash my feet?" and did not understand that his need compelled him, and his heart urged him, to see the necessity of Christ's washing him, as he said soon after, "Lord, not my feet only, but also my hands and my head." John 13:9. And our heart is in the same condition, that we wish to see the Lord Jesus present, to help us, and yet we are so timid that we are afraid of him and do not think as much of his loving kindness as we freely profess to do. For, if we considered him to be what he is, we would say as Peter did, "Wash not my feet only, but also my hands and my head," and think, now I will gladly go to him, even if I had a greater burden of sin. There is likewise another example of St. Peter in Luke 5:6-8, when they sat in the ship and caught so many fishes that their nets broke. Then Peter was amazed, fell down at Jesus' knees and said, "Depart from me, I am a sinful man, O Lord." Notice he was frightened and bids him to go away at the very time he ought to pray him to come. Thus our timid nature is ever afraid of Christ, in whom there is nothing but good, and who has come to help everybody. That is why I said, we must not make a tyrant of Christ, but suffer him to be a dear Lord and Savior, who has no other desire but to help sinners, and to invite and attract everybody by his words and example.

20. This exposition of the nature of faith is clear enough, for our great trouble is that we do not really understand the nature of faith. Therefore do this: Begin and try it and you will experience it; and the more you practice it, the more comfort and strength you will experience; and the more unworthy you feel you are, the more you must appropriate God's Word to yourself and practice it, hear or read it and speak about it, and you will always find and prove something that pleases and moves you. You should besides pray to God and say as the apostles did in Luke 17:5: "Lord, increase my faith." Thus go and you will be strengthened. But if you dwell too much on your timidity you will never go; for then you will persist to feel and not to believe. You must experience your misery and struggles of conscience. Then is the time for you to go to the Lord's Supper. Even if you are weak in faith you must not on that account step back, for he will not reject you since he has come for the sole purpose of strengthening the weak and comforting the despondent.

21. But I do not wish to have all this preached to hardened insolent characters and the fanatics, but only to consciences that are faint and weak, and occasionally fall, so that they do not despond, but know where to find help and comfort. On this point a father in the desert uttered a wise saying. When he saw that a brother was weak and faint, he said: No, my brother, thou must not withdraw thus and go back, for thou mightest go back so far that thou couldest not return. For it is to be feared that the longer we stay away, the colder and lazier we become. They ought to stay away, as we have said at length, who lead a wicked and immoral life and do not intend to amend their ways. But those who know their weaknesses and want to be rid of them and see that they cannot help themselves, they should come to the communion for help.

22. From this you see why God instituted and ordained that his Word should be preached; and therefore it ought not to be despised. It is true that the Word without the Spirit is of no use; but since God Almighty himself said, as we have heard, "My Word that goeth forth out of my mouth, shall not return unto me void," it must not be despised. For through his Word he gives the Holy Spirit into your hearts and will not suffer you to gape and wait for a miraculous sign from heaven, to be done on you, and thus to ignore his Word and sacrament. He himself highly esteems and praises the Word, for he has decreed to give his grace through it, as Christ says, "No man can come to me, except the Father that sent me, draw him." John 6:44. How does the Father draw us? Through Christ. How through Christ? By the Word. Thus he invites and calls you. If your need impels you, go then joyfully, tell your trouble bravely; but always bring the Word with you.

23. But leave it to God, how you may remain steadfast, and go now, while you have the Word and feel your misery. Then the Word itself will teach you how to prepare yourself aright. For then you must accuse yourself before God and say: Lord, I am a sinner and cannot help myself by my own strength, so I come to thee for help. If I have sufficient grace only to delight in the Word of God with my whole heart and I have joy and pleasure in it, I can surely remain steadfast. For it must be something great for God to give me his Word and cause it to be pleasing and attractive to me. Even if I am not so strong now as I ought to be, I shall grow stronger in time and at last reach the point when I can confess his grace without fear and devote my life to it. Therefore Christ says: "Ask and it shall be given you, seek and ye shall find, knock and it shall be opened unto you, for everyone that asketh, receiveth; and he that seeketh, findeth, and to him that knocketh, it shall be opened." Matthew 7:7-8.

24. Therefore I would faithfully admonish you to act wisely in this matter. We have justly condemned those who undertake to prepare themselves by their own works; but we have invited those who feel their need and see they can do nothing by their own power, and can find neither counsel nor help, for these use the Lord's Supper unto their personal salvation. Therefore, if you feel thus, go first to a pious man and tell him your distress and say, Lo, I have fallen and would like to obtain help and I ask for counsel what to do. Then he should comfort him and welcome him to the sacrament, so that he may exercise his faith and be strengthened. For it is instituted for this very purpose of ministering comfort and strength. Therefore let nothing keep you from the communion. If you feel bashful, it is well, for you must feel your unworthiness. If you however do not feel your guilt, you are not in a fit frame of mind to go, and it will be better for you to refrain from going.

25. Take the Gospel and the Holy Scriptures before you, the more the better, even if you already know them and have often read them. For it is certainly a suggestion of the devil who tries to tear from you your delight in the Word. He hates to have you come to it, for he knows very well what fruit it bears in you. If you are thus busy with the Word and strive to live it the best you can, you will see that Christ is with you and a fire is kindled in your heart. But the best is, for two or three earnestly to speak among themselves about it, so that the living voice is heard. Then you will be much stronger and the devil must yield. Thus all evil lust and thoughts disappear and thus will ensue such a light and knowledge, you have never before experienced. The only trouble is that we fools have such a great treasure lying before our doors and do not know how to use it. And the devil deceives us in order to draw us away from it and make us indifferent, because he cannot overcome it. Therefore we must prepare to resist the devil's suggestions and influence. In like manner Christ will come and reveal himself even though at first you are not aware of it; the more you speak about it and discuss it the more clearly you will recognize Christ and feel that he kindles your heart within you, as you heard in this Gospel of the two disciples journeying to, the village of Emmaus.

III. The Conclusion

26. This I had to preach now concerning the Lord's Supper and the Gospel, as God gave us the light, and I admonish you, my friends, to grasp and faithfully use it. If there be fanatics, who disgrace the Gospel, they ought to be punished by the civil authorities. But we must let them also hear, for the sake of the righteous, for we are to preach God's Word publicly to everybody, since we do not know whom it may strike.

Easter Monday. Second Emmaus Sermon. Luke 24:13-35

Three Thoughts Taught by This Gospel

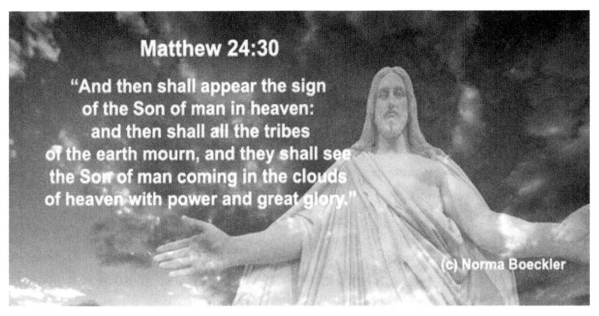

The Last Day Jesus Will Return

Luther 24:13 And, behold, two of them went that same day to a village called Emmaus, which was from Jerusalem about threescore furlongs. 14 And they talked together of all these things which had happened. 15 And it came to pass, that, while they communed together and reasoned, Jesus himself drew near, and went with them. 16 But their eyes were holden that they should not know him. 17 And he said unto them, What manner of communications are these that ye have one to another, as ye walk, and are sad? 18 And the one of them, whose name was Cleopas, answering said unto him, Art thou only a stranger in Jerusalem, and hast not known the things which are come to pass there in these days? 19 And he said unto them, What things? And they said unto him, Concerning Jesus of Nazareth, which was a prophet mighty in deed and word before God and all the people: 20 And how the chief priests and our rulers delivered him to be condemned to death, and have crucified him. 21 But we trusted that it had been he which should have redeemed Israel: and beside all this, to day is the third day since these things were done. 22 Yea, and certain women also of our company made us astonished, which were early at the sepulcher;

23 And when they found not his body, they came, saying, that they had also seen a vision of angels, which said that he was alive. 24 And certain of them which were with us went to the sepulcher, and found it even so as the women had said: but him they saw not. 25 Then he said unto them, O fools, and slow of heart to believe all that the prophets have spoken: 26 Ought not Christ to have suffered these things, and to enter into his glory? 27 And beginning at Moses and all the prophets, he expounded unto them in all the scriptures the things concerning himself. 28 And they drew nigh unto the village, whither they went: and he made as though he would have gone further. 29 But they constrained him, saying, Abide with us: for it is toward evening, and the day is far spent. And he went in to tarry with them. 30 And it came to pass, as he sat at meat with them, he took bread, and blessed it, and brake, and gave to them. 31 And their eyes were opened, and they knew him; and he vanished out of their sight. 32 And they said one to another, Did not our heart burn within us, while he talked with us by the way, and while he opened to us the scriptures? 33 And they rose up the same hour, and returned to Jerusalem, and found the eleven gathered together, and them that were with them, 34 Saying, The Lord is risen indeed, and hath appeared to Simon. 35 And they told what things were done in the way, and how he was known of them in breaking of bread.

I. Three Thoughts Taught by this Gospel

1. This Gospel brings out and enforces especially three thoughts on the article of faith concerning Christ's resurrection. First, that this narrative transpired and was written along with others as a sure witness and proof of our faith in this article of our Creed. First, in that we see these two disciples leave the company of the others, full of unbelief in the resurrection. They commune together about the things that transpired as if they despair of Christ, and he is now dead and forever buried in their hearts, who does nothing more and is unable to do anything. This appears from their own confession where they say: "We hoped that it was he who should redeem Israel. Yea, and besides this, it is now the third day since he is dead." And though they had heard from the women that these had seen a vision of angels who told them that Christ had risen and was alive, yet they urged that he had not been seen or found by anyone. In the second place — and this is the most important fact — we here see Christ not only showing himself alive to the unbelieving disciples, so that they might become assured of his resurrection and return at once to announce it to the others, and to hear the same truth from them, the testimony on both sides agreeing and being thereby established; but also that Christ, before they knew him, proved fully and clearly from the Scriptures that it behooved Christ both to die and to rise again from the dead. For this reason he upbraided them for their unbelief because they ought to have known the Scriptures concerning Christ, since he himself had taught them that his sufferings were foretold in the Scriptures.

2. The second thought this Gospel presents is an example of the power and fruit of the resurrection as manifested in these two disciples while they are talking of him and listening to his preaching. This also is nothing less than a portion of the proof of his resurrection. For Christ here proves by word and deed that he is not dead, as they believed before, but works in them and exercises his power through the Word, even before they know him, and makes believers of them who have another mind, reason, heart, and will. This they also recognize and confess, saying: "Was not our heart burning within us while he spake to us, etc?" After this manner he still works in the whole Christian church; though unseen, he yet carries on his work and shows his dominion in that, as the living Lord, he enlightens them through his Word, comforts and strengthens them, defends them with his power and keeps them against the wrath of the devil and the world.

3. As a third truth, we are here shown in what manner Christ reveals his resurrection, and how it may be known and apprehended, namely, above all first through the Word and faith, rather than through bodily vision or sensation. Therefore he is unknown to them at first when he comes to them and walks with them, though he is with them in very truth, the selfsame Christ whom they had so often seen and heard and known full well. Yet now they do not know him at all, because they know that he had died and had been buried the third day before; and hence can think of him only as a dead man. So strange and unknowable had he become to them that they would not have known him, had he stayed with them ever so long, until he announced to them his resurrection and preached about it. The text says: "Their eyes were holden, that they should not know him." It was not he who had been changed, nor was it his will to remain unknown to them, but their hearts and thoughts had become estranged and far removed from his. In the same way neither Magdalene nor the other disciples recognized him until they had heard the Word of his resurrection.

4. His purpose is to show and teach us that the power of his resurrection and dominion will be exercised here on earth, and manifest itself in this life, only through the Word, and through faith which holds fast to Christ, though it does not see him, and thus conquers sin and death in him, lays hold of righteousness and life, etc. This is a brief summary of the story contained in this Gospel, in so far as it pertains to the article of faith on the resurrection in general; of which we lately heard more.

5. But the special purpose of this Gospel is to show us how weak in faith the disciples were, and how Christ in his kingdom manifests himself to such persons of weak faith, and how he deals with them. For we see from the whole story of Christ's resurrection, as recorded in the Gospels, how the Apostles, and all the other disciples after them, were so weak in their faith in this doctrine, even to the time of his ascension, that he had to upbraid them for their unbelief and hardness of heart, because they believed not them that had seen him after he was risen, Mark 16:14. They manifested this weakness, though he had often told them from the Scriptures that he must be crucified and rise again on the third day, etc.

6. From this we learn, in the first place, that even in those who have become true Christians, weakness and frailties remain, especially in the deeper matters of doctrine and faith, they being unable to understand them or to grasp them as firmly and strongly as they ought. For faith is not so light or easy a matter as ignorant and inexperienced people fancy, and as our coarse blockheads, the popish dunces, pretend, who believe that faith is no more than to have heard the history and to know it. Having heard or read just once what the Gospel tells of Christ, these people fancy that they have fully understood and believed it, and henceforth need no longer to learn and believe it.

7. That this is naught but an idle, vain fancy, is proved by their own confession that this knowledge of the Bible story rests in their hearts as a cold, lifeless thing, a mere empty husk, lacking all life-giving power, of no use or help to them, neither giving strength nor making them better; whereas this great, exalted miracle of Christ's resurrection was performed and is to be preached, learned, and known, to the end that it may be fruitful in us, quicken and kindle our hearts, and work in us new thoughts, new knowledge, new forces, life, joy, comfort and strength. If this does not take place, the story has been heard in vain, and is dead within you, being of no more value to you than to Turks and heathen who have never heard it, or have not believed it to be true. You dare not boast of faith, though froth on your tongue, or a sound in your ears, or a dream in your memory give witness that you have heard the story, of which your heart has neither experienced nor tasted aught. The papists show plainly, in all their doctrine and life, that they do not from their hearts believe and hold fast to this article of faith, because they seek the power and effect which ought to come from the resurrection of Christ in themselves and outside of Christ, teaching that it must be sought and obtained through their own works and merits, while they condemn, blaspheme, and persecute the saving doctrine that tells us to turn from these foolish lies to Christ and to the power of his resurrection.

8. Christians, however, and true believers know by sad experience in others as well as in themselves how weak they are, and they deplore the fact that they are unable to grasp this doctrine, or to hold it fast in their hearts with as strong a faith as they ought. Their entire life is spent in combating this weakness, as even Paul says in Philippians 3:12, that he had not grasped it, nor was already made perfect, but that he was pressing on, if so be that he might lay hold of it, and obtain a knowledge of the power of Christ's resurrection, etc.

9. For though this doctrine is most delightful and comforting in itself, full of joy and blessedness, and ought to find its way gently and easily into the heart, yet it is hindered by two great obstacles which make it difficult to believe. In the first place, this work of God is much too exalted and too great in itself for us ever to understand thoroughly in this life, even if our faith were perfectly strong and without weakness; for not until we are in the life beyond will we ever truly see and feel its full force and power. In the second place, our own flesh and blood, and the hearts of all men, are by nature much too weak and too fearful to believe God's Word; and must be filled with fear and terror when they contrast the greatness of this work with themselves and their own unworthiness.

10. God cannot overlook the first cause and obstacle nor have patience with it; for this work must and shall remain as great as it is, and it dare not be belittled; yea, it must be the power to which all creatures, men, angels, the devil, and hell, must yield and be subjected, because it is necessary for our salvation. For if this were not so, we would continue in sin, death and the eternal wrath of God. The other obstacle, namely, that we are too weak to grasp this great work and power by our faith, God may overlook and have patience with; as we here see Christ doing with his disciples, who had certainly heard he had risen, and yet were full of such great and heavy doubts that they almost despaired of Christ entirely saying, "We hoped that it was he who should redeem Israel."

11. Behold, how earnestly he looks after these two of weak faith, and cares for them, doing everything to lift them out of their weakness, and to strengthen their faith. Because he sees and knows that in great sorrow and sadness they had departed from the other Apostles and do not know what to think or hope, he is determined not to leave them in such doubt and temptation. In order to help them out of it, he becomes their companion on the way, leaving behind all the other Apostles, though they too were assembled in great sorrow and very weak faith. But because these two are in great danger of total unbelief, he at once comes to them, as if he had nothing else to do now that he was risen; he speaks to them in the friendliest way, and reasons with them from the Scriptures, gives them occasion to retain him and to ask him to abide with them, to eat and to drink in their company, until their faith is quickened once more, and they are relieved of all doubts. Their faith grows so strong that they recognize him as the same Christ who had been with them before in life, and whom they had seen crucified three days ago, but had been unable to recognize on the way by reason of doubt and the weakness of their faith.

12. It is, therefore, his purpose to teach us by this narrative, given for our instruction and consolation, how his work is to be done in the Christian church after his resurrection, namely, that he will not reject nor cast out those who are weak in their faith, yea, not even those who are held in error or ignorance, or who are otherwise weak, fearful, and despairing. They are rather the very persons in whom he will exercise and manifest the power of his resurrection, not only by inviting them to come to him, but also by coming to them, and treating them in the gentlest and kindest way, talking with them, teaching and instructing them, yea, even eating with them, until at length they grow strong and secure in their faith; while their hearts, so sad and sorrowful for a time, are again filled with joy. Thus we also should know and have this comforting assurance that he is our Lord who is able to bear with our infirmities and to overlook them; that he will not reject and condemn those unable to believe and live at once as they should, if only they do not in their hearts despise and deny Christ and his Word, but delight in him and love him, and truly desire to become strong and perfect in faith and life.

13. Looking at these disciples, weak and unreasonable as they are, one sees that their hearts nevertheless were in a state that they felt kindly toward Christ, delighted both to speak of him and to hear him spoken of, and had no greater desire than that what they had heard concerning his resurrection might be true. But the thing was much too great for them to believe, so that they were as yet quite unable to accept it as true — just as it is also too high and too great for us. This our dear Lord knows and sees full well, and so he is better able to have patience with us, is satisfied and pleased if only we listen to him as his pupils and are willing to be taught and directed by him.

14. Furthermore, he thereby wishes to teach us how to conduct ourselves in his kingdom, particularly towards those who are weak and infirm in faith. We also ought not hastily to reject and condemn those whom we see erring or stumbling; but also have patience with them, even as Christ had with us and still must have every day. For though in his own person by virtue of his resurrection he is in divine might and power Lord of heaven and earth, yet he rules his Church in a way to exercise and manifest the power of his resurrection in his poor, weak band by serving them with this power and might for their consolation and growth.

15. In harmony with this example, though we be strong, we ought not to take pleasure in ourselves nor boast, but rather let our gifts and powers serve the weak, striving to uphold and reform them by instruction, consolation, encouragement, friendly admonition and reproof, etc., just as one must act kindly and considerately toward weak, frail children and invalids, nursing, lifting and carrying them until they are grown and can stand on their own feet.

16. This is one of the chief points of knowledge to be gained from the Gospel, in regard to the kingdom of Christ, how it is arranged and governed, namely that it is a government under which Christians, who have begun to believe and are holy, are nevertheless beset with frailty, ignorance, and other sinful infirmities. He bears and overlooks these shortcomings, but with the expectation that improvement shall ensue. Hence we must not dream of a church on earth in which there is neither frailty nor error in faith, as the papists boast that their church and church councils cannot err, etc. For here we are told that not only these two disciples, but all the other apostles erred in the leading and most necessary article of faith, abiding in their unbelief until Christ himself drew them out by means of many and various sermons and revelations. During the three days after Christ's crucifixion, faith in his resurrection had completely died in all hearts; indeed, that light was kept burning nowhere except with Mary, his mother, who preserved within her heart all that she had heard from him and others, and was comforted and sustained thereby in her great grief over the sufferings and death of her son.

17. For faith in Christ must always continue and be preserved somewhere in the Church; there must always be some who have the truth and confess it, though their number be small, and the most fall into error, as they did here. If there are not more, there must be a Mary to keep the faith. He permits it to happen that many great saints err and stumble, in order that we may not trust in men, though they be many, great, and holy. We must be led to rely upon the Word that is sure and cannot deceive, as here these two men, and all the others afterward, were directed to the Scriptures.

18. Aside from this, let us not overlook the example contained in this Gospel which urges and admonishes us to speak and hear of Christ gladly, and to study the Scriptures and God's Word, though it may not always be understood and affect us as it ought. The Gospel also shows us the power, blessing and effect of the Word, if approached with a sincere heart.

19. For, in the first place, although these two disciples were still filled with unbelief, yet he will not and cannot be separated from them, because they went their way communing sorrowfully with one another about Christ, and questioning together almost without result. He at once drew near and went with them and soon touched their hearts and minds. He began a beautiful, masterly sermon, such as they had never heard before, concerning the very article of faith which caused them trouble and doubt. Then, in the second place, they immediately feel its power; their hearts are no longer heavy, slow, and cold to believe as before, but are moved and kindled, and enlightened and receive a new understanding, so that now they begin to know the Scriptures aright, and what they had never understood before, becomes clear and manifest to their souls. Finally the mask and cover are taken away from their hearts and eyes, so that they no longer look upon him as a guest and a stranger, but truly know him and feel that he is no longer far from them, but at their side, and works certainty in their faith. Henceforth they no longer need bodily, visible revelations, but go forth at once to preach to others, and to strengthen and aid them against doubt and unbelief.

20. Therefore we should follow their example, and gladly hear the Word of God, without growing weary. For this is not only a needful practice for the strong and for the weak, for the wise and for the unwise, by which a knowledge of everything we need unto salvation is given — such study can never exhaust it — but it is also the punishment through which God wishes to work within our hearts, to give faith and the Holy Ghost, as St. Paul says in Romans 10:17: "Belief cometh by hearing the Word of God." If man studies earnestly, even though the heart be cold and unwilling at first, if he only continues in the work, it will not be in vain, and the effect will be produced that the unwise and erring will be brought in and made better, the weak will be strengthened, and at last the heart will be kindled and enlightened, so that Christ is better understood and known from the Scriptures.

21. And even though there were no other benefit to be derived from this study, we ought to be urged to it by the fact that it pleases God and the Lord Jesus Christ, and renders him a service. We know that he will surely not be far from us when we do so, as he himself has promised, Matthew 18:20: "Where two or three are gathered together in my name, there am I in the midst of them." If he is with us, the angels certainly are near also and take pleasure in our work, while the devil is driven away and has to retreat as he left Christ when he conquered him with the Word of God. Matthew 4:11.

22. There is a legend, telling us that an old patriarch living in the desert received peculiar visions and revelations from God. When he happened to be among young people, listening to their conversation, he saw that whenever they spoke of the Scriptures and things divine, beautiful young men consorted with them and joyfully smiled upon them; but on the other hand, whenever their conversation became wanton and silly, the same young men turned away displeased and sad, and dirty black hogs came and wallowed at their feet etc.

II. The Sermon the Risen Christ Preached to his Disciples

23. Let this be enough concerning the chief points of the story of this Gospel. There remains one other important part, the sermon Christ preached to the disciples from the Scriptures, in which he briefly showed them that it behooved Christ to suffer and thus to enter into his glory etc. Of this, sermon the Evangelist speaks as follows: "And beginning from Moses and from all the prophets, he interpreted to them in all the scriptures the things concerning himself."

24. Without doubt this was a very beautiful and a model sermon. Now it is true we all would gladly know just the passages the Lord quoted referring to himself, by which he thereby enlightened, strengthened and convinced these disciples, since Moses contains so little, or nothing, as it would seem, of a plain statement on that of which Christ here speaks, that it behooved him to suffer, and to rise on the third day, and that repentance and remission of sins should be preached in his name etc. For the Jews, who have had Moses so long and read him diligently enough even until the present day, have never yet discovered this rare truth in Moses.

25. But the Evangelist answers this and analyzes this argument by stating their heart burned within them while he opened to them the Scriptures, and in the Gospel following says Christ opened their mind to understand the Scriptures. Here is the point: Moses certainly writes concerning Christ and Christ is found in the books, of Moses; but it is necessary not only to read, but also to understand what is said. Hence Paul says in 2 Corinthians 3:14-15 that the veil of Moses remains before the face of the Jews when they read the Old Testament, which only Christ alone can take away. And to his apostles Christ says, in Matthew 13:11: "Unto you is given to know the mysteries of the kingdom of heaven; the others, however, though they see and hear, yet they do not understand."

26. Therefore the Bible is a book that must not only be read and preached, but it also requires the true interpreter, that is, the revelation of the Holy Spirit; as we learn from our own experience now-a-days that it is of no avail to prove most clearly from Scripture the articles of the true doctrine to our opponents and to point out their errors. Not a single article of faith has ever been preached that was not more than once attacked and denied by heretics, though they read the same Scriptures that we have.

27. But this revelation also requires pupils of the right kind, who are willing to learn and to be instructed, like these pious and simple-minded disciples, not wise and puffed up minds and self-made masters who reach beyond the very heavens with their knowledge. For this is a doctrine that makes our wisdom foolishness and blinds our own reason, before it can be believed and understood; for it is not born of man's wisdom, like other sciences and arts on earth, which have sprung from reason and can be grasped by means of reason. Hence it is impossible to attain to it by reason, and if you undertake to measure and reckon how far it agrees with reason, you will not succeed. All heresies from the beginning have had their origin here, and both Jew's and Gentiles, and the Turks at present, grow foolishly violent in regard to our doctrine because it does not agree with reason and human wisdom. Only the pious, simple-minded people can grasp and understand it, who are true to this rule, and say: "God hath said it, therefore will I believe it;" as Christ himself declares in Matthew 11:25 and thanks the Father with a joyful heart that he hides these things from the wise and understanding and reveals them unto babes.

28. There is no way out of it, wise people and proud reason cannot be taught these wonderful things, concerning Christ, that true man is God's Son from eternity, and yet he died and rose again, that in his human nature he has become Lord of heaven and earth, that he rules all creatures with divine power though no one sees him, and that we are saved by his merits alone, if we believe in him etc. Therefore God must needs establish the order that no one shall understand unless he is willing to be a fool, become a child, and believe in the simplicity of the heart.

29. Behold, what kind of people did he employ to be his first messengers, to proclaim and to witness his grandest work, the resurrection? Poor, ignorant women came to the sepulcher after useless expense and trouble in purchasing costly ointment and without considering that the tomb was covered with a heavy stone, yea, even sealed and guarded by soldiers. Yet these foolish persons are the first to whom Christ reveals his resurrection, and calls to be its preachers and witnesses. So also does he give these disciples a knowledge of the Scriptures which all the learned scribes did not possess, so that now they view Moses with different eyes and are forced to say: Behold, how often have I read and heard this before, but never understood it.

30. God would seem to say by this act: Very well, I see plainly that it is of no avail though everything be spoken and written in the very clearest manner; for in truth, all articles of faith are set forth clearly and tersely enough in the Scriptures. Take only the article on God and the creation, which certainly is told and given in the very plainest way; yet see the rabble of heretics it has made, Manichaeans, Valentinians, Marcionites, etc. Again, what did it avail that Christ himself, among his own people, confirmed his doctrine clearly and publicly by great miracles? Nothing more than that they began to twist both his words and his deeds, and called them the words and deeds of the devil and Beelzebub. Hence God must continue and say: Since they will not have and receive this Word as I give it to them, it shall remain hidden and unknown to them. I shall indeed have it written and preached in clear language; but reveal it to some few, simpleminded people who seek my Word. To the others it shall be mere darkness which may be felt, as among the Egyptians (though it shines and is preached most clearly), yea, it shall be naught but an offense and poison, against which they must stumble and fall in their blasphemies and contradictions, until they break to pieces.

31. Thus the Jews have had and have read Moses unto this day; yet all of them know nothing of what he speaks concerning Christ, yea, not even in minor articles of faith, just as their forefathers knew nothing of it, save some few who believed, as the prophets and the apostles after them, who elaborated their whole books from a single Bible passage. This enabled them to preach what everyone was compelled to acknowledge as true.

32. How did Christ stop the mouth of the Sadducees (who did not believe the resurrection of the dead and accepted no other Scripture but Moses), and convince them of the resurrection of the dead? He took the commonest saying in their religion, which all Jews knew and quoted every day, when God says, "I am the God of Abraham, and the God of Isaac, and the God of Jacob etc." With these words he revealed Moses and drew the following conclusion: If you believe God to be God of those that are dead, how can he be God of those who have altogether ceased to be? Therefore, if he is the God of Abraham, Isaac, and Jacob, as he himself declares, these men must be alive, though they have died as far as this life is concerned, and lie in their graves; for he cannot be God of that which does not exist. Hence Abraham, who now lies under the earth, and all the saints, must be alive before God, though they are dead before you; for this is, and will be, his name forever that he is the God of Abraham and of all who believe as he had promised him and all believers, saying: "I shall be thy God" etc.

33. Now who would have thought that these short, simple words are so full of meaning and furnish such an excellent, rich sermon, yea, that a big book might be written upon them? Though they know the books of Moses well enough, they yet declared that not a word concerning the resurrection of the dead was to be found in them. This was also the reason why they accepted Moses alone and rejected the prophets who nevertheless based all their preaching of the important articles of the faith in Christ upon Moses.

34. But let us look more closely at Christ's sermon and consider one of the passages from Moses which he quoted. Genesis 3:15 is the first word which promises grace, and was given to Adam and Eve, when he spoke to the serpent, "I will put enmity between thee and the woman, and between thy seed and her seed; he shall bruise thy head, and thou shall bruise his heel." These words are read by Jews, Turks and heathens, and by human reason, but they all find them to be only hard pebbles, yea, dead and useless words, from which they cannot take anything even by their best efforts. But as soon as revelation comes to our aid, we understand them to mean: Through sin the serpent, that is the devil, has brought upon Adam and Eve sin and the eternal wrath of God. But in order to help them out of this dreadful fall and misery, into which they were led by Satan, God in his unfathomable mercy has found within himself this remedy that by the woman's seed, that is, by the natural offspring of a woman, that very head of the serpent, that is, sin, death, and everlasting wrath, shall be crushed and robbed of his power, so that he may no longer be lord of death, nor be able to keep man either in sin, or in God's wrath and condemnation.

35. From this an entire New Testament springs forth, all the discourses of St. Paul and the apostles, who do not tell a great deal of the life and miracles of Christ, but, where it is possible, use such a passage as a flower, so to say, with which to cover a great meadow, doing so by the aid of revelation and the Holy Ghost who knows how to grind and press the words thoroughly, so that they give forth the juice and power they possess. For these words show, in the first place, that this seed must be a natural child, born of a woman, but without sin; for the Scriptures testify that whatever is born into this world of man and woman, is born in sin and is under the wrath of God, as David says, Psalm 51:5, "Behold, I was brought forth in iniquity" etc. For this flesh and blood is completely permeated and corrupted with evil lusts and disobedience against God, and as this substance is corrupted in father and mother, it must remain so in the child; hence no man can be born from man and woman without a sinful nature. God, therefore, hath ordained to take a woman alone for the conception and birth of Christ, the promised seed; without a man, she becomes, the little child's mother, by the Holy Ghost, who causes this conception and birth in her, in order that he may be a natural man, having our flesh and blood, but without sin and power of Satan, whose head he was to bruise.

36. In the second place, if he was to be lord over sin and death, to subdue the devil and pluck us out of his hand, he had to have divine, almighty power. For though a man were altogether pure and without blemish of body or soul, as Adam was first created, yet were it not in his power and strength to take away this eternal misery and corruption, and to obtain and give in their stead unchangeable blessings and eternal life. Thus it follows that his power must be greater than that of all creatures, even all angels. Such power is found nowhere except in God himself, the Lord of all creation.

37. From this follows further that if he is born of a woman he is also mortal and must die in the body as others. And since he became man for our sake, and was sent by God to deliver us from sin and death, he had to take our place, to become a sacrifice for us, to bear and atone for that wrath and curse under which we had fallen and lay. But it was not possible for him to remain in death; since he was an eternal being he could not be held by it, as St. Peter says in Acts 2:31 and in like passages; but even his body ere it had seen corruption and decay, must needs pass through death unscathed and by his resurrection and eternal life begin to rule in everlasting power and eternal glory, in order to bring his own out of sin and death, and the power of Satan unto everlasting righteousness and life.

38. Note that this is but a simple passage, which Christ surely did not overlook but interpreted from his own wealth of knowledge, as being the first and chief passage, from which later on all the others; flow. Here we see that these are words, or miracles, rather, which reason can never grasp or fathom. They can only be understood when the Holy Ghost accompanies them, and preaches and reveals them unto those who believe with singleness of heart and abide in them. Then they begin to taste the sweet savor, and receive spiritual nourishment, so that they must say: This will do it, this will enlighten the heart and set it aflame.

39. Thus the prophets viewed the saying of Moses and drew therefrom their glorious prophecies concerning Christ, as Isaiah 7:14 bases his prophecy of Christ's birth upon this passage with the plain statement, "Behold, a virgin shall conceive and bear a son" etc., also the whole 53 chapter concerning his suffering and resurrection, how that he would offer himself as a sacrifice for our sins etc. All these words Christ doubtless quoted in his sermon.

40. The apostles likewise, being ignorant fishermen, learned to know the Scriptures, not in the schools of the great scribes, but through the revelation by which Christ led them into the Scriptures. Thus they were enabled to understand and to write on the basis of a single passage a book or a sermon the world cannot understand. And if I had the same Spirit Isaiah or Paul had, I could take this passage and develop from it a New Testament, if that were not already written.

41. How did St. Peter know, or where is written in Moses that which he says in 1 Peter 10-11: "Concerning which salvation the prophets sought and searched diligently, who prophesied of the grace that should come unto you, searching what time or what manner of time the Spirit of Christ which was in them did point unto?" Who told him that the Spirit of Christ existed and prophesied of Christ, before there were prophets and, above all, before Christ and the Holy Ghost were present? Are these the words of a fisherman, or of a learned, wise scribe? Nay, it is the revelation of the Holy Spirit who had also revealed it to the prophets before. Again, where is written in Moses what the Epistle to the Hebrews says in Hebrews 1:3-4, that Christ sat down on the right hand of the Majesty on high, to be Lord over all, having become much better and higher than the angels? etc.

He certainly took it from the Old Testament, but he found it not by his own reason, but by revelation, hence he argues thus: If Christ is a Son of God and Lord of the angels, he must certainly be more and of a better nature than the angels. Now every angel is more powerful than all the world and combined human nature; yet if this true child of a virgin is to be Lord, not alone of the evil spirits, but also of the good and holy angels, he must be of one power and essence with God. This nobody will say or believe, except by revelation. Therefore I would agree to take Moses, the Psalms, Isaiah, together with the Spirit whom these men had, and make a New Testament every whit as good as that which the apostles wrote; but because we have not the same wealth and power of the Spirit, we must be taught by them and drink from the fountain which they gave us.

42. Let this be enough concerning a single portion or a single passage of the sermon Christ spoke to these disciples, and wherewith he well and fully earned, yea, paid for the entertainment they furnished him at the inn. But to set forth all the other words of Moses and the prophets which they spoke of Christ, and which he explained, would be by far too great a task for one sermon; for it would in itself amount to a book as large as the Bible. But without doubt they were the same passages the apostles quoted afterwards as they heard them from his own mouth on this occasion, and learned to understand them better on the following day of Pentecost. A goodly number of these passages were quoted by them in their sermons, in the Acts of the Apostles, and in the Epistles; and they are recommended for close study to every Christian, as he reads and ponders the Holy Scriptures. Then the Holy Ghost will be present with his power to give the right understanding, as we have heard, since he is the true interpreter, if only we treat them seriously and in the simplicity of the heart. The fruit thereof will be that we shall find Christ therein and learn to know him aright. This will quicken and kindle the heart, and fill it with comfort and joy.

Easter Tuesday or Third Easter Day. Luke 24:36-47

Christ's Manifestation after His Resurrection

TEXT: Luke 24: 36 And as they thus spake, Jesus himself stood in the midst of them, and saith unto them, Peace be unto you. 37 But they were terrified and affrighted, and supposed that they had seen a spirit. 38 And he said unto them, Why are ye troubled? and why do thoughts arise in your hearts? 39 Behold my hands and my feet, that it is I myself: handle me, and see; for a spirit hath not flesh and bones, as ye see me have. 40 And when he had thus spoken, he shewed them his hands and his feet. 41 And while they yet believed not for joy, and wondered, he said unto them, Have ye here any meat? 42 And they gave him a piece of a broiled fish, and of an honeycomb. 43 And he took it, and did eat before them. 44 And he said unto them, These are the words which I spake unto you, while I was yet with you, that all things must be fulfilled, which were written in the law of Moses, and in the prophets, and in the psalms, concerning me. 45 Then opened he their understanding, that they might understand the scriptures, 46 And said unto them, Thus it is written, and thus it behooved Christ to suffer, and to rise from the dead the third day: 47 And that repentance and remission of sins should be preached in his name among all nations, beginning at Jerusalem.

I. Christ's Manifestation after his Resurrection

1. I think, beloved, you have heard enough in these days on the resurrection of Christ, what it works, why it came to pass, and what fruit it bears. But since the Lord has commanded those who preach the Gospel to be steadfast and diligent in this proclamation, we must dwell upon it ever more and more. Our Gospel shows, first, who hear of the Lord's resurrection profitably and fruitfully, namely they that are here assembled in fear and dread behind closed doors. To them it ought also to be preached most of all, although it must be preached to all nations, as the Lord says at the end of the Gospel of Matthew. Therefore let us learn first of all what kind of persons hear the Gospel aright.

2. The disciples are gathered there together in seclusion. They are afraid of the Jews and are, indeed, in danger of their lives; they are fearful and fainthearted and afraid of sin and death. Had they been strong and courageous, they would not thus have crept into a corner; even as afterward they were made so courageous, when the Holy Spirit came and strengthened and comforted them, that they stepped forth and preached publicly without fear. This is written for us, that we might learn that the Gospel of Christ's resurrection comforts only the fainthearted. And who are these? They are the poor, conscience-stricken ones, whose sins lie heavily upon them, who feel their faint heart, are loth to die, and are well-nigh startled by the sound of a rustling leaf. To these contrite, poor, and needy souls, the Gospel offers comfort, to them it is a sweet savor.

3. This is also learned from the nature of the Gospel, for the Gospel is a message and a testimony, which declares how the Lord Jesus Christ rose from the dead, that he might remove sin, death and all evil from all who believe on him. If I recognize him as such a Savior, I have heard the Gospel aright, and he has in truth revealed himself to me. If now the Gospel teaches naught but that Christ has overcome sin and death by his resurrection, then we must indeed confess that it can be of service to none save those who feel sin and death. For they who do not feel their sin, and are not dismayed, nor see their infirmities, profit not a whit by it, nor do they delight in it. And though they hear the Gospel, it has no effect upon them, except that they learn the words, and speak of what they heard. They do not treasure them in their hearts, and receive neither comfort nor joy from them.

4. Hence it were well, if the Gospel could be preached only where such fainthearted and conscience-stricken ones are found. But this cannot be, and for this reason it bears so little fruit. For this they reproach us and say that we wish to preach many new things, and yet no one is better because of our doctrine. The fault is not in the Gospel, but in the hearers. They hear it, indeed, but they do not feel their own affliction and misery, nor have they ever tried to feel it, they simply go on, secure and reprobate, like dumb brutes. Hence none need marvel if the Gospel does not everywhere bring forth fruit. For beside the good hearers, of whom we have spoken, there are many others that have no regard for it at all, have neither a conscience nor a heart for it, and think neither of death nor of the salvation of souls. These must be driven by force, like asses and dumb brutes, and for this purpose the civil sword is established. Again there are some who do not despise the Gospel, but fully understand it, yet do not amend their lives, nor strive to walk in it. They carry away only the words and prate much about them, but neither deeds nor fruit follow. The third class, however, are they that taste it and use it aright so that it bears fruit in them.

5. This is then the conclusion of the matter, the Gospel is a testimony of the resurrection of Christ, which serves to comfort and refresh the poor, sorrowing, and terrified consciences. There is need that we have clearly apprehended this truth when we come to die, and also that we may provide for it in every other need. If you think: Behold, now death is approaching and staring me in the face; would that I had someone to comfort me, that I might not despair, then know that for this purpose the Gospel is good, here it belongs, here its use is blessed and salutary. As soon as a man knows and understands this, and believes the Gospel, his heart finds peace and says: If Christ, my Lord, has overcome my sin, and trodden it under foot by his resurrection, — wherefore should I fear, and of what should I be afraid? Why should not my heart rejoice and be of good cheer? But such comfort, peace and joy of heart, are felt by none save by the small company which was be fore greatly dismayed and full of sorrow, and felt its infirmities. Hence also the rude and impenitent understand neither this nor any other Gospel, for he that has not tasted the bitter cannot relish the sweet, and he that has not seen adversity does not understand happiness. For as in the world that man who neither cares nor attempts to do anything, and endures naught, is good for nothing; so in a more eminent degree in spiritual things it is not possible that anyone should understand the Gospel except he who has such a dismayed and terrified heart.

6. From this you should learn that it is no marvel, that many who hear the Gospel do not receive it nor live according to it. Everywhere there are many who reject and persecute it, but we must let them go and grow accustomed to their work. Where the Gospel is preached, such people will surely be found; and if it were otherwise, it would not be right, for there must be many kinds of hearers. Again, many will be found, who do not persecute it and yet do not receive it, for they bear no fruit and continue to live as before. Be not worried because of this! For even though a man preach and continue in the Gospel for many years, he must still lament and say: Aye, no one will come, and all continue in their former state. Therefore you must not let that grieve nor terrify you.

7. For note what took place at Jerusalem, where the Gospel was first heard, and where there were so many people that it is said, there were in the city at the feast of the Passover eleven hundred thousand men. How many of these were converted? When St. Peter stood up and preached, they made a mockery of it and considered the apostles drunken fools. When they had urged the Gospel a long time, they gathered together three thousand men and women. But what were they among so many? Yea, no one could discern that the Gospel had accomplished anything, for all things continued in the same state as before. No change was seen, and scarcely anyone knew that there were Christians there. And so it will be at all times.

8. Hence the Gospel must not be measured by the multitude that hear, but by the small company that receive it. They, indeed, appear as nothing, they are despised and persecuted, and yet God secretly works in them.

9. Besides this there is another thing that hinders the free movement of the Gospel, namely the infirmities of the believers. This we see in many examples. Thus although Peter was filled with faith and the Holy Spirit, yet he fell and stumbled, — he and all that were with him, — when he walked not according to the Gospel nor according as he had taught, so that Paul had to reprove him openly, Galatians 2:14. There clung to him many great and holy men, and all stumbled with him. Again, we read that Mark journeyed with Paul, but afterward fell away and withdrew from him; and in Acts 15:37 we read again that Paul and Barnabas strove together, and there arose a sharp contention between them. And, before this, we read in the Gospels how often the apostles erred in weighty matters. though they were the best of Christians.

10. These infirmities of Christians and believers darken the Gospel most of all, so that men who deem themselves wise and learned stumble and are offended in them. Few there are who can well reconcile these things so as to take no offense and hence say: Yes, these desire to be good Christians, and are still so wayward, envious, filled with hate and wrath, that one thinks the Gospel has been preached in vain. This really signifies to be offended in the weak and sick Christ.

11. It was also thus with the disciples. At first, when Christ wrought great and excellent works, and gained great honors, and began the work only to fulfill it, they remained steadfast, though many great and noble saints and learned men were offended, because he would not join them. The common man on the contrary was instructed; and the people clung to him, because they saw that with great power he wrought such excellent works; and also walked so that none could reproach him, but all must needs say: Truly this is a great and holy prophet! But when his suffering began, they all turned back and forsook him, and not one of his disciples continued with him.

Why was this? Because they considered him not the strong, but the weak Christ. He now was in the hands of the Jews, did no more works and miracles just as if he had lost all his power and was forsaken of God. Then perished completely his power and his great name. Before, they counted him a prophet, the like of whom had never appeared; now he is rated as a murderer and a condemned man. Who could now see that this was Christ, the Son of God? Here all reason must fall, yea, all the great and holy saints; for they thought: If he were the Christ, there would needs appear the fruits whereby we might know that it is he, but now we see in him only weakness and sin and death.

12. Therefore it is the highest wisdom on earth, though it is known by very few men, how to bear with the weak Christ. For if I see a pious, holy man leading a beautiful godly life, who will thank me for praising him and saying: There is Christ, and there is righteousness? For although bishops and great dunces be offended in such an one, the common people will be instructed. But if he be feeble and falter, straightway everyone will be offended and say: Alas! I had imagined him to be a good Christian, but I see that he falls short of it. However, if they look about them, they will find none without like infirmities, yea, they will perceive it in themselves. Still they think that the Gospel has come to naught. Thus might they think, if God were not able, in his wisdom, to hide it, even as he put a covering over Christ when he drew over him death and weakness, and Christ was under it, though no man could see it. Hence he told his disciples in advance, Matthew 26:31: "All, all ye, shall be offended in me, and shall no more think nor believe that I am the Christ." Hence, if we judge the Gospel, as I have said, according to the infirmity and weakness of Christians, as they stumble at times, a very great obstacle is presented at which offense is taken and the Gospel is thought to be without power.

13. Therefore he that would know Christ aright must not give heed to the covering. And though you see another stumble, do not despair, nor think all hope is lost; but rather think: God, perchance, will have this one bear the weak Christ, even as another bears the strong; for both must be and abide on earth, though the greater part appear weak and are such especially in our day. But if you pierce through such weakness, you will find that Christ lies hidden in that weak person, he will come forth and show himself.

14. That is what Paul means when he says to the Corinthians, in his First Epistle 1 Corinthians 2:2: "I determined not to know anything among you, save Jesus Christ, and him crucified." What kind of glory is this that impels him to write that he knows nothing, save Christ crucified? It is a thing, that neither reason nor human wisdom can understand, nor yet they who have studied and learned the Gospel; for this wisdom is mighty, hidden and mysterious, and seems of no value, because he was crucified and emptied himself of all power and divine strength, and hung upon the cross like a wretched, forsaken man, and it seemed as if God would not help him. Of him alone I speak and preach, says St. Paul. For the Christ, that sits on high, does wonders, comes and breaks through with power, that all may see who he is, and may quickly come to know him. But to know the weak Christ, that is hanging upon the cross and lying in death, one needs great wisdom; for they who know him not, must needs stumble and be offended.

15. Yea, some are also found who really know the Gospel, but are offended at their own manner of life. They have a desire to walk in godliness, but they feel they make no progress. They begin to despair and think that with them all is lost because they do not feel the strength which they ought to have, also earnestly desire Christ to become strong in them and manifest himself in mighty deeds. But Jehovah, our God, hereby designs to humble us, that we may see what feeble creatures we are, what wretched, lost and condemned men, if Christ had not come and helped us. Behold, that is the great wisdom we have, and at which all the world is offended.

16. But thereby we have no furlough, to continue for all time in weakness, for we do not preach that any should be weak, but that we should know the weakness of Christians and bear with it. Christ did not hang upon the cross, that he might appear as a murderer and evildoer, but that we might learn thereby how deeply strength lies hidden under weakness, and might learn to know God's strength in weakness. Thus our weakness is not to be praised, as though we should abide in it, but rather must we learn not to think that those who are weak are not Christians, nor yet to despair when we feel our own weakness. Therefore it behooves us to know our own weaknesses and ever to seek to wax stronger, for Christ must not suffer always, nor remain in the grave, but must come forth again and live.

17. Hence, let none say that this is the true course and condition. It is only a beginning, in which we must grow day by day, giving heed only that we turn not away and despair when we are so weak, as though all were lost. Rather must we continue to exercise ourselves till we wax stronger and stronger, and endure and bear the weakness, until God helps and takes it away. Hence, even though you see your neighbor so weak that he stumbles, think not that he is beyond hope. God will not have one judge another and be pleased with himself, inasmuch as we are all sinners, but that one bear the infirmity of the other. (Romans 14 and Galatians 5). And if you will not do that, he will let you fall and cast you down, and raise the other up. He desires to have us help one another and bear each other's weaknesses.

18. I have thus spoken of our infirmity in order that you may have a good understanding of it, for such knowledge is very necessary, especially at this time. Oh, if our bishops, pastors, and prelates had had this wisdom, for they needed it the most, how much better would conditions be in Christendom! They would then be able to bear with the weak consciences, and would know how to minister to them. But now it has come to this, that they look only to the strong Christians, and can never bear with the weak; but deal only harshly with them and proceed with force. In times past, when conditions were yet good, the bishops were sorely wanting in this, for, though they were great and holy men, they yet constrained and oppressed the consciences too much. Such things do not take place among Christians, for it is Christ's will to be weak and sickly yet a while, and to have both flesh and bones together, as he says here in the Gospel: "Handle me and see, for a spirit hath not flesh and bones, as ye behold me having." He would have both, not bones only, nor flesh only. Thus we read in Genesis 2:23, that when God created Eve, Adam said: "This is now bone of my bones, and flesh of my flesh." He says not flesh only nor bones only; speaks of having both himself, for he too must needs have both. So it is also with Christ and with us, and hence he says here: I have both flesh and bones, you will find in me not only bones, nor yet only flesh; you will find that I am both strong and sick.

19. Thus also my Christians must be so mingled together, that some are strong and some weak. They that are strong, walk uprightly, are hale and hearty, and must bear the others; they are the bones. The others are the weak that cleave unto the strong. They are also the greater number, as in a body there will always be found more flesh than bones. Hence, Jesus was crucified and died, and likewise was quickened again and glorified, that he might not be a spirit, as the disciples here deem him to be and were filled with fear of him, thinking that because he is not only bone and the strong Christ, it is not he, but a ghost.

20. This wisdom was diligently urged by the apostles and by Christ himself, and, beside this, I know of no book, in which it is urged. It is, indeed, sometimes touched upon, but nowhere urged. Only this one book, the New Testament, urges it constantly, and everywhere strives to set before the people the weak and strong Christ. Thus says St. Paul to the Romans 15:1-3: "Now we that are strong ought to bear the infirmities of the weak and not to please ourselves. Let each one of us please his neighbor for that which is good, unto edifying. For Christ also pleased not himself." Hence we must do the same, and this is the wisdom we are to learn here.

21. To this school belong all that are pictured here in this Gospel, whom Christ finds terrified and affrighted. The others, who do not belong here, are easily identified, for they reject and despise the Gospel. In like manner everyone can know himself, whether he truly takes pleasure in the Gospel. And if you see in another's behavior evidence of an earnest desire to be made holy, you should not despise him.

22. This Gospel therefore shows the following: First, that the Lord stands among the disciples and is now strong, having overcome sin, death, and the devil; but they do not stand as yet, but sit there, and he comes and stands in the midst of them. Where does he stand at the present time? In the midst of the weak and fainthearted company, that sit in fear and weakness, while he is strong and mighty, though it is not yet apparent to the world. But even though the world does not see it, God sees it. Secondly, he shows them his hands and his feet, and comforts them, saying: "Why are ye troubled? and wherefore do questionings arise in your hearts? See my hands and my feet, that it is I myself: handle me and see; for a spirit has not flesh and bones," etc.

23. This is nothing but a sermon that teaches us not to be offended in the weak Christ. He does not rebuke the disciples harshly, does not say: Away with you; I do not want you. You should be strong and courageous, but here you sit and are dismayed and terrified! He does not do these things; but lovingly comforts them, that he might make them strong and fearless. Hence they were also made strong and fearless, and not only this, but also cheerful and of good courage. Therefore we ought not to cast away the weak, but so deal with them that, from day to day, we may bring them to a condition that they may become strong and of good cheer. This does not signify that it is well, if they are weak, and that they should continue weak; for Christ does not stand among them for that purpose, but that they might grow in faith and be made fearless.

24. Here we may also speak, as the text gives occasion, of ghosts or walking spirits, for we see here that the Jews and the apostles themselves held that spirits roam about and are seen by night and at other times. Thus Matthew 14:25 f, when the disciples sailed in a ship by night, and saw Jesus walking on the sea, they were affrighted, as before a ghost, and cried out in fear. And here we learn that Jesus does not deny it but confirms it by his answer that spirits do appear, for he says: "A spirit has not flesh and bones," etc.

25. But the Scriptures do not say, nor give any example, that such are the souls of dead persons walking among the people and seeking help, as we, in our blindness and deluded by the devil, have heretofore believed. Hence the pope has, also, invented purgatory and established his shameful annual market of masses. We may well see in this false doctrine and abomination as a fruit, that the foundation on which it is built, namely the doctrine of the migration of souls, comes from the father of lies, the devil, who has deluded the people in the name of the dead.

26. We have good reason not to believe such apparitions of roaming erring spirits that profess to be souls. First, because the Scriptures nowhere say that the souls of the deceased, that have not yet risen, should wander about among the people; whereas everything else we need to know, is clearly revealed in the Scriptures. Not one word concerning this is given for our instruction, nor is it possible that we should grasp and understand the state of the spirits that have departed from the body, before the resurrection and the day of judgment; for they are sundered and separated altogether from the world and from this generation. Moreover, it is clearly forbidden in the Scriptures to consult the dead or to believe them who do. Deuteronomy 18:11; Isaiah 28:19. And Luke 16:31 proves that God will neither let one rise from the dead nor preach, because we have Moses and the Scriptures.

27. Know therefore that all ghosts and visions, which cause themselves to be seen and heard, especially with din and noise, are not men's souls, but evidently devils that amuse themselves thus either to deceive the people with false claims and lies, or unnecessarily frighten and trouble them. Hence with a specter that makes a pretense in the name of a soul a Christian should not deal otherwise than as with the very devil himself. He should be well girded with God's Word and faith, that he may not be deceived nor affrighted, but abide in the doctrine that he has learned and confessed from the Gospel of Christ, and cheerfully despise the devil with his noise. Nor does he tarry long where he feels a soul trusts in Christ and despise him. This I say that we may be wise and not suffer ourselves to be misled by such deception and lies, as in the past he deceived and mocked even excellent men, like St. Gregory, under the name of being a soul.

28. Now what does it, signify that he shows the disciples his hands and his feet? He would thereby say: Come, and learn to know me. Now I am strong, but you are weak, as I also was. Therefore see to it now that you become strong also.

II. The Sermon Christ Preached to His Disciples

29. The above is one chief part of this Gospel; the other follows at the end of the Gospel, where the Lord concludes by saying: "Thus it is written, that the Christ should suffer, and rise again from the dead the third day; and that repentance and remission of sins should be preached in his name unto all the nations."

30. Here you see that the Gospel is the preaching of repentance and remission of sins. And it should not be preached in a corner, but before all men, whether it be received or not, for it is to spread even farther that it may be heard and bear fruit. Hence we are not to be offended though but few receive it, nor say it has been given in vain. We should, rather, be content with it, that Christ has given command to preach it in all the world, that he who will may receive it. But we must note here in particular, that he says: 31. First, let us consider two thoughts. By repentance he means a change for the better; not as we have called it repentance, when one scourges and castigates himself and does penance to atone for his sin, or when the priest imposes this or that upon anyone for penance. Scripture does not speak of it in this sense. Repentance rather signifies here a change and reformation of the whole life; so that when one knows that he is a sinner, and feels the iniquity of his life, he desists from it and enters upon a better course of life, in word and deed, and that he does it from his heart.

32. What then is repentance in his name? Hereby he singles out the repentance that is not made in his name, and hence the text compels us to consider two kinds of repentance. First, a repentance not in his name is, when I come with my own works and undertake to blot out sin with them; as we all have hitherto been taught and have tried to do. This is not repentance in God's name, but in the devil's name. For this is striving to propitiate God by our own works and by our own strength, a thing God cannot allow.

33. But on the other hand, to repent in his name is done thus: in those who believe in Christ God through the same faith works a change for the better, not for a moment, nor for an hour, but for their whole life. For a Christian is not instantaneously or suddenly cleansed perfectly, but the reformation and change continue as long as he lives. Though we use the utmost diligence, we will always find something to sweep or clean. For even though all wickedness be overcome, we have not yet overcome the fear of death, for few have come so far as to desire death with a spirit of rejoicing; hence, we must grow better day by day. This is what Paul means, when he says in 2 Corinthians 4:16: "Though our outward man is decaying, yet our inward man is renewed day by day." For we hear the Gospel every day, and Christ shows us his hands and his feet every day that our minds may be still more enlightened, and we be made more and more godly.

34. For this reason Christ would say, let no one strive to amend his life by his own works and in his own name; for of themselves no one is an enemy of sin, no one will come to repentance and think of amending his life. Nothing will be accomplished except in my name. That name alone has power to do it, and brings with it willingness and desire to be changed. But if the works and doctrines of men be taught, I will go and say to myself: O, that I might not need to pray, nor make confession, nor go to the Lord's Supper! What will your repentance profit you, if you fail to do it gladly or willingly, but are constrained by the commandment or by fear of shame, otherwise you would rather not do it? But what is the reason? Because it is a repentance in the devil's name, in your own name or in the pope's name. Hence you go on and do worse things, and wish there were no confession and sacrament, so that you might not be constrained to attend them. This is repentance in our own name, and proceeds from our own strength.

35. But when I begin to believe in Christ, lay hold of the Gospel, and doubt not that he has taken away my sin and blotted it out, and comforts me with his resurrection; my heart is filled with such gladness that I myself take hold willingly, not through persuasion, nor of necessity, I gladly do what I ought and say: Because my Lord has done this for me, I will also do his will in this, that I may amend my ways and repent out of love to him and to his glory. In this way a true reformation begins that proceeds from the innermost heart, and that is brought forth by the joy that flows from faith, when I apprehend the greatness of the love Christ has bestowed upon me.

36. Secondly, we should preach also forgiveness of sins in his name. This signifies nothing else than that the Gospel should be preached, which declares unto all the world that in Christ the sins of all the world are swallowed up, and that he suffered death to put away sin from us, and arose to devour it and blot it out. All did he did, that whoever believeth, should have the comfort and assurance, that it is reckoned unto him even as if he himself had done it; that his work is mine and thine and all men's; yea, that he gives himself to us with all his gifts to be our own personal property. Hence, as he is without sin and never (lies by virtue of his resurrection, even so I also am, if I believe in him; and I will therefore strive to become more and more godly, till there be no more sin in me. This continues as long as we live, until the day of judgment. As he is without sin, he sets before us an example, that we might be fashioned like unto him, though while we live here, we shall be fully like the image.

37. St. Paul speaks of this in writing to the Corinthians: "We all, with unveiled face beholding as in a mirror the glory of the Lord, are transformed into the same image from glory to glory." 2 Corinthians 3:8. Christ, even as he is risen, is the image, and is set before us that we might know that he rose from the dead to overcome our sin. This image stands before us and is set before our eyes by the Gospel, and is so mirrored in our hearts that we may grasp it by faith, if we hold it to be true and daily exercise ourselves in it. Thus the glory is imparted by him to us, and it comes to pass that we become ever more glorious, and grow into the same image that he is. Hence he also says, that we are not at once made perfect and strong, but must grow from day to day till we become like him. Many similar passages are here and there in the Scriptures.

38. This then is preaching the forgiveness of sins in his name, that we do not point only to confession, or to a certain hour; for we must act in view of the fact that it deals not with our works but with the whole person. Even when we begin to believe, our sin and infirmity are always present so that there is nothing pure in us, and we are indeed worthy of condemnation. But now forgiveness is so great and powerful, that God not only forgives the former sins you have committed; but looks through his fingers and forgives the sins you will yet commit. He will not condemn us for our daily infirmities, but forgives all, in view of our faith in him, if we only strive to press onward and get rid of sin.

39. Here you may see what a difference there is between this and that which has heretofore been preached, of buying letters of indulgence, and of confessions, by which it was thought sin could be blotted out. So far as this pressed and such confidence was there put in it, that men were persuaded if anyone should die upon it, he would straightway mount to heaven. They did not know that we have still more sin and will not be rid of it, as long as we live. They supposed that all is well if only we have been to confession. Hence this is a forgiveness in the name of the devil. But see that you understand it correctly: By absolution you are absolved and declared free from sin, that is, you are put into that state, where there is forgiveness of sin that never ends. And not only is there forgiveness of past sins, but of those also you now have, if you believe that God overlooks and forgives your sins; and although you stumble still, yet he will neither reject nor condemn you, if you continue in faith. This teaching is heard indeed in all the world, but few there be that understand it.

40. Thus you have heard what the Gospel is, and what repentance and forgiveness of sins are, whereby we enter into another, a new state, out of the old. But take heed, lest you trust in this and become sluggish, thinking that when you sin there is no danger, and thus boldly persist in sin. This would be sinning in spite of God's mercy and would tempt God. But if you desire to be delivered from sin, it is well with you, and all is forgiven. So much then on the second part of this Gospel, and with it we shall, for the present, content ourselves.

Tuesday after Easter. Second Sermon. Luke 24:36-47

A Comforting Example and Picture of Christ

KJV Luke 24:36 And as they thus spake, Jesus himself stood in the midst of them, and saith unto them, Peace be unto you. 37 But they were terrified and affrighted, and supposed that they had seen a spirit. 38 And he said unto them, Why are ye troubled? and why do thoughts arise in your hearts? 39 Behold my hands and my feet, that it is I myself: handle me, and see; for a spirit hath not flesh and bones, as ye see me have. 40 And when he had thus spoken, he shewed them his hands and his feet. 41 And while they yet believed not for joy, and wondered, he said unto them, Have ye here any meat? 42 And they gave him a piece of a broiled fish, and of an honeycomb. 43 And he took it, and did eat before them. 44 And he said unto them, These are the words which I spake unto you, while I was yet with you, that all things must be fulfilled, which were written in the law of Moses, and in the prophets, and in the psalms, concerning me. 45 Then opened he their understanding, that they might understand the scriptures, 46 And said unto them, Thus it is written, and thus it behooved Christ to suffer, and to rise from the dead the third day: 47 And that repentance and remission of sins should be preached in his name among all nations, beginning at Jerusalem.

I. A Comforting Example and Picture of Christ

1. In the first part of this Gospel we have for our consolation another example showing how Christ manifests himself and how he is wont to act toward his beloved disciples. They have scarcely begun to speak of him, when he himself comes and stands in their midst and greets them with these kind and cheerful words: "Pax vobis!" (Peace be unto you!) The disciples, however, are frightened at this and suppose they behold a spirit. But he suffers them not to be thus frightened, rebukes them for allowing such thoughts to enter their hearts, and shows them his hands and feet; that they may see that he is not a spirit, nor another Christ than he has been in the past, but is of their own flesh and bones and of the selfsame nature as they. This he does that they may not be afraid of him, but may rejoice in him and be comforted, and look to him for good things.

2. For this example of his conduct is to serve as an object lesson as it were, instilling comfort into all terrified hearts; especially against that spectre called a false Christ. For the devil also has the habit of coming to people, both in public and in private, either through false doctrine or through secret inward working, and he even pretends to be Christ himself. He begins with a pleasant greeting, with a smiling "good morning;" but ere long he smites the heart with sorrow and dread, that it knows not what has become of Christ.

3. For his delight is to deceive us under the name and guise of Christ; and he is ever desirous of aping God and of imitating him in all that he sees him do. Now, when God reveals himself he employs the following manner: First, in deed, he terrifies those who have not been terrified as yet. Besides, hearts that are naturally timid always stand in dread of his words and works by reason of their timid nature. But those who are terrified already, he comforts again and speaks kindly to them. The devil imitates this and likewise comes with the name and works of Christ; but both his comfort and his terrors are counterfeit. For he reverses the two, terrifying and dismaying those who stand in need of comfort, and comforting and strengthening those who should be afraid and stand in fear of God's wrath. To shield ourselves against this deception, we should learn from this Gospel to distinguish correctly between the doctrines and ideas that come to our notice, both such as terrify and such as comfort, that we may know which of them are of God and which of the devil.

4. For, in the first place, that lying spirit, already in Paradise, began this sweet deception when he approached Eve with his courteous, kind, and honeyed words: Why, there is no danger. You need not stand in fear and dread of eating of one single tree. Do you suppose that God has really forbidden you this one fruit, that he begrudges you the eating of this one tree? Indeed, he knows, if you eat thereof, you will become much wiser and will be as God. This was, indeed, very encouraging and a pleasing sermon, but it left an abominable stench behind, and by it the whole human race was led into the evil, which we all to this day deplore. For this reason it has become a common saying among men who have striven to be devout and sought to discern the spirits, that the devil always comes with winning and cheering words at first, but leaves terror and a troubled conscience in his wake, while the Good Spirit does the contrary.

5. And it is true, this is one of the wanton tricks he practices. He creeps in unawares, like a serpent, and first makes himself attractive, in the manner indicated, and insinuates himself into favor; but before one is aware of it he strikes with his tail and leaves a poisoned wound. For this reason one should not be too credulous when a preacher comes softly like an angel of God, recommends himself very highly, and swears that his sole aim is to save souls, and says: "Pax vobis!" For those are the very fellows the devil employs to honey people's mouths. Through them he gains an entrance to preach and to teach, in order that he may afterward inflict his injuries, and that though he accomplish nothing more for the present, he may, at least, confound the people's consciences and finally lead them into misery and despair.

6. This same thing he does by means of thoughts which he causes to arise within the heart, by which he tempts people and even entices them to gross sins. Here, too, he invariably begins with the word "Peace!" that he may first cause the people to lose sight of the fear of God; making light of grave matters, and always preaching and proclaiming: "Pax et securitas!" There is no cause for worry! But much more does he do this with those great and serious sins pertaining to the faith and the glory of God, in which he moves people to idolatry and to a trust in their own works and holiness. Here he at first pretends to be holy and pious and impart the very sweetest of thoughts: Oh, there is no cause for alarm, God is not angry with you. Even as the prophets say of such. Jeremiah 6:14; Ezekiel 33:30. They will hear thee and suffer thee to preach, but they will ever comfort and bless themselves and say: Oh, there is no reason to fear; hell' is not so hot, the devil is not so black as he is painted. This is the devil's entrance and deception, even though he speak peace and extend a friendly greeting. Not until afterwards, when one is already enmeshed and cannot escape, does one see what injury and distress he has caused. Thus experience teaches that many a man falls into sin, shame, and punishment, so easily that he himself is not aware of it, being drawn in by means of subtle and pleasant thoughts, as it were by a hair or a straw.

7. Behold, this is one of his ways, by which he misleads many foolish, secure, and careless minds; he leads them to imagine that they are resting in God's lap and playing with dolls, with him. And they become so intoxicated with these imaginations and this sweet poison of the devil, so proud, hardened, and obstinate, that they simply will not listen nor give heed to anybody. However, some God-fearing people have noticed this and have warned others against the devil's wiles, declaring how he enters in so softly and pretends he is bringing divine comfort, but at last leaves a stench behind betraying that he has been about. But this is comparatively easy and a matter for younger disciples. Every Christian should certainly possess enough wisdom to be on his guard against such pleasant poison. For he who insists on learning by experience to guard against the devil's wiles, pays dearly for his learning and then he doesn't fully understand the devil's trickery.

8. His second way of doing is this: He frightens people, even in trifling matters, by means of jugglery, for example, and by apparitions. He has been very busy in the past with tappings which were supposed to be the work of departed souls. In this way, he harasses and terrifies timid and fearful hearts and thus passes on, leaving no comfort behind. Much worse, however, is it, when he comes into the heart and there begins to argue and reason, quoting even such passages as Christ himself uttered, thereby causing the heart to become so awe-stricken that it has no other thought than that it hears the voice of God and Christ. And when thoughts of this kind prevail the heart must at last despair, for where else shall it hope to find comfort when it feels that God himself, who should be its comfort, is terrifying it and aiming his arrows at it; as Job complains in 6, 4: "For the arrows of the Almighty are within me, the poison whereof my spirit drinketh up: the terrors of God do set themselves in array against me." Though it is not God that does this but the devil, who takes pleasure in thus piercing hearts with his arrows (as also he did to St. Paul, 2 Corinthians 12), yet Satan had gained such a hold on Job's heart that the poor man could say and think nothing but this: It is God that doeth these things.

9. This, then, is a much greater and more dangerous deception of Satan's, when he comes without any kindly greeting, bidding us neither "Good morning" nor "Peace" but frightens and terrifies the heart — and all in the voice and guise of God. So that man, overpowered and stricken down hereby is unable to raise himself up and think: It is the devil. For since his heart imagines and feels as if it were God, against whom no man can prevail, heaven and earth seem to him as a narrow cell, the hand of every creature is against him and everything he sees and hears affrights him.

10. As contrasted with this shameless lying Satan, Christ has here portrayed and pictured himself as he really is. For although it is true that he, too, sometimes comes with terrors, sometimes with comfort, still it is his sole and final purpose to give life and comfort and make glad the heart. And yet the heart of man is so void of understanding in both cases that it does not recognize him (the devil at the same time assisting in the delusion with his suggestions), and does not think that it is Christ, or straightway makes of him a false Christ, even as the Apostles here take him for a spirit or spectre; and they have neither heart nor mind to believe it is Christ, in spite of the fact that they see Christ's form and features. It is, therefore, the part of great art and understanding to tear the false Christ out of one's heart and to learn to picture him truly, because as has been said, one must bear in mind that the devil pictures to us a false Christ, yea clothes himself in Christ's form.

11. So then, this Gospel shows what the true Christ and his Word are, namely, in the first place, that he says, "Peace be unto you," which is a portion of the comfort that he brings; and, in the second place, that he reproves the people and will not suffer them to form false and fretful ideas of himself and says: "Why are ye troubled? and wherefore do questionings arise in your hearts?" No wealth of money or goods could ever pay for this text, because a troubled heart may learn from it and conclude: Even though the devil quote all the passages in the Bible in order to terrify the heart, yet if he continue too long and fail to bring comfort afterward, then it is surely the devil, even if you see the form of Christ as plainly as when he hung upon the cross or as he sits at the right hand of the Father. For it may, indeed, happen, that Christ comes and terrifies you at first; though it is by no means his fault, but the fault of your nature, that you do not rightly know him. But he that assails you with terrors and ceases not until he leads you into despair, is the devil himself.

12. Therefore you must clearly distinguish between the terrors of Christ and those of the devil. For even though Christ begin by terrifying, yet he is certain to bring comfort with him and does not will that you remain in terror. The devil, however, cannot cease from his terrifying although at first he comforts and acts pleasantly. This a Christian must know: he must learn to discern Christ from the devil. Especially in great afflictions, when he feels anxiety and dread, he must bear in mind that there will not be terrors only and continually, but that they will cease and that comfort will follow.

13. But, you say, it is Christ and his Word after all, for he, too, preaches about God's wrath on account of sin, as he says, Luke 13:5: "Except ye repent, ye shall all likewise perish," etc. I answer: Indeed, with this he is pleased and it must come to pass that you become terrified on account of your sins (in case you have not yet experienced this terror). Yea, by reason of your timid nature he must let it come to pass that you be terrified even at him, as these disciples were. But it is not his intention to have you remain in terror; on the contrary, he wills that you cease from it. Yes, he even reproves you for it, and says that you are doing him an injustice by such thoughts, imputing such things to him. In short, he does not desire that you should be frightened at him, but that you should take comfort and joyful assurance, thus driving away your terror.

14. Now, if these thoughts which terrify you arise from his words and works, let him thus begin with you, but then simply send him away to those who are still secure, hardhearted, and obdurate, for whom his terrors are intended. Upon them he must cry out his woes and them he must threaten with the eternal fire of hell. For they are people who in no wise fear God; on the contrary, when one wishes to put them in awe with the name and Word of God, they throw up their horns, toss their heads at God, and grow harder than steel or flint. But you, when you feel that you have become terrified (God grant it, whether the true Christ does it, or not), just remember to make an end of it and cease your fears. For if it be. Christ indeed, it is not his will that you continue thus; but if it be not he, still less should you do so.

15. Therefore mark and keep in mind this text and its example: Christ does not will that his own be terrified, and it does not please him to find you appalled at the sight of him. On the contrary, it is his will that you learn to know him as one who, when he finds you troubled and alarmed, rejoices to come to you, and that you too should rejoice over him and dismiss your thoughts of fear. And do not fail to learn that this is his way of speaking: "Why are ye troubled, and why permit ye such thoughts to arise in your hearts?" Ye picture me as a spectre and as one that cometh only to terrify you, and lo! I am come to comfort you and to make you glad.

16. For these reasons, when such oppressive thoughts concerning Christ come to you, be wise and understand that they assuredly come not from Christ but from the devil; and that even though you be terrified at him, a little sudden terror shall do you no harm. For it is in accord with our nature that it never prompts us to anything good, especially when the heart is naturally timid and fretful. Never mind your thoughts and notions. Take heed to hear Christ's words, who takes no pleasure in seeing you terrified in his name, but desires that you rejoice in him and receive him as one who would comfort your poor, sinful and troubled heart. Let the others be terrified, those headstrong, impenitent sinners, the pope, the tyrants, and all of Christ's enemies and blasphemers. These people need a sledge hammer that will shatter boulders, rocks and mountains.

17. Therefore, if there be a Christ who terrifies, he is and desires to be such only to these obstinate heads; although they themselves do not believe this, but proudly disregard it until their last hour has come, and the time when he without any mercy whatever must trample them under his feet. But he does not desire to be such to his beloved disciples and believers, who are too backward and timid as it is, insomuch that they become alarmed even in the presence of their beloved Savior. For it is by no means his intention, as St. Matthew says in 12:20, quoting from the prophet Isaiah 42:3, to utterly break and quench the bruised reed and the smoking flax; that is, broken, troubled, humbled, and fearsome consciences. Now, what if these hardened, proud, and brazen, Satanic minds do pay no heed at all to his terrifyings? Should timid, fearful hearts suffer these terrors in their stead and bring such fear upon themselves, when in short he wants them to be of good courage? Or, since no terrors and threats avail with the former, should therefore no comfort avail with the latter? In this case Christ's cause were lost entirely, and his kingdom would find no room and bear no fruit on earth.

18. Hence, if you feel terrified and faint-hearted, let your heart herein take comfort, so that Christ may find room in you; for he does not by any means find in you a proud, impenitent heart, unwilling to humble itself; otherwise you would have good cause and need to fear him as one who is set to be a judge over the wicked and the scorners. But he comes to you in order to bring and offer you grace and peace, even as you desire and pray. I say again, take care in this matter, lest you cast from you this friendly greeting and your own salvation, and lest you make a Satan of this dear Savior, or rather, lest you, instead of hearkening to Christ, hearken to the devil, who is a liar and a murderer and takes delight in vexing weak and troubled hearts. And he never desists from so doing; and if he finds himself unable to cause enough terror with one verse he comes with ten or a hundred, and continues to oppress until the heart is completely overwhelmed and drowned in sorrow.

19. Now, you as a Christian can conclude with certainty that such thoughts are not and cannot be of Christ. Yea, even if it were possible that it were Christ himself, nevertheless you here have his Word and true testimony, which you should believe more than all apparitions. And surely this is to be preferred to all private visions of Christ or of an angel from heaven, for these can err and deceive and are naught but speechless images. But here you have his living voice and Word, publicly speaking before all his disciples and reproving them for such thoughts, that we may know he is displeased with them.

20. Besides he shows the very same thing by his outward signs and works: the words with which he reproves their thoughts do not suffice him, he also shows them his hands and feet that they may feel and see it is he himself. As though he thus would say: Why will ye still have doubts concerning me and in your thoughts make a spectre of me? Ye surely have never yet handled a devil or a spirit, nor seen one having flesh and blood as I have, although they at times assume such form and deceive the senses.

21. Thus he gives them, in addition to his Word, a sure and potent sign and comforts them by his actions, that they may fear him not in the least. He shows them what he has done for them. For this is in truth a lovely, comforting, and cheerful picture, the sight of this dear Savior's hands and feet, pierced for my sake, and together with which also my sins are nailed to the cross. This he shows me as a token and testimony that he has suffered, has been crucified, and has died for me, and is by no means disposed to be angry with me and cast me into hell.

22. For this is really seeing his hands and feet, if I, through his Word and faith, perceive that what he has done was done for my good, my salvation and comfort. Here I see no executioner, surely no death nor hell, but only sweet, delightful grace toward all poor, sorrowing souls, at which grace I cannot be affrighted or terrified; excepting only in this, that his work is entirely too great for the heart sufficiently to grasp and understand. Thus he would, both by word and deed, free us from fear even though at first we be terrified at the sight of him.

23. On the other hand the devil, although at first he comforts us, at last he also shows his hands and feet; these are the horrible, abominable claws of the wrath of God and of eternal death. So finally he comes with naught but terrors, murder, and slaughter, which are his works from the beginning, He knows how to portray to the soul all the terrible scenes, examples, and histories of all the abominable sins, murders, and terrible punishments that have ever taken place, and the number and prominence of the people whom he has ever misled, blinded, and cast into perdition.

24. Now, where Christ is thus rightly understood, there, in consequence, true joy begins, and in such measure, like the Evangelist says, as to make the disciples marvel in their faith for very joy, and as to hamper them still. This again is a peculiar text and a strange saying. At first their faith was hampered by fear and dreadful thoughts; now their joy hampers their faith, a joy which even is far greater than at first their terror was. The disciples are now so full of joy at the reproof of the Lord and the sight of his hands and feet that they are still unable to believe.

25. This, too, is one of the Christian's afflictions, as we have said before, that grace is entirely too great and glorious a thing when we look upon our littleness and unworthiness in comparison with Christ, and that the comfort is so exceedingly abundant that our hearts are far too small to receive it. For who could have the boldness to conceive in his heart the truth that Christ proves himself to be so kind a Savior to me, a poor, sinful man, that he gives me at once all that he has done? Must not the heart presently start with alarm at its own boldness and say: Do you really think it is true that the great and majestic God, the Maker of heaven and earth, has so regarded my misery and so mercifully looked upon me, deeply and manifoldly as I have sinned against him, having deserved and brought upon myself wrath, death, and hell a thousand times? How can such grace and such a treasure be grasped by the human heart, or in fact by any creature?

26. To sum up all, faith in man's heart is assailed on both sides and upon both occasions, in terror and melancholy and also in joy. Either the lack or the abundance is too great, and the consolations too few or too many. At first, while the disciples were yearning for something great, all the blessings of God were too small and too insignificant to comfort their hearts, when Christ was still hidden from them; but now that he is come and shows himself to them, this is far too much for their hearts, and for very wonderment they cannot believe he is risen from the dead and is standing before them alive.

27. Finally he shows himself even still more friendly: he sits down with them at the table, eats with them of broiled fish and honeycomb, and preaches to them a beautiful sermon, to establish them in the faith, that they may nevermore fear nor doubt, but may now grow strong in the faith: and thus all their melancholy passes away.

28. Therefore let us learn from this to understand Christ's character and manner, to-wit, that when he comes and manifests himself, he thereupon takes leave and bids us adieu, leaving naught but comfort and joy; for at the last he must come with comfort, otherwise it is not Christ. But when constant fear and dread remain in the heart, you may freely conclude that it is not Christ, though it may seem so to the heart, but the accursed devil. Therefore pay no heed to such thoughts, but cling fast to the words he speaks to you, "See my hands and my feet," etc. In this way your heart will again be made glad, and afterward the fruit will follow, that you will understand the Scriptures aright, and his Word will taste pleasant to you, being naught but honey and the sweetest consolation.

II. Sermon Christ Preached to his Disciples after His Resurrection

29. The second and chief part of this Gospel is that in which Christ, after he expounded the Scripture to them and opened their minds, says in conclusion: "Thus it is written, that the Christ should suffer, and rise again from the dead the third day; and that repentance and remission of sins should be preached in his name to all the nations."

30. Here you see how the Lord again directs and leads his disciples into the Scriptures, there to strengthen and confirm their faith. So that, though he was revealing and showing himself to them in visible form, yet in the future, when they no longer beheld him, he desired them to cling to the Word and by the testimony of the Scripture make sure both their own and the faith of others. For after all, the power and the comfort of the resurrection are not understood nor received except through faith in the Word, as we have heard: although the disciples see him, still they do not recognize him, but are rather terrified at the sight of him until he speaks to them and opens their minds by means of the Scriptures.

31. Furthermore he wished to teach them by these testimonies of Scripture how his kingdom on earth is to continue and wherein it is to consist; namely, that it is not to be a new government or kingdom, concerned with earthly and temporal things, but a spiritual and divine power, whereby he would everywhere rule invisibly within the hearts of men through the Word and ministry and would cause them to pass from sin, God's wrath, and eternal death into grace and eternal life in heaven: for which purpose, in truth, he also suffered and rose again from the dead.

32. All this he shows and indicates in these few words, and in them includes the sum and substance of the entire Gospel and the chief parts of Christian doctrine, which we should at all times preach and practice in the church: namely, repentance and the forgiveness of sins. Therefore we must say something on these themes also.

33. Concerning repentance, the whole papal church has until now known nothing else to teach than that it consists of three parts, which they call contrition, confession, and satisfaction (compensation). And yet in regard to none of these could they rightly instruct the people. Now, the Latin word "satisfactio," meaning "compensation," we have, to please them, allowed to stand, hoping that by moderation on our part we might be able to lead them to the true doctrine; but with the understanding that this means not our compensation, as we in reality can render none, but Christ's satisfaction, in that he by his blood and death has paid for our sins and reconciled God. Since, however, we have heretofore so many times experienced and still plainly see that nothing whatever can be gained from them by moderation, and that they steadily continue the more violently to oppose the true doctrine, we will and must cleanly strip and sunder ourselves from them, and refuse in any way to recognize the fictitious names which they use in their schools and with which they now only strive to establish their old errors and falsehoods. For this reason also this word "satisfaction" shall hereafter in our church and our theology be null and dead, and referred to the judiciary and the schools of law, where it properly belongs and whence the papists borrowed it. Let these use this word and by it teach people who have stolen, robbed, or who are in possession of goods gotten by unrighteousness, how they are to make compensation and restitution.

34. The word "contrition" (Latin "contritio") is, to be sure, taken from the Scriptures, which speak of a "cor contritum," that is, a broken, troubled, and miserable heart, Psalm 51:17; but neither has this word been rightly understood and explained by the monks. For they have called contrition the act, extorted from one's own thoughts and free will, of sitting in a corner, hanging one's head, and with bitter meditation contemplating the sins one has committed; from which process, however, no real sorrow or displeasure on account of their sins followed, but they have rather tickled themselves with such thoughts and strengthened their sinful lust. And no matter how long they talked of it, still they could not decide how great one's contrition should be in order to be adequate to the sin. Wherefore they were compelled to console and help themselves out by this piece of patchwork, that he who could not attain to truly perfect contrition should, at least, have what they called "attritio," a sort of half-contrition, and be, at least, somewhat sorry for his sins.

35. Then they made of confession an unbearable torment and anxiety; for they thought that it was everyone's duty at least once a year to enumerate all of one's sins, mentioning all the details, including also those sins one might have forgotten and might later recall. And yet they gave men's consciences no real instruction concerning the comfort of absolution, but directed the people to trust in their own works, and informed them that when they had become sufficiently contrite to make a clean confession of sin (which was, according to their own teaching, impossible), and also render satisfaction for the same, then their sins would be forgiven. Here not a word was said of Christ or of faith, so that unenlightened and afflicted souls who earnestly desired to be free from sin and sought comfort were kept in eternal suspense on this doubtful foundation.

36. And—this was the worst feature of the matter—they did not rightly teach what constitutes sin; they knew nothing more of it than what lawyers call sin or offenses, and what comes within the sphere of the courts and of peace statutes. Their knowledge did not enable them to speak of original sin or of the inward impurity of the heart. For they even claimed that human nature and the powers of man's free will were so perfect that a man might in his own strength manage to fulfill God's law and thereby earn God's grace, and be so free from sin that he would not have need of any repentance. However, that they might nevertheless have something to make confession of, they were compelled to invent sin where there was none, just as on the other hand they invented good works of their own. And these sins they considered the greatest and most grievous of all, as for instance, when a layman chanced to touch a consecrated chalice or if a priest stammered while reading the canon in the mass, and other foolishness of that sort.

37. Such nonsensical, visionary doctrine of the papacy concerning repentance one must therefore not lose sight of, first in order to be able to convince them of their error and blindness, since they are at present in every way whitewashing themselves and disporting themselves as though they had never taught anything wrong. Secondly, in order that by contrasting the two one may better understand the true Christian doctrine. Therefore we will speak according to Scripture on what the real Christian repentance and forgiveness of sins are which Christ here commands man to proclaim in his name.

38. In the first place, these thoughts of our own invention, which the monks call "contritio" and "attritio" (whole and half contrition), are in all the Scriptures never called true contrition; but you are contrite when your heart becomes seriously alarmed at God's wrath and judgment, not only on account of outward, gross sins, but on account of the real and unyielding hardness you see and feel within, the presence in your flesh and blood of nothing but unbelief, contempt and disobedience to God, and as St. Paul says in Romans 8:7, "enmity against God," your flesh and blood being excited with all manner of evil lust and desire and the like, whereby you have brought upon yourself God's wrath and have deserved to be cast out eternally from his presence and to burn in hell fire. Contrition, according to the Scriptures, is not partial, pertaining merely to certain acts you have committed openly against the ten commandments, and leaving undisturbed the dream and delusion of the hypocritical monkish repentance which for its own convenience invents a distinction in its works and after all discovers some good in itself; but it extends over your whole person with all its life and being, yes, over your whole nature, and shows you that you are an object of God's wrath and condemned to hell. Otherwise the word "contrition" would still be too judicial, as in earthly matters one speaks of sin and sorrow as of a work one has done and afterwards thinks differently, and wishes he had not done it.

39. This contrition and earnest fear is not the product of man's own resolutions or thoughts, as the monks fancy. It must be wrought in a man by God's Word, which reveals God's wrath and smites the heart so that it begins to tremble and despair and knows not what to do with itself. For human reason cannot of itself perceive and understand that everything which lies in the power and ability of man is an object of God's wrath and, at the bar of his judgment, already condemned to hell.

40. Therefore this thing must be preached and proclaimed as Christ here says, if one is to direct and lead people to true repentance: they must be led to know their sins and God's wrath, and thus first suffer themselves to be cast by the Word beneath God's wrath and condemnation; in order that on the other hand by the preaching of the other truth, of the forgiveness of sins, they may be helped to gain true consolation, divine grace, and their salvation. Otherwise a man would never attain to a knowledge of his misery and distress and to a yearning for grace. Still less would he ever learn how he may pass from God's wrath and damnation into grace and the forgiveness of sins.

41. And this preaching of repentance, says he, shall go forth unto all nations. Surely, a sweeping accusation, one that embraces the whole world, both Jews and Gentiles, and whomsoever they wish. Without a single exception, he concludes all—as he finds them and whatever their rank and pretensions—apart from Christ under the wrath of God and says: Ye are all condemned together, with all that ye do and are, be ye what ye may, be ye ever so many, ever so great, ever so high and holy.

42. Yea, he terrifies and condemns those most of all who parade their own holiness and never once imagine that they are sinners and need repentance. Among the Jews the holiest Pharisees were such (of whom also Paul before his conversion was one), who lived and walked zealously according to the law; among the heathen certain cultured, highly intelligent, wise, and respectable people; among ourselves, those who may have been pious monks, Carthusians, or hermits, who sincerely undertook to be pious in God's sight and so lived that they were not conscious of having committed any sin unto death, and in addition to this in the severest manner chastised their bodies with fasting, vigils, sleeping on hard couches, some even with bloody flagellations and the like; so that they themselves and everybody else thought that in view of such works and such a life they surely had no need of contrition and repentance. Yes, they thought therewith, as with the best and most meritorious work, to pay for whatever sins they had previously done, and honestly to earn heaven from God by such a holy life, paying for it dearly enough. Against just such people as these this preaching of repentance should be carried on most zealously, and as with a thunderbolt it should hurl to the ground and cast into hell and perdition all who are secure and presumptuous and do not yet perceive their misery and God's wrath.

43. Even as St. John the Baptist, who prepared the way before Christ, publicly began such preaching; he courageously and spiritedly attacks the entire Jewish nation with this battle-ax and assails the holy Pharisees and Sadducees harder than all the others, saying: "Ye offspring of vipers, who warned you to flee from the wrath to come?" Matthew 3:7. For they need repentance most of all and in God's sight they also merit a greater measure of wrath than other and more open sinners (whom at least their own consciences reprove), because they lie in blindness and indulge the fancy that they have no sin, while in reality before God they are full of filth and abomination and do sin against God's law in the worst possible way, in that they lack the fear of God and make light of his wrath, and are haughty and proud and full of presumption by reason of their own good works and their own holiness, practicing idolatry with their self-chosen service of God, in addition to the fact that their hearts are full of uncleanness and inward disobedience to God's commandments, though outwardly they keep themselves from evil works; even as we ourselves in times past while pretending to be the most pious, did provoke God to the uttermost with the horrible idolatry of the mass, the worship of the saints, and our own monkish righteousness, wherewith we thought we were earning heaven to the disparagement of Christ's death and resurrection and to the lamentable delusion of ourselves and others.

44. For this reason St. John also continues his preaching of repentance and in verse 8 says to such people, "Bring forth therefore fruit worthy of repentance," etc.; that is, take my advice and do not become secure and proud from the start, but perceive your sin and God's wrath upon you, humble yourselves before him, and implore his mercy. If ye do this not, judgment is already passed upon you, yea, the ax is already laid to the tree to destroy it, both trunk and root, as one that beareth no good fruit and is good for nothing but to be cast into the fire and reduced to ashes, notwithstanding it is so tall and sturdy and has beautiful leaves: you, namely, priding yourselves upon being Abraham's children and the like.

45. This same preaching was later continued by the apostles. St. Peter, for instance, on the day of Pentecost and thereafter pointed out to the Jews what pious children they were and how they had earned God's favor by denying his dear Son, nailing him to the cross and slaying him. And St. Paul says in Acts 17:30-31: "But now he (God) commandeth men that they should all everywhere repent, inasmuch as he hath appointed a day in which he will judge the world in righteousness," etc.: that is, it is his will that all people, everywhere upon the earth, should know themselves, tremble at God's wrath, and understand that he will judge and condemn them unless they repent and obey this preaching.

46. So Christ also says in John 16:8 that the Holy Ghost will convict the world in respect of sin, etc. (by such preaching of repentance). For, as said above, such repentance reason cannot teach, much less accomplish, by its own strength; but, as Christ here says, it must be preached as a revelation, surpassing the understanding and wisdom of reason. As St. Paul also in Romans 1:18 calls it a revelation from heaven, saying, "For the wrath of God is revealed from heaven," etc. For no man's reason and no lawyer will say that I am a sinner and an object of God's wrath and condemnation if I do not steal, rob, commit adultery, and the like, but am a pious, respectable man in whom no one can find anything to reprove or censure, and I am a pious monk besides. Who would believe that I, if I be without faith, merit only God's wrath by this fine, honorable life and that I am practicing naught but abominable idolatry with this glorious service of God and this rigid training which, without God's command, I have undertaken of my own pleasure, and that thereby I am condemning myself to a deeper hell than others who are open sinners?

47. It is no wonder then, that, when the world hears this preaching unto repentance, whereby it is reproved, the lesser portion accepts it, while the greater masses, especially the knowing and righteous ones, despise it, toss their heads in defiance and say: Ho, how can that be true? Shall I suffer myself to be upbraided as a sinner and as an accursed man by people who come along with a new and unknown doctrine? Why, what have I done? I have surely kept myself with all earnestness from sin and have striven to do good. Shall all this be accounted nothing? Has all the world before our time been engrossed in errors? Have the lives and doings of all men been vain? How is it possible that God should take such a risk with the whole world and say they are all lost and condemned? Ha! The devil has commanded you so to preach. Thus they defend and confirm themselves in their, impenitence and by blasphemy and persecution of God's Word heap his wrath upon themselves all the more.

48. But in spite of this, such judgment and preaching ever continues and forces its way farther, as Christ here commands them simply to preach among all nations, to tell everybody, wherever they go, to repent, and to say that no one can escape God's wrath or be saved who does not accept this preaching. That to this end he rose from the dead, that he might found this kingdom, in order that this might be preached to them who should and would be saved and might be accepted and believed by them, though it anger the world, the devil, or hell.

49. Notice, we have considered the first part of this sermon, true repentance, which convicts not only a mass of evildoers whom all the world and the lawyers call transgressors (they, to be sure, also deserve severe punishment), but attacks the very people who in the sight of the world are the most pious and righteous, (yet are without knowledge of their sin and of Christ), and condemns them. It makes of repentance, not a work of ours brought about by our own thinking, and partial, pertaining to only a portion of our deeds and making it necessary for a man to search and consider a long time as to how, when, where, and how often he has sinned (although it is true that one single sin may give rise to this, as when David was reproved on account of adultery and murder). But repentance is a thing extending over the whole of your life and casting you all of a sudden, as by a thunderbolt from the skies, wholly and entirely under God's wrath, telling you that you are a child of hell, and terrifying your heart so that the world becomes too small for you.

50. Therefore you must make this distinction: You may refer to the repentance which may be called our own work, namely our own sorrow, confession, and satisfaction, to the schools of lawyers, or to children's schools, where it may serve for discipline and outward training; but you must keep it clearly apart from the true spiritual repentance wrought by God's Word wherever and whenever this Word smites the heart, making it tremble and quake at God's zealous and terrible wrath, and filling it so with dread that it knows not whither to flee.

51. Such contrition and repentance the Bible illustrates by means of numerous examples: as that of St. Paul when he was about to be converted, Acts 9:4, where Christ himself preaches repentance to him from heaven saying, "Saul, Saul, why persecutest thou me?" etc. And presently action and power accompany the words, so that he suddenly falls to the earth trembling and says in verse 6, "Lord, what wilt thou have me to do?" This is true contrition, not the product of his own mind; for he goes his way holding a strong conviction and assurance of his own holiness according to the law, conscious of no sin whereby he might have deserved God's wrath. But suddenly Christ shows him what he is, namely, a persecutor and murderer of Christ and of his church, a thing which hitherto he had not perceived, rather regarding his actions as manifestations of splendid virtue and of a godly zeal. Now, however, he is seized with such terror on their account as plainly indicates that with all his righteousness according to the law. he is condemned before God; and he is only too glad to hear from Christ the gracious assurance that he may obtain mercy and the forgiveness of his sins. In like manner we are told in Acts 2 how Peter stood up on the day of Pentecost and thereafter and hurled this thunderbolt at the whole Jewish nation that they were betrayers and murderers of their promised Christ, the Son of God; as the text says in verse 37: "Now when they heard this they were pricked in their heart, and said unto Peter and the rest of the apostles, Brethren, what shall we do?"

52. Behold, here too there is true repentance, which suddenly seizes the heart and fills it with mortal dread, because it feels God's wrath and condemnation weighing upon it, and begins to realize its real fault, of which it has heretofore known nothing, and is constrained to say, Ah, now what shall I do? Here is naught save only sin and wrath, a thing which hitherto, alas, I have neither known nor surmised. As St. Paul also says of the power of the Word which confronts men with God's wrath, Romans 7:9, "And I was alive apart from the law once," that is, presumptuous and secure, knowing of no sin nor of God's wrath. But when the commandment came and smote my heart then sin revived, so that I began to feel God's wrath and, thus, died; that is, I fell into fear, anxiety and despair, which I could not endure and in which I must have perished and fallen a prey to eternal death had I not again found help.

53. Now, when this has been duly preached, the other message must follow which Christ here commands us to preach, to wit, the forgiveness of sins. For it is not sufficient to speak only of sin and God's wrath and terrify the people. It is necessary, indeed, to begin one's preaching thus, so that the people may know and feel their sins and may also have a desire for grace, but this must not be our whole message, otherwise there would be no Christ and no salvation but only death and hell. Thus Judas, Christ's betrayer, made a strong enough beginning in the first part of his repentance, remorse and knowledge of his sin; yea, he was too strong on this point, because no consolation followed; so that he was unable to bear it and hurled himself forthwith into destruction and eternal death; as also did King Saul and many others. But this cannot be considered preaching aright or fully concerning repentance, as Christ would have this doctrine preached. For to this extent the devil himself is willing to serve as a preacher, though he has no call to preach, just as he is ever willing to use the name and Word of God, albeit but to deceive and work mischief. For he perverts both doctrines, comforting where comfort is not in place, or engaging solely in terrifying the people and leading them into despair. But Christ's intention is not that repentance shall be so preached as to leave the conscience in its terror-stricken state but that those who have been brought to a knowledge of their sins and are contrite in heart shall again be comforted and lifted up. For this reason he straightway adds the other part and commands us to preach not only repentance but also the forgiveness of sins. This, then, as he also says, is preaching in his name.

54. Therefore, when your conscience has become terrified by the preaching of repentance, whether it be through the spoken word or otherwise within your heart, you must remember that you are also to hear and grasp the other part Christ commanded to be preached to you, to wit: that, although you have merited eternal wrath and are deserving of hell-fire, yet God in his boundless goodness and mercy does not desire to leave you and see you perish in perdition, but he desires to forgive your sins, so that his wrath and your condemnation may be removed from you.

55. This is the comforting message of the Gospel, which a man cannot, of himself, understand as he of himself understands the preaching of the law (which was at the beginning implanted in his nature) when his heart is thereby smitten; but it is a special revelation and Christ's own peculiar voice. For human nature and reason cannot rise above the judgment of the law, which concludes and says: He that is a sinner is condemned of God. Wherefore all men would have to remain forever objects of wrath and condemnation if another and a new teaching had not been given from heaven. This teaching, in which God offers his grace and mercy to those who feel their sins and God's wrath, God's own Son himself must institute and command to be spread abroad in the world.

56. But in order that it may be apprehended and faithfully believed, this preaching must be done, as he here says, in his name; that is, not only in pursuance of his command, but also with the proclamation that sins are to be forgiven on his account and by reason of his merits. Hence we must acknowledge neither I nor any other man, with the exception of Christ, have accomplished or merited this, nor could have merited it in eternity. For how should I be able to merit it when I and all my life and whatever I may be able to do, is, according to the first part of this sermon, condemned before God?

57. But now, if God's wrath is to be taken away from me and I am to obtain grace and forgiveness, some one must merit this; for God cannot be a friend of sin nor gracious to it, nor can he remit the punishment and wrath, unless payment and satisfaction be made. Now, no one, not even an angel of heaven, could make restitution for the infinite and irreparable injury and appease the eternal wrath of God which we had merited by our sins; except that eternal person, the Son of God himself, and he could do it only by taking our place, assuming our sins, and answering for them as though he himself were guilty of them. This our dear Lord and only Savior and Mediator before God, Jesus Christ, did for us by his blood and death, in which he became a sacrifice for us; and with his purity, innocence, and righteousness, which was divine and eternal, he outweighed all sin and wrath he was compelled to bear on our account; yea, he entirely engulfed and swallowed it up, and his merit is so great that God is now satisfied and says, If he wills thereby to save, then there shall be a salvation. As Christ also says of his Father's will, John 6:40: "This is the will of my Father, that everyone that beholdeth the Son, and believeth on him, should have eternal life." Also Matthew 28:18: "All authority hath been given unto me in heaven and on earth." And in his prayer in John 17:1-2 he says: "Father, glorify thy Son, that the Son may glorify thee; even as thou gavest him authority over all flesh, that to all whom thou hast given him he should give eternal life."

58. This now he has not only actually fulfilled, but he has done and accomplished it for the very purpose of having it preached and proclaimed to us; otherwise we would know nothing of it, nor would we be able to attain to it. Therefore it is absolutely unmerited on our part and is given to us entirely free and out of pure grace, and just for the reason that we may be assured of such grace and have no cause for doubt in regard to it; for indeed, we must remain forever in doubt if we were required to look for merit of our own and to seek worthiness inhering in us, till our attainments were such that God would consider them and be gracious to us on their account. But now Christ commands that forgiveness of sins be preached in his name, so that I may know that they are undoubtedly remitted unto me on account of that which he has merited, and this he reveals and communicates to me through the Word.

59. And moreover I and everyone else for his own personal good may take comfort in this, and besides no one has any cause to be troubled and worried as to whether he dare appropriate this great mercy unto himself, for it is natural for man's heart to doubt and to argue thus with itself: Yes, I can easily believe that God has elected certain great men thereto, as, for instance, St. Peter, Paul, and others, but who knows whether I too am one of those to whom he is willing to grant grace? Perhaps I have not been ordained thereto—therefore Christ wills and herewith commands that this doctrine be spread, not in a corner nor to certain individuals only, yea, not even solely to the Jews, or to a few other nations at most, but throughout the whole wide world, or, as he says, to all nations; yes, as he says in Mark 16:15, to the whole creation. This Christ spoke in order that we may know that it is not his will that anybody anywhere should be cut off or barred out from the blessings of this preaching if he is only willing to accept them and does not bar himself out. For, as the preaching of repentance is to be a general preaching and to extend over all people so that all may perceive that they are sinners, just so general shall also this preaching of forgiveness be, and it shall be accepted by all, even as all men have stood in need of it from the beginning, and will continue so until the end of the world. For, why should the forgiveness of sins be offered and preached to all if they did not all have sin? That the truth may remain as St. Paul says, Romans 11:32: "God hath shut up all unto disobedience, that he might have mercy upon all," etc.

60. Hence this preaching also calls for faith; that is, I am to conclude from it with certainty and without a doubt, that for the sake of the Lord Jesus Christ, forgiveness of sins is granted me from the terrible wrath of God and from eternal death, and that it is God's will that I believe this preaching, not despising the proffered grace of Christ, not casting it aside, not making the Word of God a lie. For, since he commands that this Word be preached in all the world, he therewith and at the same time demands of everyone that he receive this preaching and hold and confess it to be the invariable, divine truth, that we assuredly receive these things for the sake of the Lord Jesus Christ; and, no matter how unworthy I feel myself to be, this must not hinder nor deter me from having this faith, if only my heart be so disposed that I feel sincerely displeased with my sins and heartily desire to get rid of them. For, as such forgiveness is not offered and preached to me on account of my worthiness, for I have clearly contributed nothing, neither labored to the end that Christ should merit forgiveness for me and have it proclaimed to me as he did and does; so, on the other hand, I am not to suffer any nor be deprived of forgiveness so long as I really desire it.

61. Finally, that our comfort may abound the more, Christ here makes the following arrangement respecting this preaching of repentance and of the forgiveness of sins: It shall not be merely temporary and momentary, as it were, but shall be in continual operation, never ceasing in Christendom so long as Christ's kingdom endures. For he wants us to have therein a lasting, eternal treasure and everlasting grace, which effectually worketh alway; so that we must not consider the forgiveness as being restricted to that one moment when the absolution was pronounced, nor as extending over previous and past sins only, as though thenceforward our works must render us perfectly clean and sinless.

62. For it is not possible in this present life on earth that we should so live as to be entirely free from sin and infirmity—not though we received grace and the Holy Spirit—owing to our sinful, depraved flesh and blood, which never ceases, this side of the grave, to bring forth evil lusts and desires, no, not in the saints; though they, on receiving grace, abstain from, and guard against, sin and resist their evil lusts, even as repentance requires; wherefore they too are still in daily need of forgiveness, even as they daily exercise themselves in repentance, by reason of these selfsame abiding infirmities and weaknesses; knowing, as they do, that their lives and works are yet sinful and merit God's wrath (to which they would also expose them) were it not for the fact that these things are forgiven for Christ's sake.

63. Therefore Christ has herewith instituted a kingdom on earth to be called an eternal kingdom of grace and always to be governed by the forgiveness of sins; and so powerful it is to protect those who believe that, although sin still lurks in their flesh and blood and is so deeply rooted that it cannot, in this life, be entirely eradicated, still it shall not bring injury upon them, but be remitted and not imputed to them, provided, however, that we abide in the faith and daily make endeavors to stamp out the remaining evil lust, until it has been exterminated, and utterly destroyed by death, and has rotted away in the grave and fallen a prey to the worms, that man may arise unto eternal life perfectly renewed and cleansed.

64. Yea, even though a man who is under grace and is sanctified fall away again from repentance and faith and thus lose his forgiveness, nevertheless this kingdom of grace stands firm and unmovable, so that one may at any time be reinstated in it, if one again belong to it by repentance and conversion: in like manner as the sun rises daily in the heavens, and not only banishes the past night but proceeds without interruption to shine throughout the day, even though it be darkened and covered with thick clouds, yes, even though someone close his doors and windows against its light, still it remains the selfsame sun and, breaking all barriers down, it again and again presents itself to view.

65. Behold, this is the true doctrine of the Gospel concerning Christian repentance, laid hold of and conceived in these two parts, to wit, contrition, or a sincere alarm on account of sin, and faith in forgiveness for Christ's sake. The entire papal church has hitherto taught nothing of this; and especially have they nowhere shown any knowledge of the faith in Christ which should be the chief part of this preaching: they have only directed people to their own works, and pronounced the absolution with this proviso that we have been duly contrite and properly made confession. And thus Christ has been so entirely forgotten and ignored, and the preaching he here commands has been so utterly perverted and beclouded, that there has been no repentance and absolution in his name but in our own names and for the sake of our works of contrition, confession, and satisfaction. This I call suppressing by force the faith and knowledge of Christ, yea, exterminating it, and taking from troubled consciences their comfort, leading them alone to perish in doubt, if they are not to be certain of the forgiveness of sin until they have sufficiently tortured, and made martyrs of themselves by their self-invented and involuntary contrition and confession.

66. And so the pope and all his band have by this one thing, that they have thus perverted and corrupted the doctrine of Christian repentance and forgiveness of sin, well enough deserved, and they daily still more deserve (since besides they refuse to repent of all this error and deception, which they themselves are forced to acknowledge, but rather blaspheme and storm against the plain truth) that they be cursed by all Christians into the abyss of hell, as Paul to the Galatians curses all those who teach another Gospel, etc. Galatians 1:9.

67. Here we should also say a word on the confession which we retain and which we commend as a beneficial, salutary thing. For although, properly speaking, it is not a part of repentance, and is not necessary and enjoined, still it serves us well in receiving absolution, which is nothing else than simply the preaching and announcement of the forgiveness of sins, which Christ here commands men both to preach and to hear. Since, however, it is necessary to retain such preaching in the church, the absolution should also be retained; for the only difference between the two is this: in the preaching of the Gospel the Word is publicly preached in a general way, to all who are present; and in absolution this same Word is spoken especially and privately to one or more who so desire it. This is in accord with Christ's institution, that such preaching of the forgiveness of sins should be carried on at all times and in all places, not only in a general way before a whole company but also before individual persons, wherever there are people who stand in need of it: as he says in the Gospel for the following Sunday, "Whose soever sins ye forgive, they are forgiven unto them."

68. Therefore we do not teach confession like the pope's theologians, that one must recite his sins, than which, according to the papists, there is no other way to confess, or that thereby one receives forgiveness and becomes worthy of absolution, as they say, On account of thy contrition and confession I declare thee free from thy sins. But we teach that one should use confession in order to hear the comfort of the Gospel and thus to awaken and to strengthen his faith in the forgiveness of sins, which is the main thing in repentance. So that "to confess" means not, as it does among the papists, to recount a long list of sins, but to desire absolution, which is in itself confession enough; that is, to acknowledge your guilt and confess that you are a sinner. And no more shall it be demanded or required that you mention by name all or several, many or few, of your sins, unless of yourself you have a desire to mention something which especially burdens your conscience and wherein you need instruction and advice or particular comfort, as is often necessary with young and inexperienced people, and also with others.

69. Therefore we commend and retain confession not on its own account but for the sake of absolution. And in confession this feature is the golden treasure, that there you hear proclaimed to you the words Christ commanded to be preached in his name to you and to all the world, so that even if you should not hear it in the confessional, still you otherwise hear the Gospel daily, which is nothing else than the word of absolution. For to preach the forgiveness of sins means nothing else than to absolve or to declare free from sin, which also takes place in baptism and in the Lord's Supper, which were also instituted for the purpose of showing to us this forgiveness of sins and assuring us of it. Thus to be baptized or to receive the communion is also an absolution, where forgiveness is, in Christ's name and at his command, promised and communicated to each one in particular. This forgiveness you should hear wherever and whenever you are in need of it, and should receive and believe it as though you heard it from Christ himself. For, because it is not our absolution but Christ's command and word, therefore it is just as good and valid as though it were heard proceeding from his own mouth.

70. Thus you see that everything that is taught concerning Christian repentance according to Scripture is wholly contained in the two parts called contrition, or alarm at God's wrath on account of our sins, and its antidote, faith that our sins are forgiven us for Christ's sake. For it has not been commanded that more than these two tidings be preached, to wit: the Law, which charges us with our sin and shows us the judgment of God; and the Gospel, which directs us to Christ and proclaims God's grace and mercy in him. And, to sum up all, repentance in its entirety is just that which the Scripture describes in other words in Psalm 147:11 and elsewhere, "Jehovah taketh pleasure in them that fear him, in those that hope in his lovingkindness." For there these two parts are also stated: the fear of God, which proceeds from a knowledge of our sins; and reliance upon his grace, as exhibited in the promises concerning Christ, etc.

71. What the papists say concerning "satisfaction," however, is, as said above, by no means to be tolerated; for that which in former times was called satisfaction and whereof one may still read in the writings of the ancient teachers, was nothing else than an outward and public punishment of those who were guilty of manifest vices, which they were compelled to bear before men, just as a thief or a murderer in the world's courts pays for his crime on the gallows or the wheel. Of this the Scripture nowhere teaches anything, nor does this contribute anything toward the forgiveness of sin, but may, as I have said, among other temporal things, be referred to the lawyers. But their claim that God punishes sins with temporal punishments and plagues, sometimes even when they have been forgiven, is true; but that is no satisfaction or redemption from sin, nor is it a merit on account of which sin is forgiven, but a chastisement which God inflicts to urge us to repentance.

72. .And even if one wished to retain the word "satisfaction" and explained it as meaning that Christ made satisfaction for our sins, it is nevertheless too weak and says too little concerning the grace of Christ and does not do honor enough to his sufferings, to which one should give higher honor, confessing that he not only has made satisfaction for sin but has also redeemed us from the power of death, the devil, and hell, and established an everlasting kingdom of grace and of daily forgiveness of the sin that remains in us; and thus is become for us, as St. Paul says in Corinthians 1:30, an eternal redemption and sanctification, as has been more fully discussed above.

Quasimodo Sunday After Easter. John 20:19-31

Jesus Appears to His Disciples, or the Nature, Fruit, and Power of Faith

John 20:27

"Then saith he to Thomas,
Reach hither thy finger,
and behold my hands;
and reach hither thy hand,
and thrust it into my side:
and be not faithless,
but believing."

(c) Norma Boeckler

Doubting Thomas

TEXT: John 20: 19 Then the same day at evening, being the first day of the week, when the doors were shut where the disciples were assembled for fear of the Jews, came Jesus and stood in the midst, and saith unto them, Peace be unto you. 20 And when he had so said, he shewed unto them his hands and his side. Then were the disciples glad, when they saw the Lord. 21 Then said Jesus to them again, Peace be unto you: as my Father hath sent me, even so send I you. 22 And when he had said this, he breathed on them, and saith unto them, Receive ye the Holy Ghost: 23 Whose soever sins ye remit, they are remitted unto them; and whose soever sins ye retain, they are retained. 24 But Thomas, one of the twelve, called Didymus, was not with them when Jesus came. 25 The other disciples therefore said unto him, We have seen the Lord. But he said unto them, Except I shall see in his hands the print of the nails, and put my finger into the print of the nails, and thrust my hand into his side, I will not believe. 26 And after eight days again his disciples were within, and Thomas with them: then came Jesus, the doors being shut, and stood in the midst, and said, Peace be unto you. 27 Then saith he to Thomas, Reach hither thy finger, and behold my hands; and reach hither thy hand, and thrust it into my side: and be not faithless, but believing. 28 And Thomas answered and said unto him, My Lord and my God.

29 Jesus saith unto him, Thomas, because thou hast seen me, thou hast believed: blessed are they that have not seen, and yet have believed. 30 And many other signs truly did Jesus in the presence of his disciples, which are not written in this book: 31 But these are written, that ye might believe that Jesus is the Christ, the Son of God; and that believing ye might have life through his name.

1. This Gospel praises the fruit of faith, and illustrates its nature and character. Among the fruits of faith are these two: peace and joy, as St. Paul writes to the Galatians, where he mentions in order all kinds of fruit saying: "But the fruit of the Spirit is love, joy, peace, longsuffering, kindness, goodness, faithfulness, meekness, self-control." Galatians 5:22. Thus these two fruits are also mentioned in our text. In the first place, Christ stands there among the disciples, who sit in fear and terror, and whose hearts are greatly troubled every hour expecting death; to them he comes and comforts them, saying: "Peace be unto you." This is one fruit. In the second place, there follows from this sweet word the other fruit, that they were glad when they saw the Lord. Then he further bestows upon faith power and authority over all things in heaven and on earth, and truly extols it in that he says: "As the Father hath sent me, even so send I you." And again: "Receive ye the Holy Spirit: who so ever sins ye forgive, they are forgiven unto them; whose soever sins ye retain, they are retained." Let us now consider each thought in order.

2. Faith, as we have often said, is of the nature, that everyone appropriates to himself the resurrection of the Lord Jesus Christ, of which we have already said enough; namely, that it is not sufficient simply to believe Christ rose from the dead, for this produces neither peace nor joy, neither power nor authority; but you must believe that he rose for your sake, for your benefit, and was not glorified for his own sake; but that he might help you and all who believe in him, and that through his resurrection sin, death and hell are vanquished and the victory given to you.

3. This is signified by Christ entering through closed doors, and standing in the midst of his disciples. For this standing denotes nothing else than that he is standing in our hearts; there he is in the midst of us, so that he is ours, as he stands there and they have him among them. And when he thus stands within our hearts, we at once hear his loving voice saying to the troubled consciences: Peace, there is no danger; your sins are forgiven and blotted out, and they shall harm you no more.

4. And this entrance the Lord made here through barred doors, going through wood and stone, and still leaving everything whole, breaking nothing, yet getting in among his disciples. This illustrates how the Lord comes into our hearts and stands in us, namely, through the office of the ministry. Therefore, since God has commanded men to preach his Word, one should in no wise despise a mortal man into whose mouth he has put his Word; lest we get the idea that everyone must expect a special message from heaven, and that God should speak to him by the word of his mouth. For if he imparts faith to anyone, he does it by means of the preaching of man and the external word of man. This is going through closed doors, when he comes into the heart through the Word, not breaking nor displacing anything. For when the Word of God comes, it neither injures the conscience, nor deranges the understanding of the heart and the external senses; as the false teachers do who break all the doors and windows, breaking through like thieves, leaving nothing whole and undamaged, and perverting, falsifying and injuring all life, conscience, reason, and the senses. Christ does not do thus. Such now is the power of the Word of God. Thus we have two parts, preaching and believing. His coming to us is preaching; his standing in our hearts is faith. For it is not sufficient that he stands before our eyes and ears; he must stand in the midst of us in our hearts, and offer and impart to us peace.

5. For the fruit of faith is peace; not only that which one has outwardly, but that of which Paul speaks to the Philippians (Philippians 4:7) saying it is a peace that passeth all reason, sense and understanding. And where this peace is, one shall not and cannot judge according to reason. This we shall see still farther in our Gospel lesson.

6. First, the disciples sit there behind barred doors in great fear of the Jews, afraid to venture outside, with death staring them in the face. Outwardly they indeed have peace, no one is doing them any harm; but inwardly their hearts are troubled, and they have neither peace nor rest. Amid their fear and anguish the Lord comes, quiets their hearts and makes them glad, so that their fear is removed, not by removing the danger, but in that their hearts were no more afraid. For thereby the malice of the Jews is not taken away, nor changed; they rave and rage as before, and outwardly everything remains the same. But they are changed inwardly, receiving such boldness and joy as to declare: "We have seen the Lord." Thus he quiets their hearts, so that they become cheerful and fearless, not caring how the Jews rage.

7. This is the true peace that satisfies and quiets the heart; not in times when no adversity is at hand, but in the midst of adversity, when outwardly there is nothing but strife before the eyes. And this is the difference between worldly and spiritual peace. Worldly peace consists in removing the outward evil that disturbs the peace; as when the enemies besiege a city there is no peace; but when they depart peace returns. Such is the case with poverty and sickness. While they afflict you, you are not contented; but when they are removed and you are rid of the distress, there is peace and rest again from without. But he who experiences this is not changed, being just as fainthearted whether the evil be present or not; only he feels it and is frightened when it is present.

8. Christian or spiritual peace, however, just turns the thing about, so that outwardly the evil remains, as enemies, sickness, poverty, sin, death and the devil. These are there and never desist, encompassing us on every side; nevertheless, within there is peace, strength and comfort in the heart, so that the heart cares for no evil, yea, is really bolder and more joyful in its presence than in its absence. Therefore it is peace which passeth and transcendeth all understanding and all the senses. For reason cannot grasp any peace except worldly or external peace, for it cannot reconcile itself to it nor understand how that is peace if evil is present, and it knows not how to satisfy and comfort a person; hence it thinks if the evil depart, peace departs also. When however the Spirit comes, he lets outward adversity remain, but strengthens the person, making the timid fearless, the trembling bold, changing the troubled into a quite, peaceful conscience, and such an one is bold, fearless and joyful in things by which all the world otherwise is terrified.

9. Whence does he receive this? From his faith in Christ. For if I truly believe in the Lord from the real depth of my heart, that my heart can truly say: My Lord Christ has by his resurrection conquered my need, my sin, death and all evil, and will be thus with and in me, so that body and soul shall want nothing, that I shall have all I need, and no evil shall harm me: if I believe this, it is impossible for me to be faint-hearted and timid no matter how much sin and death oppress me. For faith is ever present and says: Does sin burden you, does death terrify you, look to Christ who died for your sake and rose again, and conquered every evil; what can harm you?

Why will you then fear? So also in case other misfortunes burden you, as sickness or poverty, turn your eyes from it, lock the door to reason and cast yourself upon Christ and cleave to him, so shall you be strengthened and comforted. If you look to Christ and believe on him, no evil that may befall you is so great that it can harm you and cause you to despair. Therefore it is impossible for this fruit to remain outside, where faith is, so that peace does not follow.

10. From peace the other fruit now follows, as is taught in this Gospel. When Christ came to the disciples and said: "Peace be unto you!" and showed them his hands and feet; then they were glad that they saw the Lord. Yes, to be sure they had to be glad, for that they saw Christ was the greatest joy the heart of man can experience. Hitherto we have been permitted to see our hands, that is, we have been taught to trust in our works; this brought no gladness. But to see Christ makes us glad. And this takes, place by faith; for thus St. Paul in Romans 5:1-2 says: "Being therefore justified by faith, we have peace with God through our Lord Jesus Christ; through whom also we have had our access by faith into this grace wherein we stand; and we rejoice in hope of the glory of God."

11. Thus we have the fruit whereby we know who are true Christians. For he who has no peace in that in which the world finds nothing but unrest, and is joyful in that which in the world is nothing but gloom and sorrow, is not yet a Christian, and does not yet believe. This truth is being also sung at this season everywhere in the hymn on the Lord's resurrection; but hardly anybody understands it. He who composed it surely understood it aright. He does not stop at the Lord is risen, when he says: "Christ is risen from his Passion;" as though this were sufficient, but brings it home to us and adds: Let us all rejoice in this. But how can we rejoice in it, if we have nothing of it and it is not ours? Therefore, if I am to rejoice in it, it must be mine, that I may claim it as my own property, that it may profit me. And finally he closes: Christ will be our consolation, that we can and shall have no other consolation but Christ. He wants to be it himself and he alone, that we should cling to him in every time of need; for he has conquered all for our benefit, and by his resurrection he comforts all troubled consciences and sad hearts. This the Gospel teaches concerning faith and its fruits.

12. Now follows the office of the ministry. The power of faith now develops love. For it does not yet suffice that I have the Lord so that he is mine, and that I find in him all comfort, peace and joy; but I must henceforth also do as he has done: for it follows thus in the text: "As the Father hath sent me, even so send I you."

13. The first and highest work of love a Christian ought to do when he has become a believer, is to bring others also to believe in the way he himself came to believe. And here you notice Christ begins and institutes the office of the ministry of the external Word in every Christian; for he himself came with this office and the external Word. Let us lay hold of this, for we must admit it was spoken to us. In this way the Lord desires to say: You have now received enough from me, peace and joy, and all you should have; for your person you need nothing more. Therefore labor now and follow my example, as I have done, so do ye. My Father sent me into the world only for your sake, that I might serve you, not for my own benefit. I have finished the work, have died for you, and given you all that I am and have; remember and do ye also likewise, that henceforth ye may only serve and help everybody, otherwise ye would have nothing to do on earth. For by faith ye have enough of everything. Hence I send you into the world as my Father hath sent me; namely, that every Christian should instruct and teach his neighbor, that he may also come to Christ. By this, no power is delegated exclusively to popes and bishops, but all Christians are commanded to profess their faith publicly and also to lead

14. Secondly, if you have exercised yourself in this highest work and taught others the right way of truth, then make up your mind to keep on and serve everybody. Then the example of your life and good works follows; not that you can thereby merit and acquire anything, seeing you have beforehand everything that is necessary to salvation. Furthermore Christ now gives a command, he breathes upon the disciples and says: "Receive ye the Holy Spirit: whose soever sins ye forgive, they are forgiven unto them; whose soever sins ye retain, they are retained."

15. This is a great and mighty power which no one can sufficiently extol, given to mortal men of flesh and blood over sin, death and hell, and over all things. The pope too boasts in the canon law that Christ has given to him power over all earthly things; which would indeed be correct if the people rightly understood it. For they apply it to the civil government; this is not Christ's thought; but he gives spiritual power and rule, and wishes to say this much: When ye speak a word concerning a sinner, it shall be spoken in heaven, and shall avail so much as if God himself spake it in heaven; for he is in your mouth, therefore it has the same force as if he himself spoke it. Now it is always true, if Christ speaks a word, since he is Lord over sin and hell, and says to you: Thy sins are forgiven; then they must be forgiven and nothing can prevent it. Again, if he says: Thy sins shall not be forgiven thee; then they remain unforgiven, so that neither you, nor an angel, nor a saint, nor any creature, can forgive your sin, even if you martyred yourself to death.

16. This same power belongs to every Christian, since Christ has made us all partakers of his power and dominion; and here his is not a civil but a spiritual rule, and his Christians also rule spiritually. For he does not say: This city, this country, this bishopric or kingdom you shall rule, as the pope does; but he says: Ye shall have power to forgive and to retain sins. Hence this power pertains to the conscience, so that by virtue of God's Word I can pass judgment as to what the conscience can cleave to, so that against and above that no creature can do anything, neither sin, nor the world nor Satan. This is true power. But thereby no power is given me to rule over temporal matters, over a country and people, externally after the manner of civil governments, but a much higher and nobler power, which can in no sense be compared with it.

17. Therefore we shall thank God, that we now know the great power and glory given us through Christ in his plain Word, as St. Paul also highly praises and extols it to the Ephesians, saying: "Blessed be the God and Father of our Lord Jesus Christ, who hath blessed us with every spiritual blessing in the heavenly places in Christ." Ephesians 1:3. And again: "God made us alive together with Christ, and raised us up with him, and made us sit with him in heavenly places, in Christ Jesus: that in the ages to come he might show the exceeding riches of his grace in kindness toward us in Christ Jesus: for by grace have ye been saved through faith; and that not of yourselves, it is the gift of God; not of works, that no man should glory. For we are his workmanship, created in Christ Jesus for good works, which God afore prepared that we should walk in them." Ephesians 2:5-10.

18. Observe, what great transcendent comfort we have in that God awakens in us also the same power he exercises in Christ, and bestows upon us equal authority. As he made him sit in heavenly places, above all power and might, and everything that can be named; so has he invested us also with the same power, that those who believe have all power over heaven and earth. This we have in the words he left behind him; and they are so powerful, that when they are spoken by us, they avail as much as if he himself were on earth and spake them in the majesty and glory in which he now exists. And this is the power we have from his resurrection and ascension; there he gives us power to. kill and to make alive, to consign to the devil and to rescue from him.

19. But in this matter one must proceed carefully, and not do like the popes. For they have reached the point to have the power, that however and whatever they say, so it must be, because they say it. Nay, this power you have not, but the divine Majesty alone has. it. They say thus: If the pope speaks a word and says: Thy sins are forgiven thee, they are blotted out, even though you neither repent nor believe. They mean by this, that they have the power to bestow and withhold heaven, to open or shut it, to locate one in heaven or cast into hell; far from it that it should be so. For from this it would then follow that our salvation depended on the works, authority and power of man. Therefore, since this is in conflict with all the Scriptures it cannot be true that when you open or shut, it must be open or shut.

20. Therefore we must rightly understand Christ when he says: "Whose soever sins ye forgive, they are forgiven unto them; whose soever sins ye retain, they are retained," that this does not establish the power of him who speaks but of those who believe. Now the power of him who speaks and of him who believes are as far apart as heaven and earth. God has given us the Word and the authority to speak; but it does not therefore follow from this that it must so be done, as Christ also preached and taught the Word, and yet not all who heard it believed, and it was not everywhere done as he spake the Word, although it was God's Word. Therefore Christ's meaning is: Ye shall have the power to speak the Word, and to preach the Gospel, saying, Whosoever believeth, has the remission of his sins; but whosoever believeth not, has no remission of sin. But ye have not the power to create faith. For there is a great difference between planting and giving the growth; as Paul says to the Corinthians: "I planted, Apollos watered; but God gave the increase." 1 Corinthians 3:6. Hence we have no authority to rule as lords; but to be servants and ministers who shall preach the Word, by means of which we incite people to believe. Therefore, if you believe the Word, you gain this power; but if you believe not, then what I speak or preach will avail nothing even though it be God's Word; and if you believe not these words you are not treating me but God himself with dishonor and contempt.

21. Therefore, unbelief is nothing but blasphemy, which makes God a liar.

For if I say, your sins are forgiven you in God's name, and you believe it not, it is the same as if you said: who knows whether it be true, and whether he be in earnest? by this you charge God and his Word with lying. Therefore you better be far from the Word, if you believe it not. For when a man preaches his Word, God would have it as highly esteemed as if he himself had preached it. This then is the power given by God. which every Christian has, and of which we have already spoken much and often; hence this is enough for the present.

Quasimodo. Sunday after Easter. Second Sermon. John 20:19-31

True Piety, the Law and Faith, and Love to our Neighbor.

John 20:19 Then the same day at evening, being the first day of the week, when the doors were shut where the disciples were assembled for fear of the Jews, came Jesus and stood in the midst, and saith unto them, Peace be unto you. 20 And when he had so said, he shewed unto them his hands and his side. Then were the disciples glad, when they saw the Lord. 21 Then said Jesus to them again, Peace be unto you: as my Father hath sent me, even so send I you. 22 And when he had said this, he breathed on them, and saith unto them, Receive ye the Holy Ghost: 23 Whose soever sins ye remit, they are remitted unto them; and whose soever sins ye retain, they are retained. 24 But Thomas, one of the twelve, called Didymus, was not with them when Jesus came. 25 The other disciples therefore said unto him, We have seen the Lord. But he said unto them, Except I shall see in his hands the print of the nails, and put my finger into the print of the nails, and thrust my hand into his side, I will not believe. 26 And after eight days again his disciples were within, and Thomas with them: then came Jesus, the doors being shut, and stood in the midst, and said, Peace be unto you. 27 Then saith he to Thomas, Reach hither thy finger, and behold my hands; and reach hither thy hand, and thrust it into my side: and be not faithless, but believing. 28 And Thomas answered and said unto him, My Lord and my God. 29 Jesus saith unto him, Thomas, because thou hast seen me, thou hast believed: blessed are they that have not seen, and yet have believed. 30 And many other signs truly did Jesus in the presence of his disciples, which are not written in this book: 31 But these are written, that ye might believe that Jesus is the Christ, the Son of God; and that believing ye might have life through his name.

1. In today's Gospel is presented to us, what the life of a Christian is to be and that it consists of two parts: first, that the Lord shows Thomas his hands and feet; secondly, that he is sent as Christ is sent. This is nothing else than faith and love, the two thoughts that are preached to us in all the Gospel texts.

2. Formerly you heard, and alas! it is preached in all the world, that if anyone desires to become righteous, he must begin with human laws. This was done under the reign of the pope, and nearly all the very best preachers preached nothing else than how one is to be outwardly pious, and about good works which glitter before the world. But this is still far from the true righteousness that avails before God.

3. There is another way to begin to become righteous, which commences by teaching us the laws of God, from which we learn to know ourselves, what we are, and how impossible it is for us to fulfill the divine commandments. The law speaks thus: Thou shalt have one God, worship him alone, trust in him alone, seek help and comfort from him alone. Exodus 20. The heart hears this and yet it cannot do it. Why then does the law command such an impossible thing? In order, as I have said, to show us our inability, and that we may learn to know ourselves and to see ourselves as we are, even as one sees himself in a mirror. When now the conscience, thus smitten by God's law, begins to quake and finds that it does not keep God's commandment, then the law does its proper work; for the true mission of the law is only to terrify the conscience.

4. But there are two classes of men who fulfill the law, or who imagine they fulfill it. The first are those who, when they have heard it, begin with outward works; they desire to perform and fulfill it by works. How do they proceed? They say: God has commanded thou shalt have one God; I surely will worship no other God; I will serve him and no idol, and will have no heathen idolatrous image in my house or in my church; why should I do this? Such persons make a show with their glittering, fabricated service of God, like the clergy in our day, and they think they keep this law, when they bend their knees and are able to sing and prate much about God. By this show the poor laity also are deceived; they follow after and also desire to obey the law by their works. But the blind guides the blind and both fall into a pit, Luke 6:39. This is the first class, who take hold and imagine they will keep the law, and yet they do not.

5. The other class are those who know themselves by the law and study what it seeks and requires. For instance, when the law speaks: "Thou shalt have one God, and worship and honor him alone," this same heart meditates: What does this mean? Shalt thou bend the knees? Or what is it to have one God? It surely is something else than a bodily, outward reverence; and finally it perceives that is a very different thing than is generally supposed; that it is nothing but having trust and hope in God, that he will help and assist in all anxiety and distress, in every temptation and adversity, that he will save him from sin, from death, from hell and from the devil, without whose help and salvation he alone can do nothing. And this is the meaning of having one God. A heart, so thoroughly humble, desires to have God, namely, a heart that has become quite terrified and shaken by this commandment, and in its anxiety and trouble flees to God alone.

6. This now the hypocrites and work-saints, who lead a fine life before the world, are not able to do; for their confidence is based alone upon their own righteousness and outward piety. Therefore, when God attacks them with the law and causes the poor people to see that they have not kept the law, aye, not the least of it, and when overwhelmed by anxiety and distress, and an evil conscience, and they perceive that external works will not suffice and that keeping the commandments of God is a very different thing from what they thought; then they rush ahead and seek ever more and more, and other and still other works, and fancy that they will thereby quiet their conscience; but they greatly miss the right way. Hence it comes to pass that one wishes to do it by rosaries, another by fasting; this one by prayer and that one by torturing his body; one runs to St. James, another to Rome, this man to Jerusalem, that to Aix; here one becomes a monk, another a nun, and they seek their end in so many ways that they can scarcely be enumerated.

7. Why do they do all this? Because they wish to save themselves, to rescue and help themselves. The consequence of this is great blasphemy of God, for they also boast mightily of these works, and vaunt and say: I have been in an order so long, I have prayed so many rosaries, have fasted so much, have done this and that; God will give me heaven as a reward. This then means to have an idol. This also is the meaning of Isaiah, when he says: "They worship the work of their own hands," Isaiah 2:8. He is not speaking of stone and wood, but of the external works, which have a show of goodness and beauty before men. These hypocrites are ingenious enough to give the chaff to God and to keep the wheat for themselves. This then is true idolatry, as St. Paul writes to the Romans: "Thou that abhorrest idols, dost thou rob temples?" Romans 2:22. This is spiritual robbery.

8. Therefore you will find that there is nothing good in any man of himself. But you have this distinction, that the upright, in whom the law has exercised its work, when they feel their sickness and weakness, say: God will help me; I trust in him; I build upon him; he is my rock and hope. But the others, as hypocrites and work-saints, when trial, distress and anxiety are at hand, lament and say: Oh, whither shall I go? They must at last despair of God, of themselves and of their works, even if they have ever so many of them.

9. Such in the first place are these false and unrighteous pupils of the law, who presume to fulfill it by their works. For they have an appearance and glitter outwardly, but in their hearts they have nothing but filth and uncleanness. Therefore they also merit nothing before God, who regards not external works that are done without any heart in them.

10. In the second place they are the true and real pupils, who keep the law, who know and are conscious that they do evil, and make naught of themselves, surrender themselves, count all their works unclean in the eyes of God, and despair of themselves and all their own works. They who do this, shall have no trouble, except that they must not deceive themselves with vain fruitless thoughts and defer this matter until death; for if anyone persistently postpones this until death, he will have a sad future.

11. But we must give heed that we do not despair, even if we still feel sinful inclinations and are not as pure as we would like to be. You will not entirely sweep out of your heart all this rubbish, because we are still flesh and blood. This much can surely be done: outward wicked deeds can be prevented and carnal, shameful words and works avoided, although it is attained with difficulty. But it will never come to pass here that you are free from lust and evil inclination. St. Jerome undertook to root such inclinations out of his heart by prayer, fasting, work and torture of the body; but he found out what he accomplished; it was of no avail, the concupiscence remained. Works and words can be restrained, but lust and inclinations no one can root out of himself.

12. In short, if you desire to attain the true righteousness that avails before God, you must despair altogether of yourself and trust in God alone; you must surrender yourself entirely to Christ and accept him, so that all that he has is yours, and all that is yours, becomes his. For in this way you begin to burn with divine love and become quite another man, completely born anew, and all that is in you is converted. Then you will have as much delight in chastity as before you had pleasure in unchastity, and so forth with all lusts and inclinations.

13. This now is the first work of God, that we know ourselves, how condemned, miserable, weak and sickly we are. It is then good and God's will, that a man desponds and despairs of himself, when he hears: This shalt thou do and that shalt thou do. For everybody must feel and experience in himself, that he does not and cannot do it. The law is neither able nor is it designed to give you this power of obeying it; but it effects what St. Paul says: "The law worketh wrath," Romans 4:15, that is, nature rages against the law, and wishes the law did not exist.

14. Therefore they who presume to satisfy the law by outward deeds, become hypocrites; but in the others it works wrath only, and causes sins to increase, as St. Paul says in another place: "The power of sin is the law." 1 Corinthians 15:56. For the law does not take sin away, aye, it multiplies sin, and causes me to feel my sin. So he says again to the Corinthians: "The letter killeth," 2 Corinthians 3:6, that is, the law works death in you; in other words, it reduces you to nothing; "but the Spirit giveth life." For when he comes through the Gospel, the law is already fulfilled, as we shall hear.

15. Therefore the world errs, when it tries to make men righteous through laws; only pretenders and hypocrites result from such efforts. But reverse this and say as St. Paul says: The law produces sin. For the law does not help me the least, except that it teaches me to know myself; there I find nothing but sin; how then should it take sin away? We will now see how this thought is set forth in this Gospel. The text says: "When therefore it was evening, on that day, the first day of the week, and the doors were shut where disciples were for fear of the Jews."

16. What do the disciples fear? They fear death; aye they were in the very midst of death. Whence came their fear of death? From sin, for if they had not sinned, they would not have feared. Nor could death have injured them; for the sting of death, by means of which it kills, is sin, Corinthians 15:56. But they, like us all, had not yet a true knowledge of God. For if they had esteemed God as God, they would have been without fear and in security; as David says: "Whither shall I go from thy Spirit? Or whither shall I flee from thy presence? If I ascend up into heaven, thou art there: if I make my bed in Sheol, behold, thou art there. If I take the wings of the morning, and dwell in the uttermost parts of the sea; even there shall thy hand lead me, and thy right hand shall hold me." Psalm 139:7-10. And as he says in another place: "In peace will I both lay me down and sleep; for thou, Jehovah, alone makest me dwell in safety," Psalm 4:8. It is easy to die, if I believe in God; for then I fear no death. But whoever does not believe in God, must fear death, and can never have a joyful and secure conscience.

17. Now God drives us to this by holding the law before us, in order that through the law we may come to a knowledge of ourselves. For where there is not this knowledge, one can never be saved. He that is well needs no physician; but if a man is sick and desires to become well, he must know that he is weak and sick, otherwise he cannot be helped. But if one is a fool and refuses to take the remedy that will restore him to health he must certainly die and perish. But our papists have closed our eyes, so that we were not compelled, and not able, to know ourselves, and they failed to preach the true power of the law. For where the law is not properly preached, there can be no self-knowledge.

18. David had such knowledge, when he said: "Have mercy upon me, O God, according to thy lovingkindness; according to the multitude of thy mercies blot out my transgressions. Wash me thoroughly from mine iniquity, and cleanse me from my sin. For I know my transgressions; and my sin is ever before me. Against thee, thee only, have I sinned, and done that which is evil in thy sight, that thou mayest be justified when thou speakest, and be clear when thou judgest. Behold, I was brought forth in iniquity; and in sin did my mother conceive me." Psalm 51:1ff. Just as if David wished to say: Behold, I am so formed of flesh and blood, which of itself is sin, that I cannot but sin. For although you restrain your hands and feet or tongue, that they sin not; the inclinations and lusts always remain, because flesh and blood are present, you may go whither you please, to Rome or to St. James.

19. If now an upright heart that comes to the point of knowing itself is met by the law, it verily will not begin and seek to help itself by works; but it confesses its sin and helplessness, its infirmity and sickness, and says: Lord God, I am a sinner, a transgressor of thy divine commandments: help thou, for I am lost. Now when a man is in such fear and cries out thus to God, God cannot refrain from helping him; as in this case Christ was not long absent from the disciples tormented by fear; but he is soon present, comforts them and says: "Peace be unto you!" Be of good courage; it is I; fear not. The same happens now. When we come to a knowledge of ourselves through the law and are now in deep fear, God arouses us and has the Gospel preached to us, by which he gives us a joyful and secure conscience.

20. But what is the Gospel? It is this, that God has sent his Son into the world to save sinners, John 3:16, and to crush hell, overcome death, take away sin and satisfy the law. But what must you do? Nothing but accept this and look up to your Redeemer and firmly believe that he has done all this for your good and freely gives you all as your own, so that in the terrors of death, sin and hell you can confidently say and boldly depend upon it, and say: Although I do not fulfill the law, although sin is still present and I fear death and hell, nevertheless from the Gospel I know that Christ has bestowed upon me all his works. I am sure he will not lie, his promise he will surely fulfill. And as a sign of this I have received baptism. For he says to his apostles and disciples: "Go ye into all the world, and preach the Gospel to the whole creation. He that believeth and is baptized shall be saved; but he that disbelieveth shall be condemned," Mark 16:15-16. Upon this I anchor my confidence. For I know that my Lord Christ has overcome death, sin, hell and the devil all for my good. For he was innocent, as Peter says: "Who did no sin, neither was guile found in his mouth." 1 Peter 2:22. Therefore sin and death were not able to slay him, hell could not hold him, and he has become their Lord, and has granted this to all who accept and believe it. All this is effected not by my works or merits; but by pure grace, goodness and mercy.

21. Now whoever does not appropriate this faith to himself, must perish; and whoever possesses this faith, shall be saved. For where Christ is, the Father will come and also the Holy Spirit. There will then be pure grace, no law; pure mercy, no sin; pure life, no death; pure heaven, no hell. There I will comfort myself with the works of Christ, as if I myself had done them. There I will no longer concern myself about cowls or tonsures, St. James or Rome, rosaries or scapularies, praying or fasting, priests or monks.

22. Behold, how beautiful the confidence towards God that arises in us through Christ! You may be rich or poor, sick or well, yet you will always say: God is mine, I am willing to die; for this is acceptable to my Father, and death cannot harm me; it is swallowed up in victory, as St. Paul says in 1 Corinthians 15:57, yet not through us, but "Thanks be to God," says he, "who giveth us the victory through our Lord Jesus Christ." Therefore although we must die, we have no fear of death, for its power and might are broken by Christ, our Savior.

23. So then you understand that the Gospel is nothing but preaching and glad tidings, how Christ entered into the throes of death for us, took upon himself all our sins and abolished them; not that it was needful for him to do it, but it was pleasing to the Father; and that he has bestowed all this upon us, in order that we might boldly stand upon it against sin, death, Satan and hell. Hence arises great, unspeakable joy, such as the disciples here experience. The text says: "The disciples therefore were glad, when they saw the Lord" — not a Lord, who inspired them with terror or burdened them with labor and toil, but who provided for them and watched over them like a father is the lord of his estate and cares for his own. Aye, then first they rejoiced most on his account, when he spake to them: "Peace be unto you! It is I", and when he had showed unto them his hands and feet, that is, his works, all which were to be theirs.

24. In the same manner he still comes to us through the Gospel, offers us peace and bestows his works upon us: if we believe, we have them; if we believe not, we have them not. For the Lord's hands and feet really signify nothing but his works, which he has done here upon earth for men. And the showing of his side is nothing but the showing of his heart, in order that we may see how kind, loving and fatherlike his mind is toward us. All this is set forth for us in the Gospel as certainly and clearly as it was revealed and shown to the disciples bodily in our text. And it is much better that it is done through the Gospel than if he now entered here by the door; for you would not know him, even if you saw him standing before you, even much less than the Jews recognized him.

25. This is the true way to become righteous, not by human commandments, but by keeping the commandments of God. Now nobody can do this except by faith in Christ alone. From this flows love that is the fulfillment of the law, as St. Paul says in Romans 13:10. And this results not from the exercise of virtues and good works, as was taught hitherto, which produced only true martyrs of Satan and hypocrites; but faith makes righteous, holy, chaste, humble and so forth. For as Paul says to the Romans: "The Gospel is the power of God unto salvation to everyone that believeth; to the Jew first and also to the Greek. For therein is revealed a righteousness of God from faith unto faith: as is written, But the righteous shall live by faith." Romans 1:16-17. As if St. Paul should say: Your works will not save you but the Gospel will, if you believe; your righteousness is nothing, but Christ's righteousness avails before God; the Gospel speaks of this and no other writing does. Whoever now wishes to overcome death and blot out sins by his works, says that Christ has not died; as St. Paul says to the Galatians, "If righteousness is through the law, then Christ died for naught." Galatians 2:21. And they who preach otherwise are wolves and seducers.

26. This has been said of the first part of our Gospel, to show what is to be our attitude toward God, namely, we are to cling to him in faith; and it shows what true righteousness is that is availing before God and how it is attained, namely, by faith in Christ, who has redeemed us from the law, from death, sin, hell and the devil; and who has freely given us all this in order that we may rely upon it in defiance of the law, death, sin, hell and the devil. Now follows how we are to conduct ourselves toward our neighbor; this is also shown to us in the text, where the Lord speaks thus:

II. Of Love of Your Neighbor

"As the Father hath sent me, even so send I you."

27. Why did God the Father send Christ? For no other purpose than to do the Father's will, namely, to redeem the world. He was not sent to merit heaven by good works or to become righteous thereby. He did many good works, aye, his whole life was nothing else than a continual doing good.

But for whom did he do it? For the people who stood in need of it, as we read here and there in the Evangelists; for all he did, he did for the purpose of serving us. "As the Father hath sent me," he says here, "even so send I you." My Father hath sent me to fulfill the law, take the sin of the world upon myself, slay Death and overcome hell and the devil; not for my own sake, for I am not in need of it; but all for your sakes and in your behalf, in order that I may serve you. So shall you also do.

28. By faith you will accomplish all this. It will make you righteous before God and save you, and likewise also overcome death, sin, hell and the devil. But this faith you are to show in love, so that all your works may be directed to this end; not that you are to seek to merit anything by them; for all in heaven and earth is yours beforehand; but that you serve your neighbor thereby. For if you do not give forth such proofs of faith, it is certain that your faith is not right. Not that good works are commanded us by this Word; for where faith in the heart is right, there is no need of much commanding good works to be done; they follow of themselves. But the works of love are only an evidence of the existence of faith.

29. This also is the intent of St. Peter, when he admonishes us in Peter 1:5, to give diligence to make our faith sure and to prove it by our good works. But good works are those we do to our neighbor in serving him, and the only one thing demanded of a Christian is to love. For by faith he is already righteous and saved; as St. Paul says in Romans 13:8: "Owe no man anything, save to love one another: for he that loveth his neighbor hath fulfilled the law." Therefore Christ says to his disciples in John 13:34-35: "A new commandment I give unto, you, that ye love one another; even as I have loved you, that ye also love one another. By this shall all men know that ye are my disciples, if ye have love one to another."

30. In this way we must give proof of ourselves before the world, that everyone may see that we keep God's commandment; and yet not that we would be saved or become righteous thereby. So then I obey the civil government for I know that Christ was obedient to the government, and yet he had no need to be; he did it only for our sakes. Therefore I will also do it for Christ's sake and in behalf of my neighbor, and for the reason alone that I may prove my faith by my love; and so on through all commandments. In this manner the Apostles exhort us to good works in their writings; not that we become righteous and are saved by them, but only to prove our faith both to ourselves and others, and to make it sure. The Gospel continues: "Receive ye the Holy Spirit: Whose soever sins ye forgive, they are forgiven unto them; whose soever sins ye retain, they are retained."

31. This power is here given to all Christians, although some have appropriated it to themselves alone, like the pope, bishops, priests and monks have done: they declare publicly and arrogantly that this power was given to them alone and not to the laity. But Christ here speaks neither of priests nor of monks, but says: "Receive ye the Holy Spirit," Whoever has the Holy Spirit, power is given to him, that is, to everyone that is a Christian. But who is a Christian? He that believes. Whoever believes has the Holy Spirit. Therefore every Christian has the power, which the pope, bishops, priests and monks have in this case, to forgive sins or to retain them.

32. Do I hear then, that I can institute confession, baptize, preach and administer the Lord's supper? No. St. Paul says in 1 Corinthians 14:40: "Let all things be done decently and in order." If everybody wished to hear confession, baptize and administer the Lord's supper, what order would there be? Likewise, if everybody wished to preach, who would hear? If we all preached at the same time, what a confused babble it would be, like the noise of frogs! Therefore the following order is to be observed: the congregation shall elect one, who is qualified, and he shall administer the Lord's supper, preach, hear confession and baptize. True we all have this power; but no one shall presume to exercise it publicly, except the one who has been elected by the congregation to do so. But in private I may freely exercise it. For instance, if my neighbor comes and says: Friend, I am burdened in my conscience; speak the absolution to me; then I am free to do so, but I say it must be done privately. If I were to take my seat in the church, and another and all would hear confession, what order and harmony would there be? Take an illustration: If there are many heirs among the nobility, with the consent of all the others they elect one, who alone administers the estate in behalf of the others; for if everyone wished to rule the country and people, how would it be? Still they all alike have the power that he has who rules. So also is it with this power to forgive sins and to retain them.

33. But this word, to forgive sins or to retain sins, concerns those who confess and receive more than those who are to impart the absolution. And thereby we serve our neighbor. For in all services the greatest is to release from sin, to deliver from the devil and hell. But how is this done? Through the Gospel, when I preach it to a person and tell him to appropriate the words of Christ and to believe firmly that Christ's righteousness is his own and his sins are Christ's. This I say, is the greatest service I can render to my neighbor.

34. Accursed be the life, where one lives only for himself and not for his neighbor; and on the contrary, blessed be the life, in which one lives not for himself but for his neighbor and serves him by teaching, by rebuke, by help and by whatever manner and means. If my neighbor errs, I am to correct him; if he cannot immediately follow me, then I am to bear patiently with him; as Christ did with Judas, who had the purse with the money and went wrong and stole from it. Christ knew this very well; yet he had patience with him, admonished him diligently, although it did no good, until he disgraced himself.

35. So we are to give heed to do everything in behalf of our neighbor, and ever to be mindful, that Christ has done this and that for me; why should I not also for his sake freely do all for my neighbor? And see to it that all the works you do, are directed not to God, but to your neighbor. Whoever is a ruler, a prince, a mayor, a judge, let him not think that he is a ruler to gain heaven thereby or to seek his own advantage; but to serve the public. And so with other works, I assume to do for the good of my neighbor. For example if I take a wife, I make myself a captive; why do I do this? In order that I may not do harm to my neighbor's wife and daughters, and thus may bring my body into subjection; and so forth with all other works.

36. Thus then you have finely portrayed in this Gospel, as in almost all the Gospel lessons these two thoughts, faith and love. Through faith we belong above to God: through love below to our neighbor. That we may thus lay hold of this truth may God give us his help! Amen.

Quasimodo. Sunday After Easter. Third Sermon. John 20:19-31

The Fruit of Christ's Resurrection.

KJV John 20:19 Then the same day at evening, being the first day of the week, when the doors were shut where the disciples were assembled for fear of the Jews, came Jesus and stood in the midst, and saith unto them, Peace be unto you. 20 And when he had so said, he shewed unto them his hands and his side. Then were the disciples glad, when they saw the Lord. 21 Then said Jesus to them again, Peace be unto you: as my Father hath sent me, even so send I you. 22 And when he had said this, he breathed on them, and saith unto them, Receive ye the Holy Ghost: 23 Whose soever sins ye remit, they are remitted unto them; and whose soever sins ye retain, they are retained. 24 But Thomas, one of the twelve, called Didymus, was not with them when Jesus came. 25 The other disciples therefore said unto him, We have seen the Lord. But he said unto them, Except I shall see in his hands the print of the nails, and put my finger into the print of the nails, and thrust my hand into his side, I will not believe. 26 And after eight days again his disciples were within, and Thomas with them: then came Jesus, the doors being shut, and stood in the midst, and said, Peace be unto you. 27 Then saith he to Thomas, Reach hither thy finger, and behold my hands; and reach hither thy hand, and thrust it into my side: and be not faithless, but believing. 28 And Thomas answered and said unto him, My Lord and my God. 29 Jesus saith unto him, Thomas, because thou hast seen me, thou hast believed: blessed are they that have not seen, and yet have believed. 30 And many other signs truly did Jesus in the presence of his disciples, which are not written in this book: 31 But these are written, that ye might believe that Jesus is the Christ, the Son of God; and that believing ye might have life through his name.

1. The first part of this Gospel lesson is the same narrative we heard in the Gospel for Tuesday after Easter. The incident occurred on the evening of Easter, called by the Evangelists the first Sabbath, when Christ appeared for the first time to his frightened disciples, as they all with the exception of Thomas were assembled, and comforted and strengthened them in the faith of his resurrection. Thus we hear again what the power and benefit of Christ's resurrection are, namely, that Christ, when he comes with such a sermon, brings peace and joy; and these are the true fruits of faith as they are mentioned among the other fruits of the Spirit by St. Paul in Galatians 5:22.

2. For when he comes he finds his disciples still sitting in fear and terror both from without because of the Jews and from within because of their consciences, and yet very weak and slow of heart to believe, although they had heard from the women and some of the disciples that he had risen from the dead. But while this saddened their hearts and they were talking with one another about it, behold, Christ appears and hails them with the friendly greeting after the Hebrew custom, "Peace be unto you!" which means in our language, to wish one everything good. For we call that peace where all goes well, the heart is contented, and prosperity reigns. This is the joyful message Christ always brings with him, as he repeats it the second and third time in this narrative.

3. But this Peace of Christ is very secret and hidden from the eyes and the senses, for it is not of the nature that the world pictures and seeks, or as flesh and blood understand. For Christians can for the sake of Christ never expect any peace or any good from his enemies, the devil and the world. They must daily suffer misfortune and contention, for they are alarmed and afflicted and harassed by the devil with the terrors of sin and its punishment, by the world with its persecution and tyranny, and by the flesh with its own weakness, impatience, etc. Hence this is not a visible or tangible peace, consisting of bodily feeling, but an inner and spiritual peace, consisting in faith, which grasps and holds fast to nothing but what it hears in our text, namely, these gracious Words of Christ, which he speaks to all frightened and troubled souls: "Pax tibi; Peace be unto thee. Fear not" etc. And such a Christian, therefore, is contented and satisfied with having Christ as his friend and with having a gracious God who desires his constant welfare, even though, materially speaking, he has no peace in the world, but constant strife and contention. This is the peace of which St. Paul speaks in Philippians 4:7: "The peace of God, which passeth all understanding, shall guard your hearts and your thoughts in Christ Jesus," and of which Christ says in John 16:33: "These things have I spoken unto you, that in me ye may have peace. In the world ye have tribulation,"

4. For the devil will not allow a Christian to have peace; therefore Christ must bestow it in a manner different from that in which the world has and gives, in that he quiets the heart and removes from within fear and terror, although without there remain contention and misfortune. And this we see in the example of these disciples of Christ, who are in great fear on account of the Jews; they are behind barred doors, not daring to go forth, and are in constant dread of death. Although they have peace without and are annoyed by no one, nevertheless their hearts are all aflutter, and they have neither rest nor peace. While they are thus in fear and terror, the Lord enters; he quiets their hearts and brings them peace, not by removing the danger, but by quieting their hearts. For the wickedness of the Jews is neither removed nor changed thereby, for they are as full of hatred and rage as before, and without there is no change whatever, but within the disciples are changed, they have become courageous and bold, and the hatred of the Jews is for them now of but little concern.

5. This is the true peace, which is able to calm the heart, not in time of good fortune, but in the midst of misfortune, when without there is nothing but contention. For here is the difference between worldly and spiritual peace. Worldly peace consists in removing the external evils which cause the contention, as for example, when enemies besiege a city, there is war, but when they are gone, peace returns. Thus also, when poverty and sickness are pressing thee, thou art not contented, but when they are removed, and thou art rid of the misfortune externally, thou art again at peace and rest. But he who endures this is not changed; he remains just as discouraged when these things exist as when they do not, the only difference being that he is feeling it and that it oppresses him when it is present.

6. But with the Christian or spiritual peace we find just the opposite conditions, namely, that the evils without remain, such as foes, sickness, poverty, sin, the devil, and death. They are ever present and are surrounding us; nevertheless there is internal peace, strength and comfort in the heart, so that the heart does not concern itself about misfortune, yea, is even more courageous and joyful in the presence than in the absence of misfortune. It can therefore indeed be called a peace, which passeth all understanding. For reason understands and seeks no other peace but that which comes from without through possessions which the world can give, but which knows not how to quiet and comfort the heart in times of need, when all else fails. But when Christ comes, he does not change the outward unpleasant conditions, but strengthens the person, and makes out of a timid, a fearless heart, out of a trembling, a bold heart; and out of a disquieted, a peaceful, quiet conscience, so that the person is courageous, bold, and joyful in the midst of those things in which otherwise all the world is terrified; that is, in death, terror of sin, and all distress, in which the world with its comfort and possessions can render no help. This, then, is a true and constant peace, which remains forever and is invincible as long as the heart clings to Christ.

7. Hence, this peace is nothing else than that the heart is certain that it has a merciful God and the forgiveness of sins, for without this it can neither stand in the time of need and danger, nor be satisfied by any earthly fortune.

8. But this takes place and is accomplished only when Christ shows us his hands and his side; that is, when he shows us through the Word how he was crucified for us and shed his blood and died, in order that he might pay the debt of our sins and reconcile and avert the wrath of God. This is the sure token that comforts the frightened conscience and heart and gives assurance of divine grace and forgiveness of sin. These he shows, so that they may never doubt, but be sure that it is he himself, who is not angry with them, but is their dear Savior; for this peace is not so easily grasped by them nor by any troubled consciences, as long as they are terrified and in the conflict. Therefore he comes and strengthens them both with the Word and with visible signs.

9. This he still does constantly after his resurrection, not visibly but through the voice of the ministry, which we are to believe, even though we do not see him, as he also says at the close of this Gospel, through which he also shows how he shed his blood for us; for it is indeed sufficient that he showed this once to his disciples, to strengthen their and our faith and to show that he is truly risen and is the same Christ who for our sakes was nailed to the cross and pierced.

10. Therefore, the second thing which follows the friendly greeting of Christ, or the offering of peace, and the showing of his hands and side, if it is received by faith, is called joy, as the text says: "The disciples therefore were glad, when they saw the Lord." For it is indeed the greatest joy the heart of man can experience, again to see and recognize Christ, who had been dead to him before, and with whom all comfort and joy had fled; and when he can now again have the joyful comfort in him, and know that he has in him a dear Savior, and through him has found grace and comfort with God against all the terror of sin and death, and against the power of the world and of hell. This is what St. Paul means in Romans 5:1: "Being therefore justified by faith, we have peace with God through our Lord Jesus Christ; through whom also we have had our access by faith into this grace wherein we stand" etc.

11. Of this we sing also at this season in the old Easter hymn on the resurrection of the Lord: "Christ is risen from all his pangs," for we are not only told of the story of his resurrection, but it is also brought close to us, and we are told to rejoice in it as our treasure and salvation, through which we have peace and every good gift from God. For how could we rejoice in him, if we had nothing of him nor appropriated as our own possession that which he has done for us. Therefore he also wishes to teach us that Christ is our comfort, and this comfort we should surely obtain and desire no other on which we can depend in every time of need. For through his resurrection he has conquered all and bestows upon us as our own all that he has done and suffered.

12. But from the fact that Christ comes to the disciples through the door that is closed, we are to learn that after his resurrection and in his kingdom here upon earth he is no longer bound by bodily, visible, tangible and worldly things, as time, place, space and the like, but that he is to be recognized and believed in as one who through his power can reign everywhere, who can be present with us at all places and at all times, when and wherever necessary, and who will help us without being taken captive and hindered by the world and its power.

13. In the second place, he also shows that wherever he comes with his government and rule, through the office of the Word, he does not come with a great noise, with storm and commotion, but very orderly; not changing nor breaking anything in the outward affairs of human life and government. He simply permits these things to remain in their condition and office as he finds them, and governs Christendom in a way that orderly government is neither abolished nor weakened upon the earth. Thus he does not derange and displace anything in man, neither his senses nor his reason; but he illuminates and changes for the better his heart and reason.

14. The devil, on the contrary, disorganizes and ruins everything through his factious and disturbing spirits, his ratling and boisterous servants, in the external and worldly government and life as well as internally in the hearts of men, whom he really makes insane and blind by his evil spirits, as we now have experienced with his insurrectional prophets, fanatics, and Anabaptists.

15. This the first part of this Gospel treats of how Christ comforts and gladdens his dear disciples through his resurrection, and resurrects them, together with himself, from the heavy death and sorrow of their hearts, in that Christ was now lost and eternally dead to them. And as they now have this benefit and fruit, and in order that this power and comfort of the resurrection be made known to others, he continues and gives the command to spread the same in the world through their office, as we read:

II. The Government and Office of the Keys Christ Instituted

"Jesus therefore said to them again, Peace be unto you; as the Father hath sent me, even so send I you. And when he had said this, he breathed on them and saith unto them. Receive ye the Holy Spirit: whose soever sins ye forgive, they are forgiven unto them; whose soever sins ye retain, they are retained."

16. The Lord shows with these words what he accomplished through his resurrection, namely, that he established a government, which shall have nothing to do with money and gold, or anything that pertains to the temporal life, or how we are to acquire and keep them. For such a government already existed, being established from the beginning of the world, and being made subject to the reason of man through the Word of God, as he says in Genesis 1:28: "Have dominion over the fish of the sea, and over the birds of the heavens, and over every living thing that moveth upon the earth." This is the ancient government, in which the worldly power legislates and executes, for which the Holy Spirit is not needed, and concerning which little need be taught in Christianity. Jurists may counsel and help as to how that shall be carried on.

17. But in addition to this there is another government, which is above the conscience and is concerned with things that relate to God. This government is of two kinds: One was founded by Moses, and the other the Lord established here, when he said: "As the Father hath sent me, even so send I you," etc. The government of Moses is to serve to the end that it may teach us what sin is and what sin is not, and it belongs to those who neither know nor feel sin, as at present the Antinomians who say the law need not be preached. It is fruitless to teach much of grace among these people, for if the law is not preached, we cannot know sin, as St. Paul says: "Without the law sin is dead," which means where no law is, there is no transgression; for sin, no matter how great it may be, and the wrath of God, are known only through the law. Therefore, when the law is not preached, the people become perfect heathen, and think they do right, although they sin grossly against the commandment of God.

18. Worldly authority indeed may punish and restrain open sin; but it does this too little, though it take to its aid all the books of the jurists, in order to illustrate or teach what sin is before God. Therefore the law is given that people may learn from it what is sin. Where sin continues unknown we cannot understand, much less desire, forgiveness and grace. Yea, even grace itself is then of no avail, for grace should fight and conquer in us against the law and sin, that we despair not. Just as a good physician must be experienced in his profession, first to know the nature of the disease, for otherwise, if he wishes to help the patient without knowing the cause of the sickness, he might give him dangerous poison instead of helpful medicine. Thus sin must first be known and experienced before we can preach grace. But the law is needed to gain such a knowledge, and it is necessary to instruct the people in the catechism, and diligently to teach them the ten commandments. For, as I have already said, human reason with all its wisdom and all the skill of the jurist, is unable to gain this knowledge. And although there is implanted into it a little of this knowledge, yet this is too insignificant; therefore God established the preaching of the law of Moses, which he had first received from the patriarchs.

19. Such preaching Christ himself instituted, when he commanded his disciples, as we have heard in the last Gospel lesson, first to preach repentance in his name; and John 16:8 says: "The Holy Spirit will convict the world in respect of sin" etc., for although it really belongs to the government of Moses to expose sin, nevertheless, that Christ may come to his government and work the beginning must be made by preaching the law where there is no consciousness of sin; for where that is not done, sin cannot be forgiven.

20. The other government or kingdom is that founded on the resurrection of Christ, for thereby he desired to establish a new kingdom which has to do with sin that has been awakened by the law, and with death and hell. This does not teach us anything about marriage, the household, the rule of a city and country, how to preserve the worldly peace, how to build and plant etc., but its aim is to show us where we may abide when this temporal, perishable kingdom and existence have passed away, when we must leave behind possessions, honor, home, farm, world and all that is upon the earth, together with this life, as we expect every moment. Now to this end has been established the kingdom of Christ, who is enthroned therefore as an eternal King, that he is Lord over sin and righteousness, over death and life. His kingdom has to do with, and to rule over, these things. This is what the Lord means when he says: "Receive ye the Holy Spirit: whose soever sins ye forgive, they are forgiven unto them; and whose soever sins ye retain, they are retained." Here you can see that his object is to deliver the people from sin, or to permit them to remain in sin, and show that they are condemned.

21. Certainly, we cannot say that he has thereby founded a worldly kingdom, as the pope boasts of his power of the keys, that he has the power to loosen and to bind even that which is not sin, yea, even that which Christ neither binds nor loosens, thereby making of it a worldly power. But Christ shows clearly enough here what his keys are, namely, they are not to make laws and abolish them again, as the pope is doing, but to remit or retain sin. He wishes to say: For this purpose shall my kingdom exist: First, that people may become conscious that they are sinners. This I have commanded Moses to teach, not for the purpose, however, of binding them, for they are indeed already bound; neither for the purpose of creating sin nor having anything to do with created sin, as the pope through his commandments and with his power of the keys is doing, creating sin where there is no sin: but for the purpose of dealing with those transgressions which naturally are sins against the commandments of God, as for example, despising God and unbelief, blaspheming his name, despising his Word, disobedience etc., which are indeed not sin by virtue of the commandments of the pope, but sins in truth, which are ingrained into the flesh and blood of man, which cannot be absolved nor removed through the loosing key of the pope as he uses it, but remain in man until he is in his grave.

22. It is the purpose of the kingdom of Christ that we may know now how we may be freed from sin. It is, therefore, called not a temporal or earthly kingdom, but the kingdom of heaven; for it shall just commence when this temporal kingdom ceases through death, in order that the people may know how they shall then reach heaven. This kingdom, he says, shall begin and continue thus: "As the Father hath sent me, even so send I you."

23. With these words he takes away from his disciples first their carnal mind, which they still possessed after his resurrection, that he would, like a temporal King and Lord, rule and reign with external and carnal power. Therefore he says: You have now seen what kind of an office I have filled upon the earth, for which I was sent by my Father, that I should establish a spiritual kingdom against that of the devil, sin and death, and thereby to bring them that believe on me to eternal life. This I have now done, and finished it as far as my person is concerned, and have not taken upon myself anything of a worldly character and rule. Yea, I have also been put to death by the world because of this my office and service, and am separated from it, but now through my resurrection I have entered into that glory where I shall reign forever over all creatures at the right hand of my Father. Therefore I send you also forth in like manner to be my messengers, not to engage in temporal affairs, but to conduct the same office as I have hitherto filled, namely: to preach the Word you have heard and received from me, an office through which people are delivered from sin and death, who experience sin and death, and wish to be delivered from them.

24. By means of this office the apostles and their successors are exalted also as lords unto the end of the world, and there is given to them such great authority and power as Christ, the Son of God, himself possessed, in comparison with which the power and dominion of all the world is nothing (although before the world it neither resembles nor is called dominion). And yet this office shall not and cannot extend further than over that alone which before God is called sin; so that wherever sin begins and works their government or rule shall also begin and work, and everything that lives and is called human upon the earth, shall be in subjection to their rule, whether it be emperor or king, great or small, no one is excluded. Therefore he says: "Whose soever sins ye remit." This "whose soever" means nothing else than that all are included, Jews, Gentiles, great and small, wise and ignorant, holy or unholy; that no one shall enter heaven and come to eternal life, except he receive it from you, that is, through the office which you have received.

25. For they all are also subject to and concluded under sin through these words, by which he shows that upon earth they shall find nothing but sin, and he pronounces the judgment, that all mankind to whom the apostles and their successors shall be sent are sinners and condemned before God in their person and life, and that one of two things must take place: either their sins are forgiven, if they confess and desire forgiveness, or they must remain eternally bound in sin unto death and condemnation.

26. Now in order to exercise and accomplish the end of this authority and government, special power is required that is not human but divine. Therefore he does not give them swords and weapons, neither does he equip them with armor and worldly power, but he breathes on them and says: "Receive ye the Holy Ghost," namely, they are to know that such an office and work cannot be carried on in their own strength, but in his power through the Holy Spirit, who operates through their office and word; and it shall thus be the office of the Holy Spirit, who is given for this purpose by Christ, that although the message seems but weak, and nothing more than a weak breath out of the mouth of man, yet such power shall be exercised through it, that sin, God's wrath, death, and hell must yield to it.

27. For this we can also easily give an answer, if anyone should ask and critically question how can man forgive sins, since this belongs to God alone? For it is indeed true that it is not in the power nor ability of man, nor of his merit and worthiness, to forgive sins, even though he were as holy as all the apostles together and all the angels in heaven. Therefore we condemn the pope himself with his monks, who promise the people forgiveness of sins by virtue of their own merit, works and holiness, and give them absolution, and thus shamefully deceive the poor people, who long for true and sure comfort.

28. But here we must make a true difference, which the papists and their rabble neither know nor can give, namely, between that which man is able to do by his own power and worthiness, and that which is commanded to be done in the name of Christ, and which he accomplishes through his power. It avails nothing, to be sure, when a barefooted trickster comes along and undertakes to give absolution and forgiveness to a poor conscience by virtue of his own sorrow and repentance, and the merits of the saints and his order, as indeed their indulgences read (of which they can be convicted through the letters of their brotherhood which they have sold to the people): "The merits of the sufferings of Christ and of Mary, the blessed Virgin, and all the saints; the merits of this severe and grievous order, the humility of thy repentance and sorrow of heart, and all good works that thou hast done or shalt do, shall serve thee to the forgiveness of thy sins and eternal life," etc. This is indeed nothing else than fearful blasphemy of Christ, and the perversion of the right absolution, for even though they remember his sufferings, yet they are not sincere in it, for they do not consider it efficacious enough for the forgiveness of sins, but must add the merits of Mary and of the saints, and especially of their own order and monkish doings and put them on an equality with Christ's sufferings. This they do without any command from Christ; yea, against his Word and command. This is not from the Holy Spirit, but from their own spirit, the devil, who is the father and founder of this false doctrine.

29. But for the absolution to be right and efficacious, it must spring from the command of Christ, which is as follows: I declare thee free from all thy sins, not in my own name, nor in the name of any saint, nor for the sake of any human merit, but in the name of Christ and by the authority of his command, who has commissioned me to say to you that all your sins are forgiven, hence, not I but he himself by his own mouth forgives thee thy sins, and thou art under obligation to receive this and believe it firmly, not as the word of man, but as if thou hadst heard it from the lips of the Lord Christ himself.

30. Therefore, although this power to forgive sins belongs to God only, we should nevertheless know that he exercises and imparts this power through this external office, to which Christ has called his apostles, and commands them to proclaim in his name forgiveness of sins to all who desire it. Sins, are forgiven, therefore, not by human will and power, but by the command of Christ, for this purpose he then also sends the Holy Spirit, namely, in order to forgive sins.

31. God also does this for our welfare, so that we need not look up to heaven in vain, when we receive it not, and be compelled to say as St. Paul does, when he quotes Moses: "Who shall ascend unto heaven?" etc. But he does this that we may have the assurance of it, he has placed the forgiveness of sins in the public office and the Word, in order that we may continually have it with us, upon our lips and in our hearts. There we shall find absolution and forgiveness, and we know that where we hear this message proclaimed to us by the command of Christ we are bound to believe it as if it were announced to us by Christ himself.

32. Behold, such is the authority given through this office of the apostles to the church which extends farther and higher than all the authority upon earth, that without it no one, and it matters not how great and mighty he may be, shall come nor can come to God, nor have the comfort of conscience, nor be free from God's wrath and eternal death. For although all emperors and kings were to concentrate their might and power, their money and possessions, they could deliver neither themselves nor any human being from the least sin, for if the heart of man is intimidated, what matters it whether he be a mighty king or emperor? What did it help the great and mighty king Nebuchadnezzar of Babylon when he became insane, so that he was rejected by his people and had to lie with the irrational beasts of the field and eat grass, and nothing could help him except that the prophet Daniel had to absolve him from his sins?

33. But who can express what an unspeakable, mighty and blessed comfort it is that a human being can with one word open heaven and lock hell to a fellow mortal? For in this kingdom of Grace Christ has founded through his resurrection, we do indeed nothing else than open our mouth and say, I forgive thee thy sins, not on my account, nor by my power, but in the place of, and in the name of, Jesus Christ, for he does not say: ye shall forgive sins on your own account, but: "I send you, as my Father hath sent me." I myself do not do this of my own choice or counsel, but I am sent by the Father. This same commandment I give to you unto the end of the world, that both ye and all the world shall know that such forgiveness or retaining of sin is not done by human power or might, but by the command of him who is sending you.

34. This is not said alone to the ministers or the servants of the church, but also to every Christian. Here each may serve another in the hour of death, or wherever there is need, and give him absolution. If you now hear from me the words, "Thy sins are forgiven thee," then you hear that God wants to be gracious to you, deliver you from sin and death, and make you righteous and blessed.

35. Yea, you say, thou hast indeed given me absolution, but who knows whether it is certain and true with God that my sins are forgiven? Answer: If I have done this and said this as a man, then thou mayest well say: I do not know whether thy absolution is effective and efficacious or not, but that thou mayest be sure concerning this, thou must be instructed in the Word of God, that thou canst say, I have been absolved neither by the minister nor by any other man; for thus the minister has not taught me to believe: but God has spoken and done it through him; of this I am sure, for my Lord Christ has commanded and said: As my Father hath sent me, so also send I you. Here he indeed puts those to whom he gives the command on an equality with himself, because they are sent by him to accomplish that for which he is sent by God, namely, to remit and retain sins. There it rests and that does it, otherwise, without such a command, absolution would amount to nothing.

36. If thou, therefore, art sad and worried on account of thy sins, and art afraid of death, with which God eternally punishes sin, and thou hearest of thy minister, — -or if thou canst not have access to him, — -of a Christian neighbor comforting thee with these or similar words: Dear brother or sister, I see that thou art timid and in despair, and fearest the wrath and judgment of God on account of thy sins, of which thou art conscious, and on whose account thou art terrified — listen to me and let me announce to you, Be of good comfort and cheer, for Christ thy Lord and Savior, who came into the world for the sake of sinners in order to save them, has given the command through the public office to his called servants, and wherever necessary, to everyone in particular, that one is to comfort another for Christ's sake, and in his name acquit him of his sins. I say, when thou therefore hearest this comfort, then receive it with joy and thanksgiving, as if thou didst hear it from Christ himself; then thy heart shall indeed be at peace, established and comforted, and thou canst then joyfully say: I have heard a man speak to me and comfort me; for the sake of himself I did not believe a single word, but I believe my Lord Christ, who has established this kingdom of Grace and forgiveness of sins, and has given this commandment and authority unto men to remit and retain sins in his name.

37. Therefore every Christian when the devil attacks him and suggests that he is a great sinner, and he must be lost and condemned etc., should not long contend with him or remain alone, but go or call to him his minister, or any other good friend, lay his difficulty before him, and seek counsel and comfort from him, and remain firm in that which Christ here declares: "Whose soever sins ye remit etc.," and as he says in another place: "Where two or more are gathered together in my name, there am I in the midst of them," and whatever this person says to him in the name of Christ from the Scriptures, let him believe it, for according to his faith it shall be done unto him. For two or more come together in the name of Christ when they converse with one another, not on temporal things, how money and riches may be acquired or gained; but on what would be of service for the salvation and happiness of their souls; as for instance, when thou art in the confessional or anywhere else art making known thy weaknesses and temptations, and he to whom thou art disclosing it sees that Moses through the law has thee in a dilemma; that thy sin is oppressing thee; that death is alarming and frightening thee, and thou groanest and complainest concerning thine own life, so that even words like these are apt to fall: Oh, that I had never been born, or, Oh, that God would prolong my life, I would amend my life, etc.

38. If then thy pastor of anyone else begins to comfort thee, not in a worldly way nor for the sake of money, but because he sees thou art in anxiety and fear of sin and death, and says to thee, Let everything go that is upon earth — -money, goods, everything that pertains to man, and pay now attention to this; thy heart is indeed in great pangs and asks: Can I be freed from my suffering, misery, and evil conscience? How can I escape Moses with his fearful threats? I say, listen to him when he speaks to thee in this manner: I say to thee in the name of the Lord Christ, who died for thy sins, that thou art to permit thyself to be comforted, to believe and be sure that thy sins are forgiven, and that death cannot harm thee.

39. Yea, my dear brother, you say, how wilt thou prove that this is true? Answer: Christ our Lord said to his disciples and to entire Christendom: I command and bid you, that ye shall forgive and retain sin. Whatever ye do then in this, ye do not of yourselves; but because ye are doing it at my command and bidding, therefore I do it myself. Therefore thy minister or pastor as the one who cares for thy soul (Seelsorger), or any Christian in such a case is called for and sent to comfort thee. And because he is seeking only the salvation of thy soul, thou art, therefore, bound to believe him as though Christ were standing there himself and would lay his hand upon thee and speak the absolution.

40. Behold, this is the way we deal with sins, retaining or forgiving them. Besides this there is no counsel nor help for them; as the pope pretends to do with his false doctrine, points the people to their own works or sufficiency, tells them to go into cloisters, to Rome, to the saints, torture themselves, build churches, heavily endow cloisters, hold mass, etc. This is indeed not the right way. Thou canst indeed employ thy going, money, and works in a better manner. Here the matter is entirely different, as has already been said. For when Moses comes with his fearful threats, that is, when he through the law reveals to thee thy sins and shows how great and many they are, and brings thee into great fear and despair, when thou art no more in the great, wicked, and hardened multitude, but with the little flock, which realizes and feels, its misery and despair, and would therefore indeed be frightened even at the rustling of a leaf, then this is the only help: I, I have founded, says Christ, the kingdom of Grace. It shall consume and destroy sin and death, and bring to light righteousness and life.

41. Therefore do not say: Where shall I find this? Shall I go to Rome or Jerusalem for it? Not in this way; yea, even if thou couldest ascend to heaven, and if possible on a golden ladder, thou couldst accomplish nothing; but it must come thus: give heed to his Word and command when he says: "I send you," etc., as if he wanted to say: I must first come to you to announce to you the will of my Father through the Gospel; institute the holy sacraments: and absolution. You should not come to me in a different way. But since I cannot be bodily at all places in the whole world, and shall not be visibly present with you always, I will do as my Father hath done.

He took a small corner of the earth, namely, the land of Judea, to which he sent me, that I should be a preacher there; I traveled through Galilee and Judea; so much I could accomplish personally; I preached the Gospel to the comfort of the poor sinners among the Jewish people, healed the sick and raised the dead etc. This, you will notice, was the work entrusted to him.

For this purpose he was sent by the Father. There he was found, not in the courts of kings among the debauchers, not with Annas, Caiaphas, and other holy, rich, and learned people; but among the blind, lame, lepers, the deaf, the dead, and the tempted, the poor and afflicted sheep. To this he brings help for soul and body. He brings to them the most costly treasure, which no one has, much less can give, unless he receives it from him, namely, righteousness and salvation. And thus, he says, ye shall also do at all places wherever ye go, and to this purpose I send you, that ye shall run as my messengers through the entire world. And besides you and after you I will ordain others who shall run and preach, as I sent you, even unto the end of the world, and I will continue to be with you that ye may know that it is not you who are accomplishing this, but I through you.

42. From this command we also have the power to comfort the sorrowful consciences and to absolve from sin, and we know that, wherever we exercise this office, not we but Christ himself is doing it. Therefore every Christian, in this case as well as when he hears the Word preached in the pulpit, should hear the same, not as the word of man, but as the Word of God himself; then he can indeed be sure and need not doubt a moment that he has the forgiveness of sins, for Christ has established through his resurrection that whenever a called servant of the Church, or someone else in the time of need, absolves his neighbor who is distressed and desires comfort, it shall count as much as if Christ had done it himself, because it was done at his command and in his name.

43. Therefore, when two deal thus with each other they are gathered together in the name of Christ, for, as we have said before, none is seeking the money or goods of the other, as the servants of the pope are doing, who speak to the sick and say: My dear man, the time is at hand when thou must die. Where shall thy possessions go? Think of thy poor soul and give a portion to us and we will pray to God for thee, and do much with it afterwards etc.; instead he ought to speak to the sick and say: This is no time to be occupied with your money and property, let others care for that. I see very well thy heart is despondent and terrified; thou art wrestling with doubts and canst not help thyself nor deliver thyself; but Christ has established upon the earth a comforting and blessed kingdom, when he says: "As my Father hath sent me, so send I you." He has consecrated us all to be priests, in order that one may proclaim to the other forgiveness of sins. Therefore I come to thee in the name of this our blessed Lord Christ, and tell thee not to be so despondent and terrified as though there were no comfort, help, and counsel any more to be had. Dost thou not hear what Christ says, that he came for the sake of the sinners, not the righteous, to save them? Therefore be at peace, receive these glad tidings with joy and thank him for them most heartily, that he permits me to announce to thee without any trouble and expense on thy part; yea, he even gives command to the effect that thy sins are remitted. Therefore I absolve and make thee free from all thy sins, in the name of the Father, and of the Son, and of the Holy Ghost. To this thou shalt reply joyfully: I thank thee, merciful God, thou heavenly Father, that thou hast forgiven me my sins through thy dear Son Christ; and do not doubt that thou art surely absolved by God the Father himself.

44. From this you can see that this paragraph concerning the office of the keys does not at all confirm the tyranny of the pope, but it is there for the purpose, not that thou makest me, or I thee, rich, nor that I be thy Lord and thou my subject, as the pope, the arch-rogue and denier of God, indeed is making out of it worldly pomp and power; but that I can come to thee, when thy conscience is worried, to help and counsel thee in thy last hour, or at other times, and say: Power, money, honor and goods, everything must be set aside; we have now only to speak of the kingdom of Christ — only through this and through nothing else must thou be helped from sin and death.

45. This signifies indeed not an external and worldly dominion or power but a service, for I am seeking nothing from thee, I want to serve thee and bring thee a great and precious treasure, but not gold and silver; because thy heart desires to be comforted and to have a merciful God in heaven I come to thee and bring thee this joyful message, not of my own will or choice, but at the command and commission of Christ, who says: "Come unto me, all ye that are weary and heavy laden, and I will give you rest." Also, "Whatsoever ye shall loose on earth, shall be loosed in heaven," or as he says in this connection, "Whose soever sins ye remit, they are remitted unto them."

46. Cannot this be called a service and the gratuitous bringing of an unspeakable, heavenly, eternal treasure, which neither thou nor the world can purchase with all its possessions and riches? For what are all the treasures of the world and all the crowns of kings, gold, silver, precious stones, and whatever the world counts great in comparison to this treasure called the forgiveness of sins, through which thou art made free from the power of the devil, of death and of hell, and art assured that God in heaven will now be gracious unto thee, and gracious in a way that thou shalt be his child and heir, and the brother and joint-heir of Christ, for the sake of Christ? Therefore it is impossible to sell such a precious treasure for money, or to purchase it with money, as our Judas Iscariot, the pope, has done. This treasure must be given and received gratuitously or thou art not helped by it, for the gift of God cannot be purchased with money. Acts 18:20.

47. But this I say not to the end that people shall give nothing to the servants of the Church, who teach God's Word in its truth and purity, as, alas, they are eager to do, and many are ready to begrudge their minister every bite, and, if they could they would rob the possessions of the Church and ministers, and prove by their actions that they would gladly starve out their minsters and get rid of them. But what a wild state and calamity would follow, would be soon experienced, if the government did not intervene. Nay, this is by no means my meaning. Your pastors should be properly supported, for if they have nothing to eat, drink and wear, and for their other needs, they cannot very long fill their office, for they would have to think on how to support themselves in other ways. Thus the Gospel would not continue long, and it is this that the devil is seeking through these people.

48. But that we are under obligations properly to support our pastors is also stated by Christ himself, when he says in Luke 10:7: "The laborer is worthy of his hire." As St. Paul says in Galatians 6:6: "But let him that is taught in the Word, communicate unto him that teacheth, in all good things," adding in verse 7 a sharp word, "Be not deceived; God is not mocked," and in 1 Timothy 5:17: "Let elders, or priests, that rule well be counted worthy of double honor, especially those who labor in the Word and in teaching." We support others, who are engaged in worldly offices, in which they serve the public, in order that they may be able to perform their service. How much more do we owe it to them that serve in the Word of God, as St. Paul says, they are "worthy of double honor."

49. And in order that the doctrine of the Gospel may remain pure in our pulpits in the future, and that our posterity may retain and hear these doctrines, we are not only bound properly to support those who serve the Church, but we must also with all diligence see to it that our schools are supplied with competent teachers, who should also be properly supported, so that the people may be trained to become not only common ministers, who are simply prepared to instruct the Christian congregation in the Word, but learned men, who will be capable of contending against the rabble and factious spirits. To this end it is the duty of everyone to contribute willingly and cheerfully, not alone the princes and lords, but also the citizens and peasants.

50. From what has been said each one can see for himself what a great and precious treasure it is to hear the Gospel or the absolution in its true meaning from the preacher or pastor. If he comes to thee in the time of sickness and comforts thee, then thou canst be assured that Christ the Lord himself visits and comforts thee. For no one could possibly come to thee in this capacity without divine commandment, and he would know neither how to help nor to counsel; but since thou hearest that he himself has commanded it, thou canst be fully assured and say joyfully: Here Christ himself comes to me in my confessor, for he does not speak his own word, but the Word of God, to do which he is sent, and the command to do it he has.

51. Here thou hast then sure support against the terror and despair of conscience. Thou dost not need to float and bob in uncertainty, as the doctrine of the pope would teach us, which never absolves anyone from sin unless he has been sorry enough and confessed enough until he is clean. There was not the least thought about faith and the power of the keys as instituted by Christ, for such doctrines and knowledge was so completely unknown that I myself, a Doctor of Divinity, who should indeed have known better, did not hold and teach differently than that my sins were forgiven, if my penitence and confession were sufficient. But if our sins are not forgiven, before we outweigh them with our sorrow, penitence and good works, we can never hope to receive forgiveness. For I can never come to the conclusion that my sorrow and repentance have been sufficient; hence, no man, be he called pope or anything else, is able for that reason to absolve or acquit me.

52. In this manner the conscience has been lamentably misled from the Word of Faith and the commandment of God to their uncertain sorrow and repentance, through the falsehoods of the pope. This has brought a large income, and from it have been built many churches, cloisters, chapels, altars, that are richly endowed. Yes, there are still extant bulls and letters of the pope that refer to this, and confirm these things, through which he has deceived the world woefully, so that it is impossible to estimate much less to describe the damage and the sorrow that have arisen therefrom. For this reason we are faithfully and constantly admonishing, and let him who can help so that we may maintain schools, ministers and pulpits that such or worse error may not increase among us, as the devil indeed desires.

53. This is the true doctrine concerning the kingdom of Christ and the office of the Keys, and if we act accordingly, then we will remain Christians, and are prepared for everything in our relation to God and man. We will also heartily thank God that he has delivered us from the constraint and tyranny of the pope, who made out of the power of the Keys a mere show and worldly dominion, although they were established and ordained by Christ to help the whole world obtain a treasure that cannot be bought with money.

54. Let us therefore be truly grateful to our dear Lord and Savior, who through his resurrection founded this Kingdom of Grace, which is established for the purpose that we should constantly find therein for all our needs and anxiety sure help and comfort. And we need not go very far for this precious treasure, nor do we need to secure it at any great expense, for he has given command and full power to his apostles and their successors, and in case of need to every Christian, even unto the end of the world, that they should comfort and strengthen the weak and discouraged souls, and should remit unto them their sins in his name etc.

Quasimodo. Sunday after Easter. Fourth Sermon. John 20:-19-31

Thomas Delivered from His Unbelief.

Jesus Raises Lazarus

KJV John 20:19 Then the same day at evening, being the first day of the week, when the doors were shut where the disciples were assembled for fear of the Jews, came Jesus and stood in the midst, and saith unto them, Peace be unto you. 20 And when he had so said, he shewed unto them his hands and his side. Then were the disciples glad, when they saw the Lord. 21 Then said Jesus to them again, Peace be unto you: as my Father hath sent me, even so send I you. 22 And when he had said this, he breathed on them, and saith unto them, Receive ye the Holy Ghost: 23 Whose soever sins ye remit, they are remitted unto them; and whose soever sins ye retain, they are retained. 24 But Thomas, one of the twelve, called Didymus, was not with them when Jesus came. 25 The other disciples therefore said unto him, We have seen the Lord. But he said unto them, Except I shall see in his hands the print of the nails, and put my finger into the print of the nails, and thrust my hand into his side, I will not believe. 26 And after eight days again his disciples were within, and Thomas with them: then came Jesus, the doors being shut, and stood in the midst, and said, Peace be unto you.

27 Then saith he to Thomas, Reach hither thy finger, and behold my hands; and reach hither thy hand, and thrust it into my side: and be not faithless, but believing. 28 And Thomas answered and said unto him, My Lord and my God. 29 Jesus saith unto him, Thomas, because thou hast seen me, thou hast believed: blessed are they that have not seen, and yet have believed. 30 And many other signs truly did Jesus in the presence of his disciples, which are not written in this book: 31 But these are written, that ye might believe that Jesus is the Christ, the Son of God; and that believing ye might have life through his name.

1. John the Evangelist further writes that Thomas was not present when the Lord appeared the first time to his assembled disciples on Easter evening. Now that the Lord comes just at the time St. Thomas is the first time absent does not take place without a reason; for Christ could have easily chosen an hour when Thomas could have been found in company with the other apostles. But it took place for our instruction and consolation that the Lord's resurrection might receive more and stronger evidence and documentary testimony. Now, on Easter he appeared to the assembled eleven; one week later, that is today, he appeared to them again and at the same time also to Thomas for whose sake alone this appearance or revelation took place which is more beautiful and glorious than that of eight days before.

2. Here we see what a poor thing the human heart is when it begins to grow faint, that we cannot strengthen and comfort it again. Both the other disciples and Thomas did not only hear during the time they were with the Lord that he taught the people with great authority, and later also saw how he confirmed his doctrine by the great miracles performed on the blind, the lame, the lepers, the dumb etc., whom he cured; but also that he raised three persons from the dead, especially Lazarus who had been four days in his grave. And, as it appears, St. Thomas was the most fearless and courageous of all the disciples, in that he said when Christ wished to go again into Judea to Lazarus who was dead: "Let us also go, that we may die with him," John 11:16. Such fine characters were the disciples of Christ and especially St. Thomas, who it appears, had a more manly heart than the others, and besides had recently witnessed how Christ raised Lazarus who had been in the grave four days, and ate and drank with him; yet he could not believe that the Lord himself arose from the dead and was alive.

3. Moreover, we see in the apostles that we are truly nothing when Christ withdraws his hand and we are left to ourselves. The women, Mary Magdalene and the others, announced it, and now the disciples themselves proclaim that they had seen the risen Lord. Yet St. Thomas is stubborn and will not believe it; yea, and he will not be satisfied even if he see him, unless it be that he sees the print of the nails in his hands and puts his fingers into the print of the nails and his hand into his side. And the beloved disciple will thus himself also be lost and condemned, in that he will not believe. For there can be neither forgiveness of sins nor salvation if one believes not, since therein lies all the virtue and power of faith and eternal life, as St. Paul says: "And if Christ hath not been raised, then is our preaching vain, your faith is also vain; ye are yet in your sins. Then they also that are fallen asleep in Christ have perished," etc. 1 Corinthians 15:14-18. To perdition will St. Thomas also go, he will not be saved but wills to be lost, because he will not believe that Christ is risen. And he would have perished and been condemned in his unbelief had not Christ rescued him from it by this revelation.

4. So the Holy Spirit illustrates and teaches now in this example that without faith we are simply blind and completely hardened, as we see everywhere in the holy Scriptures that the human heart is the hardest thing in the world, harder than steel and adamant. And on the other hand, if it be bashful, despondent and soft, there is no water nor oil so soft as the human heart.

5. You find many examples and narratives illustrating this in the Scripture. Pharaoh, before whom Moses performed so many terrible signs and wonders that he could not reply to them, yea, he had to admit that it was God's finger and therefore also confessed he had sinned against God and his people etc.: yet his heart became harder and more obdurate continually until the Lord drowned him with all his army in the sea. Likewise also the Jews; the more powerfully Christ proved both by word and deed that he was the one who was promised by their fathers that he should be a blessing to them and to the whole world, the more vehemently and bitterly they raged against him and their hatred, blasphemy and persecution knew no measure nor end until they condemned their Lord and God to the most ignominious death and crucified him between two malefactors, nothing could prevent it although Pilate the judge himself declared against them that he was innocent, creation acted differently than usual and thereby testified that its Lord and Creator hung there on the cross etc.; likewise the thief freely confessed publicly, although Christ truly hung there and died, yet he was a king who had an eternal heavenly kingdom; and the heathen centurion publicly cried: "Truly this was the Son of God," etc. Matthew 27:54. This all, I say, helped nothing to bring about this conversion.

6. This is the way the godless, condemned world does: the more grace and kindness God shows it, the more unthankful and wicked it becomes. Now it is meet and right for us all to thank God from our hearts that he has revealed his holy Word so pure and clear before the day of judgment, from which we learn what inexpressible treasures he has given us in Christ, namely, that we are saved by him from sin and death, and shall now be righteous and blessed, etc. What is the attitude of the world to this? As its custom is, it does not know how to abuse, blaspheme and condemn this Word of grace and life enough, and wherever possible to persecute and destroy those who confess it, and although the world hears that God will severely punish such sin with hellfire and eternal condemnation, it thinks little about it, goes ahead securely and obdurately, as if it were nothing, and enjoys its sport as we clearly see now in the pope and his following. And yet it is such horrible and dreadful wrath that all creatures are terrified by it. Therefore it is certainly true that no stone, steel, adamant, yea, nothing on earth is as hard as the impenitent heart of man.

7. On the other hand, if the heart loses courage and is terrified it is softer than water and oil, so that, as Scripture says, it is frightened at a rustling leaf. And when such a person is alone in a room and hears a little cracking of a rafter or a beam, he thinks thunder and lightning are striking him and he is in such anxiety and fear (as I have often seen), that no one can comfort or strengthen him, and all the preachers and all consoling proverbs are too few to calm him. So there is no moderation with the human heart; it is either entirely too hard like wood and stone, that it inquires about neither God nor Satan, or, on the other hand, it is entirely too timid, fickle and despondent.

8. Thus the apostles are here too scared and terror-stricken by the scandal they saw in their Lord being so ignominiously mocked, spit upon, scourged, pierced and finally crucified, so that they no longer had a heart in their bodies, who before while they had Christ among them were so bold and courageous, that James and John ventured to bid fire to come down from heaven and consume the Samaritans who would not receive Christ, Luke 9:54. They also knew how gloriously to boast that the devils were in the name of Jesus subject unto them; and Thomas admonished the others and said: "Let us go that we may die with him;" and Peter, more impetuous than the others, smites with the sword among the crowd when they wished to seize and take Christ captive. But now they lie prostrate in great fear and terror, locked up, and will let no one come to them. For this reason they were also terrified at the Lord when he comes and greets them, and they still think (which is indeed a sign that they are completely overcome by fear and despair) they see a spirit or a ghost. So soon they had forgotten all the miracles, signs and words they had seen and heard from him, that the Lord had enough to do during the forty days after his resurrection before he separated from them, in his appearances and revelations in various ways, now to the women, then to the disciples, both individually and collectively, besides eating and drinking with them; all for the purpose that they might be assured that he is risen. Yet it is so hard for this truth to enter their hearts.

9. Likewise, when after forty days he spoke with them out of the Scriptures about the kingdom of God, which should now commence and be a kingdom in which should be proclaimed in his name repentance and the forgiveness of sins among all nations, they raise the cry and ask him when he was about to ascend from them in a cloud, and say: "Lord, dost thou at this time restore the kingdom to Israel?" they have entirely different thoughts of the kingdom of Christ than those he had been teaching them. Here you see how exceedingly difficult it is for bashful and despondent hearts to be comforted and strengthened, even after being rightly instructed, so that they know what kind of a king Christ is and what he has accomplished by his death and resurrection.

10. Thus both the obduracy and the bashfulness of the human heart are indescribable. When out of danger it is hard and obdurate beyond measure, so that it cares nothing for the wrath or the threatening of God. Although it hears for a long time that God will punish sin with eternal death and condemnation, yet it goes ahead and is drowned in pride, avarice, etc. On the other hand, when the heart begins to fear it becomes so despondent that it cannot be again reclaimed. It is indeed a great pity that we are such wicked people. If we are not in want we continue to live on in sin without the least fear or shame, yea, to grow stiff like a dead corpse; what is spoken to us is as if spoken to a rock. On the contrary, if there is a change in us that we feel our sins, we are terrified by death, God's wrath and judgment; we on the other hand grow stiff at the great anxiety and sorrow, so that no one can strengthen us; yea, we are even terrified before that which should comfort us, like the disciples were before Christ, who came to them for the very purpose that they might be comforted and made happy. Although he does not at once set them right he has to doctor them during the forty days, as I said. He takes and uses all kinds of comfort and medicine and still he can hardly strengthen them again, until he gives them the right strong drink, namely, the Holy Spirit, of which they drank and were comforted in the right way so that they are no more as before, bashful and terrified.

II. Thomas Saved from his Unbelief

11. Finally, we have in St. Thomas an illustration of the power of Christ's resurrection. We just heard how firm and even stiff-necked he was in unbelief, that although the other disciples unitedly testified that they had seen the risen Lord, yet he simply will not believe it. He appears to have been a fine and brave character who had thoroughly concluded that he would not so soon believe the others. For he had seen that the Lord only three days before was put to death on the cross and the nails driven through his hands and feet and the spear pierced his side. This picture was so indelibly and deeply impressed upon him that he simply could not in the least believe what the others told him, that Christ was risen. Therefore he promptly and defiantly says: "Except I shall see in his hands the print of the nails, and put my finger into the print of the nails, and put my hand into his side, I will not believe." He thus utters a hyperbole, an exaggerated statement, that he will not believe his eyes alone, but will feel and grope about Christ's body with his hands. As if he would say: No one shall persuade me to believe, but I will stand so firmly upon no, that I will not believe even if I see him, as you say you saw him. But should I believe it, then he must come so near to me, that, if it were possible, I may touch his soul and put my hands into his eyes.

12. That is to be steeped very firmly and deeply in unbelief. And it is wonderful what he means by it that he at once proposes a thing absurd, to put his hand and finger into the openings of his wounds. For he had always been so smart as to think: Since Christ was again alive, had conquered death and was rid of all the bruises from the scourging and the crown of thorns, he would surely have healed and removed also the five wounds.

13. Now, this has happened for our example and consolation, that the great apostle also had to fail and stumble, in which we see how Christ shows and conducts himself toward his weak disciples, that he can tolerate also such who are still as hard and stubborn as St. Thomas is here, and that he will not on that account condemn and disown them, if only in other respects they sincerely wish to continue to be his disciples, and not maliciously blaspheme him and become his enemies; and by this he teaches us that we should become neither offended nor despondent because of that; but in harmony with this his example gently go on with them, serve their weakness, with our strength until they become established and grow strong.

14. But it serves more to the end, as I began to say, that the resurrection of the Lord is not only clearly shown and proved by this unbelieving and stubborn Thomas, who persevered for eight days in his unbelief, and he lay there grown almost stiff; but also that the power of the resurrection becomes known, and is of benefit to us; as appears in Thomas who thereby was brought from unbelief to faith, from doubt to certain knowledge and to a beautiful and glorious confession.

15. Now it happens, says the Evangelist, first on the eighth day after his resurrection, when Thomas had established himself in his unbelief in the face of the testimony of all the others, and by this time he is dead and no one hopes he will show himself in a special manner to Thomas. Just then Christ comes and shows him the same scars and wounds, as fresh as he had shown them to the other disciples eight days before, and tells him to reach hither his finger and hand and place them into the prints of the nails and into his side. Christ yields to Thomas so much that he not only sees as others did, but he also seizes him and feels, as he had said: "Except I shall see in his hands," etc., and he says in addition: "Be not faithless, but believing."

16. Here you see Christ is not satisfied to stop with the narrative; but he is concerned only that Thomas becomes believing and is resurrected from his stubborn unbelief and sin. This follows in a powerful way in that St. Thomas soon begins and says to Christ: "My Lord and my God!" There is at once a different man, not the old Thomas Didymus (which means in English a twin, not a doubter, as has been wrongly interpreted from this text), as just before, when he was so cold and stiff and dead in his unbelief, that he would not believe unless he puts his finger into his wounds; but he commenced suddenly to deliver a glorious confession and sermon about Christ, the equal of which no apostle to that time had yet preached, namely, that the person, the risen one, is true God and man. For they are admirable words he utters: "My Lord and my God! He is not drunken, he is not jesting nor mocking; he does not mean a false God; therefore he certainly does not tell a lie. Besides he is not here chastised by Christ, but his faith is confirmed, and it must be the truth and sincere.

17. It is now the power of the resurrection of Christ that St. Thomas, who was so deep and obdurate in unbelief, even more than any other disciple, was so suddenly changed, becomes an entirely different man, who publicly and freely confesses that he not only believes that Christ is risen but is also enlightened by the power of Christ's resurrection so that he firmly believes and confesses that he, his Lord, is true God and man, through whom, as he is now resurrected from unbelief, the fountain of all sin; so he will also arise from the dead at the judgment day and live forever with him in indescribable glory and blessedness. And not only he, but all who believe thus, as Christ himself further says to him: "Thomas, because thou hast seen me, thou hast believed: blessed are they that have not seen, and yet have believed."

18. Finally, that Thomas puts his finger into the wounds. I will not argue whether Christ always after his resurrection retained the wounds and prints of the nails; yet I argue they did not appear hideous, as otherwise they might, but fresh and comforting. And whether they were still fresh, open and red as artists paint them, I will leave for others to decide. Otherwise it is a fine idea to picture them before the ordinary person so that he has a memorial and a picture that will remind and admonish him of the sufferings and wounds of Christ. It is possible that he retained the same signs or marks which will likely enlighten much more beautifully and gloriously at the day of judgment his whole body and he will show them before the whole world, as the Scriptures say: "They shall look unto me whom they have pierced," Zechariah 12:10. This I would commend to every devotional exercise for consideration.

19. The leading thought, however, for us to learn and retain from this Gospel is, that we believe that Christ's resurrection is sure and that it works in us so that we be resurrected both from sin and death; as St. Paul richly and consolingly speaks of it, and Christ himself here, when he says: "Blessed are they that have not seen, and yet have believed," and St. John concluding this Gospel teaches and admonishes about the use and benefit of the resurrection: "These are written, that ye may believe that Jesus is the Christ, the Son of God; and believing ye may have life in his name."

20. This is indeed a powerful and clear passage, which highly praises faith and gives the testimony that we certainly have eternal life through the same; and that this faith is not an empty, dead thought on the history about Christ, but that which concludes and is sure that he is the Christ, that is, the promised King and Savior, God's Son, through whom we all are delivered from sin and eternal death; for which purpose he also died and rose again; and that we alone for his sake acquire eternal life, in a way that is called in his name, not in Moses' nor in our nor any other man's name, that is, not because of the law, nor of our worthiness and doings, but alone on account of Christ's merits, as Peter says in Acts 4:12: "There is none other name among men, wherein we must be saved," etc.

Recent Books from Martin Chemnitz Press

Illustrated by Norma Boeckler

The Augsburg Confession

Catholic, Lutheran, Protestant: A Doctrinal Comparison of Three Christian Confessions

Creation Gardening: By Him Were All Things Made

The Faith of Jesus: Against the Faithless Lutherans

Introduction to the Christian Faith: Jesus, Priceless Treasure

Jesus, Lord of Creation

Liberalism: Its Cause and Cure: The Poisoning of American Christianity and the Antidote

Making Disciples: The Error of Modern Pietism

My Lutheran Hymnal

The Lost Dutchman's Goldmine: Luther's Biblical Doctrine of the Word

The Story of Jesus in Pictures

Thy Strong Word: The Efficacy of the Word in the Scriptures and Lutheran Confessions

Luther's Sermons, Lenker Edition, The Next Project

Books by Norma Boeckler

The Art of Norma Boeckler

The Augsburg Confession

Religious Art

A Treasury of Inspirational Quotes

Printed in Great Britain
by Amazon

41318626R00165